DATE DUE

ANNAPOLIS PASTS

A N N A P O I

Historical Archaeolog

The University of Tennessee Press / Knoxville

IS PASTS

ı Annapolis, Maryland

Edited by Paul A. Shackel · Paul R. Mullins · Mark S. Warner

Chapter 12, "The Archaeology of Vision in Eighteenth-Century Chesapeake Gardens," by Elizabeth Kryder-Reid, was originally published in "Site and Sight in the Garden," a special issue of the *Journal of Garden History* 14 (1) (Jan.–Mar. 1994): 42–54, guest-edited by Elizabeth Kryder-Reid and D. Fairchild Ruggles. It is used here by permission of the publisher.

Title page photos: (from left to right) William Paca, courtesy of the Collection of the Maryland Historical Society, Baltimore; Eugenia Brown, courtesy of Mr. Philip L. Brown; anonymous priest, courtesy of the Maryland State Archives/Special Collections, Robert G. Merrick Collection, MSA SC 1477-4038; anonymous, courtesy of the Maryland State Archives/Special Collections, Mame Warren Collection, MSA SC 985-251; Natalie Hammond, courtesy of Mr. Jacques Kelly; Henry Darnall III, courtesy of the Collection of the Maryland Historical Society, Baltimore; Edwin Dennis, courtesy of Mr. Philip L. Brown; project archaeologist, courtesy of Amy Elizabeth Grey.

Except for maps produced from historical sources, all of the maps and many figures were prepared by Amy Elizabeth Grey. Unless otherwise noted, illustrations are reprinted by permission of the authors of the chapters in which they appear.

Library of Congress Cataloging-in-Publication Data

Annapolis pasts : historical archaeology in Annapolis, Maryland / edited by Paul A. Shackel, Paul R. Mullins, Mark S. Warner.—1st ed.
    p.   cm.
Includes bibliographical references and index.
ISBN 0-87049-996-3 (cloth: alk. paper)
1. Annapolis (Md.)—Antiquities. 2. Annapolis (Md.)—History. 3. Excavations (Archaeology)—Maryland—Annapolis. 4. Archaeology and history—Maryland—Annapolis. 5. Historic sites—Maryland—Annapolis.   I. Shackel, Paul A.   II. Mullins, Paul R., 1962–   .
III. Warner, Mark S.
F189.A647A56   1998
975.2'15601—dc21   97-21071

To the people and the city of Annapolis for
their continuous support of the Archaeology
in Annapolis project

and with gratitude to Amy Elizabeth Grey,
who prepared the illustrations

Contents

Part I. Presentation of the Past

Part II. Everyday Lifeways

Part III. Landscapes and Architecture

Illustrations

Figures

Maps

Tables

Acknowledgments

Many of the papers in this book were presented in the 1991 Society for Historical Archaeology meetings in Richmond, Virginia. A session dedicated to Annapolis archaeology was organized and chaired by Barbara J. Little. Barbara turned over the reins of compiling these works into a single volume to the current editors. We appreciate her efforts in gathering these works in the form of a symposium and for allowing us to continue to pursue this project and create this edited volume.

The editors, as well as many of the authors, appreciate the opportunity given to us by Mark P. Leone by allowing us to participate in the Archaeology in Annapolis Project. The Archaeology in Annapolis project has been a training ground for M.A. and Ph.D. students and it has launched many careers in the field. The Archaeology in Annapolis project is a collaborative venture between the University of Maryland, College Park, and the Historic Annapolis Foundation. The Port of Annapolis Foundation, the Banneker-Douglass Museum, the City of Annapolis, and the Maryland Historical Trust have also been instrumental in providing assistance for the project. Personnel at the Maryland State Archives have also been extremely helpful in our research efforts. Lynn Jones, former laboratory director for the Archaeology in Annapolis project, provided necessary support and information to many of the authors.

We appreciate Russell Skowronek and the many anonymous reviewers for their helpful comments. Jeff Hantman also provided valuable input at the beginning stages of this manuscript. Amy Grey has graciously provided numerous hours of her own time to standardize the graphics in the book. We appreciate her hard work and her dedication to creating an excellent product.

From the University of Tennessee Press, Jennifer Siler was very supportive of this project, and we appreciate her encouragement. Kim Scarbrough and Scot Danforth of the press have also provided necessary support.

Introduction: The Archaeology in Annapolis Project

*Paul A. Shackel, Paul R. Mullins,
and Mark S. Warner*

This volume is a cross-section of the substantive and theoretical issues explored by the Archaeology in Annapolis project. These essays are archaeological in their focus on the material world, but the issues which they explore—racism, class structure, historical interpretation, landscape symbolism, industrialization, consumer society—are familiar to many researchers commonly considered outside the disciplinary boundaries of archaeology. Such subjects clearly are not research problems which are the concern of archaeologists alone; yet, historical archaeologists once were (and sometimes still are) wary to examine some of these issues or accept them as appropriate subjects for archaeological study. Archaeology in Annapolis researchers have been among a burgeoning number of contemporary historical archaeologists who are ambitious enough to confront the relationship between such broad anthropological and historical problems and everyday material culture. This volume uses the archaeological interpretation of one city to probe how apparent everyday minutia, such as food, gardens, architecture, and tablewares, have been significant mechanisms which have reproduced, modified, and resisted capitalist society over three hundred years.

Archaeology in Annapolis was developed in 1981 by Richard Dent, Mark Leone, and Anne Yentsch as a cooperative project between the University of Maryland and the Historic Annapolis Foundation. Initially the project's primary goal was to provide a comprehensive, yet relatively basic archaeological study of the socioeconomic development of an eighteenth-century port town. That inquiry began, conventionally enough, as an investigation of mostly elite contexts and basic colonial institutions, such as taverns and warehouses. Yet, it soon became clear that these sites could not be understood in isolation from a city of enslaved Africans, impoverished and middle-class Anglo-Americans, and women, all of whom had been slighted to varying degrees by conventional historiography and archaeology. Like many other historical archaeologists, Archaeology in Annapolis researchers recognized that one of archaeology's contributions could be the illumination of such people who are invisible in or poorly represented by dominant historiography. It also became clear that Georgian mansions and colonial craft sites could not be understood as part of the same society without probing the emergence and growth of capitalism. Annapolis's extensive archaeological data reflected how capitalism has been a dynamic market force for three centuries, but they also emphasized that capitalism has been an equally dynamic body of social rules. Perhaps most significantly, the genesis of many contemporary social practices and class relations was reflected in the archaeological record. Instead of accepting capitalism as a self-evident socioeconomic system or simply probing *how* capitalism has worked, Archaeology in Annapolis has attempted to confront *why* capitalism works, to identify ways it breaks down, and to illuminate how class relationships are negotiated, contested, and resisted through material culture.

A second objective of our work has been to make archaeology accessible to broader constituencies than the scholarly community. To accomplish this, Archaeology in Annapolis created a public outreach program which has presented archaeological method and interpretation to Annapolitans and tourists for fifteen years. The program is based on site tours which display the excavation methods and interpretive strategies of archaeological investigation, allowing visitors to follow our excavation and interpretive strategies and subsequently accept, probe, or even reject our interpretations. The public interpretation program emphasizes how everyday material objects such as plates, forks, and gardens are implicated in the emergence and development of ideological practices such as personal etiquette and landscape planning.

Exposing the origins of these practices in capitalism and tracing their two-century elaboration demonstrates that our modern lifestyle is not inevitable or "natural." Instead, it is the product of identifiable historical dynamics which can be illuminated through material culture.

History of Annapolis

Maryland was established in 1634. The Annapolis area was first settled by Protestant Virginians in 1649. Early colonists exploited the region's rich, well-drained soils and grew tobacco as a staple crop. The many creeks and rivers draining into the Chesapeake Bay facilitated the shipment of tobacco to England. Present-day Annapolis was inhabited by Thomas Todd, a boatwright, by 1651, and he continued his trade there for 20 years. The boat yard along contemporary Shipwright Street remained active into the 1730s. Several families resided in the immediate area, including a tavern keeper, Robert Proctor, who lived somewhere at the foot of Duke of Gloucester Street (figs. 0.1 and 0.2). Proctor also owned and planted six hundred acres nearby, and operated a mill.[1]

In the mid-seventeenth century the area became known as the "town lands at Proctors." In 1684, one hundred acres of the area were surveyed to encourage settlement and development of the town, and the surveyed site was named Arundelton. Arundelton was intended to serve as a port of entry for the tobacco trade; officially designated ports of entry were the only legal areas where tobacco could be shipped. The 1684 survey by James Beard only measured about half of the required area, and it certainly did not accelerate settlement of the area: little development occurred in Arundelton or in many of the region's other "port of entries" for ten years.[2]

In 1694 Governor Francis Nicholson moved Maryland's provincial capital away from the Catholic stronghold of St. Mary's City to the politically stable, non-Catholic Arundelton. The town, which was renamed Annapolis, was still predominately rural. Nicholson ordered a resurvey of the area and attempted to make it more urbane by adding elements of Baroque design to a new town plan.[3] John Reps notes that the Baroque features of Nicholson's Annapolis plan included formal symmetry, imposing open spaces, street vistas closed by important structures, and major buildings placed on commanding sites.[4] A knoll, the highest point in the area, was chosen by Nicholson as the appropriate location for the State

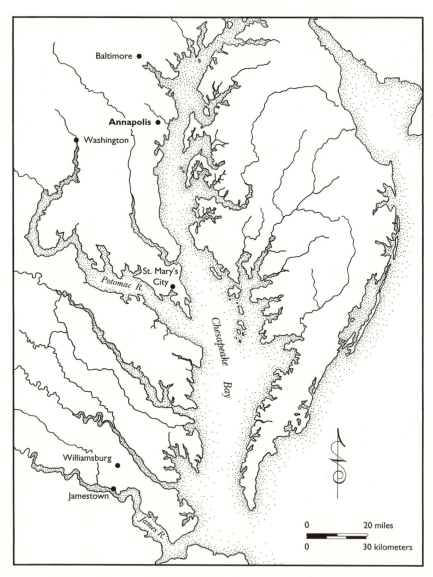

Map 0.1. The Chesapeake Bay region.

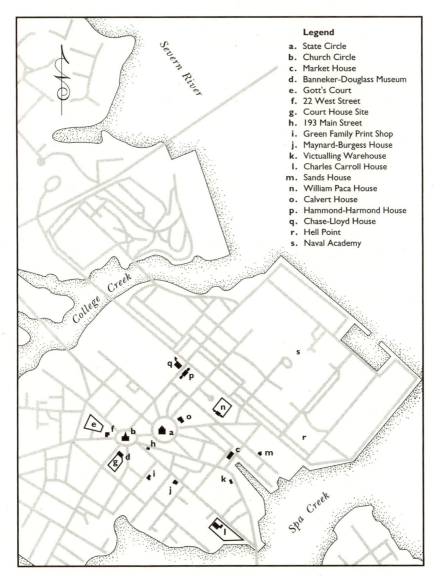

Legend

a. State Circle
b. Church Circle
c. Market House
d. Banneker-Douglass Museum
e. Gott's Court
f. 22 West Street
g. Court House Site
h. 193 Main Street
i. Green Family Print Shop
j. Maynard-Burgess House
k. Victualling Warehouse
l. Charles Carroll House
m. Sands House
n. William Paca House
o. Calvert House
p. Hammond-Harmond House
q. Chase-Lloyd House
r. Hell Point
s. Naval Academy

Map 0.2. Major Annapolis landmarks and excavations conducted by Archaeology in Annapolis.

House, and the structure was enclosed by a 250-foot-diameter circle. Church Circle, a 125-foot-diameter road which enclosed the Anglican Church, was placed just west of the State House on the second-highest elevation in town. These areas quickly developed into the social and political centers of Annapolis.[5] The town's new asymmetrical street plan radiating from the two circles did not conform to Arundelton's pre-existing layout. Several of the streets in the 1684 and 1694 plans are similarly located, though, so it appears likely that Beard's 1684 orthogonal-like plan was at least partially incorporated into Nicholson's Baroque-inspired design.[6] The layout of Annapolis's historic district today is essentially unchanged from Nicholson's plan.

Despite Nicholson's best efforts, early Annapolis was by no means a Baroque metropolis comparable to the European cities on which it was modeled. For instance, a 1699 account of the town indicated that Annapolis was simply a small village consisting of about forty wood structures. Ten years later a poem described Annapolis houses as so poorly constructed that only a few could even keep out rain.

Substantial expansion did not occur in Annapolis until the late 1710s and 1720s, when the town was transformed into a bureaucratic center. The Calvert family regained proprietorship of the Maryland colony in 1715, and in 1718 they resurveyed Annapolis, a clear indication that they did not intend to move the government seat back to St. Mary's City. The increased sense of stability resulted in a period of intense land speculation in Annapolis and growth in the numbers of craftspeople and artisans working in the city. Entrepreneurs sensed that investment in Annapolis offered reasonable promise, and their land and market speculation stimulated the city's growth. Many elite colonists were drawn to the city as a center of colonial power, and their immigration supported a merchant class catering in luxury goods and a burgeoning enslaved African labor force. By the 1740s and 1750s, luxury craft production catering to the city's elite had increased substantially, and it continued to flourish through the 1770s.[7]

The city's high style reached its apogee in the 1760s and 1770s, when many colonists considered Annapolis a major political and social center in America. Historians often call the era between about 1763 and 1786 Annapolis's "Golden Age." The bustling sea port grew rapidly, and the town became a center of stylish decorum with amenities like theaters and social clubs. Annapolis became home to a series of formal gardens and ostentatious buildings which included several impressive five-part brick

Georgian mansions. By 1774 over a dozen major Georgian-style structures had been built, many of which served as winter retreats for plantation owners. The town was considered prosperous and genteel, even though the general conditions in the city were far from perfect for the masses.[8]

Annapolis's development was interrupted by the American Revolution. The city served as the capital of the United States for six months at the end of the war, but Annapolis's zenith in socioeconomic influence and prosperity was passed. By war's end many of the local elite and some emergent industries moved to other urban centers, and in 1785–86 Annapolitans found themselves in the midst of an economic depression. By 1790 the town had lost much of its economic and social power.[9] Many of the city and region's elite flocked to Baltimore, where tax rates were more favorable and deeper shipping ports were available. Annapolis was reduced to the status of a local port town, and the city struggled throughout the nineteenth century to maintain itself as the seat of Maryland's government. By the start of the twentieth century Annapolis was a small town of 8,500 residents whose primary employers were the U.S. Naval Academy and the state government. The decline of Annapolis and its sluggish development were archaeologically fortuitous: Annapolis escaped the nineteenth-century industrialization which destroyed the archaeological record in many other colonial cities, and much of the city's eighteenth- and nineteenth-century landscape remains undisturbed today.

Since Annapolis lost its colonial luster at the end of the eighteenth century, scholars have been relatively uninterested in the city's nineteenth- and twentieth-century histories. Until recently, there also was hesitancy to write about the lives of everyday colonial Annapolitans, because the town was peopled by many famous figures who garnered most scholarly attention. Perhaps most prominently neglected is the central role that African Americans have played in the development of Annapolis and, indeed, the state of Maryland. By 1710, ninety-five African Americans were living in Annapolis, a total which was roughly 24 percent of the city's modest population. From the 1730s through today, about a third of all Annapolitans have been African Americans.[10] Enslaved African Americans initially were an important source of labor who afforded planters' profits and built and maintained many of Annapolis's homes. After the mid-eighteenth century, free African Americans also became an increasingly important part of Annapolis's socioeconomic landscape. The African American community impacted all aspects of the city as laborers and consumers, both free and enslaved. African Americans provided the bulk of the labor force for the Naval Academy after its construction in 1845, and they filled most of the city's service jobs as laborers, carters, waiters, and servants. Several African Americans acquired significant amounts of property and were among the city's wealthiest residents. For instance, William Butler at one time had a net worth of over $24,000, and William Bishop held over $8,000 in assets in 1859.[11] Many lived more quietly and thrived in Annapolis despite the persistent adversities of racism, legalized segregation, and white racist violence.

During the 1950s Annapolis once again began to develop into an important American social center. The primary catalysts for the revitalization of Annapolis were an aggressive historic preservation movement focused on the city's eighteenth-century history and the growth of Annapolis as a major boating center. Today Annapolis's major industry is tourism, a trade which relies significantly on the perception and presentation of the city's colonial heritage.

Summary of Archaeological Projects

Archaeology became increasingly important when Annapolis's historic preservation movement emerged in the 1950s. Amateurs and professionals received private funding to conduct a few excavations, but most of these digs were quite limited and, unfortunately, poorly documented. Since Archaeology in Annapolis's founding in 1981, approximately forty sites have been examined. The scope of work conducted on these projects has ranged from the monitoring of construction projects to brief testing of individual house lots to long-term excavations. The excavations have been supported by research grants, contracts, and local preservationists. A significant amount of Archaeology in Annapolis's recent work has been compelled by development which would have destroyed archaeological resources. Other excavations have been driven primarily by the site's research potential. This ongoing balance between contract archaeology and continuing research has clearly documented Annapolis's archaeological record and ensured continuing archaeological research on the socioeconomic development of the city.

The sites excavated by Archaeology in Annapolis encompass many social groups and time periods in the city's history. Archaeological research has been done at the homes and businesses of tavern keepers, craftspeople, physicians, priests, enslaved and free African Americans, a royal governor, and two signers of the Declaration of Independence. The following review of the archaeological excavations in Annapolis is by no means complete; rather, it briefly surveys the excavations which are discussed at length throughout this volume.

Archaeology of the Masses

One of the largest bodies of information recovered from excavations in Annapolis has been of the city's middling and lower classes. Until quite recently, scholars commonly slighted or ignored the everyday life of common people. However, historical archaeologists recognize that the archaeological record offers a distinctive if not unique glimpse into the apparently mundane material world of everyday life. The elite are well known through their own records, the accounts of contemporaries, and subsequent histories, but the lives of common people went largely unacknowledged. Historical archaeology offers a crucial insight into the elusive workings of American homes, labor, and material consumption, and archaeologies in Annapolis have contributed to better understandings of the everyday world of common people and the relationship between the Chesapeake elite and the masses.

The Sands House is one of the earliest archaeologically documented sites in Annapolis. Originally inhabited by Evan Jones, the structure served a variety of functions. Jones used the structure as a tavern, and he probably printed there while serving as Maryland's public printer. Archaeology conducted in 1987 recovered the remains of a kitchen garden dating to the early eighteenth century. Other material culture recovered reveals dramatic changes in the architectural and archaeological record in the 1720s, probably during Jones's occupation. Archaeologists found post holes underneath the corners of the house, indicating that the structure originally was built on wood blocks. During the 1720s Jones converted the house to a more permanent building and laid it upon a fieldstone foundation. These changes occurred during socioeconomic growth and restructuring of the city and correspond with other local and regional material culture changes.[12]

William Wilkins, a successful middling merchant, occupied the structure where the Victualling Warehouse now stands. After the Revolutionary War he purchased the waterfront warehouse and used it as his store

and residence until it burned in 1790. Wilkins relocated his business and
the lot remained vacant into the nineteenth century. A fire created a burn
layer that sealed the archaeological record dating prior to 1790, and archaeologists uncovered a large ceramic assemblage from the Wilkins
household.[13]

One of the project's most extensive excavations was conducted at the
Green House, home to the *Maryland Gazette* printers for over one hundred years. Jonas Green served as the official printer for the province of
Maryland, and in 1737 he began printing the principal newspaper in the
city, the *Maryland Gazette*. When Green died in 1767, his wife Anne
Catherine succeeded him as the official printer. She eventually took her
son Frederick into partnership in 1772, and Frederick replaced his mother
as official printer after her death in 1775. The Green family printing business continued until 1839, when Frederick's son Jonas disbanded the
business because of financial difficulties. The print shop burned in the
late-eighteenth century and eventually was filled, sealing a rich material
assemblage. Over 10,000 pieces of printer's type consisting of 157 different fonts were found at the site. Excavations and an examination of
probate inventories indicate the changing uses and functions of space
as the head of household changed across several generations of Green
printers.[14]

The Main Street site was located in the upper block of Main Street, near
Church and State Circles. The site was first inhabited in the 1690s, and,
like the Sands House, it probably served as a tavern as well as a residence.
Thomas Hyde, who began his career as a tanner and shoemaker, removed
the early tavern structure and constructed a five-bay, two-story brick
building and several outbuildings in 1767. Hyde became a merchant and
by 1783 was the fourth wealthiest Annapolitan. Unlike many of the elite
sites in Annapolis which contained ornamental landscapes, the Hyde
backyard reflects relatively typical everyday activities. Several outbuildings related to the Hyde occupation were located, including a kitchen and
a possible milk house. During the late nineteenth and early twentieth
century the property was occupied by a physician and his household.
Archaeologists located a privy from the physician's occupation which
contained a dense deposit of late-nineteenth-century household refuse.[15]
Among the ceramics, bottles, and food discards recovered from the privy
were several human bones which had been sawn and probably were from
an amputation.[16]

The Elite

The wealthiest colonial Annapolitans also were among the richest and most powerful men in colonial America. Two of Maryland's four signers of the Declaration of Independence—William Paca and Charles Carroll—had Annapolis homes which have been studied archaeologically. Other members of the city's gentry, such as the Calverts and Thomas Bordley, played important roles in state and national politics, and their residences also have been excavated. Not surprisingly, historians have studied these men and their elite peers extensively.[17] However, archaeologists can make an important contribution to the historiography of the elite, particularly by probing how the elite utilized material culture to reproduce and reinforce their prominence in Annapolis society.

William Paca, a lawyer who signed the Declaration of Independence and served as the first governor of Maryland, lived in a five-part Georgian mansion in Annapolis.[18] Built in the 1770s, the home fronted a large formal garden whose terraces and beds have been recreated with the aid of archaeology. Some excavations were performed adjacent to the house during its restoration in the 1960s, and over the past twenty-five years archaeologists have conducted extensive work in the garden.[19] The garden used sloping topography and lines of sight to manipulate perspective and distort a viewer's perception of the garden's size.[20] Built during a period of socioeconomic instability for elite such as Paca, the garden demonstrated Paca's understanding of nature and his class's ability to mold that nature. Ostentatious gardens, like Georgian architecture, displayed elite power and even attempted to legitimize that power. Such gardens were one mechanism members of the elite developed in an effort to legitimize and fortify their eroding influence on the eve of the Revolution.

The Calvert House was the residence of two royal governors in the early eighteenth century. Excavations were conducted from 1982 through 1984, including work in the backyard, the interior of the structure, and the front yard. The quantity and quality of artifacts from this occupation form one of the most extensive assemblages from early-eighteenth-century Annapolis. The site also included impressive architectural features, such as the remains of a hypocaust, a dry-air heating system based on Roman technology. The room above the hypocaust may have served as a greenhouse for growing exotic plants.[21] The feature is on display today through a plexiglass floor where it has been incorporated into the structure's contemporary use as a hotel.

Excavations were conducted at the Charles Carroll House from 1987 through 1991. From at least the mid-eighteenth century until 1853, the property was owned and inhabited by the Carroll family. Although the Carrolls were Catholic, their power and wealth made them important participants in state and national politics: Charles Carroll was the only Catholic signer of the Declaration of Independence. Carroll, like William Paca, built a large formal garden on the eve of the Revolution. After 1853 the Carrolls gave the property to a Roman Catholic order, the Redemptorists, who still own it.

Five seasons of excavations were conducted on the property. An early-eighteenth-century frame house, eighteenth-century deposits from a filled cistern, and numerous artifact deposits associated with the Redemptorists were excavated during those seasons. The intact eighteenth-century formal garden constructed during Charles Carroll's residency was surveyed extensively. Similar to William Paca's garden, Charles Carroll's 1770s garden used a series of geometric formulae to construct terraces, ramps, and slopes in patterns which manipulated lines of sight and perspective.[22]

Excavations on the interior of the house identified an African American component to the site. It was well known that the Carroll family owned significant numbers of slaves, but the location of quarters was unknown, and there was no clear material evidence reflecting African Americans' lives at the home. However, 1991 excavations inside the eighteenth-century structure recovered a cache of crystals, stones, disks, and incised ceramics which were common elements of African religious practices. The basement of the Carroll House apparently was where some of the enslaved Africans resided and worked, and the artifacts and their placement near the room's doors is consistent with religious practices identified in west Africa.[23]

African American Annapolis

Since 1989 Archaeology in Annapolis has explored the history of African American Annapolis and the complicated relations between African Americans and white Annapolitans. Excavations have been conducted on three African American domestic sites, in addition to the African American materials excavated at the Carroll House. The most extensive work was done at the Maynard-Burgess House from 1990 to 1992. The house lot was purchased by John Maynard in 1847. Sometime during the 1850s Maynard and his household built the structure which still stands at the site today. The Maynard family continued to live at the Duke of Gloucester

Street house until the early twentieth century, when the Burgess family acquired the house. The Burgesses, who were related to the Maynards through marriage, lived in the home until the early 1980s.

Archaeology at the site recovered a large and diverse assemblage of material culture from the first seventy-five years of the household's occupation. The earliest assemblage was recovered from below the floorboards of a circa 1874 addition to the main block of the house. This pre-1874 deposit included almost four thousand animal bones alongside ceramics, glass, and other household refuse. A post-1889 cellar and a post-1905 privy containing dense deposits of household refuse, particularly bottle glass and canned goods, also were excavated.[24] The rich assemblage of national brand bottled goods and canned foods reflects rapid and devoted consumption of brand-name goods by the households. The presence of many nationally advertised goods suggests that at least some African Americans embraced emergent mass consumption, despite the common archaeological assumption that African Americans were too impoverished or too culturally distinctive to quickly become part of consumer culture.

Two less extensive excavations of African American neighborhoods were conducted by Archaeology in Annapolis on the Courthouse Site and Gott's Court. The Gott's Court site was a brief excavation at the location of a circa 1907–1950s African American alley community. The neighborhood consisted of twenty-five connected frame dwellings occupied by working-class African American renters.[25] The Courthouse Site was a predominantly African American neighborhood occupied by both homeowners and renters from the mid-nineteenth century into the 1960s. The Phase II excavations identified several structural remains, backyard refuse, a barrel privy, and a pet burial.[26] Phase III excavations of the property were conducted by Archaeology in Annapolis during the summer of 1994. Perhaps the most important contribution of these two modest excavations was the beginning of an oral history project. In addition to providing straightforward information on African American neighborhoods and everyday life, African American memoirists have directed us toward subjects of interest to the contemporary community and guided interpretations of archaeological materials.

Town Plan

In addition to archaeology which has focused on specific households, several excavations have focused on the town's plan. Baroque design was incorporated into the Annapolis grid plan when it succeeded St. Mary's as Maryland's capital in 1694. The Baroque-style grid had radiating circles on the town's two highest points, and circles containing the State House and Church were placed upon those two points. Extending from the two prominent circles were long streets which formed vistas that channeled sight toward the Church and State House. It has been modified continually for three centuries, yet that Baroque grid remains the most striking feature of the contemporary Annapolitan landscape. The numerous apparently meaningless modifications of the grid reflect the social and economic crises which Annapolis has weathered since 1694. Archaeology throughout the plan has charted and placed firm chronologies on numerous alterations which reflect continual social and economic change in the city.

In 1985 excavations were done in the front yard of the State House Inn on State Circle, and archaeologists monitored the excavation of utility lines across State Circle. Excavations located mid-eighteenth-century post holes lining State Circle about ten feet from the present curb. Examination of the trench across State Circle indicates that during the late eighteenth century the lands surrounding the capital were graded. This evidence indicates that the areas within and surrounding State Circle were constantly changing from the late seventeenth century, suggesting consistent reconceptualization of the town plan.[27]

This hypothesis was explored in greater detail in 1989–90, when Archaeology in Annapolis conducted additional excavations around the entire perimeter of the circle. These excavations again identified a number of modifications of the circle over time.[28] Archaeologically identified changes indicated that, over time, the circle has been a place of business, a center for state government, a transportation venue, a residence, a historic site, and a tourist trap. These functions often have conflicted with one another, and various parties have attempted to satisfy their interests by modifying the Annapolis landscape. Consequently, the movement of sidewalks, widening of roads, and grading of streets are some apparently insignificant activities which reflect quite different perceptions of the meaning of the cultural landscape.

The Volume

Scholarly work on Annapolis has been conducted on varying scales, from the level of isolated backyards to local, regional, and national perspectives. The research questions which have explored these different scales also have utilized diverse classes of information ranging from ceramic dishes to food refuse to formal landscapes to historical texts. The theoretical orientations of members of this project consequently varies from processual to Marxist to post-structuralist. Despite such variation, all the project's researchers have used Annapolis's archaeological data to interpret the emergence and elaboration of capitalism as a dynamic market force and an equally dynamic body of social rules.

Consequently, the research questions and theoretical frameworks represented in this volume are necessarily interrelated. They are connected in one sense by the shared analytical methods and interpretive approaches of anthropology as an academic discipline. Yet, these essays reflect that even within these disciplinary boundaries archaeologists design and exercise many creative research strategies which borrow heavily from other disciplines. The authors in this volume also are connected by a common interest in the development and expansion of a dominant European and Anglo-American socioeconomic system. The essays illustrate that this dominant socioeconomic system is heterogeneous and has fostered distinctive experiences across ethnic, gender, and class boundaries. These experiences, taken together, provide considerable insight into the dynamism and pervasiveness of European capitalism.

We have organized the volume by dividing it into three sections which illustrate the project's central research themes.

The first part, "Presentation of the Past," examines how archaeologists and nonarchaeologists construct historical knowledge and present that interpretation. The articles are concerned with how archaeologists recognize the effects of contemporary social context in shaping their research questions and interpretations. We also examine how marginalized people, such as African Americans, cultivate group-based histories which contrast to, subvert, or consciously spurn dominant historical accounts of "their" past. Archaeology in Annapolis has attempted to use archaeology to create history in dialogue with the peoples who feel proprietorship of certain historical interpretations. Archaeologies produced by archaeologists and contemporary people working together promise important implications for archaeological interpretation. More significantly, an archaeology shaped by issues which are pertinent to contemporary people can be an empowering voice for groups that are commonly neglected or ignored by archaeologists. These chapters suggest how to produce interpretations which can be conscious of contemporary social conditions and socially useful to a broad range of contemporary people.

The second part, "Everyday Lifeways," examines some of the unobserved forms which embrace, negotiate, resist, and rebuff dominant social practices. Capitalism certainly took the well-studied forms of socioeconomic hierarchies, ostentatious architecture, and a series of distinct political and economic systems, but it also is reflected in material minutia such as food remains, community craft networks, and vernacular architecture. The interests of dominant society are not simply indicated by the goals of powerful groups like the colonial elite; they also are expressed in the everyday material objects and cultural practices which surround all social agents. Indeed, much of the success of modern capitalism can be attributed to its dissemination in the apparently innocuous form of everyday material goods. This section includes an archaeology of groups which the discipline has ignored, slighted, or reduced to dominant Eurocentric terms. These chapters are interested in the alternative identities subordinated groups constructed for themselves, identities which resist dominant cultural characterizations while negotiating social inequality. These people "without" histories, such as African Americans, women, and the working class, are obviously an integral element in the fabric of the past, despite their lack of historical visibility. Illuminating them harbors one of historical archaeology's greatest potential contributions.

The third part, "Landscape and Architecture," is concerned with two broad senses of landscape. The first is the physical landscape; i.e., the buildings, space, and topography which people manipulate and negotiate. The second, intimately related sense of landscape is the cultural landscape, the meanings which people construct for the houses, gardens, and cityscapes they confront. The chapters in this section reflect the project's interest in both dominant society's effort to express power through landscape management and the way social agents actively modify, accept, or reject those meanings.

One volume cannot cover the entire range of work performed by historical archaeologists working in Annapolis,[29] and it does not aspire to provide a plan for how historical archaeology should be done everywhere else. Annapolis itself provides a particularly rich but by no means unique resource: similarly challenging work has been done in other places, and it certainly could be done in many more. This collection instead demonstrates how archaeologists convincingly can interpret many different social, temporal, and theoretical pieces of a city's history. The volume is a cross-section of some of the questions and perspectives which have been developed by archaeologists in Annapolis. We hope readers will find in these essays some answers, some questions, and numerous stimuli to promote further work from many other perspectives.

Notes

1. Nancy Baker, "Annapolis, Maryland 1695–1730," *Maryland Historical Magazine* 81 (3) (1986): 191–209; Constance Werner Ramirez, *Urban History for Preservation Planning: The Annapolis Experience* (Ann Arbor, Mich.: Univ. Microfilms International, 1975), 33.

2. Edward Papenfuse, *In Pursuit of Profit: The Annapolis Merchant in the Era of the American Revolution, 1763–1805* (Baltimore: Johns Hopkins Univ. Press, 1975), 8; Elihu Riley, *The Ancient City: A History of Annapolis, in Maryland 1649–1887* (Annapolis: Record Printing Office, 1887), 46–53.

3. Riley, *The Ancient City*, 54–58.

4. John W. Reps, *Tidewater Towns: City Planning in Colonial Virginia and Maryland* (Williamsburg, Va.: Colonial Williamsburg Foundation, 1972), 121.

5. Mark P. Leone, Julie H. Ernstein, Elizabeth Kryder-Reid, and Paul A. Shackel, "Power Gardens of Annapolis," *Archaeology* 42 (2) (1989): 34–37, 74–75; Paul A. Shackel, *Personal Discipline and Material Culture: An Archaeology of Annapolis, Maryland, 1695–1870* (Knoxville: Univ. of Tennessee Press, 1993).

6. Ramirez, *Urban History*, 38–40.

7. Jean Russo, "Economy of Anne Arundel County," in *Annapolis and Anne Arundel County, Maryland: A Study of Urban Development in a Tobacco Economy; 1649–1776*, ed. Lorena S. Walsh, N.E.H. Grant RS-20199-81-1955 (Maryland State Archives, Annapolis, 1983), appendix.

8. Aubrey Land, ed., *Letters from America by William Eddis* (Cambridge: Harvard Univ. Press, 1969), 13.

9. Papenfuse, *In Pursuit of Profit*.

10. Robert J. Brugger, *Maryland: A Middle Temperament, 1634–1980* (Baltimore: Johns Hopkins Univ. Press, 1988), 46; Sallie Ives, "Black Community Development in Annapolis, Maryland, 1870–1885," in *Geographical Perspectives on Maryland's Past*, ed. Robert D. Mitchell and Edward K. Muller (College Park: Dept. of Geography, Univ. of Maryland), 133; Papenfuse, *In Pursuit of Profit*, 14.

11. Ives, "Black Community Development," 147; James M. Wright, *The Free Negro in Maryland, 1634–1860* (1921; reprint, New York: Octagon Books, 1971), 191.

12. Paul A. Shackel, "Town Plans and Everyday Material Culture: An Archaeology of Social Relations in Colonial Maryland's Capital Cities," in *Historical Archaeology of the Chesapeake*, ed. Paul A. Shackel and Barbara J. Little (Washington, D.C.: Smithsonian Institution Press, 1994), 85–96.

13. Constance A. Crosby, *Excavations at the Victualling Warehouse, Jan. 14, 1982:*

Preliminary Report (Annapolis: Historic Annapolis Foundation, 1982); Marlys J. Pearson, *Archaeological Excavations at 18AP14: The Victualling Warehouse Site, 77 Main St., Annapolis, Maryland 1982–84* (Annapolis: Historic Annapolis Foundation, 1991).

14. Barbara J. Little, *18AP29, Jonas Green Print Shop: Printers' Type from the 1983 Excavation* (Annapolis: Historic Annapolis Foundation, 1984); Little, *Ideology and Media: Historical Archaeology of Printing in Eighteenth-Century Annapolis, Maryland* (Ann Arbor, Mich.: Univ. Microfilms International, 1987), 118–29; Little, "'She Was . . . An Example to her Sex': Possibilities for a Feminist Historical Archaeology," in *Historical Archaeology of the Chesapeake*, 189–204.

15. Paul A. Shackel, *Archaeological Testing at the 193 Main Street Site, 18AP44, Annapolis, Maryland* (Annapolis: Historic Annapolis Foundation, 1986); Shackel, *Personal Discipline.*

16. Robert Mann, Douglas Owsley, and Paul A. Shackel, "A Reconstruction of 19th-Century Surgical Techniques: Bones in Dr. Thompson's Privy," *Historical Archaeology* 25 (1) (1991): 106–12.

17. See, for example, Ronald Hoffman, *"Anywhere so Long as there be Freedom'" Charles Carroll of Carrollton, His Family and His Maryland* (Baltimore: Baltimore Museum of Art, 1993); Gregory A. Stiverson and Phebe R. Jacobsen, *William Paca, A Biography* (Baltimore: Maryland Historical Society, 1976); Anne E. Yentsch, *A Chesapeake Family and Their Slaves: A Study in Historical Archaeology* (New York: Cambridge Univ. Press, 1994).

18. Stiverson and Jacobsen, *William Paca.*

19. Stanley A. South, *The Paca House, Annapolis, Maryland* (Annapolis: Historic Annapolis Foundation, 1967); South, *Method and Theory in Historical Archeology* (New York: Academic Press, 1977), 224, 229, 258; Laura J. Galke, *Paca Garden Archaeological Testing, 18AP01, 186 Prince George Street, Annapolis, Maryland* (Annapolis: Historic Annapolis Foundation, 1990); J. Glenn Little II, Archaeological Research on Paca Garden, 8 November 1967, 24 May 1968 (Unpubl. field notes, Historic Annapolis Foundation, 1967–68); K. G. Orr and R. G. Orr, *The Archaeological Situation at the William Paca Garden, Annapolis, Maryland: The Spring House and the Presumed Pavilion House Site* (Annapolis: Historic Annapolis Foundation, 1975); B. B. Powell, *Archaeological Investigations of the Paca House Gardens, Annapolis, Maryland* (Annapolis: Historic Annapolis Foundation, 1966); Anne E. Yentsch, "Spring House at Paca Garden, 16 March 1982," unpublished letter, Historic Annapolis Foundation, 1982.

20. Mark P. Leone, "Interpreting Ideology in Historical Archaeology: Using the Rules of Perspective in the William Paca Garden in Annapolis, Maryland," in *Ideology, Power and Prehistory*, ed. Daniel Miller and Christopher Tilley (Cambridge: Cambridge Univ. Press, 1984), 25–35; Leone, "Rule by Ostentation: The Relationship between Space and Sight in Eighteenth-Century Landscape Architecture in the Chesapeake Region of Maryland," in *Method and Theory for Activity Area Research: An Ethnoarchaeological Approach*, ed. Susan Kent (New York: Columbia Univ. Press, 1987), 604–33; Barbara Paca-Steele with St. Clair Wright,

"The Mathematics of an Eighteenth-Century Wilderness Garden," *Journal of Garden History* 6 (4) (1987): 299–320.

21. Anne E. Yentsch, "The Calvert Orangery in Annapolis, Maryland: A Horticultural Symbol of Power and Prestige in an Early 18th-Century Community," in *Earth Patterns: Essays in Landscape Archaeology*, ed. William M. Kelso and Rachel Most (Charlottesville: Univ. Press of Virginia, 1990), 169–87; Yentsch, *A Chesapeake Family*.

22. Elizabeth Kryder-Reid, "'As Is the Gardener, So Is the Garden': The Archaeology of Landscape as Myth," in *Historical Archaeology of the Chesapeake*, 131–48; Leone and Shackel, "Plane and Solid Geometry in Colonial Gardens in Annapolis, Maryland," in *Earth Patterns*, 153–67.

23. George C. Logan, Thomas W. Bodor, Lynn D. Jones, and Marian C. Creveling, *1991 Archaeological Excavations at the Charles Carroll House in Annapolis, Maryland, 18AP45* (Annapolis: Historic Annapolis Foundation, 1992).

24. Paul R. Mullins and Mark S. Warner, *Final Archaeological Investigations at the Maynard-Burgess House (18AP64), An 1850–1980 African-American Household in Annapolis, Maryland* (Annapolis: Historic Annapolis Foundation, 1993).

25. Mark S. Warner, *Test Excavations at Gott's Court Annapolis, Maryland, 18AP52* (Annapolis: Historic Annapolis Foundation, 1992); R. Christopher Goodwin, *Phase II/III Archaeological Investigations of the Gott's Court Parking Facility, Annapolis, Maryland* (Annapolis: Maryland Historic Trust, 1993).

26. Mark S. Warner and Paul R. Mullins, *Phase I–II Archaeological Investigations on the Courthouse Site (18AP63), An Historic African-American Neighborhood in Annapolis, Maryland* (Annapolis: Historic Annapolis Foundation, 1993).

27. Mark P. Leone and Paul A. Shackel, "Archaeology of Town Planning in Annapolis, Maryland," (Final report to the National Geographic Society, NGS Grant Number 3116-85; Annapolis, Historic Annapolis Foundation, 1986); Paul A. Shackel, Joseph W. Hopkins, and Eileen Williams, *Excavations at the State House Inn, 18AP42, State Circle, Annapolis, Maryland. A Final Report* (Annapolis: Historic Annapolis Foundation, 1988).

28. Esther Doyle-Read, Mark P. Leone, Barbara J. Little, Jean B. Russo, George C. Logan, and Brett Burk, *Archaeological Investigations Around State Circle in Annapolis, Maryland* (Annapolis: Historic Annapolis Foundation, 1990).

29. Anne Yentsch and Richard Dent were unable to participate in this volume. However, several references to their Annapolis work can be found in this book's bibliography.

Part I

Presentation of the Past

For many years archaeology was a fascinating curiosity, a magnetic yet enigmatic pursuit. Archaeology apparently was engaged in by cool-headed scientists who unearthed hidden truths in front of tourists' eyes. Anyone who visited an archaeological site or saw archaeological artifacts recognized that interpretation demanded highly specialized knowledge, yet interested constituents rarely were able to push beyond the mystery of that specialization.

Today, archaeologists are increasingly self-conscious of how the past is interpreted and archaeologists' relationship to the public. One of the most significant insights of New Archaeology was that the meaning of the objects we dig up is not self-evident, and today archaeologists are examining the interpretive process more aggressively than ever before.[1] There are no manifest research questions beneath the surface of every site; indeed, the very research questions we choose are shaped by the world in which we live today. Perhaps most significantly, archaeologists are working hard to make archaeology accessible, interesting, and pertinent to the many people who find something compelling in our interpretations.

How we interpret our excavations and the things we recover can vary quite dramatically, and the ways archaeologists develop research questions reflect many different perceptions of appropriate roles for historical archaeology. Consequently, archaeologists with many different theoretical perspectives have examined their internal philosophical assumptions and have come to a predictably wide range of conclusions. Perhaps the most prominent strain of self-reflection in historical archaeology stresses methodological rigor and clarity in interpretation as the means to defuse bias. Stanley South has most articulately championed empirical rigor and precise statements about how archaeological patterning relates to cultural processes.[2] South underscores the fundamental significance of explicit arguments which define the relationship between observed material culture patterns and social processes. Examples of historical archaeologists in this vein include John Solomon Otto and Kenneth Lewis.[3] Some historical archaeologists have borrowed from myriad textual theories which stress reader and authorial positionality. The archaeological thinking for that approach has been most clearly articulated by Ian Hodder.[4] Historical archaeologists who adapt various veins of such thought include Mary Beaudry, who stresses structuralist insight; Margaret Purser, who emphasizes authorial position; and Barbara Little, who examines textual metaphors in archaeological interpretation.[5] Still other historical archaeologists base self-reflection upon a fusion of disparate theories which stress power relations. Archaeologically, such thinking tends to build on the work of Michael Shanks and Christopher Tilley. Shanks and Tilley idiosyncratically borrow from structuralism, post-structuralism, and Marxism, yet they remain wedded to interpreting how archaeological knowledge is related to power relations. Historical archaeologists who borrow from this approach include Russell Handsman, who extensively integrates post-structuralism, and Terrence Epperson, who fuses post-structuralism and Marxism.[6] Yet another line of self-reflexiveness is firmly grounded in various strains of Marxism. Charles Orser and Robert Paynter, for example, each lean on well-developed Marxian thinking on class and self-consciousness.[7] Mark Leone emphasizes ideology, borrowing from Frankfurt School critical theory and Louis Althusser's structural Marxism.[8] Parker Potter blends Frankfurt School critical theory with hermeneutics, an approach articulated by Daniel Miller.[9] There certainly is no consensus among these archaeologists, but they clearly share concern about the construction of archaeological knowledge.

Such self-awareness of ourselves as a discipline and individual prac-titioners is not universally embraced. One concern is that increasing at-tention on the interpretive process itself forebodes a descent into pure philosophy or even political doctrine which will diminish archaeology's well-established empirical rigor.[10] A more extreme criticism is that archae-ology should be as depoliticized as possible and report "just the facts" in the most unbiased manner feasible. These and numerous other percep-tions of archaeology's role in the contemporary world are constantly played out on archaeological sites and in professional literature.

Like most contemporary archaeology projects, Archaeology in Annapo-lis always has opened its excavation sites to the public and been concerned that archaeology contribute to the community's sense of its history. The project's public programs encourage visitors to identify the evidence used to support historical interpretations, recognize how that data is used to interpret a research issue, and critically examine interpretations, particu-larly those that are presented as self-evident facts. Our interpretive pro-gram builds on the idea that self-critical visitors will be most likely to ask questions which will challenge inherited perceptions of history and ex-amine the relationship between the contemporary world and the past. Archaeology offers a particularly vital means to build such a critical aware-ness because the process of interpretation can be made clearly visible on an archaeological site. Every person who visits an archaeological site immediately realizes that there is virtually nothing self-evident about its meaning; to an untrained eye, the scatters of artifacts, soil strata, and dis-tinctive equipment on an archaeology site appear almost incomprehen-sible. Visitors can see that archaeological knowledge is constructed, but to most visitors the systematic techniques and the logic of research are often mystifying or simply ignored. Rather than dwell upon fascinating excavated objects, our tours introduce the basic methods of excavation—stratigraphy, tools, record-keeping, artifact analysis, and so on—so that visitors can begin to move beyond the mystification of wondering how ar-chaeologists know the things they know.

Like any knowledge, historical archaeology is produced in the contem-porary world for concrete historical, social, and class interests. We have been quite open about our research questions on sticky and unsettling issues such as racism, class conflict, and capitalism. We work to demon-strate how apparently disconnected phenomena such as class structure and ceramic plates were implicated in the same social transformations.

This makes for interesting but challenging archaeological tours. Our philosophy runs counter to the school of thought that visitors simply want to be entertained. There perhaps is some truth to that, but it is short-sighted at best and arrogant at worst to assume that nonarchaeologists cannot critique interpretations or contribute to the development of research questions. Like most archaeologists today, we perceive visitors to our sites as constituents who will engage us when we explore historical questions which are important to them. Visitors may enter a site simply as a curious audience, but we want them to leave with a clear sense that archaeology has something to say about their society. Every archaeologist who has done regular public presentations realizes that this makes for engaging, challenging, and unpredictable archaeology. Teenage African Americans, for instance, are among the most incisive social critics of our African American archaeology projects, and some visitors to our eighteenth-century excavations are quite willing to openly celebrate and defend their willing incorporation into capitalist society. The vitality of such dialogues on an archaeological site reflects that people realize that historical presentations are political. With encouragement they can penetrate and reject socially naive archaeologies as quickly as they become bored by simplistic historical tours.

Archaeology in Annapolis clearly is not alone in the effort to systematically present archaeological interpretations and develop increasingly challenging archaeologies. The chapters in this section examine some of the approaches project researchers have taken to generate research questions and present our interpretations. Paul Mullins's essay probes some of the unexamined interpretive logic in archaeological scholarship. His study examines how the project's use of critical metaphors derived from Marxism have added to and critiqued some of archaeology's dominant perspectives. Using examples from the project's research on formal gardens and African American consumption, Mullins demonstrates that self-reflexiveness and consciousness of contemporary social structure will not necessarily disable archaeology's empirical rigor. Contrary to some caricatures of Marxism and the overwhelming sway of ideology, Mullins argues that archaeologies building on Marxism are compelled to confront the complexity of power relations and the genuine leverage of myriad forms of resistance.

Parker Potter examines how ethnographic methods are critical to the way in which the project developed its research questions and has attempted to produce an archaeology which is both historically pertinent and socially challenging to contemporary Annapolitans. Potter argues that many contemporary practices which superficially have nothing to do with the past—the use of parking spaces, Annapolitans' views of tourists, or the local newspaper—actually say a great deal about a community's perception of its history. He offers some examples of how he did archaeological ethnography over several years of living in Annapolis and writing about the relationship between tourism, history, archaeology, and a living community.

George Logan charts the development of Archaeology in Annapolis's African American archaeology project and examines the potential for similar community-based archaeological programs which seek to make historical interpretations more inclusive. Logan explains what Archaeology in Annapolis tries to accomplish through its public interpretation programs and discusses the distinctive aspects of the African American project. The African American archaeology project required new strategies for promoting community involvement and developing research questions, and community input influenced virtually every educational activity in the project. Logan stresses the importance of listening to our constituents and concedes that some of our own strategies were ineffective or misguided. He concludes that project-community interaction must be an integral part of the planning process as well as a goal of educational programming.

The section concludes with Hannah Jopling's study of the oral history project, which she has directed as part of Archaeology in Annapolis research. Jopling examines how her oral histories of two marginalized Annapolitan communities demonstrate the fluidity of communal definition and reflect the ways in which marginalized peoples remember their past community to empower themselves in the present. Jopling argues that her memoirists attempt to shape history to negotiate contemporary society and provide some coherent bridge between their past and present. One group of memoirists from an ethnically mixed neighborhood known as Hell Point tended to use their neighborhood's past marginalization to display their subsequent achievements. Members of the other group from the working-class African American community known as Gott's Court more often used their perception of the past to negotiate problems in their contemporary neighborhoods. Jopling demonstrates that the way communities are remembered from both the "inside" and "outside" is a quite fluid negotiation of their relationships with other groups in Annapolis and their historical experience since leaving their former neighborhoods.

Notes

1. For example, compare Robert W. Preucel, ed., *Processual and Postprocessual Archaeologies* (Carbondale: Southern Illinois Univ. Press), and Michael Shanks, *Experiencing the Past* (London: Routledge, 1992). For a discussion of self-reflection in new archaeology, see Alison Wylie, "The Interpretive Dilemma," in *Critical Traditions in Contemporary Archaeology*, ed. Valerie Pinsky and Alison Wylie (Cambridge: Cambridge Univ. Press, 1989), 18–27.

2. Compare Stanley South, *Method and Theory in Historical Archaeology* (New York: Academic Press, 1977), and "Santa Elena: Threshold of Conquest," in *The Recovery of Meaning: Historical Archaeology in the Eastern United States*, ed. Mark P. Leone and Parker B. Potter Jr. (Washington, D.C.: Smithsonian Institution Press, 1988), 27–71.

3. John Solomon Otto, "Race and Class on Antebellum Plantations," in *Archaeological Perspectives on Ethnicity in America: Afro-American and Asian American Cultural History*, ed. Robert L. Schuyler (Farmingdale, N.Y.: Baywood, 1980), 3–13; and Kenneth E. Lewis and Helen W. Haskell, *The Middleton Place Privy: A Study of Discard Behavior and the Archaeological Record* (Columbia, S.C.: South Carolina Institute for Archaeology and Anthropology, 1981).

4. Ian Hodder, *Reading the Past* (Cambridge: Cambridge Univ. Press, 1986).

5. Mary C. Beaudry, ed., *Documentary Archaeology in the New World* (Cambridge: Cambridge Univ. Press, 1988); Margaret Purser, "Consumption as Communication in Nineteenth-Century Paradise Valley, Nevada," *Historical Archaeology* 26 (3) (1992): 105–16; and Barbara Little, ed., *Text-Aided Archaeology* (Boca Raton, Fla.: CRC Press, 1992).

6. Russell G. Handsman, "The Still-Hidden Histories of Color and Class: Public Archaeology and the Depot Village of West Kingston, Rhode Island," paper presented at the Conference on New England Archaeology, 1995; and Terrence W. Epperson, "Race and the Disciplines of the Plantation," *Historical Archaeology* 24 (4) (1990): 29–36.

7. Charles E. Orser Jr., *The Material Basis of the Postbellum Tenant Plantation: Historical Archaeology in the South Carolina Piedmont* (Athens: Univ. of Georgia Press, 1988); and Robert Paynter, "Steps to an Archaeology of Capitalism: Material Change and Class Analysis," in *The Recovery of Meaning*, 407–33.

8. Mark P. Leone, "Interpreting Ideology in Historical Archaeology: Using the Rules of Perspective in the William Paca Garden in Annapolis, Maryland," in *Ideology, Power, and Prehistory*, ed. Daniel Miller and Christopher Tilley (Cambridge: Cambridge Univ. Press, 1984), 25–35.

9. Parker B. Potter Jr., *Public Archaeology in Annapolis: A Critical Approach to History in Maryland's "Ancient City"* (Washington, D.C.: Smithsonian Institution Press, 1994); and Daniel Miller, *Material Culture and Mass Consumption* (Oxford: Basil Blackwell, 1987).

10. For example, see Michael Brian Schiffer, "Review of *Experiencing the Past: On the Character of Archaeology*," *American Antiquity* 59 (1) (1994): 158–59.

1

Expanding Archaeological Discourse: Ideology, Metaphor, and Critical Theory in Historical Archaeology

Paul R. Mullins

Contemporary historical archaeology is populated by a spectrum of functional, structural, and post-processual currents which probe a wide range of research questions. It would be self-deceiving, though, to suggest that historical archaeologists do not persistently concentrate on a narrow range of subjects which are interpreted through a handful of perspectives. A diverse range of archaeologists have contemplated how the discipline can build and expand upon these key questions and perspectives.[1] This chapter focuses on how the central research questions and interpretive approaches of Archaeology in Annapolis have attempted to contribute to this expansion of historical archaeology. Archaeology in Annapolis is a participant in a widespread effort to illuminate the emergence and development of capitalism, scrutinize the diversity of historically slighted experiences, and suggest how archaeological interpretation can be enriched by a diversity of contemporary voices both within and outside the discipline. Archaeology in Annapolis's Marxian-derived emphases on ideology, public interpretation, and self-reflection are distinctive, but they are by no means unique, definitive, or exclusive to Marxian thinkers; indeed, the discourses examined in this essay borrow from a diverse range of archaeological scholars.[2]

The first section examines the key metaphors historical archaeologists have forged to interpret the material world. Despite its abstraction, some of the scholarship on metaphor has been quite creatively appropriated by archaeologists, and it harbors the potential to make a significant contribution to the discipline.[3] The predominant metaphors in contemporary historical archaeology revolve around status.[4] The section examines how the metaphors embedded in status studies reflect the discipline's construction of a distinctive (and occasionally self-restrictive) methodological and interpretive niche. I then suggest how Archaeology in Annapolis's public program has attempted to confront the flexible metaphors different people use to understand the past.

The second section examines metaphors based in Marxism, concentrating on the concept of ideology. Archaeology in Annapolis's central research questions are based on these metaphors, particularly in the critical theory developed by Mark Leone, Parker Potter, and Paul Shackel.[5] I examine a well-known case study from Annapolis, Leone's study of William Paca's formal garden, to scrutinize the strengths and shortcomings of Marxian insights in historical archaeology.[6] My intention is to defuse the criticism that Marxian-influenced archaeologies in general and ideology in particular inevitably slight or ignore the myriad ways the masses subvert and impact domination.

I close this chapter by pondering how to address some of critical theory's shortcomings yet preserve its distinctive and compelling insights. As an archaeological example of the expansion of critical theory, I examine African American archaeology in Annapolis. Material culture from turn-of-the-twentieth-century African American sites stresses the complex tension between dominant ideologies and the everyday resistance to and reproduction of domination. African American archaeologies can persuasively draw on both appreciation of dominant ideologies as well as perspectives which concentrate on resistance to such ideological domination.

Perceiving Pasts: Archaeological Metaphors

> What then is truth? A mobile army of metaphors, metonyms, and anthropomorphisms—in short a sum of human relations which have been enhanced, transposed, and embellished poetically and rhetorically, and which after long use seem firm, canonical, and obligatory to a people. . . .
>
> —Friedrich Nietzsche, "On Truth and Lie in an Extra-Moral Sense"

An examination of metaphors is essential to understanding how any discipline defines and interprets its subjects. Metaphors establish an identity between dissimilar subjects by describing the unknown in terms of known phenomena, which requires that some phenomena have accepted literal meanings.[7] Metaphors are necessary linguistic mechanisms which register similarities and differences in research subjects and clarify them by linking them with better-known subjects.[8] Like any discourse, historical archaeology uses a distinctive range of metaphors to create meanings.[9] Those metaphors include, among other things, concepts such as site significance, cost-status and consumer behavior, and systemic relationships. The discipline uses these concepts to define research interests and establish particular relationships between contemporary society and historical subjects.

All archaeological interpretation uses distinct conventions for constructing questions, defining data, and establishing some sort of relationship between the past and present. Systems theorists, structuralists, and functionalists, for instance, each rely on particular metaphors which use different strategies to define and examine research issues and establish relationships between past and present. There is no way to escape such a process; however, in conceptualizing certain inquiries as part of "proper" archaeological discourse, other questions and meanings are inevitably neglected, peripheralized, or rejected.[10]

Most of the thinking on metaphor comes from philosophy and literary criticism. Critics of such theory's emergence in archaeology are quick to lament that it marks an inevitable "descent into discourse" in which words can mean anything.[11] However, the universe of metaphors used in our discipline (and every other) is finite and not prone to continual revolutionary change: if there were endless metaphors and constant transformation, we would be left with neither disciplinary standards nor any remotely coherent interpretation. Rather than caricature this literature, our attention should focus on how the discipline establishes standards, evaluates competing interpretive perspectives, and produces something distinctive from competing ways of interpreting material culture.

Status and Archaeological Metaphors

The most pervasive metaphors in historical archaeology come from the study of "socioeconomic status." Historical archaeology's archetypal status study

is John Solomon Otto's examination of relative intra-plantation material variation and status differences at the Georgia plantation called Cannon's Point.[12]
Subsequent status research has borrowed most clearly from George Miller's
ceramic indices, which base interpretation of status upon the original cost of
English ceramics.[13] A stream of models in the wake of Otto and Miller examine relative artifact value or original cost and cast that analysis within a socioeconomic status ranking, which has been taken to mean myriad things.[14]
The recent tide of consumer behavior studies follow Miller's lead, privileging initial exchange value and illuminating the relationship between consuming masses and worldwide commodity exchange systems. However, studies
which stop at the analysis of goods' values risk imposing an absolute comparative scale which defines and even values consumers by the cost of their
artifacts. Status studies pose significant heuristic insight, but they always
hazard even unintentionally imposing a universal interpretive logic. A fixation
on initial cost risks reducing objects' meanings to a reflection of disposable
income and economic value, neglecting wholly meaningful symbolism which
has little or nothing to do with an object's cost. Historical archaeologists cannot discard such genuinely useful methods and insight; we simply should
remain conscious of their limitations.

Effective archaeological metaphors make the past "visible" by identifying the past as different from the present, if not alien.[15] Archaeology in this
sense is neither a mechanical documentation of an objective past nor a mere
projection of the present onto the past. Instead, archaeology illuminates the
way in which we define relations between the past and present.[16] Archaeological tours in Annapolis have stressed that the past "changes" because it
can be interpreted differently across time and between groups. Today, for
instance, guides in colonial garb spirit visitors through Annapolis's streets in
the footsteps of George Washington, who came to Annapolis for everything
from haircuts to the resignation of his Continental Army commission.[17] Of
course, reducing Annapolis to "Washington's town" is a transparent marketing tool, and it inevitably slights experiences that complicate the simplicity
of the canned tour. Washington's Annapolitan experience certainly was radically unlike that of the Africans sold into servitude on the Annapolis docks.
While most white Annapolitans have literally or figuratively profited from the
city's historicity, African Americans systematically were displaced from the
historic district during the 1960s and 1970s, including many of the streets
Washington traveled along.[18] The African American experience of this same
space was and still is one shaped by racism. By fixating almost exclusively

on white elite history in Annapolis, tours craft an illusory white genteel history as the backdrop against which all Annapolitan experiences should be defined. A critical African American tour of the city clearly would be a quite different experience than the contrived optimism and tacit whiteness of a George Washington tour.

Through our public program, Archaeology in Annapolis has attempted to demonstrate how archaeology in general and our project in particular investigate and interpret the past. The public interpretation program explains the mechanics of excavation, discusses how we develop our interpretations, and encourages visitors to interrogate our perceptions of the past. The intent of this program is to promote a continual dialogue on the construction of the past: we attempt to demonstrate how we methodologically assemble archaeological data and why we choose certain research subjects.

The significance of this dialogue seems clear: archaeology constructs the past for the present; the past simply does not exist without interpretation developed by and for people in the present. This hint of relativity is not widely embraced within archaeology. The most conventional criticism is that such logic risks rendering all interpretations equal. Unconvinced by the instability of metaphor, some archaeologists argue that muddy interpretation of an objective archaeological context harbors no criteria for judging between right and wrong.[19]

This argument deflates itself on at least two counts. First, it assumes that we share the same criteria for evaluating an interpretation, implying that we must all share the identical way of defining and analyzing our subjects. Yet, if we were to ask any group of archaeologists to define apparently self-evident concepts such as class or status, there would be a range of legitimate, albeit contrasting perceptions of how such concepts are defined or interpreted archaeologically. Second, it assumes that there is an essential reality to the past, a truth at which proper method inevitably converges.[20] But of course a single archaeological assemblage can accommodate various interpretive foci (e.g., women's experiences, class identity, and so on), and the same sites can accommodate analyses which stress different types of data (e.g., ceramics, primary texts, landscape, and so on). If a research interpretation is not persuasively supported by a particular assemblage, then practitioners can and will reject the explanation. Obviously, there must be disciplinary consensus on basic issues and methods, but those issues and methods are not self-evident; instead, they are determined by concrete debate among archaeologists.[21]

To concede the contingency of archaeology's basic metaphors does not mean that the way we discuss our subjects will undergo constant, "postmodern" transformation: if anything, a discipline's most basic concepts persist and change rarely.[22] Disciplinary standards change gradually, but their stability ensures that every metaphor simply is not as good as the next. Ultimately, the discipline and each practitioner evaluates interpretations and determines whether to accept them, remain unconvinced, perceive contradictions, or reject the perspective entirely. It is that process which slowly yet systematically erodes established interpretive approaches and promotes new perspectives.

Critical Archaeological Theory

Archaeology in Annapolis has been less interested in *how* society works than *why* it has worked in the face of 250 years of considerable social and economic inequality; i.e., we have attempted to identify the concrete social and material practices which have persuaded or compelled people to accept or tolerate often overwhelming inequality. Our research questions have concentrated on the way people negotiate class inequality, metaphors which were developed by Marx and a subsequent century of thinkers.[23] Like other scholars who use elements of Marxian theories, our questions revolve around Marxism's emphases on contradiction; its focus upon the social whole rather than its isolated parts; the contingency of knowledge; and Marxism's critique of class-based injustice.[24]

For various reasons, some archaeologists are immediately repelled by the specter of Marxism. Some scholars uncomfortable with Marxism's critique of capitalism do not see the critique of our own society as part of historical archaeology's mission. Others are apprehensive of the media caricature of Marxism as a totalizing instrument to engineer social control and extinguish personal freedoms. Still others are simply uneasy that archaeology should assertively advocate for any social interest, and such advocacy is fundamental to Marxian critique.[25] Archaeology in Annapolis has used elements of Marxian thought to emphasize our position in a capitalist world, to appreciate the historical roots of contemporary dilemmas, to acknowledge the objective restrictions which capitalism imposes, and to recognize the often-ignored creativity, subversion, and fulfillment which has existed within, yet defied and shaped, capitalism.

The critical archaeology elaborated by Archaeology in Annapolis adapts the thinking of the Frankfurt School of critical theory. The critical theorists were a group of scholars based in the Institute for Social Research in Frankfurt from 1923 until the 1930s.[26] The institute was composed of thinkers who wanted to retool Marx's critique of capitalism. As scholars trained in traditional Marxism, the critical theorists were sobered by the absence of a proletarian revolution in the face of profound material crises in the 1920s and 1930s. A half-century earlier, Marx had viewed such revolution as an inevitability in the cyclical destabilization of capitalist economies. The critical theorists believed twentieth-century capitalism and emerging fascist states had somehow defused working-class revolutionary consciousness.[27] They were particularly wary of mass cultural forms, including popular music, film, art, and mass-produced commodities, concluding that popular culture was an obstacle to social change which harbored little or no emancipatory potential. Through such seemingly innocuous popular forms, the critical theorists believed capitalism came to dominate every aspect of the masses' lives.

The basic ideas of the Frankfurt School continue to resonate in the work of many contemporary scholars.[28] Critical theorists share a fundamental desire to emancipate people from oppression and rationally reorder society. Critical theorists view the exposure of social illusions as the means to raise consciousness about objective inequalities and work toward changing them. In contrast, post-structuralists and postmodernists tend to favor great relativism, shrink from normative critique, and focus on deconstruction itself.

The critical theory developed by Leone, Potter, and Shackel borrows heavily from the Frankfurt School's notion of ideology as a totalizing, class-interested illusion. The Frankfurt School incorporated emergent psychoanalytic theory to envision ideology as a collective social illusion which permeates every idea and legitimizes social structure. In other hands, ideology has been taken to mean everything from imposed "false consciousness" to a general worldview.[29] In most Marxian definitions, ideology distorts material relations, and one class's dominance, to reproduce material inequality.[30] In Leone, Potter, and Shackel's formulation, ideology fragments consciousness of shared experiences among subordinated classes. In this vein, Parker Potter has argued that Annapolis's historical accounts are ideological in their polarized fragmentation of black and white histories and the cleavage of Naval Academy history from the history of Annapolis. These divisions obscure fundamental tensions which connect African Americans with whites and the Naval Academy with Annapolis:

ideologies extinguish challenges to established power relations by creating distinctions where none exist. These shared systems of understanding are the essential building blocks for class consciousness, a consciousness which elites attempt to deny to subordinated groups.[31]

Ideology in the Garden: A Marxian Archaeology of the William Paca Garden

The most widely discussed interpretation of ideology in Annapolis has been Leone's study of the William Paca Garden.[32] In the 1760s, lawyer William Paca built a Georgian mansion fronting a "pleasure garden." Paca, who later signed the Declaration of Independence and became a prominent constitutional lawyer, was one of a series of Chesapeake gentry who built such formal gardens during the 1760s and 1770s. The gardens have rolling topography (i.e., flat terraces alternating with sloping falls) and carefully manicured spaces which contain shrubs, trees, some exotic plants, ponds, and fountains arranged in geometric forms like the Georgian architecture they mirror. The perception of distances and the relative size of objects in the gardens is distorted by the effect of the topography and prominent features (such as gazebos, houses, or vegetation) which manipulate a visitor's line of sight within the garden's volume. A series of such gardens was built by elite Annapolitans including Paca and Charles Carroll of Carrollton, who also signed the Declaration of Independence.[33] Formal gardens were built throughout the Chesapeake during this period.

Leone argues that formal gardens were one of the Chesapeake elite's material responses to pre-Revolutionary socioeconomic instabilities. The power of the domestic elite was destabilized during the twenty years leading up to the American Revolution, and Leone argues that members of this elite began to seek new ideological mechanisms to re-establish, legitimize, and cling to their class influence. This line of thinking builds on Rhys Isaac's argument that between 1740 and 1790 the Tidewater gentry became increasingly detached from other groups both within and outside the colonies.[34] The Crown, on the one hand, attempted to recoup increasing debts through increasingly restrictive socioeconomic policies which formerly reproduced the power of the domestic elite. On the other hand, the economic power of the colonial American elite relied upon the production and oppression of enslaved Africans and increasingly alienated Anglo masses. Threatened by the progressive deterioration of these relations with both the Crown and the masses, Isaac argues that the elite developed a cohesive class identity reflected in Georgian material culture and social practices.

In the Chesapeake, this new material culture included the building of formal gardens. Leone suggests that gardens served two fundamental ideological effects: they ordered nature in a specific way, and they constructed a distinct past for that nature. The ordering of nature involved systematic observation of the garden, which enabled the gardener to predict natural growth cycles, and the manipulation of sight within the garden. Gardeners' ability to display their comprehension of natural law and control optics in the garden created a social space which displayed the gentry's ability to order nature itself. The ordering of nature, Leone argues, was openly displayed in formal gardens as part of the elite's effort to legitimize and reproduce their eroding domination. The gardens attempted to make the elite appear unique, demonstrate their exclusive knowledge, and suggest that their class power was based in a rational nature, rather than objective socioeconomic domination.

Landscape manipulation attempted to persuade viewers that gentry domination was appropriate, but that ideology could only be persuasive through a wide range of material mechanisms and social discourses. Those other discourses and material practices are at best tacit in Leone's analysis. Clearly, though, the construction of formal gardens was simply a single material strategy in the Annapolitan gentry's ongoing campaign to reproduce and legitimize its social power. The gardens could never have been remotely persuasive if they were viewed in isolation from the gentry's full range of ideological mechanisms. Our own assessment of the gardens' ideological persuasiveness is likewise compelled to consider gardens as just one element among many related strategies which had varying degrees of persuasiveness.

A measured critique of Leone's Paca analysis (and ideology in general) is compelled to probe how people actually resist dominant ideologies. However, Leone hazards exaggerating the force of landscape ideology by slighting resistance; i.e., he neglects how people in gardens (or peering over their walls or ignoring them altogether) subverted or ignored the gentry's bid to ground its power in "natural law." Rather than scrutinize scattered resistance as a force in pre-Revolutionary War social change,

Leone primarily situates that change in interdependent shifts in material wealth distribution and behavioral ideologies (e.g., individualism, science, etiquette, etc.).

Leone privileges material wealth as the predominant factor determining the local forms capitalism assumed. However he acknowledges that *local* responses to economic change and disciplinary ideology structured the contours of American class and social structure. This concession of the sway of local agency and variation is crucial (albeit understated), because it admits the potential power of resistance. Leone concludes that capitalism tends to eventually absorb resistance and homogenize alternative cultural practices, so his concession of resistance risks ringing hollow. To nuance Leone's analysis of Annapolis gardens, it is vital to more aggressively probe for resistance to landscape ideologies and demonstrate how such resistance impacted, frustrated, and changed dominant ideology. Even if people are incorporated into dominant ideology, that incorporation does not preclude conflict: ideology can produce disciplinary acquiescence and can muffle mass aspirations without producing automatons mystified by material power relations.[35]

Georgian ideology undoubtedly was effectively resisted by the masses in infinite ways, and traces of such resistance lurk in mainstream documents as well as material culture. For instance, in June 1770 Charles Carroll of Carrollton placed the following warning in the *Maryland Gazette:* "And whereas several idle disorderly Persons are continually forcing their Way into the Garden of the Subscriber, in this City, either by breaking down the Rails or leaping over them, in order to steal Fruit, and have done considerable Damage to the Trees and Shrubs in the said Garden; this is to give Notice, that if any Person or Persons are detected in being Guilty of this Offense for the Future, they will be punished with utmost Severity."[36]

These "disorderly Persons" pilfering fruit from Charles Carroll do not appear to have been utterly persuaded by the gentry domination fashioned in Carroll's garden. Indeed, they may well have targeted Carroll's garden precisely because it symbolized elite power and betrayed his apprehension that he could not reproduce that power. Even the gardeners themselves might resist. In July 1766, for example, William Paca placed this notice in the *Maryland Gazette:* "Ran away from the Subscriber, about a Fortnight ago, a Convict Servant Man, named John Morgan, by trade a shoemaker, and pretends to be a Gardener. . . . Whoever secures the said

Servant, so that the Subscriber may have him again, shall have Twenty Shillings Reward."[37] The desertion of John Morgan suggests that he was not convinced that William Paca deserved any "natural" right to control Morgan's life and labor. Viewed as two isolated acts, the pilfering of Carroll's garden and John Morgan's escape are innocuous challenges to elite power. Yet, with widespread repetition such tactics challenged and changed dominant ideology, and they illuminate the ways in which the masses penetrated ideologies.

Such everyday resistance was not universal. Some marginalized Annapolitans—often the very same people who resented the influence of the local elite—purchased clocks, telescopes, and individual ceramic table settings. The masses could loathe the elite's dominance over their lives, but they could also simultaneously desire the material trappings and self-determination of that same elite. To desire such material objects and power was not a lapse into "false consciousness." It is unreasonable to reduce the myriad experiences of ideology to either monolithic assimilation or completely willful resistance. Colonial consumers were not hypnotized by fashion or blindly drawn into elite emulation; nor did they simply fall prey to manipulative marketing subterfuge.[38] Nevertheless, the masses became convinced that they could improve their lives by appropriating elements of Georgian ideology and material culture. The consumption of mass-produced tableware certainly promoted distinct behaviors with a concrete relationship to dominant class interests, but it did not transform consumers into ideological automatons. For many people, the mass-produced bounty of consumer goods harbored real material and symbolic betterment, but consuming mass-produced commodities inevitably involved some willing incorporation as well as some unintended submission to the dominant class.

Although it seems contradictory, such consumption could both critique dominant ideology and reinforce domination. Resistance to ideology can appear empowering at the very moment it fortifies domination—capitalism thrives on such ambiguities. There always are empowering possibilities lurking within or concealed by dominant ideology, and the discovery of such possibilities forces change in ideologies.

Leone's analysis focuses on the construction of ideology and how the elites attempted to preserve power and define themselves through material culture like formal gardens.[39] Nevertheless, he demonstrates that it is impossible to examine resistance without an appreciation of ideology's structuring capacity. Different social groups undoubtedly perceived and subsequently accepted, rejected, or redefined ideologies in many different ways. The end of garden construction after the Revolution certainly argues that the construction of gardens was either an inadequate ideological mechanism or inferior to subsequent strategies. Indeed, perhaps resistance to gardening ideology ultimately defused gardens as ideological mechanisms.

This does not imply that ideology is monolithic or reduce ideology's penetration to a "trickle-down" effect.[40] It is clear that multiple socioeconomic groups penetrate ideologies and sometimes manipulate them to their own advantage—if they did not, why would the elite encourage *any* social change? At one extreme, critics of ideology's structuring capacity tend to caricature it as a conscious, wholly instrumental deception capable of always delivering its intended effects. At the other extreme, a watered-down version of ideology defined merely as the production of ideas (most commonly called a "worldview") ignores that the effort to distort social relations is most coherently articulated by dominant groups who share common material interests.[41] If we were to venture further and dismiss completely the concept of ideology, we would be left with the dilemma of identifying from where social coherence emerges; i.e., how is it that so many people come to understand society in such a remarkably coherent fashion? We could conclude (quite ideologically) that social coherence is "natural," and many historical archaeologists appear to have implicitly embraced just that conclusion. However, then individual agency—which critics of ideology zealously protect—is reduced to either mere variations of "natural" social behavior or purely random action.

Leone argues that dominant groups must reproduce their power through the *acceptance* of subordinated groups.[42] The profound enigma Leone confronts is *why* the masses conceded to or accepted Annapolitan class inequality. He concludes that the Chesapeake underclass generally acceded to class domination because they became convinced that they shared the elite class's interests and should also share its way of describing the world. The construction of formal gardens was not the way some elite colonial men instrumentally constructed social relations for every other social group; it instead was their *wish* for how social relations would be comprised.[43] To acknowledge such dominant ideology does not inevitably assume monolithic false consciousness or ignore everyday resistance. There are cogent ways to accept the persistent structuring capacity of dominant ideology and still appreciate these subtle yet significant ways in which ideologies are embraced, accepted, modified, and rejected.

Alternative Metaphors: African America and Consumer Culture

Since 1988, Archaeology in Annapolis has examined how African America has confronted dominant ideologies through material tactics ranging from conscious concession to subversiveness to complete rejection of racist boundaries. African America's negotiation of racism demonstrates how historical archaeology can exploit Marxism's appreciation of ideology and still acknowledge the meaningful everyday tactics people use to defy and change those ideologies.

Archaeology in Annapolis has excavated three African American domestic sites.[44] The Maynard-Burgess House was a home to two African American families, the Maynards and Burgesses, from the 1850s to 1980s.[45] The Courthouse Site was a predominately African American–occupied block of homes from about 1850 to the 1960s.[46] Gott's Court was a complex of connected frame houses on a block interior which was home to about twenty-five African American households from 1907 until 1952.[47] All three sites had rich assemblages of nineteenth- to early-twentieth-century consumer goods, including ceramics, glass, food remains, and household artifacts.

In the late nineteenth and early twentieth centuries, the increased volume of mass-produced commodities, pervasive advertising, and the visible abundance of mail-order catalogs and department stores fostered a widespread hope in America's material affluence.[48] Optimism in the social potential of abundance was not really justified, because consumer culture was structured by considerable racial, class, and regional inequality. However, there was a genuine profusion of material goods: anyone who has excavated turn-of-the-century sites recognizes that they typically contain an overwhelming volume of mass-produced commodities.

In the second quarter of the nineteenth century, racial ideologues began to construct caricatured behavioral and genetic attributes for blacks, as well as for Irish, Italian, German, Jewish, and Asian Americans, and these racial caricatures were projected onto material consumption after the Civil War.[49] Racial ideology attempted to make consumer space's symbolic privileges exclusive to whites and hinder (or completely obstruct) African America's access to many consumer venues. Nevertheless, African Americans consumed mass-produced goods, frequented most consumer outlets, and aspired to social self-determination and material security.

Many African Americans vested considerable hope in material consumption, particularly because post-Reconstruction politics and surging Jim Crow racism harbored little potential for positive change. The symbolic significance material consumption had for many African Americans typically was dismissed by white contemporaries, just as African American culture remained mysterious (or nonexistent) to most Whites. Jacob Riis, for instance, saw the mass-produced goods in African American homes as an irrational contradiction to poverty. He noted that "in the art of putting the best foot foremost, of disguising his poverty by making a little go a long way, our negro has no equal. . . . Pianos and parlor furniture abound in the uptown homes of colored tenants and give them a very prosperous air. But even where the wolf howls at the door, he makes a bold and gorgeous front."[50] Rather than see consumption as African America's aspiration to gain an equitable foothold in American society, Riis reduced African Americans' consumption to a meaningless "front" which simply contradicted (or even intensified) their economic marginalization.

African Americans were compelled to make their social behavior and material world appear innocuous to white society, because the appearance of willing deference to or emulation of white society was a practical survival strategy: to risk appearing conspicuously different was hazardous for African Americans. In 1880, for instance, an African American told a *Harper's Weekly* correspondent that "[w]e have been accustomed to look upon white people as beings to be conciliated at any cost, and so we hide ourselves behind a mask that *reflects their moods and opinions*."[51] The *Harper's* writer agreed, confessing that "[i]t was only after many weeks of familiar visiting in their cabins that I discovered a shrewd thoughtfulness about public events, and an anxious carefulness about the future of their families and their race, which no one would have suspected to exist beneath the mask of jest or indifference worn outside their homes." In a rare concession of the illusion of blackness, the correspondent acknowledged that African Americans failed to conform to predominant racist caricatures (e.g., universal happiness, irrepressible sexual power, excessive laziness, social backwardness, etc.).

White observers often reduced genteel African American behavior (e.g., fashion, etiquette, etc.) to racially innate emulation of whites. In a typical

1860 comment on the fashion of enslaved African Americans, dime nov-
elist J. H. Ingraham concluded that "imitation is one of the most remark-
able features of the negro race. They originate nothing, imitation is nature in them and irresistible."[52] In 1863, English traveler Catherine Cooper
Hopley noted that an enslaved carpenter's "manners and appearance,
though quite negro-ish, were undoubtedly those of a superior rank; a thing
one often perceived in house servants, which may be accounted for in their
strong power of imitation."[53] Such observers cast African American social
life and material consumption as deficient imitation of dominant (implicitly white) standards. Convinced of white racial supremacy, whites almost
universally accepted racist caricatures of blacks and overlooked the symbolic significance of the African American material world.

The Contradictions of Affluence: An Archaeology of Genteel African American Consumption

Recognizing the boundaries Victorian racists attempted to impose on African America, archaeologists can examine African American material assemblages and appreciate that they reflect a variety of ways African Americans
resisted racist ideology and subverted black caricatures. That negotiation in
African American Annapolis included a range of consumer choices which
variously embraced, modified, or completely rejected different ideologies.
Consumption reveals how African Americans used material goods and the
display of appropriate consumer discipline to combat the racial ideology that
consumer society and its embedded citizen rights were restricted to whites.
African American consumers persistently subverted racist caricatures and
struggled to demonstrate they could be both genteel Americans and black.

Glass and ceramic assemblages from African American sites in Annapolis reflect the myriad ways African American consumers displayed
their cultural, nationalist, and class identities and aspirations. At
Maynard-Burgess, for instance, eighty-seven glass vessels (including eight
table vessels) were recovered from a post-1889 cellar. The assemblage's
late mean production date of 1882 indicates that most of these vessels
were purchased, consumed, and discarded in a relatively short span of
time. The assemblage contained no locally bottled products, but it did
contain twenty-six nationally advertised brands. The cellar also included
forty-two ceramic vessels. The ceramics, in contrast to the bottles, were
overwhelmingly older ware and older decorative types (including

pearlware and mid-nineteenth-century whiteware), and none had matching decorative motifs. There is no indication of any piecemeal assembly of matching or similar ceramics; i.e., there are no uniform colors, styles, or wares, suggesting the household rejected showy Victorian ceramic etiquette.

The Maynard-Burgess pattern of a high percentage of bottles, few glass table vessels, small quantities of ceramics, and all unmatched wares was reproduced at Gott's Court. Of fifty-four glass vessels recovered at Gott's Court, only twelve were table vessels, and, like Maynard-Burgess, no local bottlers were included (table 1.1). Gott's Court also contained no matching ceramics. The tenants of Gott's Court, probably much like the Maynards, were consuming high quantities of bottled goods and discarding them rapidly; both assemblages contained low quantities of glass table vessels; and the melange of ceramic decorative types and forms suggests vessels were being obtained in small lots, with no strategy to accumulate matching or similar wares.

Stylish Victorian tables contained specialized glass vessels and matching decorative sets. An Annapolis illustration of such consumption comes from the Main Street site, a white physician's household two blocks from the Courthouse neighborhood.[54] A privy at Main Street contained thirty-one glass table vessels and a large assemblage of stylish matched ceramics, including several ironstone sets and a French porcelain set.[55] The assemblage's large quantity of recent, stylish ceramics, large number of glass table vessels, and very few bottles is directly opposite the ceramic and bottle consumption pattern at Maynard-Burgess and Gott's Court.

Table 1.1

Maynard-Burgess Cellar Glass Manufacture-Deposition Lag

Functional Type	Mean Production Date	Lag[a]
Pharmaceutical	1886.42	2.58
Food	1884.00	5.00
Whisky/liquor	1877.81	11.19
Fresh beverage	1877.25	11.75
Wine/champagne	1870.00	19.00
All other vessels[b]	1886.04	2.96

SOURCE: Mullins and Warner 1993.

NOTES: [a]I.e., difference from assemblage TPQ 1889. [b]Includes dated table vessels.

A Share of Affluence: African American Status and Aspiration

Racial ideology presumes dramatic contrasts between black and white households. Yet, the variation between, on one hand, the Maynard-Burgess House and Gott's Court, and, on the other hand, Main Street, should not be reduced to a black/white contrast. Unlike Maynard-Burgess and Gott's Court, a circa 1890 African American privy at the Courthouse site contained ten table vessels in a deposit of thirteen glass vessels (table 1.2). This may seem like an inconsequential quantity to be ignored in favor of "richer" deposits. Yet, a combined total of only twenty-five glass table vessels were recovered in extensive excavations at Maynard-Burgess and Gott's Court. It is tempting to consider the Courthouse table glass deposit a reflection of higher "status" than that of the other Annapolitan African American assemblages, since table glass was relatively costly and its presence suggests the household was following dominant table etiquette. The remainder of the assemblage, though, does not reflect clear cost status or uniform stylishness. Between 1880 and 1900 the household was occupied by a farm laborer and cook whose wife was "keeping house," and the remainder of the privy contained buttons, marbles, a few whiteware vessels, and a small faunal deposit which are comparable to the artifacts in most late-nineteenth-century household refuse. Viewed as one element of the assemblage, the glass table vessels in the Courthouse privy probably do not reflect social or economic status; instead, they suggest aspiration which fashioned the *appearance* of status. At best, the status reflected in the table glass is equivocal when compared to other materials from the same assemblage. The assemblage reflects that these households may have expressed aspirations through mass consumption, but their consumption did not seamlessly reproduce material ideologies or simply reject them altogether. Instead, they developed a range of variable consumer strategies (e.g., high-style table glass and mundane ceramic dishes) which showed that they presented their identity and "status" in a variety of different material forms. Such disparities within assemblages clearly were the norm among the vast majority of Victorian consumers.

Many archaeologists would recognize the contradictions of the Courthouse table glass assemblage and resist reducing it to a flat reflection of "status." However, it might still be tempting to suggest that the household was attempting to "assimilate." Assimilation is a problematic explanation for social change, because it begs the question "assimilation to *what?*" Turn-of-the-

Table 1.2

Comparison of Bottle and Table Glass Percentages from
Annapolis Sites

Site	Bottles (No./%)	Table glass (No./%)
Maynard-Burgess cellar (1889 TPQ)	79 90.80%	8 9.19%
Main Street privy (1889 TPQ)	43 58.10%	31 41.89%
Courthouse site privy (ca. 1890)	3 23.07%	10 76.92%
Gott's Court (1898 TPQ)	42 77.77%	12 22.22%
Maynard-Burgess privy (1905 TPQ)	18 78.26%	5 21.73%

SOURCE: Warner and Mullins 1993.

century observers toyed with the notion of assimilation extensively, building a backdrop of whiteness against which all social differences were defined. The tenacious resort to assimilation as a means to explain social and cultural change reflects that archaeology itself is embedded in a societal bedrock which assumes whiteness to be the gauge against which all difference is evaluated.

At the turn of the twentieth century, the burgeoning potential of mass-consumed goods was enticing to all Americans, so it is unreasonable to think that African America would not want a share of that affluence. In 1890, for example, the Washington, D.C., African American newspaper *The Bee* argued that "the quickest way to solve the Negro problem is for the Negro to purchase property. . . . The white people are opposed to us because we have no money, no property, no education and the like. These are the barriers to the races [*sic*] success. Take our advice and buy property."[56] However, the investment of such hopefulness in material consumption does not mean that African Americans willingly rejected their cultural traditions or tolerated white domination for mass-produced baubles. The consumption of mass-produced goods clearly demanded some transformation in African American culture, just as it impacted all consumers.

Many African Americans, though, were wary that such changes were being promoted by white advertisers, merchants, and producers. *The Bee,* for example, observed in 1885 that African American consumers "must not be so easily flattered out of our money by the white citizens . . . the greatest estimate which we place upon life, is fine dress, and the only people benefited are the whites."[57]

The dilemma was not material goods themselves; instead, the problem was the racial exclusivity of consumer space. African Americans recognized the effort to construct consumer culture as a white space, so consumption was something to be embraced judiciously. Consequently, African Americans developed diverse strategies which attempted to secure the benefits of consumer goods and privileges yet escape racist marginalization.

The Paradoxes of African American Resistance

African American consumer resistance is typically more ambiguous and conflicted than revolutionary. The rejection of stylish glass table vessels and ceramics at Maynard-Burgess and Gott's Court suggests some renunciation of etiquette and dominant status measures. Yet, these households did not reject all Victorian consumer ideology. All of the African American assemblages included a large volume of glass bottles which reflect persistent consumption of mass-produced goods. In addition to the Maynard-Burgess cellar's bottles, the feature also contained nearly eight hundred can fragments, indicating that the household was consuming a steady volume of canned foods as well. Each of the African American assemblages reflected a marked preference for national goods over local bottled products. Mass-produced bottled and canned goods were distributed and advertised widely during the late nineteenth and early twentieth centuries. Although brands were more costly than locally produced goods sold loose, their consistent quality and pricing evaded the underweighing, adulteration, and deceit routinely directed at African American consumers buying locally produced goods. These bottles and cans reflect that many African American households did not reject or rebuff consumer space; instead, they resisted everyday racist mechanisms of local marketers.

These consumption patterns were subtle negotiations of racist marketing. For instance, the predominately mid-nineteenth-century age of the Maynard-Burgess ceramics, their decorative variety, and heavy use-wear suggest that many vessels were recycled between households or generations. Consuming recycled ceramics minimized racism because it reduced consumption in the white-dominated local market. Economically, such tactics were prudent; socially, such exchange bound African Americans together in exchange networks. For African America, alternative consumption venues such as barter with neighbors, street peddling, or even theft minimized the everyday power racist merchants had over African American consumers. Through such apparently innocuous tactics, African Americans could exert modest yet meaningful influence over material exchange.

Dominant ideology and resistant symbolism could lurk together in even the most trivial object. An example of such paradoxical material symbolism is reflected in bric-a-brac, such as mass-produced statues, vases, figurines, and pictures. Such apparently innocuous trinkets typically featured exotic motifs, stylized adaptations of classical art, or historic personages, and they were abundantly manufactured for Victorian homes.[58] Archaeologists routinely find such objects and dismiss them as curiosities with little or no interpretive significance.

The 1889 cellar at the Maynard-Burgess House included two such pieces of ceramic bric-a-brac, and examples were recovered from Gott's Court and the Courthouse site. The archaeological quantities may seem inconsequential, but the modest number of such objects reflects an unusually low breakage rate (much as ceramic assemblages tend to overrepresent "everyday" versus "Sunday" tableware). For instance, an African American who grew up in the Courthouse neighborhood acknowledged that "we had knick knacks in our living room. In fact, we had quite a few of them. We weren't allowed to touch them. My mother didn't like to see her stuff broken up. . . . We weren't barred from the living room, we just weren't allowed to touch them."[59]

Bric-a-brac created a cluttered appearance of exoticism and affluence in the parlors of many marginalized Americans. Jacob Riis believed that the ubiquitous knick-knack decoration in New York tenements was an effort to mask poverty, noting that even "the poorest negro housekeeper's room in New York is bright with gaily-colored prints of his beloved 'Abe Linkum,' General Grant, President Garfield, Mrs. Cleveland, and other national celebrities, and cheery with flowers and singing birds."[60] Such goods were cheap and widely available. In 1897 the *Boston Cooking School Magazine* observed that "these days, when the artificer can give us almost perfect copies of the artist's works, at a nominal sum, there is scarcely a home so humble that it may not have a Raphael, a Corot, a Millet, speaking from its walls."[61] These inexpensive, mass-produced knick knacks did not really display socioeconomic standing, but they could distort status. In 1993, for example, a woman who grew up in the Gott's Court neighborhood examined an excavated figurine and determined that "evidently when you worked for white families they would give you these things. Because I'm more than sure black people did not have the money to buy a lot of expensive things."[62] These objects actually were cheap, but to some people they apparently fostered a deceiving appearance of "cost status."[63]

Bric-a-brac did not simply mask or creatively redefine poverty. Instead, knick knacks also were implicated in the reproduction of racialized labor; i.e., labor structure and opportunity were based upon the presumption of white racial superiority to blacks and more recent European immigrants. An untold number of knick knacks were given by whites to African American domestics, usually passing from white to African American women. One man's mother did housework and "would bring them off jobs. People would give them to her. Sometimes the people who she worked for would go away and when they came back they would bring a little gift."[64] Another African American who lived in Annapolis during the Depression noted that his home also "always had knick knacks . . . [from when] somebody bought my mother something."[65]

Some white employers probably gave domestic workers gifts without conscious ulterior motives. Most gift giving to African American laborers, though, was driven by paternalistic benevolence and racist rationalization. To many white employers, token gifts tacitly encouraged reliability, legitimized African American subordination, and discouraged defiance (e.g., thievery). Yet, some African Americans viewed mass-produced exotics as reflections of their ascendance toward gentility and affluence. Consequently, bric-a-brac could potentially recast racial inequality by symbolically demonstrating an African American's gentility; simultaneously, a white could see it as confirming the very ideology which reproduced racial inequality.

Obviously, many commodities had the slippery potential to be viewed as both resistant symbols and ideological assimilators. The empowering power and the assimilative power of material goods are bound together as a constantly negotiated contradiction, and critical archaeologies attempt to identify those contradictions and evaluate the possibilities and oppression different interpretations harbor. This makes for complex, albeit enigmatic, research, because ideologies are confronted in circuitous ways: people disregard, misinterpret, modify, and acquiesce to ideologies in ways which make inequalities seem palatable or even appropriate. If an ideology was so transparent that it could be easily defined and subverted, it would never work in the first place. The line between empowering resistance and ideological domination is always this ambiguous, but archaeologies which work across that boundary offer valuable ways of appreciating both the boundaries of ideology and the capacity to subvert and change domination.

Expanding Historical Archaeology Discourses

Archaeology interprets particular facets of the past which our methodological, theoretical, and social metaphors evoke. Through concrete disciplinary debate, certain perspectives have predominated and have laid a rich and sound foundation for the expansion of the field. Yet, the potential for taking some insights from Marxism and structuralism alike and listening to the cacophony of marginalized voices does not threaten to devolve into frustrating theoretical and methodological discord. Likewise, it seems unlikely that the discipline will become mired in disabling reflexive theory because of hermeneutics, African American voices, or other unsettling phenomena. There certainly are few if any archaeologists eager to forsake the discipline's basis in empirical analysis in favor of solipsism.[66] Clarity in research methods and interpretive goals clearly can make analyses increasingly persuasive and amplify historical archaeology's distinctive insights.

Archaeology in Annapolis is simply one of an increasing number of projects confronting the consequence of archaeological interpretation and the society which shapes archaeology. Archaeology in Annapolis is among the historical archaeology projects which have attempted to produce an increasingly flexible discourse that is attentive to both ideological domination and the myriad ways people accept, modify, and reject that domination. This self-critical flexibility ultimately can turn the dilemmas of paradigmatic conflict and restrictive disciplinary metaphors into a positive energy which will productively expand historical archaeology.

Notes

Glass minimum vessel analyses and newspaper research presented in this essay were supported by a Wenner-Gren Foundation Predoctoral Grant. Ceramic analyses at Maynard-Burgess were supported by a Sigma Xi Grant-in-Aid of

Research. Victorian domestic manuals and travel literature were researched under a Winterthur Research Fellowship; thanks to Neville Thompson and the Winterthur Library staff for their help with these resources. Marlys Pearson identified the *Maryland Gazette* notices during her own research and suggested how they fit into this chapter. Russell Skowronek provided very helpful suggestions to focus the essay. Thanks to Mark Leone, Helan Page, Bob Paynter, Marlys Pearson, Paul Shackel, and Mark Warner for commenting on various ideas in this version or earlier drafts. The shortcomings of the chapter are completely my own responsibility.

1. For example, Mary C. Beaudry, ed., *Documentary Archaeology in the New World* (Cambridge: Cambridge Univ. Press, 1988); Mark P. Leone and Parker B. Potter Jr., eds., *The Recovery of Meaning: Historical Archaeology in the Eastern United States* (Washington, D.C.: Smithsonian Institution Press, 1988); Barbara J. Little, ed., *Text-Aided Archaeology* (Boca Raton: CRC Press, 1992); and Randall H. McGuire and Robert Paynter, eds., *The Archaeology of Inequality* (Cambridge: Basil Blackwell, 1991). For examples not limited to historical archaeology, compare Valerie Pinsky and Alison Wylie, eds., *Critical Traditions in Contemporary Archaeology* (Cambridge: Cambridge Univ. Press, 1989); and Michael Shanks and Christopher Tilley, *Reconstructing Archaeology* (London: Cambridge Univ. Press, 1987).

2. For instance, self-reflection was central to the New Archaeology's project; Wylie, "The Interpretive Dilemma," in *Critical Traditions*, 18–27. Compare Robert W. Preucel, "The Philosophy of Archaeology," in *Processual and Postprocessual Archaeologies: Multiple Ways of Knowing the Past*, ed. Robert W. Preucel (Carbondale: Southern Illinois Univ. Press, 1991), 17–29.

3. For example, Wylie, "The Interpretive Dilemma"; Shanks and Tilley, *Reconstructing Archaeology*, 20–21; Shanks, *Experiencing the Past: On the Character of Archaeology* (London: Routledge, 1992); Mary C. Beaudry, "Words for Things: Linguistic Analysis of Probate Inventories," in *Documentary Archaeology*, 43–50; and Anne E. Yentsch, "The Symbolic Divisions of Pottery: Sex-Related Attributes of English and Anglo-American Household Pots," in *The Archaeology of Inequality*, 192–230.

4. George L. Miller, "Classification and Economic Scaling of Nineteenth-Century Ceramics," *Historical Archaeology* 14 (1) (1980): 1–40, and "A Revised Set of CC Index Values for Classification and Economic Scaling of English Ceramics from 1787 to 1880," *Historical Archaeology* 25 (1) (1991): 1–25. The archetype for status studies is John S. Otto, *Cannon's Point Plantation, 1794–1860: Living Conditions and Status Patterns in the Old South* (Orlando: Academic Press, 1984).

5. Mark P. Leone, Parker Potter Jr., and Paul A. Shackel, "Toward a Critical Archaeology," *Current Anthropology* 28 (3) (1987): 286–302; Potter, *Public Archaeology in Annapolis: A Critical Approach to History in Maryland's "Ancient City"* (Washington, D.C.: Smithsonian Institution Press, 1994); and Shackel, *Personal Discipline and Material Culture: An Archaeology of Annapolis, Maryland, 1695–1870* (Knoxville: Univ. of Tennessee Press, 1993).

6. Mark P. Leone, "Interpreting Ideology in Historical Archaeology: Using the Rules

of Perspective in the William Paca Garden in Annapolis, Maryland," in *Ideology, Power, and Prehistory*, ed. Daniel Miller and Christopher Tilley (Cambridge: Cambridge Univ. Press, 1984), 25–35.

7. Richard Harvey Brown, *Society as Text* (Chicago: Univ. of Chicago Press, 1987), 98; and David E. Cooper, *Metaphor* (Cambridge: Basil Blackwell, 1989), 20–21. Compare Richard Rorty, *Philosophy and the Mirror of Human Nature* (Princeton: Princeton Univ. Press, 1979); Richard Rorty, *Contingency, Irony, and Solidarity* (Cambridge: Cambridge Univ. Press, 1989); and Steven A. Tyler, "Post-Modern Ethnography: From Document of the Occult to Occult Document," in *Writing Culture: The Poetics and Politics of Ethnography*, ed. James Clifford and George E. Marcus (Berkeley: Univ. of California Press, 1986), 122–40.

8. The precise definition of metaphor is a thorny issue. Nietzsche, for instance, believed all literal meaning was derived from metaphors. The definition of metaphor here includes words, sentences, and embedded concepts which do not have generally accepted and clearly defined literal meanings (Cooper, *Metaphor*, 5–12).

9. The best-known study of how a discipline is constructed is still Thomas S. Kuhn, *The Structure of Scientific Revolutions*, 2d ed. (Chicago: Univ. of Chicago Press, 1970).

10. See Rorty, *Contingency, Irony, and Solidarity*, 22.

11. See Michael Brian Schiffer, "Review of *Experiencing the Past: On the Character of Archaeology*," *American Antiquity* 59 (1) (1994): 158–59.

12. Otto, *Cannon's Point Plantation*.

13. Miller, "Classification and Economic Scaling," and "A Revised Set of CC Index Values."

14. Compare the chapters in Suzanne M. Spencer-Wood, ed., *Consumer Choice in Historical Archaeology* (New York: Plenum Press, 1987). For a valuable critique of the methodological failings of ceramic analysis, see George L. Miller, "Thoughts Towards A Users' Guide to Ceramic Assemblages," *Council for Northeast Historical Archaeology Newsletter* 18 (Apr. 1991): 2–5.

15. Shanks and Tilley, *Reconstructing Archaeology*, 20–21; compare Wylie, "The Interpretive Dilemma," 19.

16. Compare Walter Benjamin's discussion of the "sediments" of history; "The Storyteller: Reflections on the Works of Nikolai Leskov," in *Illuminations*, ed. Hannah Arendt (New York: Harcourt Brace and World, 1969), 83–109.

17. Potter, *Public Archaeology*, and George C. Logan, chap. 4, this volume.

18. See Philip L. Brown, *The Other Annapolis, 1900–1950* (Annapolis: Annapolis Publishing Co., 1994).

19. For instance, compare Schiffer's critique of Michael Shanks's post-processualism: "When a logical argument becomes too threatening (perhaps by calling for evidence), a postmodern archaeologist need only break out sideways, seek an appropriate metaphor, and disappear down the nearest rabbit hole" ("Review of *Experiencing the Past*," 158–59).

20. Rorty, *Contingency, Irony, and Solidarity*, 75.

21. See Kuhn, *The Structure of Scientific Revolutions*, 182–87.

22. The notion that there actually could be a "postmodern" archaeology does not ring true with most postmodern theory. The methodical, generalizing logic of archaeology, if not all social sciences, runs directly counter to the extreme reflexivity in most postmodernism. Postmodernisms attempt to construct knowledge "without foundation" and create spaces for as-yet undetermined forms of knowledge; consequently, if a "postmodern archaeology" actually arrived, how would we know this was it? Compare Tyler, "Post-modern Ethnography," 136.

23. Karl Marx, *Capital*, vol. 1 (1867; reprint, New York: International Publishers, 1967); compare Theodor Adorno, *Negative Dialectics* (New York: Seabury, 1973); Louis Althusser, *For Marx* (New York: Pantheon, 1969); Antonio Gramsci, *Selections from the Prison Notebooks* (New York: International Publishers, 1971); Jürgen Habermas, *Legitimation Crisis* (London: Heinemann, 1976); Max Horkheimer and Theodor Adorno, *Dialectic of Enlightenment* (New York: Herder, 1972); George Lukacs, *History and Class Consciousness* (Cambridge: MIT Press, 1971); and E. P. Thompson, *The Making of the English Working Class* (New York: Pantheon, 1963).

24. McGuire, *A Marxist Archaeology* (New York: Academic Press, 1992), 83–84. Compare Russell G. Handsman, "Historical Archaeology and Capitalism, Subscriptions and Separations: The Production of Individualism," *North American Archaeologist* 4 (1) (1983): 63–79; Charles E. Orser Jr., *The Material Basis of the Postbellum Tenant Plantation: Historical Archaeology in the South Carolina Piedmont* (Athens: Univ. of Georgia Press, 1988); Thomas C. Patterson, "Exploitation and Class Formation in the Inca State," *Culture* 5 (1985): 35–42; Paynter, "The Archaeology of Inequality," *Annual Review of Anthropology* 18 (1989): 369–99; and Preucel, "The Philosophy of Archaeology," 21–25.

25. I use *Marxian* to describe theory derived from Marx's thinking, following the lead of Orser, *The Material Basis*, 9. Orser uses *Marxian* to distinguish between philosophy derived from Marx's work and *Marxist*, which often is attached to states using totalitarian adaptations of Marxism.

26. Stephen Eric Bronner and Douglas MacKay Kellner, ed., *Critical Theory and Society: A Reader* (London: Routledge, 1989). Frankfurt School thinkers include Horkheimer and Adorno, *Dialectic of Enlightenment*; Leo Lowenthal, *Literature, Popular Culture and Society* (Englewood Cliffs, N.J.: Prentice-Hall, 1961); and Benjamin, *Reflections* (New York: Hart, Brace, Jovanovich, 1979).

27. Terry Eagleton, *The Ideology of the Aesthetic* (Cambridge: Basil Blackwell, 1990), 359.

28. Jürgen Habermas, *The Philosophical Discourse of Modernity* (Cambridge: MIT Press, 1987).

29. Raymond Williams, *Marxism and Literature* (Oxford: Oxford Univ. Press, 1977).

30. Roland Barthes saw mythical metaphors in much the same vein. Barthes argued that the bourgeois used myth to "transform history into nature" and "freeze" power relations so that they seem inevitable and appropriate; see *Mythologies* (New York: Hill and Wang, 1972), 129. Compare Brown, *Society as Text*, 116, and Cooper, *Metaphor*, 41–42.

31. Leone, Potter, and Shackel also stress reflexivity; i.e., self-reflective attention to how archaeologists' contemporary identities and social context shape interpretation.

Reflexivity itself is not a sentiment unique to Marxians, but attention to the historical roots of contemporary material oppression is distinctive to critical Marxisms.

32. Leone, "Interpreting Ideology." For critiques, see Ian Hodder, *Reading the Past: Current Approaches to Interpretation in Archaeology* (Cambridge: Cambridge Univ. Press, 1986); Martin Hall, "Small Things and the Mobile, Conflictual Fusion of Power, Fear, and Desire," in *The Art and Mystery of Historical Archaeology: Essays in Honor of James Deetz*, ed. Anne E. Yentsch and Mary C. Beaudry (Boca Raton: CRC Press, 1992), 373–99; Yentsch and Beaudry, "Introduction," in *The Art and Mystery of Historical Archaeology*, 3–21; Lauren J. Cook, "Tobacco-Related Material Culture and the Construction of Working-Class Culture," in *Interdisciplinary Investigations of the Boott Mills, Lowell, Massachusetts, Volume III: The Boarding House System as a Way of Life*, ed. Beaudry and Stephen A. Mrozowski (Boston: National Park Service, 1989), 209–30; and Beaudry, Cook, and Mrozowski, "Artifacts and Active Voices: Material Culture as Social Discourse," in *The Archaeology of Inequality*, 150–91.

33. Compare Elizabeth Kryder-Reid, chap. 12, this volume.

34. Rhys Isaac, *The Transformation of Virginia, 1740–1790* (New York: W. W. Norton, 1982).

35. James C. Scott, *Domination and the Arts of Resistance: Hidden Transcripts* (New Haven, Conn.: Yale Univ. Press, 1990), 73–74.

36. *Maryland Gazette*, June 28, 1770.

37. *Maryland Gazette*, July 24, 1766.

38. Scholars examining material consumption have relied heavily on middling and underclass emulation of elite consumers to explain the emergence of mass consumption. For example, see Neil McKendrick, John Brewer, and J. H. Plumb, *The Birth of a Consumer Society: The Commercialization of Eighteenth-Century England* (Bloomington: Indiana Univ. Press, 1982). This logic was most clearly articulated by Thorstein Veblen, *The Theory of the Leisure Class* (1899; reprint, Boston: Houghton Mifflin, 1973). The problems with emulation as an explanatory mechanism have been examined by Colin Campbell, *The Romantic Ethic and the Spirit of Modern Consumerism* (Oxford: Basil Blackwell, 1987).

39. Mark P. Leone, "The Georgian Order as the Order of Merchant Capitalism in Annapolis, Maryland," in *The Recovery of Meaning*, 235–61.

40. Hodder, *Reading the Past*, 166–67. Compare Hall, "Small Things and the Mobile"; Yentsch and Beaudry, "Introduction"; and Cook, "Tobacco-Related Material Culture," 213.

41. Williams, *Marxism and Literature*, 66.

42. Compare Gramsci, *Selections from the Prison Notebooks*, 52–55.

43. Leone, "The Georgian Order," 257.

44. The project also has excavated an early-nineteenth-century site which contained material evidence of African cultural practices. George Logan, Thomas W. Bodor, Lynn D. Jones, and Marian Creveling, *1991 Archaeological Investigations at the Charles Carroll House in Annapolis, Maryland 18AP45* (Annapolis: Historic Annapolis Foundation, 1992).

45. Paul R. Mullins and Mark S. Warner, *Final Archaeological Investigations at the*

Maynard-Burgess House (18AP64), An 1850–1980 African-American Household in Annapolis, Maryland (Annapolis: Historic Annapolis Foundation, 1993).

46. Mark S. Warner and Paul R. Mullins, *Phase I-II Archaeological Investigations of the Courthouse Site (19AP63), An Historic African-American Neighborhood in Annapolis, Maryland* (Annapolis: Historic Annapolis Foundation, 1993); Elizabeth A. Aiello and John L. Seidel, *Three Hundred Years in Annapolis: Phase III Archaeological Investigations of the Anne Arundel County Courthouse Site (18AP63), Annapolis, Maryland* (Annapolis: Historic Annapolis Foundation, 1995).

47. Mark S. Warner, *Test Excavations at Gott's Court, Annapolis, Maryland (18AP52)* (Annapolis: Historic Annapolis Foundation, 1992).

48. Examples of the rich literature on consumer culture include the following: Jean-Christophe Agnew, "Coming Up for Air: Consumer Culture in Historical Perspective," *Intellectual History Newsletter* 12 (1990): 3–21; Daniel Horowitz, *The Morality of Spending: Attitudes Toward the Consumer Society in America, 1875–1940* (Baltimore: Johns Hopkins Univ. Press, 1985); and Warren I. Susman, *Culture as History: The Transformation of American Society in the Twentieth Century* (New York: Pantheon, 1984). Historical archaeologists who have studied consumption include Margaret Purser, "Consumption as Communication in Nineteenth-Century Paradise Valley, Nevada," *Historical Archaeology* 26 (3) (1992): 105–16; and Ann Smart Martin, *Buying into the World of Goods: Eighteenth-Century Consumerism and the Retail Trade from London to the Virginia Frontier* (Ann Arbor, Mich.: Univ. Microfilms International, 1993).

49. Compare Eric Lott, *Love and Theft: Blackface Minstrelsy and the American Working Class* (New York: Oxford Univ. Press, 1995); and David R. Roediger, *The Wages of Whiteness: Race and the Making of the American Working Class* (New York: Verso, 1991).

50. Jacob A. Riis, *How the Other Half Lives* (1890; reprint, New York: Dover, 1971), 118.

51. Anonymous, "Inside Southern Cabins," *Harper's Weekly* 24 (1246) (1880): 733–34.

52. J. H. Ingraham, *The Sunny South; or, The Southerner at Home* (Philadelphia: G. G. Evans, 1860).

53. Catherine Cooper Hopley, *Life in the South from the Commencement of the War* (1863; reprint, New York: Augustus M. Kelley, 1971), 180.

54. Paul A. Shackel, *Archaeological Testing at the 193 Main Street Site, 18AP44, Annapolis, Maryland* (Annapolis: Historic Annapolis Foundation, 1986).

55. Paul R. Mullins, *Analysis of Feature 12 Ceramic Assemblage, Main Street Site (18AP44)* (Annapolis: Historic Annapolis Foundation, 1988); and Michele Beavan, *Analysis of Bottle Glass Recovered from Feature 12, Main Street (18AP52)* (Annapolis: Historic Annapolis Foundation, 1988).

56. *The Bee,* Nov. 22, 1890, 2.

57. *The Bee,* Nov. 14, 1885, 2.

58. Compare Susan Stewart, *On Longing: Narratives of the Miniature, the Gigantic, the Souvenir, the Collection* (Baltimore: The Johns Hopkins Univ. Press, 1984).

59. Hannah Jopling, unpublished oral history interview, 1992. On file at Archaeology in Annapolis, College Park, Md.
60. Riis, *How the Other Half Lives*, 118.
61. Clara H. Parker, "The Use and Abuse of Ornamentation in the House," *Boston Cooking School Magazine* 2 (1) (1897): 8.
62. R. Christopher Goodwin, *Phase II/III Archaeological Investigations of the Gott's Court Parking Facility, Annapolis, Maryland* (Annapolis: Maryland Historic Trust, 1993), 11.
63. For instance, *Spelman's Fancy Goods Graphic* 3 (3) (Feb. 1883) "Bric-A-Brac" section priced "Vase with Roses," "Terra-Cotta Figure," and "Basket of Darkies" each at $5.00 per 100. See page 3.
64. Jopling, unpublished oral history interview, 1992. On file at Archaeology in Annapolis, College Park, Md.
65. Ibid.
66. See Schiffer, "Review of *Experiencing the Past*," 159.

2 Ethnography in Annapolis

Parker B. Potter Jr.

In 1981 Archaeology in Annapolis was established. At some point between then and now, Archaeology in Annapolis became archaeology among Annapolitans, and a primary reason for this transformation is the title of this chapter, "Ethnography in Annapolis." This shift from doing archaeology "in Annapolis" to doing our work "among Annapolitans" is an important one because it illustrates one of the ways in which archaeology, as a social product, can be made to meet the mandate for relevance that has been articulated within the discipline at various times over the last twenty years.[1]

This chapter is based on my own experience with "Archaeology in Annapolis," gained primarily through living in the city and working for "Archaeology in Annapolis" between 1983 and 1987.[2] I will begin by presenting a brief theoretical framework for thinking about the various applications of ethnography to the practice of archaeology, and the balance of the chapter will focus on ethnographic strategies, specific findings, and the application of ethnographic findings to both archaeology and archaeological interpretation.

Theoretical Framework

There are at least three reasons for introducing ethnographic techniques into archaeological practice: 1) to get answers to archaeological questions; 2) to find important questions for archaeology to answer; and 3) to learn how to integrate archaeology into a particular local social context. In addition, several anthropologists and archaeologists have studied both archaeological field crews and the discipline of archaeology in a manner that is essentially ethnographic, but that kind of work lies beyond the scope of this chapter.

The most obvious reason for introducing ethnography into archaeology is to locate answers to archaeological questions. As Elizabeth Tooker noted over a decade ago, "archaeologists have increasingly turned to doing their own ethnography . . . in a rather new fashion to help answer questions that have arisen within archaeology."[3] Of course, the "rather new fashion" to which Tooker referred is ethnoarchaeology.

I suspect that I speak for many archaeologists in finding ethnoarchaeology tremendously fascinating; even the most mundane collection of facilities and objects can make for riveting reading or viewing once living human actors have been added to the scene. Even so, there's something missing in quite a lot of ethnoarchaeology, and the key to what's missing may be found in Tooker's phrase, "questions that have arisen within archaeology." Unlike archaeologists, who deal strictly with artifacts, features, and strata that do not speak for themselves (because they *cannot* speak at all), ethnoarchaeologists, like ethnographers, are often faced with informants who find their research questions to be puzzling, trivial, irrelevant, ridiculous, stupid, offensive, or even dangerous. And as often as not, the informants have a point: the fact that a research question has arisen within archaeology (or ethnology) is no guarantee that the question is sensible, or that answers to it will have any real utility. The answer an informant gives is only as good as the question that he or she has been asked.[4]

Of course, there are advantages to using ethnography to answer questions about material culture. First of all, many ethnoarchaeologists *have* gained a great deal of valuable information this way, information that may have been otherwise inaccessible. Second, and of greater interest to me, there is the social side of this kind of information gathering. Anyone who is able to answer an ethnographer's question has earned the right to think of him or herself as an expert, a status that seems to be highly valued cross-culturally.

But, if we think about things a bit more closely, just who is the expert in such an information exchange? Asked another way, who has more authority: the person who *answers* a question or the person who *asks* it? This leads to a second archaeological use for the tools of ethnography. An important part of Archaeology in Annapolis and of this chapter has been the use of ethnography to help frame archaeological questions. In a variety of ways, a succession of Archaeology in Annapolis team members have tried to learn just what people in Annapolis think they want—or need—to know about their city's history. To whatever extent informants feel empowered by having the chance to provide information, it stands to reason that they would feel even more empowered by having the chance to help select and phrase the questions. By enlisting the aid of informants in framing archaeological research questions, local residents gain the benefits of empowerment. At the same time, archaeologists gain the benefits of utilizing the knowledge and skills of their informants much more fully than they would if archaeological ethnography was simply a tool for asking a roomful of people to identify a tableful of enigmatic artifacts.

In addition to trying to learn what the people of Annapolis say they want to know about local history, we have formed our own opinions about what contemporary Annapolitans need to know about the history of their city. And often we have been pushed toward forming these opinions by observing situations that seem on the surface to have nothing at all to do with the past. Here I refer to situations we have examined in a mildly ethnographic way in order to integrate our project smoothly into the local community, which is the third use of ethnography noted at the beginning of this section.

The Archaeology of Parking Spaces

A case in point is our treatment of parking spaces. I sometimes have joked that the best use Archaeology in Annapolis has ever made of ethnography is our discovery that for most of the year parking spaces in downtown Annapolis are both rare and valuable. On the basis of this high-level ethnographic finding, which is duplicated hundreds of times each day by people with credentials no more lofty than a valid driver's license, Archaeology in Annapolis has been very careful about proposing excavation work that would take parking spaces out of use. Paul Shackel's initial survey of the Main Street site, which was then a parking lot, was conducted incrementally, two parking spaces at a time.

At one level, our discovery that Annapolis parking spaces are valuable, and the project's use of this knowledge, would appear to be little more than simple project logistics tinged with common sense. In fact, when I talk about Archaeology in Annapolis ethnography, I usually begin with the parking space example and make a pitch for ethnography as a useful tool for getting the lay of the land and keeping out of hot water with local hosts. Ethnography, I argue, is a tool for finding out that a piece of real estate that I might define and value as an archaeological site is defined and valued in any number of ways by people with perfectly valid interests that just happen to be different from my interests. Typically, I talk about parking spaces as an ice breaker and as an introduction to my discussion of the two more "serious" applications of ethnography noted above.

However, people do not need parking spaces unless they're coming from somewhere and going somewhere else: a place with an acute need for parking spaces is clearly a destination, and "places" don't become "destinations" without an "electorate" voting with their feet (or their gas pedals). Furthermore, anytime someone goes from one spot to another, he or she has a reason, even if the reason is simply to enjoy the experience of the trip itself. The point is that Annapolis's insatiable need for parking spaces is not an independent, free-standing ethnographic fact; it is connected to other parts of local life, principally Annapolis's dual status as the capital of Maryland and the home of the United States Naval Academy, and the city's current role as a popular tourist destination.[5] What's more, these aspects of life in Annapolis are big business; Annapolis's top three sources of income are state government, the Naval Academy, and tourism, and this basic economic pattern—dependence on outsiders—has been in place for nearly three centuries.[6] Thus, in relatively short order we can move from a casual observation about the local importance of parking spaces to the recognition of a key theme in Annapolis history.

Our discoveries about the value of parking spaces in the downtown Historic District of Annapolis don't just help us keep from alienating local residents; they also can help us articulate archaeological research questions and establish a framework for archaeological interpretation. While we have not done so explicitly, I would have no trouble designing an archaeological approach to the history of parking spaces in Annapolis, and the value of such a study would be its attention to the historical origins of an economic system that has allowed Annapolitans to make a living from visitors for almost three hundred years.

In its broad outlines, the archaeological site tour I would write to interpret the history of parking spaces in Annapolis would be fairly similar to the George Washington tour that was given in 1986 at the Main Street site.[7] In that tour, we gave a history of the activity that had brought most visitors to the Main Street site, namely tourism. We talked about the very real needs of a city of thirty-two thousand people to guide and control the behavior of more than one million visitors each year, and we suggested that one way that Annapolis has found to encourage deferential visitor behavior is by embracing and presenting for public consumption pictures of the past that portray George Washington, the Father of His Country, as a wealthy, sophisticated, and, above all, polite overnight visitor during his twenty or more trips to Annapolis. We pointed out the striking parallels between the Washington who appears in histories of Annapolis and descriptions of the "quality tourist" which appeared regularly during the 1980s on the front page of the Annapolis *Capital*. We also pointed out the incongruity: Washington is presented more or less as a model tourist, despite the fact that tourism as we know it today postdates the life of Washington by a half century, if not more.

In pulling back the curtain on Annapolis's creative but out-of-time portrait of Washington as a tourist, we gave a history to tourism. We suggested that tourism, as a widespread cultural activity, is about one hundred years old in this country, rather than two hundred years old, but we also argued that the key concepts that enable tourism (separations between work and home and between work time and leisure time, along with the idea of the self-regulating, experience-collecting possessive individual) were beginning to enter American life in the early eighteenth century, several decades *before* Washington ever visited Annapolis. We argued, in addition, that the artifactual record of eighteenth-century life in Annapolis contains evidence for the introduction and penetration of these new ways of thinking and living.

In the same way, we could give a history to parking spaces or, rather, to the various patterns of work and leisure that have inspired or required millions upon millions of Americans to obligate themselves in a dozen different ways to a veritable army of automobile dealers, loan officers, insurance agents, state motor vehicle administrators, toll collectors, emissions inspectors, mechanics, traffic cops, meter maids, and parking lot attendants—all in the name of maintaining the right to operate a machine that is promoted by its manufacturers, through their advertising campaigns, as giving its users all manner of freedom. Automobiles and, by extension, the need for parking spaces did not come to Annapolis until the turn of the twentieth century, but the pattern of life that created a set of needs that automobiles could fill has archaeologically discernible roots in the early eighteenth century. In Annapolis the part of this history that matters most is the story of a local economy that depends heavily on the discretionary spending of outsiders—nearly all of whom drive into town and need to park their cars.

So, in fact, knowing about the value of parking spaces in Annapolis is not useful simply as a way of keeping on the good side of our local hosts; it is also useful as a serious guide to what parts of the present we should try to give a history archaeologically. The fact that most contemporary Annapolitans probably would not think to link twentieth-century parking spaces with eighteenth-century creamware plates simply strengthens my argument for the importance of rigorous ethnography. The need for parking spaces, the high social value placed on them, and the entire social and economic pattern of life that frames these needs and evaluations is largely taken for granted, unexamined, and unchallenged. The purpose of a critical archaeology such as Archaeology in Annapolis is to open up to public scrutiny and discussion precisely those aspects of contemporary life that are so deeply taken for granted that they are treated as immutable facts of nature rather than as products of culture. The goal of an Archaeology in Annapolis parking space tour would be to help the people of Annapolis to learn as much as they could about the local history that makes parking spaces so sacrosanct. Everyone, I should think, would be better served by discussions in which people said, "Don't touch that parking space" thoughtfully and self-reflectively rather than just loudly.

How I Did Ethnography in Annapolis

When I first started planning to study the creation and use of history in Annapolis, I explained the project to my dissertation committee as a case study in the ethnography of history, designed to provide findings useful for the establishment of a program of public archaeological interpretation. My reasoning was that if the Archaeology in Annapolis public program intended to provide historical information to the public, those of us responsible for the interpretive program needed to know: 1) what Annapolitans already knew about their city's history; 2) what they said about their city's history to themselves and to visitors; and 3) how they used stories about the past to live in the present. I went into the field determined to collect ethnographic data that would allow Archaeology in Annapolis to understand how our archaeological interpretation of Annapolis history might or might not fit into what people already knew and said about local history. On this basis, I presumed that my ethnography of history would consist mainly of studying explicit discussions of the past as enacted in historic house tours, public history lectures, and local celebrations of historical events, such as the two-hundredth anniversary of the ratification of the Treaty of Paris. Initially, I intended to do a long-term version of Leone's visit to Raleigh Tavern or Shakertown at Pleasant Hill, with some participant observation thrown in for good measure.[8] Ultimately, I did do some of this kind of research, but this turned out to be somewhat less useful than—or at best, only as useful as—data collection that was substantially less oriented toward explicitly historical discourse.

Put simply, for more than four years, I was an Annapolitan. I lived in the downtown historic district for my first three years in the city. I had a residents' parking sticker. I paid the city income tax. I voted in local elections, and opened my front door to candidates as they canvassed my neighborhood. I subscribed to the Annapolis *Capital*. I shopped downtown. And like most of my neighbors, I struggled each day to make sure I had some place to park my car. Furthermore, I took great pains to understand all of these experiences as data, rather than as a series of everyday annoyances I needed to deal with in order to have a chance to do my "real" historical and archaeological work.

At the risk of greatly oversimplifying the process of archaeological ethnography, it is fair to say that there is one tremendously powerful key to this kind of work. That key is the careful redrawing of the line that separates data from nondata. To do successful archaeological ethnography means staying "on duty" after five o'clock, after the end of the archaeological field day. Valuable data are there to be found, around the clock, on the way to the site (or the lab) first thing in the morning, at happy hour after work, at the grocery store, in the newspaper at the end of the day, virtually everywhere.

Despite my intention of doing the "ethnography of history," I found that only a part of what I needed to know was to be found in what would seem to be the obvious places. I read all the major histories of Annapolis, toured the city's historic house museums, and even took the Historic Annapolis tour guide training course. All of these were valuable sources of information, but what I learned from these sources would have meant virtually nothing without the context provided by what I learned from keeping tabs on the City Council, from being a voter whose ballot was coveted by various candidates for office, and from all the other mundane aspects of daily life in Annapolis. Of course, this "flash of insight" is old news to any field ethnographer, but it does move an important step beyond the ethnoarchaeological strategy described by Tooker in which the archaeologist queries (or observes) living informants in order to answer a rather narrow range of rather narrow archaeological questions.

I can make this point most clearly through an example. Midway through my time in Annapolis, the City Council spent a good bit of time—and the *Capital* spent a good bit of ink—on the issue of public urination. It seems that downtown residents were growing tired of having their front yards used as an open-air restroom by patrons of the twenty or more bars that lined the city dock. Bar-hoppers (presumably from out of town) who had grown weary of long restroom lines were taking advantage of the trek from one bar to another to relieve themselves outdoors, on private property. This issue came before the City Council because the police were reluctant to intervene strongly, since the only crime with which they could charge public urinators was indecent exposure, which is a felony. The City Council's contribution to solving the problem was the establishment of urination in public as a misdemeanor, separate from indecent exposure. Their hope was that the availability of a less serious charge would encourage the police to take action against visitors they found watering the plants in an inappropriate fashion.

Interestingly, while this story came right off the front pages of the *Capital*, this set of current events related directly to long-standing themes in Annapolis history. For nearly three hundred years, Annapolis has made a good living from inviting outsiders to visit or settle in town. Built into this economic strategy is the need to control the behavior of individuals and institution who answer the invitation; without careful attention to activities of any current crop of visitors, there is the possibility that today's visitors will ruin Annapolis for the next wave of potential visitors. In effect, the City Council's urination legislation was just one of the more recent in a long line of local decisions intended to guide the behavior of outsiders.

Conversely, in the same way that many of the contemporary events I studied had a lot to do with Annapolis history, much of the seemingly historical data I collected had surprisingly much to do with contemporary Annapolis. For example, Historic Annapolis's interpretive focus on the late-eighteenth-century "golden age" seemed to mirror quite directly the aspirations of many members of Historic Annapolis who wanted to establish bona fide connections to a city in which they had not lived for very many years.[9] The golden age is a useful slice of history for Annapolis newcomers seeking strong local ties because many of the late-eighteenth-century worthies celebrated by the historic preservation movement—men such as Thomas Stone, William Paca, Samuel Chase, and Charles Carroll of Carrollton—were themselves eighteenth-century newcomers to Annapolis and/or transient, short-term residents. These are important historical figures with whom contemporary Annapolis newcomers can easily identify.

At many turns, I found that what I was studying was not necessarily what it appeared to be. Many current events were all about history, or historical issues, while much of what called itself history was actually a complex discourse on contemporary politics. And again, this quality of life in which one thing stands for another, in ways that are not immediately obvious, is bread and butter to any good ethnographer.

How to Do Archaeological Ethnography

To the extent that every archaeological and ethnographic situation is unique, it is impossible—or at least unwise—to write out a step-by-step instruction manual for archaeological ethnography. There are, however, several broad observational strategies that are likely to pay good dividends. These bits of advice will not lead the archaeological ethnographer directly to the data needed, but they will help put him or her into a position to learn what needs to be known.

First, pay attention to—and trust—first impressions. Within two weeks of arriving in Annapolis I got a strong sense that contemporary Annapolis shares with most earlier versions of itself a strong desire to be both genteel and connected to the water; any institution or activity that has allowed Annapolis to have this dual identity has succeeded, while institutions or activities that have provided one or the other but not both have failed. Of course, I didn't learn all of this in just two weeks, but my initial impression of the city gave me a tremendously productive frame of reference for posing research questions and evaluating data. Initial impressions can show, with some clarity, what is obvious, and, paradoxically, things that are obvious are often among the first things to become murky or fade into the background as the archaeological ethnographer trains attention on smaller details and obscure data. So, take advantage of these first impressions; they're only available once.

Second, and it is difficult to stress this bit of advice too strongly, archaeological ethnography—just like any other ethnography—depends on adequate exposure, which simply means spending enough time, and the right kind of time, in enough of the right places. What I'm suggesting here is the same basic level of exposure that ethnographers gain from long-term participant observation. Some of what I learned in Annapolis came from searching for a particular fact in a book or in a public lecture. But as much if not more came from the daily routine of being a year-round Annapolitan. My ethnography, like all ethnography, benefited from my being in the right place at the right time, but these places and times cannot be selected with surgical precision; ethnographic epiphanies often come when least expected, and are best thought of as a reward for all the long hours spent waiting for them.

Third, in addition to redrawing the line that separates data from nondata, it is important to be able to peer over the walls that scholars typically build between different categories of data. For example, the basic idea behind the George Washington tour resulted from my simultaneous participation in three very different research activities, one ethnographic, one historical, and one archaeological.

On the archaeological side, as I was working on the early drafts of the George Washington tour, Paul Shackel was working on formulas for using eighteenth- and nineteenth-century ceramics to measure the degree to which occupants of a given site had accepted the principles of the Georgian order.[10] The George Washington tour and the ceramic formula were both developed during the course of our writing an essay, "Toward a Critical Archaeology," with Mark Leone. While the ceramic formula is Shackel's creation, the entire staff of Archaeology in Annapolis—myself included—had turned its collective attention to the problem of devising archaeological measurements of the acceptance of a worldview based on balance, order, symmetry, segmentation, and standardization.

On the historical side, I was in the midst of reading every local guide-book and history book I could get my hands on, in an attempt to learn the history of history in Annapolis.[11] In reading these books, I paid particular attention to patterns of emphasis and to underacknowledged themes, expressed both on and below the surface of the texts I was reading. Among the themes I discovered were a three-century-long invitation to outsiders, an emphasis on the eighteenth-century golden age, and a very specific—if somewhat skewed—picture of George Washington, based on the social and domestic aspects of his twenty or more visits to the city.[12] This view of Washington, based on his social and domestic life to the exclusion of his economic and political life, has been in place for at least seventy-five years, if not longer.

Finally, on the ethnographic side, I witnessed a very public discussion of just what kind of tourist town Annapolis wanted to be. The term "quality tourist" seems to have been defined—at least for Annapolis—during the mid-1980s in the local newspaper, and tourism was a major issue in the 1985 mayoral election. Annapolis decided, or decided to tell itself, that it prefers overnight guests to day-trippers, wealthy people to less wealthy people, white collars to blue ones, eaters to drinkers, shoppers to souvenir hunters, families to singles, and, if push came to shove, sail-boaters to powerboaters. Above all, the city decided that it wanted to attract polite, deferential tourists who would spend heavily while treading lightly on the qualities of the city that attracted them.

It would be conventional to think of these three research projects, one archaeological, one historical, and one ethnographic, as entirely separate. It is distressingly uncommon these days for a scholar trained in one of these disciplines to know much at all about either of the other two. However, the key to archaeological ethnography is ignoring this convention. The George Washington site tour drew equally on techniques and findings from all three disciplines: 1) it discussed explicitly Annapolis's legitimate need to control visitor behavior (discovered through ethnography); 2) it demonstrated Annapolis's use of George Washington stories to teach deferential visitor behavior (discovered through ethnography and history); 3) it outlined the history of the ideas that led, several generations after Washington's death, to modern tourism (illustrated by archaeological finds); and 4) it suggested to visitors that anytime they expose themselves to a historical interpretation, that version of the past is trying to get them to think a certain way or act a certain way. Our point in putting this all on display was not to chastise Annapolis for its creative use of George Washington (much of which is probably unconscious anyway), nor was it our purpose to discourage polite visitor behavior. Rather, we feel strongly that the interests of all parties, both residents and visitors, are better served by a more direct discussion of the issues at hand. George Washington was not a tourist, because he could not have been one, but both residents and visitors will be the losers if uncontrolled visitor behavior leads to the destruction of the key features that make Annapolis such an attractive place to visit. Mutual self-interest rather than mild historical misrepresentation should be the basis for establishing a social relationship between residents and visitors.

Who Might Do Archaeological Ethnography Elsewhere?

There is no question that Archaeology in Annapolis, and in particular the project's public program, has had many advantages, both financial and logistical. Consequently, it is easy to dismiss the project's interpretive program and its ethnographic component as pie-in-the-sky luxuries that are fine for us, but ill-suited to the conditions under which most American archaeology is conducted. I heartily disagree.

I have argued elsewhere that the next wave of advances in archaeological method and theory, at least with respect to critical archaeology, could well come not from academics but from public archaeology of the sort paid for by government agencies and conducted by contract firms.[13] This suggestion would have been laughable twenty years ago, but not today. While many grant-funded academic archaeologists still work wherever NSF will send them and often discount the archaeological value of their own backyards, many contract archaeologists are developing rich local data bases and strong local roots. They are becoming, in some ways, the cooperative extension agents for archaeology that many academics have chosen not to become. As a result, some contract archaeologists are extremely well-positioned to undertake archaeological ethnography in areas they know especially well. Furthermore, because of the nature of their work, studying sites just ahead of new construction, most contract archaeologists have the opportunity to be extremely well-informed about the social, political, and economic contexts in which they work. All that needs to be done to transform this kind of knowledge into useful data is to recognize it as such by redrawing the line between data and nondata. Once this step is taken, it is easy to imagine a wide variety of ethnographically informed contract archaeology projects.

The possibilities for work of this sort are especially promising in—but by no means limited to—historical archaeology. Take, for example, the case of an archaeological survey conducted along a roadway that has been used continuously for several hundred years, in anticipation of an upgrading of the roadway. In such a case, the historical trend that produced most of what would be recovered by the required archaeological project *also* would be the cause of the archaeological project itself. Thus, a CRM project that studied transportation history along this corridor would, in essence, be excavating and writing *its own history,* in an intellectual process not unlike that contained within the George Washington site tour, which was a tour about tourism delivered to tourists. I am certain that, in situations like this, a broad ethnographic understanding of contemporary circumstances can lead to the establishment of better, more meaningful archaeological research questions.

Both historical archaeology and prehistoric archaeology offer opportunities to explore the roots of issues that are still open and unsettled. And if archaeology is to be relevant to contemporary life—as archaeologist have claimed for twenty years the discipline should be—then we are obligated to understand equally well the past and the present, both the historical information we attempt to recover *and* the society to which we attempt to relate that information. And the tool that will help us understand the contemporary context to which we hope to link our work is ethnography, done the way ethnographers do it—over the long term, and with the idea that virtually everything we see, hear, read, or feel is potential data.

Notes

1. See Parker B. Potter Jr., *Public Archaeology in Annapolis: A Critical Approach to History in Maryland's "Ancient City"* (Washington, D.C.: Smithsonian Institution Press, 1994), 13–25, for a detailed discussion of this issue.

2. Post-1987 ethnography in Annapolis has been conducted by both George Logan (this volume, chap. 4) and Paul R. Mullins (this volume, chap. 1).

3. Elizabeth Tooker, "Foreword," in *Ethnography by Archaeologists,* 1978 Proceedings of the American Ethnological Society, ed. Elizabeth Tooker (Washington, D.C.: American Ethnological Society, 1982), vii.

4. This same point has been made with regard to archaeological hypothesis-testing by James Deetz, "Scientific Humanism and Humanistic Science: A Plea for Paradigmatic Pluralism," *Geoscience and Man* 23 (1983): 30.

5. Potter, *Public Archaeology,* 45–68.
6. Ibid., 69–88.
7. Mark P. Leone, Parker B. Potter Jr., and Paul A. Shackel, "Toward a Critical Archaeology," *Current Anthropology* 28 (3) (1987): 286–302, 289–91; Potter, *Public Archaeology,* 184–90.
8. Mark P. Leone, "Archaeology's Relationship to the Present and the Past," in *Modern Material Culture: The Archaeology of Us,* ed. Richard A. Gould and Michael B. Schiffer (New York: Academic Press, 1981), 5–13; Leone, "The Relationship Between Artifacts and the Public in Outdoor History Museums," in *The Research Potential of Anthropological Museum Collections,* ed. A. M. Cantwell, J. B. Griffin and Nan Rothschild (New York: Annals of the New York Academy of Sciences, 1981), 301–13.
9. Potter, *Public Archaeology,* 116–32.
10. Leone, Potter, and Shackel, "Toward a Critical Archaeology," 287–89; Barbara J. Little and Shackel, "Scales of Historical Anthropology: An Archaeology of Colonial Anglo-America," *Antiquity* 63 (240) (1989): 495–509; Shackel, *Personal Discipline and Material Culture: An Archaeology of Annapolis, Maryland, 1695–1870* (Knoxville: Univ. of Tennessee Press, 1993), 30–42.
11. Potter, *Public Archaeology,* 89–115.
12. Walter B. Norris, *Annapolis: Its Colonial and Naval Story* (New York: Thomas Y. Crowell, 1925); William Oliver Stevens, *Annapolis: Anne Arundel's Town* (New York: Dodd, Mead, and Company, 1937).
13. Potter, *Public Archaeology.*

3 Remembered Communities: Gott's Court and Hell Point in Annapolis, Maryland, 1900–1950

Hannah Jopling

Remembered communities can be imagined communities whose members recall themselves as a homogeneous, bounded, and harmonious entity while they ignore the conflict and differences that existed among them. Community identity is first based on relationships among people living in a defined space. How they see themselves in terms of those living outside of their neighborhood; how they think they are being perceived by the outsiders; and who they let into their neighborhood can strengthen their sense of community. In other words, friendly relations with neighbors create a sense of belonging to a group, and unfriendly relations with outsiders enhance the ties among community members who can overlook their class, racial, and ethnic tensions and differences.[1]

This chapter is about two communities in the town of Annapolis from 1900 to 1950. One was a working-class African American community in an alley that was torn down in 1952, the other an ethnically and economically mixed group living near the waterfront in a neighborhood demolished in 1941.

I pose three questions about these communities. First, what kind of community do largely working-class residents of a small neighborhood remember forming? Second, what role does the residents' sense of what outsiders think of them affect their image of themselves as a community? And third, what happens when communities try to reassemble years after they have been dispersed?

Oral History Projects

This essay is based on interviews with former residents of two small neighborhoods in Annapolis, Maryland—Gott's Court and Hell Point.[2] (map 3.1) In February 1992, I recorded a group discussion with a dozen former Gott's Court residents—three men and nine women—who had lived in Gott's Court until it was torn down in 1952. The men ranged in age from forty to sixty years old; the women from fifty-five to about eighty-five years old. Their memories covered the period of the 1920s to the 1950s. They had spent either their childhood or early adulthood in Gott's Court. Most are still working class and living in subsidized housing.

The meeting had been organized by two former residents who were upset by an article in a November 15, 1991, issue of the *Arundel Sun* about Gott's Court which called their homes "ramshackle." They wanted to respond to the article and used the meeting with me to discuss among themselves how to reply to the paper and plan a reunion. Some members of the group continued to meet on a monthly basis for a year to talk about a reunion and a response. In May, I recorded a second group discussion—now two men and seven women. During that summer, I conducted individual hour-and-a-half interviews with five of the former residents (four women and one man). I asked them questions about daily life in Gott's Court and their relationship with people living outside the neighborhood.

The sample of Hell Point residents was much larger. In the summer of 1993, twenty students from the University of Maryland Archaeological Field School, whom I trained in oral history techniques, conducted interviews with twenty-three former residents of Hell Point.[3] This was a neighborhood acquired by the Naval Academy in 1941 and subsequently demolished in 1942 to build an athletic field house.

Most of the people interviewed were members of the Hell Point Association, an organization formed in the early 1980s by several former Hell Point residents to organize reunions. The group's president recommended many of the memoirists for the interviews. The memories of this group span

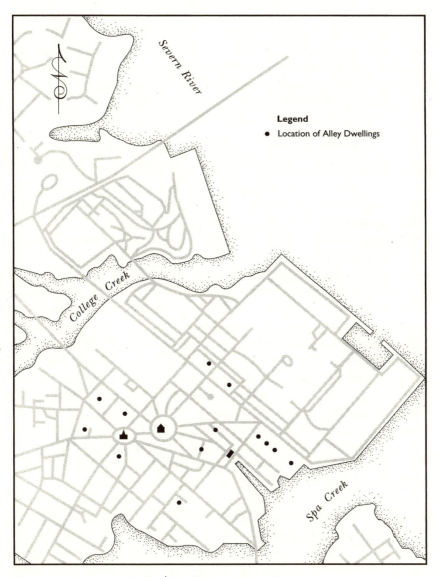

Map 3.1. Location of alley dwellings, Annapolis.

from the 1910s to the 1940s, when the neighborhood was taken over by the Naval Academy. Nine of the memoirists were European American of unknown origin. Additionally, there were various different ancestral groups represented: four of Jewish ancestry, two Italian, two Greek, two Filipino, one Scottish, two English, one Irish, and one African American. Thirteen were men and ten were women. Many of the former Hell Point residents grew up in working-class homes; some are now members of the middle class; and some are now successful lawyers and real estate investors.

Two Communities: Gott's Court and Hell Point

Gott's Court and Hell Point were very different neighborhoods. Gott's Court was two rows of attached wooden houses located inside a triangular block on the west side of Annapolis (fig. 3.1). The houses were two-story, four-room structures, approximately twelve feet wide by twenty-four feet deep, built in 1907. Nineteen houses were owned by a W. G. Gott and the other six by Harry Ivery. The only other buildings inside this block at that time were a few sheds. By 1921, garages had been built behind some of the houses, according to the Sanborn Insurance map of that year. The buildings were sold by Gott's son Winson to the city of Annapolis in 1951.[4] A year later they were torn down to make room for a municipal parking lot.

According to some former residents, the rents in the 1930s were about twelve dollars a month. At that time, a laundry worker at the Naval Academy made about eighteen dollars a week. A woman could earn eight dollars a week doing "day's work," that is, domestic work. According to the 1939 *Polk's Annapolis Directory,* of those male residents of Gott's Court whose professions were listed, one was a carpenter, one a building attendant at the Naval Academy, and six were laborers. Two women were listed as domestics. As many as eleven, and as few as one person, lived in a house. Sometimes members of three generations lived together. Three families took in boarders.

The tenants were responsible for maintaining the houses, which, according to some, were in bad repair. The thirty-foot-wide street between the two rows of houses was dirt, though most Annapolis streets were brick by the 1930s. As a woman now in her fifties described it as follows: "It was a beautiful place to live. We lived with dirt streets, no sidewalks, but we lived clean. We had four-room houses. We had water inside, and a flush toilet outside."

The Gott's Court houses were alley dwellings, hidden from view from the nearby streets. A former resident who lived in Gott's Court as a young

Fig. 3.1. Late-nineteenth-century view of Gott's Court. Courtesy of James E. Beans Jr. Family Photo Collection.

mother and is now in her seventies explained that "Gott's Court was off bounds. You could come down West Street and walk right past Gott's Court and wouldn't know nobody lived up there."

Alley dwellings have housed working-class people in American cities such as Boston and Philadelphia since the eighteenth century.[5] The alley communities in Annapolis were built at the turn of the century, the Sanborn Insurance maps reveal. According to the maps, some of the alley communities developed slowly, over a number of years. In other cases, such as Gott's Court, the houses were built within two years.[6] While most of the alley communities in Annapolis consisted of four to ten houses, Gott's Court had twenty-five houses. In some alley dwellings, there was no running water or electricity, in contrast to the houses on the main streets. The memoirists recall that by the late 1930s, many houses had electricity. Initially, working-class European Americans and working-class African Americans rented the small houses. By the 1920s, mostly African Americans lived in the alley dwellings, according to the census.

Gott's Court was surrounded by three streets. One was West Street, a main commercial thoroughfare where butchers, grocers, a druggist, and clothiers were located. Residences occupied by African Americans ran along the other two streets, Northwest Street and Calvert Street. The town jail was at the end of Calvert Street. Around the corner, part way up Northwest Street, was the "Colored" Episcopal church, which middle-class African Americans attended. Homeowners, some teachers and doctors, and some Naval Academy workers lived on Clay Street, located in the largest African American district, a block from Gott's Court.

Also constructed at the turn of the century, Hell Point was a fifteen-minute walk from Gott's Court, down by the waterfront, next to the market area and the Naval Academy. It consisted of two blocks in which there were four small alley communities (map 3.2). The Hell Point absorbed by the Naval Academy was bounded by Randall Street on the north, King George Street on the east, and Prince George Street on the west.

This neighborhood of approximately ninety-three households was ethnically and, to some degree, economically mixed. A 1941 housing assessment commissioned by the navy and oral history interviews reveal an apparent hierarchy of residency. The more middle-class families, most of whom owned their homes, lived in the upper block—between Randall and Holland Streets—farthest away from the waterfront.[7] Retired naval personnel, Naval Academy employees, including officers, musicians, and firemen, and the mayor of Annapolis were among the homeowners in this

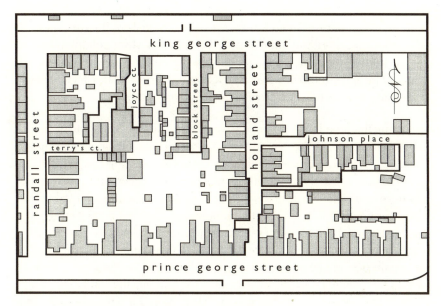

Map 3.2. Hell Point neighborhood, Annapolis.

part of the neighborhood. On lower Prince George Street the houses were mostly rented by clerks and mechanics whose wages were about $150 to $200 a month in 1941. The rents were from $25 to $70. Filipinos, European Americans, and African Americans lived on Holland Street, where more houses were rented than owned. Rents there were about $15 to $21 a month, according to the 1941 assessment. African Americans rented the alley dwellings on Terry and Joyce Courts, Johnson Place and Block Street. In 1941, the monthly rent for one of the five room houses in Terry's Court— 11 feet by 29 feet, with outside toilet—was $15 a month, according to the assessment. Joyce Court houses, also rented, did not have electricity. Block Street rents were $12 to $16. The streets of all three alleys were dirt. A Jewish man who lived on the middle-class end of Prince George Street described the class hierarchy, without mentioning any class conflict:

> Towards the lower part of Prince George's Street, which is also part of Hell Point, I would say you had your blue collar workers. It was a good mix, a good ethnic mix. But most of the houses between the street which is now missing, Holland Street, and Randall Street were what you might term townhouses, and some prominent citizens [were] living in those houses. It was just a great place to grow up . . .

there were mixtures of all kinds of people. There were Italians, there was Jewish, there was some Polish. . . . It was a white neighborhood that fronted off Prince George, but directly behind it, was a nonexistent [alley] street known as Block Street [which] was a black community, unfortunately a very poor black community.[8]

During the time Hell Point and Gott's Court existed, Annapolis was a legally segregated community. African Americans went to separate schools, churches, and movie theaters and drank from separate drinking fountains. In some clothing stores they were not allowed to try on clothes, and in others they had to go to the back door and point to the merchandise they wanted to buy. They were not permitted in restaurants except to pick up take-out orders. African Americans lived primarily in the western section of Annapolis. Jews also faced restrictions. They were not permitted into certain clubs or beaches and could not buy homes in certain neighborhoods, according to a Jewish woman whose father owned a small grocery store around the corner from Gott's Court in the largest African American neighborhood. Filipinos also had a limited choice of residence and employment. They worked in low-level positions at the Naval Academy mess and laundry and rented homes in the poorer section of Hell Point. The other Hell Point ethnic categories—among them Italians, Scots, Greeks, and Irish—were more dispersed in the neighborhood, living according to class distinctions. The poorer Scots and Irish lived at the lower end of Prince George Street, for example.

In 1941, the poorer section of Hell Point, from Holland Street to the waterfront and part of Randall and King George Streets, was acquired by the Naval Academy as the site of a new athletic facility. By the fall of 1942, the buildings were torn down, and Hell Point residents moved to different parts of the city. In 1953, the athletic field house and a parking lot were built on the land.

Accounts of Community in Hell Point and Gott's Court

The picture that emerges from the interviews with Gott's Court and Hell Point residents is one of groups of individuals living in a defined space who describe themselves as a harmonious community, when in fact they were not. Benedict Anderson's discussion of the rise of nationalism and the imagined community is applicable even to these very small neighborhoods because, as he says, all communities are "imagined" and are seen by their members "regardless of the actual inequality and exploitation that may prevail in each . . . always . . . as a deep, horizontal comradeship."[9] Additionally, Albert Hunter writes that members of a community define themselves as a place of friendliness and unqualified good, a view that was mentioned repeatedly by Gott's Court and Hell Point residents.[10]

These former residents often spoke of their community as a "big family." Some only wanted to focus on their similarities, and differences were played down. For example, a woman whose mother had been a domestic worker and who grew up in Gott's Court in the 1930s and 1940s said that "far as I'm concerned Gott's Court was beautiful. We would fight. Our parents would get mad with each other, but the next day everybody was still friends."

A Hell Pointer who experienced poverty as a child and was the daughter of a Filipino father and Scots mother echoed the same theme: "What I liked about Hell Point was we knew everybody. You know, everybody was friendly. Everybody was close." Another Hell Pointer whose father owned a shoe store recalled a sense of solidarity, despite differences: "You can't change what made us Hell Point because economically, you draw closely when you all feel like you're in the same boat. We helped each other, the families were very close. If someone went on to get an education, everyone was proud."

The oral history interviews reveal an intricate and complex picture of these neighborhoods and the residents' sense of community and how they related to one another during this period. For some, there were racial, ethnic, and class hierarchies that were reinforced by their relations with each other. As their comments reveal, they considered these relationships normal; they do not attribute any conflicts to structural constraints.

However, race, class, and ethnic identities are not always clear dividing lines among people. Some Hell Pointers only associated with people of the same race and class—some by choice, some by necessity. Others mixed with people of different backgrounds. Some felt stigmatized by neighbors for their race and class, but others were not. A Greek woman whose family owned a restaurant around the corner from Hell Point described how some people segregated themselves because they had to: "The colored people and the Filipinos, they knew their place and they would stay with their own, they never mix up, you know what I mean?" And the daughter of a Jewish owner of a grocery store on Holland Street explained why some chose ethnic separation in Hell Point to create a sense of solidarity amongst themselves: "We didn't have too many Jewish people in that area. But we mostly stuck to ourselves, we didn't go looking for the goyim to be friendly. Some might inter-marry—

we didn't do that. We stuck to our own. And I think it gave us a little more strength. When you don't stick together, you kind of dissipate."

A middle-class Jew who chose not to segregate himself and played with African American and European gentile boys, described his quandary over how to interpret the anti-Semitism which was "accepted back then": "The boys at the end of the day would say, 'Let's get a soda at the Jew store.' I heard that all my life. I didn't know whether to take it offensively."

A Filipino male told of two types of racial segregation in Annapolis at that time: "There was one between the white establishment and all others—anyway as I perceived it. There was [one between] the African American community and the Filipino community."

A former Hell Point resident, a middle-class woman whose ancestors were English, recalled how her parents segregated her. She was told to avoid the alleys where the African Americans lived, and Holland Street, where a number of Filipinos lived: "We were not allowed to go on Holland Street after a certain time. As it began to get dark. There were a lot of, umm [long pause], well, what my parents considered bad elements down there."

A successful European American businessman who grew up in a working-class family on an integrated street remembered a more flexible segregation, but one that he did not question: "We lived on an integrated street. Played together, grew up together, were friendly, but we didn't go to school together [with African Americans]. For that matter we couldn't . . . we couldn't go together to get ice cream soda on account, 'cause they didn't serve blacks in there."

Another Hell Pointer of European descent who played ball with African Americans sometimes had a different experience. He only hinted at the tensions and the fights which took place between African Americans, Filipinos, and whites when he described being "watched" when he went into Block Court, where African Americans lived: "Yeah, there was no reason we couldn't all go down in there [Block Street, Joyce Court, Terry's Court, or Johnson Place], but any alley groups of people like that would watch any visitors they had from different parts of the city, and the kids would think nothing of having a little fight."

For some, divisions existed along class lines as well. Several women remembered "snooty" next-door neighbors who ignored them, a rejection that enhanced their sense of solidarity and community with neighbors of the same class. An Italian women whose family had been working class recalled the class boundaries of the neighborhood: "Holland Street was almost like a dividing line, okay. All the neighbors, this end, were very friendly, neighborly. Right across on the opposite corner was a family . . . in a big house and in a child's mind, I mean big [laughter]. We always felt that they were rich, and they would go in and out, and never look left or right."

A woman of Scottish origin was married to a waterman and had fourteen children, one of largest and one of the poorest families in Hell Point. She recollected her experience of being supported by members of her own working class and rejected by middle-class residents when she lived on Dock Street, adjacent to Hell Point: "Course the people on Prince George Street, the next street up and down, they thought we were a bunch of poor trash. We might have been poor trash, but we certainly did take care of each other."

An upper middle-class woman of English descent who lived on upper Prince George Street and did not consider herself part of Hell Point, hedged about class tensions: "But nice people lived all up and down Prince George Street and nice people lived on Holland Street and nice people lived on King George Street. But there was an element, too, that was rough and ready. The children [from Holland and Upper Prince George Streets] didn't get along. They called us the 'Prince George Streeters' and they were the [laughter] 'Hell Pointers.' They didn't come up very often."

The divisions and clusters of people in Gott's Court, a much smaller community in which only African Americans lived, were much more subtle. Moreover, the sample was much smaller; therefore, less information was collected from this group. The former residents who met with me as a group only alluded to problems; they wanted to emphasize how well everyone got along. Few were willing to discuss their differences. White racism was only briefly mentioned. Distinctions between the Gott's Court residents were made over who had electricity, an inside toilet, a summer kitchen, and for whom you worked. Day laborers had less status than a plumber with a full-time job or a cook at the Naval Academy. Women who were domestics for upper-class white families had higher status than those who worked for middle-class families. The woman who moved into Gott's Court as a young mother described how people would help each other despite their differences, of which they were very aware: "Everybody helped everybody. If you lived across the street and them people knew you didn't have no food, everybody would give you something."

The sharing that took place both amplified the distinctions that existed between the Gott's Court residents and fostered a sense of community between these alley dwellers. One former Gott's Court resident whose father was a plumber described how he learned what it was like to be better off than some of his neighbors: "Some families were fortunate, like my father, and couple of others. They used to pitch [in] together during Christmas or holiday times and [help] those [who] were less fortunate. But I didn't think I was no better."

Few brought up racial conflicts between African Americans and whites or among African Americans themselves. A man whose skin was light brown was punished for his racist slurs: "I used to have a habit of calling people black. My father's father was a white man and his mother was most Indian. Her hair, she could sit on it. Like I used to call people black. This one told him [his father], and he would take that hard whip and whip me." Another Gott's Court resident at first described how all the children growing up in Gott's Court played together. A year later she mentioned to me one Gott's Court mother's racial and class prejudice toward her: "Me and Alice were the best of friends. I can remember when we wanted to play with each other, her mother and grandmother wouldn't let her play with me because I was too black."

How They Saw Outsiders

Residents of Hell Point and Gott's Court were asked what happened when they told someone where they lived, or what it was like when someone found out they were from Hell Point or Gott's Court. (Interviews have not been conducted with Annapolitans who lived outside of Gott's Court and Hell Point to ascertain their opinions of the people living in these two neighborhoods.) From the interviews conducted, it is apparent that some residents of Gott's Court and Hell Point felt stigmatized by where they lived. They sensed that people reacted negatively to them when people found out where they came from. These experiences were not the only basis on which these communities developed, however. Rather, they enhanced the sense the residents of these two communities already had of belonging to a group. As a number of scholars suggest, the sense of community develops in part as a result of the members of the community defining themselves against outsiders.[11] In the case of Gott's Court and Hell Point, the residents' definition of themselves as community was primarily based on their relationships with each other. This was then heightened by their perceptions of outsiders' opinions of them.

Residents of Gott's Court and Hell Point felt that their neighborhoods were seen as bad places. Their reaction to this was twofold. To some degree they pulled inward, staying within their community. But they also asserted themselves, defending their territory, putting themselves on display outside their community or correcting what they perceived to be an inaccurate impression held by outsiders.

Gott's Court residents felt that they were looked down upon because of their dirt street and "ramshackle" houses that were the result of a neglectful town administration and landlords. In their discussions with me, the Gott's Court residents rarely brought up the white racism they must have experienced. When asked to relate what it was like to say that they had come from Gott's Court, they spoke of the prejudice they experienced within the larger African American community. For example, no one remembers children from other African American sections of town coming into the court to play. Some of the Gott's Court children visited family members who lived a couple of blocks away in the largest African American district, but the children in that neighborhood did not want to play with children from Gott's Court: "They just thought that we were a little different than what they were. Like the kids on Washington Street, we couldn't go play with them. . . . To them we were dirt." Adults from the alley communities such as Gott's Court and Larkin Street felt as though they were treated differently by people who lived in better circumstances: "We, as children, and our parents, were not accepted with a lot of black people that had like a six-room house with a basement, and a big yard, and a porch and a hedge."

The residents of Hell Point also felt stigmatized. They thought outsiders saw Hell Point as a place where there were rowdy, drunken sailors and rough poor people. A number of Hell Pointers said that such behavior was associated with the people who lived there as far back as the late nineteenth century, when Hell Point was known as a menace to the Naval Academy. More than forty years later, a 1941 housing appraisal described the area as an "undesirable environment" and "less desirable residential section."[12]

Some told what it was like to be associated with the neighborhood. One man whose parents worked at the Naval Academy remembered that "As a kid, four or five of us would walk up King George Street. . . . The mother used to say 'here comes those Hell Pointers' and get her son and bring him in the house." An Italian working-class woman lived next door to an upper-class family that ignored her, and she recollected stories about Hell Pointers visiting classmates who lived outside the neighborhood: "Well, the minute the mother [of the classmate] would know that child lived in Hell Point, you know, never again were you invited." The owner of the Greek restaurant around the corner from Hell Point recalled the problems in hiring staff: "Well, at one time people were afraid to go down there, cause the first years when we had the restaurant, we were trying to get waitresses and no one would want to work there."

Members of the communities reacted to the outsider's view, as they saw it, by asserting themselves in various ways. They created their own world within their communities. They sometimes prevented others from coming into the neighborhood. When they went out of the community, they put themselves on display. In Gott's Court, one former resident whose mother was a domestic described their world: "There wasn't no outsiders. We all stayed together, we played together, we went to school together. We studied together." A person who lived on West Street above a store owned by his parents described the time he tried riding his bike up into the Court, when he would not let anyone in the Court ride it: "I would go all the way back here and turn around and come back up. By the time I got up here I had a pint bottle up the side of my head." One woman described how they felt different from other children, but how they went out of Gott's Court: "You didn't feel it too much, you know, we wasn't like shunned, but we felt a little different, a little bit different. . . . People thought that we was living in what people call the slums . . . because their streets were paved, and we had clean dirt. And they looked down on us. And um, you know, when we came out of Gott's Court, we were all dressed, starched."

In Hell Point, some residents boasted of how outsiders could be treated, as one working-class resident did: "I don't say it was a reputation, but I can remember if you wasn't from that area you just didn't come down and fool around. It just was [that] simple." Or, as another described, "If you were a stranger, you didn't wander around Hell Point. Word spread fast in Hell Point, 'Somebody's down there.' For whatever reason, I don't know what they were upset about, but, I guess it was protecting their turf."

According to some stories, Hell Pointers asserted themselves in other ways outside the neighborhood. They were the only ones allowed to sit in the first four rows of the local movie theater.[13] One Hell Pointer explained how well the Hell Point baseball team did: "We won the league championship, because I knew that if Hell Point put a team in there, they would be very competitive, because that was the nature of the upbringing."

Only Subjective Communities

Residents of Gott's Court and Hell Point imagined themselves as cohesive communities, as people who shared values because of their shared experience with some of their neighbors. Their idea of being a "family" overlooked the slights they withstood or the conflicts they had with higher-class people or people of a certain race and ethnicity. On the other hand, their sense of community was heightened by their experience of feeling shunned or looked down upon by people who lived outside their neighborhoods.

While they may have seen themselves as a tightly knit community, they did not act like one when their neighborhoods were threatened. They did not coalesce or organize themselves into groups to oppose the destruction of their neighborhoods, as other threatened communities have done.[14]

For Hell Pointers among those who experienced the destruction of their neighborhood in the 1940s, it is apparent the community was divided. Some residents were pleased to move into better homes but sad to leave their neighborhood. Others were bitter about the disruption and amount of compensation they received for their homes and businesses. Some fought the acquisition. Some felt they had to acquiesce because it was wartime, or because the Naval Academy threatened to leave Annapolis if it could not expand into Hell Point, a departure that would mean loss of employment.

Gott's Court was demolished in the early 1950s as part of an urban renewal project.[15] Many of those interviewed were teenagers then and did not recall the response of the adults in Gott's Court. Some were glad to move to a house in better condition with running water and an inside toilet.

Communities Reassembling Themselves

While these groups of people could not prevent their communities from being demolished, their remembered sense of belonging to a community motivates their reunions today. The communities of Hell Point and Gott's Court are reassembling themselves forty years after the buildings were torn down and the people dispersed. Some Hell Pointers have been getting together every few years since the early 1980s for big reunions attended by over two hundred people and sometimes marching in the Fourth of July parade.[16] People who lived outside Hell Point also want to come to the reunions. Some of the participants who grew up in struggling working-class families are now successful lawyers, real estate developers, and politicians. Others have moved up from working-class to middle-class status. They want to correct what they consider to be outsiders' perceptions of them as trouble-makers and to show off their new identities: "We had families that came from this environment that went on to be very successful."

Many of the memoirists have fond memories of their childhoods (and in some cases adulthoods) in Hell Point and enjoy reconstituting themselves: "I think the people down there had character. When we get together, there's so much joy and togetherness."

Some of the residents of Gott's Court are involved in a similar process of remembering. The present influences their reminiscences of the past.[17] As mentioned at the beginning of this chapter, a group of former residents of Gott's Court met in February 1992 to discuss a newspaper article that described Gott's Court residents as living in "ramshackle" houses. To them, "ramshackle" implied slovenly people. They wanted to correct the negative impression of their old neighborhood which they thought was conveyed in the article: "It didn't look like Gott's Court. . . . Right out there in Gott's Court. It was clean. It was real clean."

One women who has worked as a cook and is a community activist mentioned how she has to confront the negative opinion she thinks people form of her when they learn she is from Gott's Court: "People still look down on you when you say you are from Gott's Court until you let them know that you know just as much, if not more, about the world affairs as they know." A young mother who had moved into Gott's Court when she was seventeen and is now in her seventies expressed pride in the accomplishments of her former neighbors: "They [outsiders] thought they were just a little bit above us. But today, whole lot of Gott's Court people have gotten just as far as they have."

An informal group of about a dozen people met monthly for a year to reminisce and plan a reunion. Attendance was sometimes sparse, however. Members of the group met with their city alderman who helped them draft the wording for a plaque which would describe Gott's Court as they remembered the neighborhood, a close-knit community of people who helped one another. The plaque would be attached to a brick wall in a park bordering a parking lot that was being built on top of their old homes. All that remained to be done was to raise the funds to pay for the plaque, not an easy job for a largely working-class group.

Setting the record straight about Gott's Court residents with the plaque and holding a reunion will take longer than planned because more pressing matters take up the Gott's Court community members' time. These former Gott's Court residents are also working in their new communities to reopen a neighborhood school, feed the homeless, volunteer in their churches, run a food give-away program for the elderly and a breakfast program for the neighborhood children.

• • •

While the former Gott's Court and Hell Point residents resemble clusters of individuals living in a defined space more than cohesive communities, their memories of their past as members of a strong community motivates their present actions.[18] Their reassembling their communities again is also a response to their feeling denigrated because of where they lived. They differ in their use of history to correct what they perceive to be an inaccurate picture of themselves.

The Hell Point residents use their past to show what they have become, contrary to what they think were the expectations of the outsiders who they think scorned them when they were children. Through their reunions and participation in the Fourth of July parade, they put themselves on display as a community, celebrate their achievements, and tell themselves the others were wrong about Hell Pointers.

Gott's Court residents use the past in several ways. They also want to reassemble themselves to celebrate their former community. And they want to correct the negative impression they think outsiders had of them, not by putting themselves on display, but with a plaque that recognizes them as their imagined community of supportive families. They use the past also to distinguish themselves from the present. Their recollections of a supportive community and helpful neighbors are interrupted continuously by references to the problems in their present-day neighborhoods. It is with these accounts of the past that they contrast themselves with present-day communities marred by crack houses and unattended children. But it is these problems in the present that take precedence over celebrating their past and reassembling their old community.

The remembered communities of Gott's Court and Hell Point are based on the relationships the former residents had within their community and outside of it, how they saw themselves then and how they see themselves now. Such reminiscences reveal the complexity of communities of the past and exemplify how oral history provides archaeologists a rich context in which to place their data.

Notes

I would like to thank the members of the Gott's Court and Hell Point communities who so willingly shared their memories. A number of people have provided me with helpful guidance and support, namely, Mark Leone, Joan Vincent, Vincent Crapanzano, Nan Rothschild, Delmos Jones, Barbara Little, Christopher Matthews, and Lynn Jones. This chapter was presented in a shortened version as a paper for a panel organized by Julie Ernstein for the Society for Historical Archaeology Conference in Vancouver. I am particularly grateful to the three editors of this volume for their valuable suggestions.

1. Benedict Anderson, *Imagined Communities: Reflections on the Origin and Spread of Nationalism* (London: Verso, 1991), 1–7; Frederik Barth, *Ethnic Groups and Boundaries* (Boston: Little, Brown, 1969); James Brow, "Notes of Community, Hegemony, and the Uses of the Past," *Anthropology Quarterly* 63 (1990): 1–6; Grady Clay, *Close-Up: How to Read the American City* (New York: Praeger, 1972); Anthony Leeds, "Locality of Power in Relation the Supralocal Power Institutions," in *Urban Anthropology: Cross-Cultural Studies of Urbanization*, ed. Aidan Southall (New York: Oxford Univ. Press, 1973), 15–41; Barbara J. Little, "Echoes and Forecasts: Group Tensions in Historical Archaeology," *International Journal of Group Tensions* 18 (1988): 243–57; Leith Mullings, *Cities of the United States: Studies in Urban Anthropology* (New York: Columbia Univ. Press, 1987), 1–19; Jay O'Brien and William Roseberry, *Golden Ages, Dark Ages: Imagining the Past in Anthropology and History* (Berkeley: Univ. of California Press), 1–18; Amos Rapoport, *Human Aspects of Urban Form* (Oxford: Pergamon Press, 1977); Nan A. Rothschild, *New York City Neighborhoods: The 18th Century* (New York: Academic Press, 1991); Roger Sanjek, "Urban Anthropology in the 1980s: A World View," *Annual Review of Anthropology* 19 (1990): 151–86; Gerald D. Suttles, *The Social Order of the Slum* (Chicago: Chicago Univ. Press, 1968); William K. Tabb and Larry Sawers, *Marxism and the Metropolis: New Perspectives in Urban Political Economy* (Oxford: Oxford Univ. Press, 1978); Joan Vincent, "The Structuring of Ethnicity," *Human Organization* 33 (1974): 375–79; and Eric Wolf, *Europe and the People without History* (Berkeley: Univ. of California Press, 1982).

2. Other sources include Annapolis, Anne Arundel County, Maryland Census of Population (National Archives Microfilm Publ. T623, roll 605); Twelfth Census of the United States, 1900 (National Archives Microfilm Publ. T624, roll 550); Thirteenth Census of the United States (National Archives Microfilm Publ. T625, roll 653); Fourteenth Census of the United States, 1920, Records of the Census, Record Group 29, National Archives, Washington, D.C.; *Map of the City of Annapolis, Maryland* (New York: Sanborn Insurance Company, 1885, 1891, 1897,

1903, 1908, 1913, 1921, 1930); *Polk's Annapolis Directory* (New York: R. L. Polk & Co., Inc., 1939); "1941 Valuation and Conclusions, Extension of the U.S. Naval Academy," Thomas C. Worthington Collection MSA SC 2375, Maryland State Archives, Annapolis; Philip Brown, *The Other Annapolis* (Annapolis: Annapolis Publishing Co., 1994); Mame Warren, *Then Again . . . Annapolis, 1900–1965* (Annapolis: Time Exposures, Ltd., 1990); Eric Goldstein, "Surviving Together: African Americans and Jews in Annapolis, 1885–1968," Historic Annapolis Foundation; Ann Jensen, "Remembering Hell Point," *Annapolitan* (Nov. 1989): 38–43, 62–66; Christopher N. Matthews, "A Reconstruction of Hell Point, Annapolis Maryland: Material Culture and Memory," unpubl. MS; and Mark S. Warner, *Test Excavations at Gott's Court Annapolis, Maryland 19AP52* (Annapolis: Historic Annapolis Foundation, 1992).

3. This oral history project was funded by a Legacy Grant from the U.S. Navy Dept. to collect historical and archaeological data about properties acquired by the Naval Academy.

4. Warner, *Test Excavations.*

5. Compare James Borchert, *Alley Life in Washington: Family, Community, Religion and Folklife in the City, 1850–1970* (Urbana: Univ. of Illinois Press, 1982); Sam Bass Warner, *The Private City* (Philadelphia: Univ. of Pennsylvania Press, 1968); and Oscar Handlin, *Boston's Immigrants: A Study in Acculturation* (Cambridge: Belknap Press, 1958).

6. Warner, *Test Excavations.*

7. Compare Matthews, "A Reconstruction of Hell Point."

8. In 1941 the Naval Academy acquired all the land from Holland Street to the waterfront and part of Randall and King George Streets. By the fall of 1942, the area had been razed, but the sports arena and parking lot were not built on the site until the mid-1950s.

9. Anderson, *Imagined Communities,* 7.

10. Albert Hunter, "Persistence of Local Sentiments in Mass Society," in *Perspectives on the American Community,* ed. Roland L. Warren (New York: Rand McNally, 1983), 178–93.

11. Barth, *Ethnic Groups;* Gavin Smith, "The Production of Culture in Local Rebellion," in *Golden Ages, Dark Ages: Imagining the Past in Anthropology and History,* ed. Jay O'Brien and William Roseberry (Berkeley: Univ. of California Press, 1991), 180–208; Rapoport, *Human Aspects;* and Delmos Jones, personal communication, 1993.

12. "1941 Valuation and Conclusions."

13. Jensen, "Remembering Hell Point."

14. Smith, "The Production of Culture," 180–208.

15. Warner, *Test Excavations.*

16. Jensen, "Remembering Hell Point."

17. Mark P. Leone, "The Relationship Between Artifacts and the Public in Outdoor History Museums," in *The Research Potential of Anthropological Museum Collections,* ed. A. M. Cantwell, J. B. Griffin, and N. A. Rothschild (New York: Annals of the New York Academy of Sciences, 1981), 376; David Lowenthal, *The Past*

Is a Foreign Country (Cambridge: Cambridge Univ. Press, 1985); Anderson, *Illuminations* (New York: Harcourt, Brace, and World, 1968), 255–269; and Gertrude Fraser and Reginald Butler, "Anatomy of a Disinterment: The Unmaking of Afro-American History," in *Presenting the Past: Essays on History and the Public*, ed. Susan Porter Benson, Stephen Brier, and Roy Rosenzweig (Philadelphia: Temple Univ. Press, 1986), 121–32.

18. O'Brien and Roseberry, *Golden Ages, Dark Ages*, 1–18.

4 Archaeologists, Residents, and Visitors: Creating a Community-Based Program in African American Archaeology

George C. Logan

In 1989, Archaeology in Annapolis initiated a program that focused specifically on researching and interpreting aspects of the city's African American past. The archaeological work also provided an opportunity to develop an ongoing oral history project and varied educational programs. Support for these efforts from both residents and tourists indicates not only that the initiative has made a welcome contribution to the study of Annapolis's past, but also that community-based programs similar to this one, which seek to make interpretations of the past more inclusive, could also succeed elsewhere.

This chapter explains what Archaeology in Annapolis tries to accomplish through its public programs. It discusses the genesis of the African American initiative and highlights the public educational programs, research projects, and outreach activities that were all part of the first two seasons of the program's focus on African American history, including an on-site tour program; a museum exhibit that presented work-in-progress and preliminary results; oral history interviews with people who had been residents of one neighborhood; and participation in the annual Kunta Kinte

Festival in Annapolis, which celebrates African American heritage. High-lighting the ways in which community involvement influenced the creation and development of the public programs is a theme that binds these discussions together. Since the activities were designed to encourage us to ask questions and listen to local residents and interested visitors, community input influenced virtually every educational activity. Undoubtedly some opportunities were missed, but by stressing the importance of listening, Archaeology in Annapolis was better equipped to develop public outreach activities that others recognized as being relevant not only for interpreting the past but also for addressing current issues related to historic preservation and other community interests.

Through these educational activities we succeeded in achieving some of our most basic goals, but we also fell far short of others. By identifying the strengths and weaknesses of our most recent public programming efforts, we hope that this essay will help other archaeologists and educators learn from our experiences and make project-community interaction not just a goal of educational programming, but also an integral part of the planning process.

Background

"Archaeology in Public" was established as the public education component of Archaeology in Annapolis soon after the project began in 1981. The public programs encourage people to act in three ways when they visit historic sites and museums: first, to identify the evidence used to support historical interpretations; second, to recognize how interpretations are created based on that evidence; and third, to question and challenge interpretations, especially those that are presented as facts beyond question. Once visitors recognize how historical interpretations are created and realize that they are not revealed truths from the past, we expect they will consider interpretive messages more carefully in the future, and they may be more likely to challenge versions of the past with which they do not agree.[1] These programs have been developed to encourage people not only to actively interpret the past, but also to explore how connections are made between the past and present, and to examine how historical interpretations are used to influence perceptions of modern life in ways that are not always apparent.[2]

Limitations of Public Outreach

After seven years of excavation, analysis, and interpretation, Archaeology in Annapolis had accumulated data from a number of different sites in the city. On-site programs had focused on the eighteenth-century planter-elite class, tavern owners, merchants, and blacksmiths, as well as on broader topics such as the Annapolis town plan and the U.S. Naval Academy's relationship with the city. Yet, despite efforts to critically interpret the past through public programs which would serve the entire Annapolis community, public outreach had achieved only limited contact with some local constituencies, most notably with the African American community.

Soon after Archaeology in Annapolis formed, Parker Potter examined how Annapolis has viewed its past over the last century by studying written histories, conducting interviews, and taking guided historical tours of the city.[3] He hoped to get a sense of how residents thought about the city's past and about how that past has been presented since the 1880s, a period when the city began to recognize itself primarily as a historic town. He concluded that interpretations of the past have contributed to fragmented histories by making few connections between certain time periods, population groups, and community institutions. Significantly, eighteenth-century history continues to be separate from nineteenth-century history, the history of the city of Annapolis remains separate from the history of the Naval Academy, and black history is separate from white history.[4] The fragmentation has been so complete that, according to Potter, a comprehensive and coherent view of how all the parts fit together cannot be found.[5]

Although not a surprising discovery, this characterization helps us see how historical interpretations can affect contemporary society. In this case, fragmented histories have led people to think about Annapolis in terms of clear dichotomies focusing on some specific topics while ignoring others. Historical interpretations also have played a part in maintaining physical separations between racial and economic groups in present-day Annapolis.

Two developments have contributed to physical separations of groups according to differences in class and race. Many people, including a significant number of African Americans, have moved out of downtown over the last century, initially as a result of Naval Academy expansion and then as a result of urban renewal projects. More recently, gentrification of downtown neighborhoods and a resulting overall rise in property values have encouraged other residents to move, changing the character of the downtown from one based on a local economy to one based on tourism.[6]

During this same period, the Annapolis past that has dominated historical interpretations has focused on the city's "golden age" of the later 1700s, with most attention paid to the colonial period's most wealthy citizens, such as William Paca and the Carroll and Calvert families. From the beginning of the city's preservation movement in the 1950s until quite recently and even to the present, an impression among local African Americans has been that the Historic District is about white history. This observation is based on informal conversations with individuals over the past several years and may not be representative of the broader population. If it is, however, then it would suggest that local African Americans consider many of the historical programs in Annapolis to be irrelevant and even insulting, so they choose not to participate. We did not critically examine the extent to which this local impression is shared, nor did we initiate discussions with visitors about it as a formal part of our tours. Maybe we should have: such examinations would most likely have added significantly to a better understanding of Potter's observations on the controversial and sensitive issue of fragmentation.

Archaeology in Annapolis may have contributed to this interpretive and physical separation by not addressing sooner the extent to which African American history is underrepresented in Annapolis. Until the 1989 excavation project on the Gott's Court site, Archaeology in Annapolis had not addressed in any great detail the African American presence in Annapolis. In public programs, we had not explored the African American contributions to the individual sites already excavated, nor how such contributions might have been explicitly identified in the archaeological record. These issues would become central concerns as our research of African American sites increased and related public programs took shape.

Addressing the City's African American Past

Archaeology in Annapolis used existing data from a historic buildings survey and from previously completed research to identify a number of historic African American sites that also had potential for archaeological investigation. Two of these sites had been residential neighborhoods, bought up and demolished in the mid-twentieth century to construct parking lots. In the late 1980s, these two properties were again under consideration as sites for new construction, and this time the work would destroy all surviving archaeological remains on both sites. Before testing the sites to determine archaeological integrity, Archaeology in Annapolis met with senior staff members of the Banneker-Douglass Museum. The museum is dedicated to interpreting African American heritage throughout the state and is the center for the Maryland Commission on African American History and Culture. We hoped the meetings could lead to the development of research questions that could be tested archaeologically. Answers to some of the following questions and concerns at this planning stage would affect the rest of the project. What should be the focus of this archaeological initiative? Are there groups or individuals in the community that would be interested in participating in such a project? What would be effective methods for encouraging people to get involved in the research? Instead of supplying answers for the community about African American sites in Annapolis, we began the work by approaching members of the community and asking them to help develop research questions and ideas for public outreach programs.

Given our apparent sudden interest in the city's African American past, the museum staff initially was skeptical, but during the discussions that followed in 1988 and 1989, participants identified a number of mutual research interests. In particular, three questions that came out of one of the first meetings helped us frame our archaeological work. First, do African Americans have an archaeological past in Annapolis that can be specifically identified and studied? Second, we know something about slavery, but is there archaeology in Annapolis associated with freedom and early African American success stories? Third, is there anything left suggesting African cultural influence?[7] We hoped that the first question could be answered during initial field testing, but the second and third questions would almost certainly require additional research.

The first excavation project on Gott's Court (map 4.1) began in August 1989 and lasted only about three weeks, but results proved that the site contained archaeological remains associated with its early-twentieth-century African American occupation. A series of twenty-five connected frame houses had been constructed there in 1907 on the interior of the city block. The buildings on the court were rented exclusively by African Americans, so we expected that research on this site would provide data useful for interpreting working-class African American lifestyles during the years soon after the court's construction.[8] Since relatively little was recorded or known about the daily lives of this turn-of-the-century community, project coordinators convinced city and county planners that the site was archaeologically and historically significant. This limited project was a first step toward including African Americans in our historical interpretations. As a result of the work, city and county officials decided that additional archaeological research, required prior to construction, must address this period of the site's history.

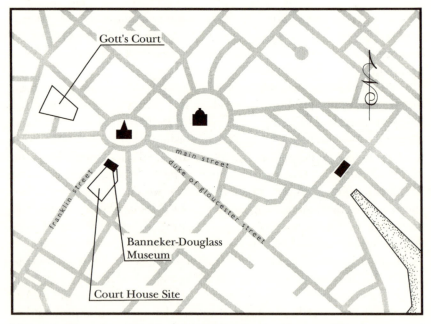

Map 4.1. Banneker-Douglass Museum, Gott's Court, and the location of the Courthouse Site excavations, Annapolis.

A Public Program about African American History: Learning to Listen

During the summer of 1990, we began a full season of excavations on the proposed site of the Anne Arundel County Courthouse expansion—the second historic African American site threatened by construction (map 4.1). The area had been part of a predominantly African American neighborhood for more than one hundred years, occupied since at least the 1870s by both African American property owners and renters.[9] The last remaining houses on this part of the block were purchased by the county and torn down in the early 1970s to complete a parking lot for the county courthouse. More recently, the county identified the lot as a favored location for a major courthouse expansion, and it was this proposal that raised concern over the archaeological resources that may be destroyed as a result of construction. Again, arguing for the site's historical significance and with support from Historic Annapolis Foundation and the Banneker-Douglass Museum, Archaeology in Annapolis took the opportunity to determine whether or not the Courthouse site contained preserved archaeological deposits from its nineteenth- and early-twentieth-century occupation. Based on preliminary results, we determined that yard areas behind the demolished foundations were still relatively undisturbed and identified the site as an important historical resource for learning more about the city's turn-of-the-century African American population.

During the three-month dig in 1990, archaeologists offered an on-site public program with a primary educational goal of initiating a dialogue with members of the community about how historical interpretations of the city could be made less racially segregated. The Courthouse site program was designed according to a general framework used for previous Archaeology in Annapolis on-site programs.[10] Site tours were complemented by large informative placards and free brochures offered to visitors at the conclusion of tours.[11]

Site Placards

Placards framed an entrance to the site, which otherwise would have been difficult for visitors to navigate, because it was dominated by scattered excavation units, hanging screens, backdirt piles, and broken asphalt. The placards also provided site information for visitors to read in case they had to wait a few minutes for a tour. Most of the first placard's text consisted of excerpts taken from oral history interviews with people who once lived in the neighborhood.[12] The purpose of this placard was to highlight the program's interdisciplinary approach and the importance of oral history to the project.

Placard One: The Community Remembers

People who lived in this large area from Franklin Street to South Street remember many things about its past. As part of this project, former residents have been talking with archaeologists to tell about the neighborhood during the first half of this century. Here are some excerpts from those conversations.

It was a lovely home. It was the kind of home that had a very large living room. As you walked in the door you just walked into this big room. The stairway came down into the living room. Then in the next room was the dining room, then the next was the kitchen. All the rooms opened into each other.

Lulu Hardesty, Franklin Street

All these people had fences and alleyways between their houses— what you would call now townhouses—one, two, three, all the way down the street.

George Phelps, Jr., South Street

On South Street everybody knew everybody. There were a lot of kids over here. We grew up together—a lot of boys—we played ball, we crabbed, we fished, we had good times.

There was an effect on them, because many of them, with this urban renewal, had to give up their homes. It was a really thriving community before things began to happen.

Henry Holland, South Street

I lived at 125 [South Street] and [that] was where the man went through with his horses to his stables. He was a contractor [a gardener], but he didn't have trucks, he had horses and wagons. When all the people were buying trucks, he was getting up in age and never did buy a truck. He stuck with the horses clear up until, oh gosh, I guess the war had started, I guess about '44 or '45.

I went in the service in '47 and all this was still intact. I came home three years later and it was gone. I came home and my family had moved.

Norvain Sharps, South Street

Personal memories cannot be recovered through archaeological research. On the other hand, oral history cannot reveal information about Annapolis as it existed in the 1800s. By taking an interest in all their historical resources, Annapolitans are producing an account of the city's history that is meaningful to everyone.

The second placard introduced an archaeological perspective. It presented some preliminary results from analysis of the Gott's Court site artifact collections. The text emphasized comparative analysis of historic African American sites with other sites in the city in an effort to show that black history and white history should not be interpreted separately, but as aspects of a single, coherent past.

Placard Two: The Archaeology

Some aspects of the past are particularly well suited for archaeological study. For example, by digging this site we will learn more about forgotten aspects of daily life of African-Americans in Annapolis over 100 years ago. The lives and history of black Annapolitans are said not to be well documented and African-American history is currently underrepresented in most presentations of the city's past. Results from archaeological excavations can help remedy this.

"Archaeology in Annapolis" recently compared artifact collections from two sites dating to the late 1800s and early 1900s. One site, known as Gott's Court, was composed of rental properties built between 1906 and 1908 and occupied by African-American families. Most of the renters were listed in census records as either semi- or unskilled laborers.

The other site, on Main Street, was owned and occupied by a European-American physician and his family. The Gott's Court collection of dishes or "ceramics" contains relatively more storage vessels than the Main Street site. The limited excavations at Gott's Court yielded only mismatched vessels, in contrast to the matched sets of ceramic vessels at Main St. Both collections have mostly vessels such as plates and saucers and very few bowls. The Gott's Court ceramics reveal that the people living there were probably processing and storing more of their own food. They were participating in the local economy, but had little purchasing power. Nevertheless, the similarities in the collections suggest that people at both sites shared social conventions about organizing and serving meals.

The artifact collections excavated from beneath this courthouse parking lot suggest that by the 1850s people living here were thoroughly middle class in their cooking and eating preferences. They were free, independent and middle class, even if they generally bought less expensive goods.

Gott's Court, the Courthouse, and the Main Street sites are only three small areas within the Historic District. We need to compare more sites to better understand the city's past and its people, but first we must ask: *"Does this research matter?"*

This excavation is devoted to learning more about the African-American past in Annapolis. As you walk around the site consider this question: "Will archaeologists' contributions be relevant and important to Annapolis in general and to African Americans in particular?" See what you think.

The two placards were created as complements to one another. One provided information about the site and its history through personal memories. The other explained one way in which historical archaeologists interpret the past. The intention of the second placard was to emphasize the importance of comparative analysis in archaeological research; however, there are problems with the way we tried to convey this message. The discussion of the Gott's Court–Main Street study was premature, since it was based on a limited comparison between collections that were from two very different kinds of deposits. The conclusion was based more on our expectations about how Gott's Court residents may have lived than on what we could prove based on the initial excavations. Terms used in describing occupants of the Courthouse site may have been unintentionally mislead-ing, since no additional clarification of "thoroughly middle class," "free," or "independent" were offered. The results of comparative study and the descriptive terms were deliberately used to confront and challenge mod-ern-day negative stereotypes about nineteenth-century African American households. The problems arose from attempting to compose a provoca-tive and coherent message in a limited space. This is a dilemma common to all history museum presentations and one that is rarely negotiated suc-cessfully. More than ten years of experience in Annapolis has shown us that visitors do take time to read placard texts, sometimes even more than once, so we use these large signs both as props for marking off sites and as introductions to thought-provoking tours.

Site Tours

More people have participated in tours of ongoing archaeological digs than any of our other educational programs. There are a number of unifying themes common to these site tours. Using specific examples during each tour, guides are able to point out that historical interpretations are created in the present, that they inevitably have subjective elements and are, therefore, open to ques-tion. During tours, we also point out that historical interpretations not only shed light on the past, but they also provide useful insights into understand-ing modern society. Any historical research project is conducted because it serves current interests, and the results reflect those interests, whether they are social, political, religious, or economic in nature, or usually some combi-nation. Historical interpretations present and, therefore, support particular views of the past, views which serve contemporary interests. Because many presentations about the past do not identify and examine the modern inter-ests the work may be serving, the presentations may actually be supporting hidden interests either inadvertently or by design. Therefore, as we examine established interpretations of Annapolis's past and as we develop our own, we also attempt to identify the modern interests that each may serve. Unfor-tunately, this is a characteristic we find lacking in many historical American museum settings.[13]

On-site tours conducted by working archaeologists formed the core of this interpretive program, as they have at previous excavations open to the public. Archaeologist/guides, trained in public speaking, developed their own styles of giving fifteen-minute tours. Although some aspects of the tour changed as excavations progressed, three sets of ideas were included in each guide's tour.

A brief introduction welcomed visitors to the site and acquainted them with the Archaeology in Annapolis program. This information answered initial questions. Who sponsors this dig? Is everyone here a student? The first portion of tours introduced some historical information about African Americans in Annapolis and, more specifically, provided visitors with some background about the project area. The information, much of which was also included in the site brochure, helped visitors understand why the site was considered historically significant.

After a site orientation and a discussion about why we were interested specifically in the Courthouse site, guides explained archaeological techniques and field methods so that visitors would understand something about all the various activities going on around them, which otherwise could be very distracting. Main points for this portion of the tour included: deciding where to dig; establishing a site grid; explaining excavation techniques; emphasizing the importance of taking notes and drawing maps; and pointing out that research must continue in the archaeological laboratory in order to complete the research.

The third portion of the tour focused on ways in which archaeologists use material culture to develop interpretations about aspects of past communities. For example, guides explained how the study of food remains, ceramics, and glassware may indicate economic status, or it may suggest culturally influenced food preferences of people who lived in the area. It also was stressed that, in the postbellum period, African Americans may have maintained their ethnic identity through conscious choices associated with diet, dress, leisure activities, or other aspects of daily life. During this discussion, guides noted that archaeologists all too often focus on economic issues rather than (or at the cost of) addressing issues associated with ethnic identity. Guides also noted that the comparative method will bring things to light that aren't possible by looking at only one site.

Guides frequently posed rhetorical questions during tours as a way of encouraging people to think about some of the same issues that the archaeologists would be addressing. How were people in this neighborhood part of the broader Annapolis community during the late 1800s and the early 1900s? In what ways did they participate in the local market economy? Were free African Americans somehow limited in the ways they could participate, and, if so, to what degree were they able to free themselves

from those social and economic limitations? Such questions usually did
not prompt responses during the tours, but in discussions that followed
and in questionnaire responses, visitors expressed strong interest in looking for answers to these and other questions.

The tour concluded by stressing once again the importance of archaeology in learning more about the history of African Americans in Annapolis. Such research, the guides explained, would help create interpretations
that more effectively represent this historically significant group which has
lived and worked in the city since its founding. Guides ended tours by
pointing out that the need to incorporate groups left out of traditional historical interpretations is not unique to Annapolis, but can be seen throughout Maryland and across the country.[14]

The Brochure

The final component of the Courthouse site interpretive program was a brochure offered to visitors at the end of the tour. The purpose of the plain,
one-color pamphlet was not to impress, but rather to inform and reinforce
points made during the tours. It presented concepts related to archaeological research, community participation, and the significance of historic
sites occupied by African Americans. The following numbered sections
served as the brochure's interior panels.[15]

1. Why Do This Project?

Archaeologists have been excavating historic sites in Annapolis for
more than twenty years. The excavations have studied everything
from formal pleasure gardens of the Colonial period to mercantile
warehouses of the nineteenth century. As diverse as these research
projects may seem, they have shared one characteristic. Excluding
one small-scale project, all have centered around the European-
American community in Annapolis. No major archaeological excavation has focused primarily on African Americans.

The parking area behind the Anne Arundel County Courthouse
is now the focus of such an excavation. Until the 1970s this block
had been an African-American neighborhood for generations. Remains of this historic site still lie beneath the surface, but these archaeological resources are now in danger of being destroyed.

Anne Arundel County is considering plans for a courthouse annex on this property. Before construction begins "Archaeology in Annapolis" is conducting excavations to learn more about the history of African Americans in Annapolis, a population often missing from traditional presentations of Annapolis history.

Members of the African-American community in Annapolis, like African Americans across the country, have expressed an interest in archaeology as another way of exploring their heritage. At the same time, Annapolis, just like the rest of contemporary America, would have a richer heritage if it included the stories of African Americans. Archaeology is one means of achieving such an integrated history.

2. You Can Help!

Before excavating a site, historical archaeologists decide on specific aspects of the past they want to investigate. Based on these interests, archaeologists ask questions that will guide the research. Examples of these questions include: "How did people prepare and serve meals?"; "How did people spend their leisure time?"

"Archaeology in Annapolis" staff is working to compose guiding questions that are of interest to local citizens. We hope this project is of interest to other archaeologists, but we are more concerned with its meaning to the people of Annapolis. We are using several different methods to help us achieve this goal. We are searching historic documents—maps, photographs and written records—that will help in understanding what the neighborhood was like in the past and how it has changed over the years. By interviewing local citizens we are learning what daily life was like in the neighborhood during the first half of this century. Participation by members of the community in everything from digging to interpreting the discoveries will contribute to a history that is truly meaningful to all of us.

3. This Is An Important Place.

The people who lived in this neighborhood represent an integral part of Annapolis society. African Americans have made up a third of the city's population since the 1700s. In 1850, one quarter of Annapolis' entire free population was African-American, and before the Civil War, more free African Americans lived in Maryland than in any other state.[16]

Despite Maryland's significant African-American population for centuries, their history is not well understood. Written documentation on the lives and contributions of African Americans is slim, but archaeological research can help us begin to fill in the gaps.

This area we call the Courthouse site has been important to African Americans for nearly 200 years. There was an African Methodist Episcopal congregation in Annapolis by 1803, but the exact location of the first church is unknown. The Mt. Moriah AME Church was built along Franklin St. in 1874. Today this historic structure houses the Banneker-Douglass Museum, a division of the Maryland Commission for Afro-American History and Culture.

Land deeds tell us that at least some properties on this block were owned and occupied by African Americans in the early 1800s. Both owners and renters lived here until the early 1970s. The archaeology of this site will help us learn more about an economic cross-section of African Americans living in Annapolis during important historical periods.

4. What We Will Learn.

This project focuses on free African Americans, and does so for two reasons. Some African Americans are interested in how the lives of their ancestors compared with the lives of European Americans, and others are interested in learning what aspects of African culture their ancestors were able to bring with them.

To compare free African Americans with other Annapolitans, we will look for similarities and differences in residential patterns, housing construction and costs, room arrangements within houses, and patterns of garbage disposal. We will also study foodways including food preparation, consumption, and disposal.

To search out African influences, we will study decorative items, cooking traditions, and evidence of folk medicines. We will then compare these items with those from African cultures.

Ultimately, we want to move beyond the idea of "black sites" and "white sites," so we can see, for example, all the forms of African-American labor that went into the great mansions of Annapolis. It is appropriate to begin this project with African-American sites, but the goal of creating an integrated history should enable us to use archaeology to see the imprint of African-American lives *throughout* Annapolis.

This on-site program emphasized that the history of African Americans has been largely absent from most presentations of the city's past—presentations offered to tourists, but these are not the only Annapolis histories. For generations, African American residents have recognized the importance of their contributions and those of their ancestors to Annapolis society. Historical records have been curated by individuals, churches, and public repositories such as the Maryland State Archives. Recently, Philip L. Brown, an Annapolis educator and historian, wrote *The Other Annapolis: 1900–1950* "to provide a permanent record of the life and times of colored Annapolitans during this period, thereby preserving this era of African American history."[17] Through narrative text, photographs, and other documentary sources, he presents a rich and comprehensive view of "the other Annapolis" during this period of institutionalized segregation. Archaeology in Annapolis shares Mr. Brown's goals and those of other residents; i.e., to recognize and interpret African American history "as a part of the overall history of Annapolis."[18]

As an extension of the on-site public program, Archaeology in Annapolis participated in the Kunta Kinte Commemoration and Heritage Festival. The annual festivals commemorate the arrival of Kunta Kinte in Annapolis and celebrate the creative spirit and perseverance of African American culture. We created a photographic exhibit for a booth on the festival grounds in 1990 and also spoke to area students about the project during a festival-sponsored "Youth and Educators' Day." These two forums helped attract more than 350 people to the site during the weekend-long festival, enabling us to offer the program to a broader audience of African Americans and European Americans which included both Annapolis residents and out-of-town visitors.

This excavation attracted close to one thousand visitors during the three-month season including the festival, a low visitation rate when compared to several previous open projects in Annapolis. Even though the Courthouse site is located in the Historic District, it is not in an area that gets heavy tourist traffic; unfortunately, archaeological digs even a short distance from main attractions do not attract numbers of visitors comparable to those conducted near the downtown waterfront area.

Two observations should be highlighted regarding visitation. Tour logs indicate that 44 percent of all those who visited the site from late June through the September festival were African Americans, which stands in stark contrast to almost no African American visitation to previous archaeology digs in Annapolis. Also, 26 percent of those who filled out evaluation forms were from Annapolis, compared to an average of 10 percent local representation at previous programs. However, even though a significantly higher percentage of courthouse visitors were local residents, this is not based on large numbers of people. Tourism still accounts for the vast majority of site visitation.

We invited visitors to evaluate the program during the festival by asking them to complete one-page questionnaires at the end of tours. Respondents represented slightly over 10 percent of total project visitation, essentially the same rate of response gathered during previous projects. The high rate of return, the number of written compliments about the program, and the suggestions for future research indicate that this research initiative has made a real contribution to interpreting Annapolis's past.[19]

The first question on the form asked "What connection do you see between this site and everyday life today?" Two of the main themes identified from among the wide range of answers pointed out that such work would help create better public understanding of the past and it could also help improve current social relations. Selected responses referring to the educational potential include: "It helps the Maryland community/American community to understand our history or roots"; "As an African American who has been miseducated in America, it has reinforced my understanding of a need to better educate people"; "What is found on this site will help to fill a large gap in our history"; "This new information will help us better understand a long overshadowed segment of our society"; and "As an African-American, I am pleased to know that we can integrate the past with the future and present. What a wonderful way to introduce our children to their own cultural past." Responses that focused on the potential for examining and improving community relations include: "*This* site could help build bridges among groups in the community, not just add to the lore of academia"; "Much of Annapolis life during the 1800s (i.e., black/white relations) seemed to be setting the pattern for the relations between the races today"; "Studying all people's history gives values to all people—thus a tolerance for all"; and "It is difficult to understand the present and how its problems can be solved, and how prior ones were, without knowing how the present community came to be."

The second question was "What did you learn about the history of

African Americans in Annapolis?" With 73 percent of respondents answering, many echoed messages in the tours, and others pointed out what they did not know about African American history, reflecting the general lack of accessible programs about the African American past. Selected responses include: "I didn't know this was a 'black' area of the town"; "The fact that there *were* African Americans in Annapolis"; "Never knew the population of African Americans in Annapolis was as large in the past and as large in the present"; "There were African Americans that were free and well-to-do in Annapolis prior to the Civil War"; and "About the range of their occupations and about comparisons (similarities) between their life and that of others living in Annapolis."

The third question asked "What did you learn about archaeology that you did not know before you visited the site?" Again, the range of answers was quite broad, and a number of people wrote of what they had learned about excavation and analysis, but some visitors used this space to write about their perceptions of how historical research and interpretation has been affected by racial bias. Such observations include: "That archaeologists are interested in historical America and black America in particular"; "I learned that there are probably few African Americans engaged in the field probably again due to miseducation and racism and a need to focus on survival"; and "It is not what we learned, it's the fact that some majority Americans are giving recognition to others."

When asked what people would like to see in future programs, many respondents suggested that archaeologists display more of the excavated artifacts. As a direct result of these suggestions, the Banneker-Douglass Museum and Archaeology in Annapolis mounted a museum exhibit several months later entitled "The Maryland Black Experience as Understood Through Archaeology" as a way of presenting the research in progress. Ultimately, the entire exhibit opened in three different Maryland museums: Banneker-Douglass Museum in Annapolis; Historic Annapolis's Shiplap House; and the Jefferson-Patterson Park Museum in Calvert County. Portions of the full exhibit also have been displayed in the Annapolis City Hall, in two locations on the campus of University of Maryland, College Park, and for a second time in the Shiplap House.

In collaboration, museum professionals and archaeologists combined artifacts, maps, photographs, oral history excerpts, and narrative texts to express the exhibit's guiding theme that plural voices compose the past.

Quotes about daily life were taken from the oral history interviews and linked spatially in the exhibit to excavated artifacts. Our intention was to present something close to the original significance of the objects as they functioned in households. Narrative texts, produced by archaeologists, were intended to provide different perspectives on the same objects. The idea behind the presentation was to produce a dialogue with the viewer about the nature of interpretation. Neither source of textual material was inaccurate or inappropriate, but by presenting both perspectives, the exhibit encouraged viewers to think about how each serves to enhance our understanding of the city's past. Seen and discussed together, the two perspectives increased overall understanding of the city's African American past as well as the workings of archaeology.[20]

• • •

More than any other project undertaken by Archaeology in Annapolis, this program was a community-based endeavor. Well before any excavations began, project members recognized that listening to the interests, concerns, suggestions, and doubts of members of the African American community should play a central role in the development of the research design. As research continued, this idea not only helped the archaeologists fashion research questions that would more effectively address community interests, it became one of the concepts central to educational activities associated with the excavation project. As a result, the public outreach developed a character which distinguished it from previous public programs. During previous programs, discussions with visitors about the past developed from the archaeological discoveries and on-site interpretations. During this initiative, the public programs, as well as the archaeological research and interpretation, were influenced by insights gained during discussions between archaeologists, residents, and visitors about interpreting the African American past. In other words, the dialogue helped structure the research and interpretation as much as the research and interpretation influenced the continuing dialogue. Therefore, project-community interaction was as important to the archaeological research as it was to the public programs.

There are a number of ways in which a program like this could be improved. In particular, even though the rate of local visitation increased somewhat and African American interest increased dramatically from previous excavation projects, fewer people visited the site than we had expected. Except for our participation in the Kunta Kinte Festival, a strategy for drawing attention to the site and attracting visitors was probably one of the least successful aspects of the program. This is because our strategies did not match our goals. We relied on local advertising techniques that had worked well in the past for drawing out-of-town visitors, but for this initiative we were more interested in encouraging participation from within the community. Other public programs of this type would enjoy even greater success if project members started by devoting much more time and energy to visiting churches, civic groups, schools, and other local institutions. This sounds obvious, but with the time and budgetary constraints so common in archaeological research, grass-roots community involvement is not even considered for many projects, much less given priority. By putting more time and effort into local outreach, this program would become familiar to more residents, and the community would then be more likely to use the archaeological information to serve its own interests.

Archaeology in Annapolis's experience has shown that a deep commitment to public education and community outreach is well worth the effort for everyone involved. The courthouse site excavations and associated public programs helped initiate an ongoing dialogue between archaeologists and residents about interpreting the African American past through archaeology. What began as an experiment in community-based research in African American archaeology is not finished, but continues to broaden its scope more than five years since it began.

Notes

1. Mark P. Leone, "The Role of Archaeology in Verifying American Identity: Giving a Tour Based on Archaeological Method," *Archaeological Review from Cambridge* 2 (1) (1983): 44–46.
2. Mark P. Leone, "Method as Message: Interpreting the Past with the Public," *Museum News* 62 (1) (1983): 34–41.
3. Parker B. Potter Jr., *Archaeology in Public in Annapolis: An Experiment in the Application of Critical Theory to Historical Archaeology* (Ann Arbor, Mich.: Univ. Microfilms International, 1989), 150–94.
4. Ibid., 185–93; Mark P. Leone, Parker B. Potter Jr., and Paul A. Shackel, "Toward a Critical Archaeology," *Current Anthropology* 28 (3) (1987): 283–302, 285–87.
5. Potter, *Archaeology in Public*, 187.
6. For a more detailed discussion of Annapolis's twentieth-century development see Potter, *Archaeology in Public*, 82–119.

7. Mark S. Warner and Paul R. Mullins, "Community Activism and African American Archaeology: Excavations at the Maynard-Burgess House, Annapolis," paper presented at Third Annual Anne Arundel Archaeology Conference, Annapolis, 1992, 9.

8. Ibid., 3.

9. Sallie M. Ives, "Black Community Development in Annapolis, Maryland, 1870–1885," in *Geographical Perspectives on Maryland's Past,* ed. Robert D. Mitchell and Edward K. Muller (College Park: Dept. of Geography, Univ. of Maryland, 1979), 129–49.

10. Leone, "Method as Message," 37; Leone, Potter, and Shackel, "Toward a Critical Archaeology," 289; Potter, *Archaeology in Public,* 315–17.

11. For a more detailed discussion of previous site tours created by Archaeology in Annapolis, see Potter, *Archaeology in Public,* 311–57.

12. Additional oral history excerpts are presented in Mark P. Leone, Barbara J. Little, Mark S. Warner, Parker B. Potter Jr., Paul A. Shackel, George C. Logan, Paul R. Mullins, and Julie A. Ernstein, "The Constituencies for an Archaeology of African Americans in Annapolis, Maryland," in *"I Too Am America," Studies in African American Archaeology,* ed. Theresa Singleton (Charlottesville: Univ. Press of Virginia, in press).

13. For a critique of education in history museums, see Parker B. Potter Jr. and Mark P. Leone, "Liberation Not Replication: 'Archaeology in Annapolis' Analyzed," *Journal of the Washington Academy of Sciences* 76 (2) (1986): 97–105.

14. Excerpts from a Courthouse site tour are presented in Leone et al. "Constituencies for an Archaeology of African Americans."

15. George C. Logan and Parker B. Potter Jr., *African-American Archaeology in Annapolis, Maryland* (Annapolis: Historic Annapolis Foundation, 1990).

16. For a detailed discussion of nineteenth-century Maryland that focuses on its African American heritage, see Barbara J. Fields, *Slavery and Freedom on the Middle Ground: Maryland During the Nineteenth Century* (New Haven: Yale Univ. Press, 1985).

17. Philip L. Brown, *The Other Annapolis: 1900–1950* (Annapolis: Annapolis Publishing Co., 1994), 8.

18. Ibid.

19. Visitors' responses are reviewed in Mark P. Leone and George C. Logan, Project Director Evaluation to the Maryland Humanities Council for Grant #032-L, a report submitted to the MHC on the results of the interpretive program entitled "Historical Archaeology and African American Heritage in Annapolis: A Program of Public Interpretation for the Community," which was supported in large part by the MHC. The evaluation report was submitted to the MHC and a copy is on file with the Historic Annapolis Foundation. See also Leone et al. "Constituencies for an Archaeology of African Americans."

20. For a more thorough discussion of the exhibit "The Maryland Black Experience as Understood through Archaeology," see Mark P. Leone, Paul R. Mullins, Marian C. Creveling, Laurence Hurst, Barbara Jackson-Nash, Lynn D. Jones, Hannah Jopling

Kaiser, George C. Logan and Mark S. Warner. "Can an African American Historical Archaeology Be an Alternative Voice?" In *Interpreting Archaeology: Finding Meaning in the Past,* ed. Ian Hodder, Micheal Shanks, Alexandra Alexandri, Victor Buchli, John Carman, Jonathan Last, and Gavin Lucas (London: Routledge, 1995), 111–24.

Part II

Everyday Lifeways

In spite of the richness and diversity of the historical record, there are things we want to know that are not to be discovered from it. Simple people doing simple things, the normal, everyday routine of life and how these people thought about it, are not the kinds of things anyone thought worthy of noting.

—James Deetz, *In Small Things Forgotten*

One of the most significant challenges scholars have focused on in the last few decades has been the investigation of everyday life in the past. As James Deetz noted, the lives of "everyday folk" and their routines are not as readily accessible as those of prominent individuals and events. While exceptional individuals or events are frequently recorded, the seemingly mundane experiences of daily life certainly harbor more insight into the historic circumstances of most Americans' lives. Over the past thirty years or so, historians, folklorists, anthropologists, economists, and American studies scholars have dedicated a considerable amount of time and effort to more effectively explore everyday lifeways. The result has been an impressive array of material which has included many studies of the lives of the disenfranchised, the enslaved, recent immigrants, women, children, and the ever-shifting relations of power between groups.[1] Among this body of scholarship is the work of historical archaeologists, who have been numbered among the most active contributors to this broad area of study.

One of the most basic and long-standing claims of historical archaeology has been the discipline's singular ability to explore people's everyday experiences in the past. The detritus of everyday life provides historical archaeologists with unique avenues to explore past human experiences. As has been widely acknowledged, material remains reflect on past human experiences in ways which are unique from historic texts, reflecting behavior which is comparatively free from the intentionality generally implicit in the written word.[2] This does not mean that historical archaeology somehow has more direct access to the past, because the discipline is fraught with its own intrinsic methodological problems. However, it does suggest that the material remains of everyday life unquestionably can be seen in a different light through archaeology.

Much like other fields of study, archaeological work on everyday lifeways has been quite voluminous, utilizing a wide range of theoretical perspectives and forms of material culture.[3] Over the past fifteen years, Archaeology in Annapolis has been among the contributors to this body of work. Early archaeology in Annapolis often focused primarily on mechanisms used by members of the Annapolis elite to establish and reinforce their positions of power.[4] This starting point was quite understandable given the continuing prominence that Annapolis accords many of its past elite residents and their surviving homes. In short, research began with the places that were among the most prominent (both in the past and today) and accessible (in contemporary society).

Unquestionably this initial research addressed the everyday lives of the non-elite; yet, they were present only implicitly in many of the resulting archaeological texts. In response to this shortcoming a substantial amount of recent work has focused on families and households who did not occupy the uppermost economic strata of the city. The chapters in this section illustrate some of the current threads of research currently being explored in Annapolis. As a group, the chapters pertaining to everyday lifeways illustrate differing perspectives on the themes that Archaeology in Annapolis consistently has addressed. Consistent throughout all of the chapters is an awareness of the dynamic and fluid nature of social and class relationships in Annapolis and how those relationships are constantly being accepted, modified, or challenged by individuals and/or groups. All of the chapters build upon archaeological data to address the myriad strategies that Annapolitans utilized in various elements of their lives to negotiate and/or contest their position in Annapolis society.

The chapters generally reflect broad intellectual similarity, but what is perhaps more striking is the diversity of scholarship they also represent. The contributions included here illustrate a broad range of questions which can be asked about everyday lives. Furthermore, the essays also reflect a wide range of theoretical approaches and archaeological assemblages that can be utilized in investigations of people's everyday lives. The scope of people studied in this section range from middle-class households with upper-class aspirations (the Green family) to members of white, working-class Annapolis, to African American Annapolitans. Methodologically, these chapters include detailed quantitative analyses, explorations of the symbolism of particular forms of material culture, the shifting utilization of the built environment, and the impact of changing social relations on building types. As an "assemblage," these chapters provide illustrations of the intellectual diversity within the Annapolis, and, more important, they provide insight into the diversity of everyday life in Annapolis over the past three centuries.

The explorations of everyday lifeways begin with Paul Shackel's investigation of the earliest property that has been excavated in Annapolis. Shackel argues that the relations between craftspeople and elite patrons extended considerably beyond their functional purpose of maintaining and repairing earthfast structures. He argues that the maintenance relations necessary to repair earthfast housing in the seventeenth and early eighteenth century also maintained social ties within the community, which transcended wealth differences. Using contrasting examples from the Sands House and the Main Street excavations in Annapolis, he argues that the demise of impermanent architecture (and the necessary maintenance relations) in the eighteenth century was attributable to the shift to a more stratified, consumer society. The construction of more permanent structures and the end of maintenance relations exacerbated the development of more rigid class distinctions and social distance within Annapolitan society.

The chapters by Laura Galke and Julie Ernstein also explore the issue of the rise of consumer society and individual responses to this change.

Each author examines the changing use of space and how the discrete changes reflect much broader social changes. Galke demonstrates how a single household's use of space changed over time, while Ernstein compares the changing use of space at a house lot occupied by members of the "working class" in Annapolis with a similar property in Baltimore.

Galke uses quantitative methods, specifically cluster analysis, to identify distinct activity areas at the Green family print shop during the second half of the eighteenth century. She identifies a clear lack of distinct activity areas during the nineteenth century, a finding which corresponds to historic accounts of the shift of the family print shop to a separate location. Galke argues that the separation that she identifies corresponds to the widespread documentation of the separation of work and domestic spheres. This separation was part of a broad change that involved a shift from a communal to a more segmented and hierarchical society.

Ernstein also explores the separation of work and domestic spaces over time, noting the differing circumstances of this change in Annapolis and Baltimore. Using a combination of archaeological and historical sources, Ernstein addresses the shifting uses of two lots from domestic properties to mixed home-businesses and, ultimately, in the case of the Baltimore property, to exclusively industrial use. The development of Annapolis is reflected in earlier modifications of the 22 West Street property and the comparatively later development of the 1609–1611 Thames Street property in Baltimore. Finally, she demonstrates how the relative fortunes of Annapolis and Baltimore are reflected in changing use of the two lots.

The other contributions in this section address how particular households use material culture as part of the negotiation of status within a community. Mark Warner compares bottle and ceramic assemblages from three sites in Annapolis. Two of the excavations, the Maynard-Burgess House and Gott's Court, were occupied by African Americans, and the third, the Main Street site, was occupied by a white physician and his household. The comparisons explore the complicated process of how members of the African American community in Annapolis attempted to reinforce economic and social class differences within their community while also maintaining social difference from the city's white community. Warner examines the social role that serving tea and the acquisition of teawares played in African American Annapolis and the contradictory meanings that tea consumption held for different segments of Annapolitan society.

Justin Lev-Tov's exploration of status differences is based on the comparison of the faunal remains from the Green family print shop, occupied by a middle-class household with upper-class aspirations, and the Calvert site, the residence of one of the wealthiest and most powerful families in Maryland. Lev-Tov argues that despite the Green family's frequent social interactions with city elite their diet clearly did not parallel that of the Calvert family. While the Calverts had the resources to acquire and consume a wide variety of foods, the Green family diet was considerably more uniform, reflecting a greater degree of economic conservatism and dependence on the products that were available in the market place.

Taken as a group, the essays presented in this section reflect a diverse cross-section of archaeological contributions to the ongoing explorations of everyday lifeways in Annapolis. They utilize food, glasswares, ceramics, printer's type, the build environment, architectural features, and labor relationships to show aspects of how everyday lives of many Annapolitans were negotiated. They should demonstrate how archaeology can expand on established knowledge of the elite to provide a richer understanding of everyday life in America.

Notes

1. For example, Ruth Schwartz Cowan, *More Work for Mother* (New York: Basic Books, 1983); William Cronan, *Changes in the Land* (New York: Hill and Wang, 1983); Robert Blair St. George, ed., *Material Life in America, 1600–1860* (Boston: Northeastern Univ. Press, 1988); Henry Glassie, *Folk Housing in Middle Virginia* (Knoxville: Univ. of Tennessee Press, 1975); Rhys Isaac, *The Transformation of Virginia: 1740–1790* (Chapel Hill: Univ. of North Carolina Press, 1982); Gary B. Nash, *Red, White, and Black: The Peoples of Early America* (Englewood Cliffs, N.J.: Prentice-Hall 1974); and Anthony F. C. Wallace, *Rockdale* (New York: W. W. Norton and Co., 1972).
2. See, for example, Kenneth Ames, "Material Culture as Non-Verbal Communication," *Journal of American Culture* 3 (1980): 619–41; Jules David Prown, "Mind in Matter: An Introduction to Material Culture Theory and Method," *Winterthur Portfolio* 17 (1982): 1–19; Thomas J. Schlereth, *Cultural History and Material Culture* (Ann Arbor, Mich.: UMI Research Press, 1990).
3. A selected listing of this work would include: Deetz, *In Small Things Forgotten*; Deetz, *Flowerdew Hundred: An Archaeology of a Virginia Plantation* (Charlottesville: Univ. Press of Virginia, 1993); Charles E. Orser Jr., *The Material Basis of the Postbellum Tenant Plantation* (Athens: Univ. of Georgia Press, 1988); Theresa A. Singleton, ed., *The Archaeology of Slavery and Plantation Life* (Orlando: Academic Press, 1985); and Anne E. Yentsch, *A Chesapeake Family and Their Slaves* (Cambridge: Cambridge Univ. Press, 1994).

4. For example, Mark P. Leone, "Interpreting Ideology in Historical Archaeology: Using the Rules of Perspective in the William Paca Garden in Annapolis, Maryland," in *Ideology, Power, and Prehistory*, ed. Daniel Miller and Christopher Tilley (Cambridge: Cambridge Univ. Press, 1984), 25–35; and Leone and Paul A. Shackel, "Forks, Clocks, and Power," in *Mirror and Metaphor, Material and Social Construction of Reality*, ed. Daniel W. Ingersoll and Gordon Bronitsky (Lanham, Md.: Univ. Press of America, 1987), 69–84.

5 Maintenance Relationships in Early Colonial Annapolis

Paul A. Shackel

Impermanent earthfast building techniques dominated Chesapeake architecture through most of the seventeenth and early eighteenth centuries, although forms of permanent architecture are also found throughout the region, especially in urban centers.[1] Impermanent architecture consists of wood posts or wood blocks for a structure's foundation. These adequate, but somewhat temporary foundations were a relatively quick construction method which suited the immediate needs of Chesapeake planters who spent the majority of their time caring for their tobacco crops.[2] Foundation materials were continually exposed to environmental elements that accelerated decay. Since earthfast structures survived on the average of five to ten years before major repairs were needed—and in some cases even longer—planters regularly faced the decision to either abandon the structure or perform periodic maintenance. Repair sometimes included the replacement of foundation members in order to stabilize the building, an activity that may have involved several community participants, or specialists.

Neiman, Carson et al., and Kelso, among others, have convincingly shown the proliferation of impermanent architecture among the elite and poor in the seventeenth-century Chesapeake.[3] Even those who had the means to build brick houses or frame houses with brick chimneys constructed post-in-the-ground structures with mud chimneys. Some of these earthfast structures lasted for over thirty years. Most of these long-term occupations were made possible by regular maintenance, including the replacement of posts and blocks. For instance, seventeenth-century earthfast structures at Hampton were occupied for thirty to forty years, and they were kept habitable by undergoing several repair episodes, including bracing and shoring. Neiman's work at Clifts Plantation indicates that the site was occupied for sixty years. He meticulously demonstrates that the building underwent four phases of repair, including the replacement of many of the posts. The lack of post or block repairs has often been interpreted as a short-term occupation; however, there are exceptions. Archaeological documentation from St. Mary's City and the Kingsmill Plantation show that major buildings existed for at least a couple of decades without repair.[4]

Alain Outlaw's observations of the general material culture patterning at the Governor's Land site, which contained first- and second-quarter seventeenth-century habitation sites, is worth noting. The site demonstrates the shift toward the building of community networks. The earlier sites contained mostly imported goods from England. Much like other contemporary second-quarter seventeenth-century sites, such as those found at Kingsmill Plantation and Carter's Grove, there is increasing evidence of a developing local economy. The presence of locally made ceramics and pipes indicate the development of a local economy and community networks. Some explain that the local economy developed in response to the tobacco depression in the 1630s and 1640s and the decreasing supply of expendable money among planters.[5] Also of importance is that this new economy also created new social and economic networks.

Similar to the findings at seventeenth-century Jamestown, impermanent architecture coexisted with permanent architecture in Annapolis, Maryland, until the early eighteenth century. Some evidence exists for the interrelationship between impermanent architecture and community maintenance relationship. Archaeology demonstrates that this architectural tradition did not uniformly disappear from all parts of the city at the same time. Rather, the disappearance of impermanent architecture is linked to a change in the town's maintenance relationships and shifting social and economic structures linked to the development of a consumer society.

Maintenance relationships were important in structuring the social relations in Annapolis and throughout the Chesapeake. One form of maintenance reciprocity relied on impermanent architecture for the persistence of community relationships and social relations.[6] Maintenance related tasks "insured a fundamental continuity in economic, as well as social, relations in communities. . . . [This allowed owners to] seek periodic contractual obligations with a local worker capable of mending the product."[7] St. George explores why craftsmen and builders would enter into maintenance relationships, especially when maintenance only accounted for about 5 percent or less of their total income. He reasons that such relationships probably existed for both economic profit and social reasons.

Socially, labor was at the center of the community relations and the development and maintenance of social relations. From this perspective, members of all wealth groups built earthfast buildings for over a century as a way of structuring social relations by maintenance relationships. People also purchased locally made wares which further aided in the development of community networks. The change to a more permanent and more maintenance-free architecture, and increasing participation in a consumer society, is understood more completely when considering the complexities of defining social relations.

Maintenance relationships may develop in three distinct forms. First, formal relationships are created where a laborer is hired to perform a task. These are explicit and created and characterize urban and industrial relations. Second, maintenance relationships may be established in the form of balanced or general reciprocity where neighbors or relatives may be called upon to aid in a task. These are implicit and expected relations and are typical of rural, agrarian communities. Third, work might be performed in-house either by the owner or servants and slaves. The latter two cases may have predominated during the early Chesapeake settlement. But as the native population increased and urban areas began to develop at the turn of the eighteenth century, settlers began to differentiate between social and economic exchange. Hiring labor to perform maintenance tasks became increasingly important.

St. George asserts that the "maintenance of material forms implies, perhaps is identical with, the maintenance of social forms."[8] An economy based on maintenance-related tasks would insure a continuation of economic and social relations as well as guarantee that contractual obligations of local workers were necessary. Maintenance relationships create a form of reciprocity and may symbolically create a form of communality. As Glassie notes, vernacular technologies involve local materials and local labor. The actors are diverse and interlock their talents. When people start opting for more permanent architecture and consumer goods, they withdraw from the "local economic system/exchange relations,"[9] and there is a radical change in the existing social order. The change in house forms and material culture forms are associated with the reorganization of community social relations. No longer are people relying on the community to organize their social relations.[10] Instead, they take these responsibilities upon themselves. An appreciation of the changing maintenance relations, and the development of consumer society in Annapolis, may be gained via the examination of two contemporaneous tavern sites.

One tavern, known as the Sands House, was built around 1700 near Annapolis's waterfront (map 5.1). The remains of an earthfast structure that was underpinned with a stone foundation in the 1720s survives at the site. The second tavern, the Main Street site, was located in the social and political center of town, and it was originally built with a fieldstone foun-

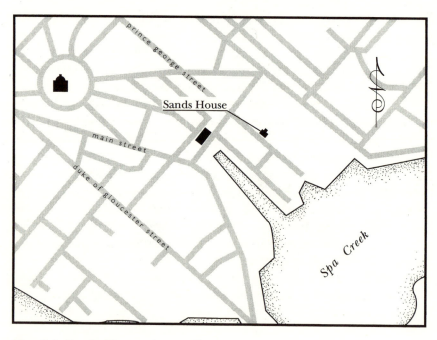

Map 5.1. Sands House, Annapolis.

dation around 1700. The two buildings stood only a few blocks from each other. As people in the center of town participated in new commercial and consumer activities in the early eighteenth century, people in the waterfront area continued to rely on maintenance activities and community relations. The disappearance of earthfast structures coincides with the social and economic restructuring of town. With the dramatic shifts in wealth in 1720s Chesapeake, along with the development of new commercial and consumer activities along the waterfront, material culture patterning in the Sands House neighborhood became similar to that found in the commercial district where the Main Street site lies. Architecture and material goods played a different role in community relations; they became symbols of power and economic wealth as well as an indication of the degree of participation in the rules of the new consumer society.

Early Annapolis and the Early Consumer Revolution

Many early-eighteenth-century Annapolitans were wealthy planter/merchants whose families resided in the surrounding countryside. Other settlers included merchants and craftsmen from St. Mary's City who relied on the government for a living. These included tavern keepers like Garrett Van Sweringen and the colonial printer Dinah Nuthead. The largest number of Annapolitans came from surrounding Anne Arundel County and were either planters establishing mercantile trades or craftsmen.[11]

By 1710, many of the original Annapolis landowners no longer lived in the town. Instead, four gentry members began to accumulate large quantities of land in the city.[12] In the early eighteenth century one citizen noticed that "most of the Lotts in the Said Town and Porte are ingrossed into three or four Peoples hands to the great Discouragement of the neighbors who would build and Inhabitt therein could they have the opportunity of taking up Lotts."[13] Landless Annapolitans were subjected to a leasehold system which persisted throughout the colonial period.[14]

By 1700 several craftsmen had established themselves in Annapolis, although the largest influx of craftsmen occurred after 1710. Many craftsmen and other service industries established themselves along West Street, Maryland Avenue, upper Main Street, and upper Duke of Gloucester Street, adjacent to the political (State Circle) and religious (Church Circle) centers of town. These newcomers included butchers, barbers, watermen, carpenters, tavern keepers, attorneys, luxury craftsmen, a portrait painter, and tanners. Many were subject to a leasehold system by four of the major landholding families, Carroll, Garrett, Bordley, and Bladen, who owned about half of the city's real estate. While the wealthy and poor gained wealth during the 1710s and 1720s, the amount of wealth accumulated by the gentry far outpaced the town's laborers, craftsmen, and merchants.[15] The area developed into an economy that relied on commodity consumption activities.

As mercantile enterprises and crafts developed rapidly near the church and state house, the waterfront remained relatively undeveloped and unexploited by commercial activities. Residents, merchants, and craftsmen did not participate in the new economic order like other communities did elsewhere.[16] Shipbuilding developed slowly, although a boat yard existed along Shipwright Street (map 5.2). Several boatwrights worked in the area sporadically during the first several decades of the eighteenth century. The city dock area, where the Sands House site is located, developed its boat-building industry, although it remained void of craft and mercantile activities into the 1720s. In 1696 the assembly designated this area specifically for shipwrights. In 1719 Robert Johnson, a shipwright, petitioned the assembly to use lands along the harbor for his business. By 1735 shipbuilding along the Annapolis harbor became a competitive industry, and by 1740 other associated crafts (i.e., blockmaking, sailmaking, ropemaking) established themselves in the area.[17] With an increasing division of craft and labor, consumer activities probably became very much like those found in the established centers of town.

With the disintegration of the traditional order and the penetration of the effects of consumerism, a radical transformation occurred concerning the amount and type of goods used in Annapolis.[18] Material culture, including architecture and other artifacts, has symbolic meaning which actively shapes and creates society through the purchase, display, and usage by individuals and groups. Indeed, some scholars have argued that material objects are the most fundamental but unnoticed aspect of the socialization process. They not only play an important role in social reproduction, but also they can form a bridge between the mental and physical world and between the conscious and the unconscious.[19] Each tavern operator at the Sands and Main Street sites participated in community relationships in varying ways. They used material culture and the built environment in different ways. Their acquisition and use of goods reflect whether consumers, including owners and customers, chose to participate in or resist modernization.

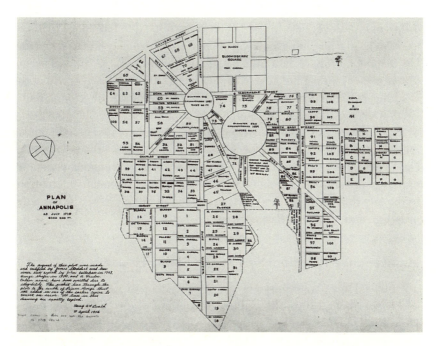

Map 5.2. The 1718 town plan of Annapolis. Courtesy Maryland State Archives, MS SC-1427-4.

Goods which had relatively static symbolic meanings during times of unquestioned hierarchy were more active in creating meanings and reinforcing social asymmetry in 1720s Annapolis. With the increased production of consumer goods, emulation of the higher groups by those lower in the social order became increasingly popular. Subaltern groups may have also created alternative meanings from the dominant group in order to create their own identity. Demand for goods increased with ambiguity of the social hierarchy. New goods, new behaviors, and new social actions were necessary for the elite to keep their social distance, a job that was accomplished by controlling the access to knowledge about the goods.[20]

Probate inventory data documents this transformation in early-eighteenth-century Annapolis consumerism. When probate data from the first two decades of eighteenth-century Annapolis were analyzed, the upper and lower wealth groups owned similar types of material goods. The primary difference between the two groups is that the wealthiest people owned more. During the 1710s and 1720s, however, the elite began to acquire different types of goods. In the 1720s items related to formal, individualized dining and grooming and hygiene first appear among Annapolis's elite. For instance, probate data indicates that consumer goods such as sets of plates, sets of forks, and sets of knives were found in the majority of the wealthiest estates from the 1710s, while the lower wealth groups had a smaller proportion of these disciplining items.[21]

Behavioral guide books also first appear in probate inventories during the 1720s.[22] These etiquette books provided new rules of behavior associated with the influx of new consumer goods. These changing consumer patterns appear to be associated with the social and economic fluctuations in the city during the 1720s, such as demographic increase, tobacco depression, and wealth redistribution.

Maintenance Relationships at the Sands House

The Sands House was constructed along the sparsely developed Annapolis harbor about 1700. The original inhabitant of the Sands House was Evan Jones. In many ways Jones participated in a community maintenance relationship. He was a jack of all trades. He was involved in the community as a bookseller, innkeeper, and public servant.[23] Although he was not involved in a labor or craft maintenance job, he held many positions which allowed him to be in contact with many residents and easily participate in the maintenance of the community. For example, one of his jobs included warning all citizens twice nightly about their fires and making sure that public buildings were secure. Like the craftsmen who spent a small portion of time and received a small amount of their total income through maintenance relationships, this community service allowed Jones the chance to become part of the community network. Jones also held several other positions in Annapolis, including deputy collector of customs, clerk to the council, and assistant clerk to the assembly. In 1718 and 1719, he was commissioned to print the laws of the Maryland Assembly. Another printer was hired in 1720–21, but by the end of 1721 Jones was rehired to do public printing until his death in 1722. His wife and son may have continued to live in the house for a while, but how long is unknown. By 1739 the Joneses were living in Prince George County and had sold the Sands House and lot to Dr. Charles Carroll.[24] Jones's participation in many activities placed him in the center of the community network and community-based maintenance relationships. Archaeological and architectural evidence also provide additional information about Jones's involvement in community-based maintenance relations, and these data show how these relationships changed with Carroll's ownership.

Architecture and Archaeology at the Sands House

Archaeological and architectural evidence suggest that, after the initial construction of the Sands House, some of the earthfast posts for the house fell into disrepair and had to be replaced. Jones may have relied on some type of maintenance relationship to repair the structure. Yet, by the 1720s or 1730s modifications to the house reflect the changing worldview of the household and their conformity to changing community social relations.

The Sands House, a frame building, was originally built as a hall-and-parlor design with an entrance lobby and an H-shaped central fireplace (fig. 5.1). The earliest section of the house measures 35 feet by 20 feet. Each of the rooms are 14 feet by 20 feet; the central lobby was originally 7 feet wide. These findings are an anomaly when compared to Neiman's study of 65 Chesapeake impermanent seventeenth-century structures found archaeologically. He notes that in the Chesapeake lobbies were often not centered and they disappeared in the 1680s.[25]

Four building phases can be described for the Sands House. First, the original construction of the house probably dates to about 1700. The main structural members, such as the corner posts, girts, the center post for the stairs, all measure 9 inches square, while the studs are 4 inches square. The 7-foot-by-5-foot central chimney sits on its original foundation. A chair rail in the hall possibly dates to this period as well. Between about 1720 and 1730 the house underwent a second renovation phase that coincides with the selling of the Sands House and the changing community relations in town. During this era the new architectural additions to the house included changes to the baseboards on the first floor, the door in the first-floor hall leading to the western room, and three window casings on the second floor, and the kitchen door was removed (and later reused in the twentieth-century addition). The third phase of alterations dates to the late eighteenth or early nineteenth centuries. New features included some flooring, a downstairs parlor mantle piece, and a western room addition. The fourth and final phase dating to the late nineteenth century includes the additions of the exterior doorway on the front of the house, the downstairs windows, and the mantle in the hall.[26] These phases of construction relate to the modernization, stabilization, and repair to the structure and they coincide with noticeable changes in the archaeo-logical record found directly beneath or adjacent to the house.

Test units were placed within the west wing or eighteenth-century exten-sion of the house while additional testing was done in the backyard. Several archaeological features were located that may reflect the persistence and eventual restructuring of social relations in Annapolis. First, post holes were

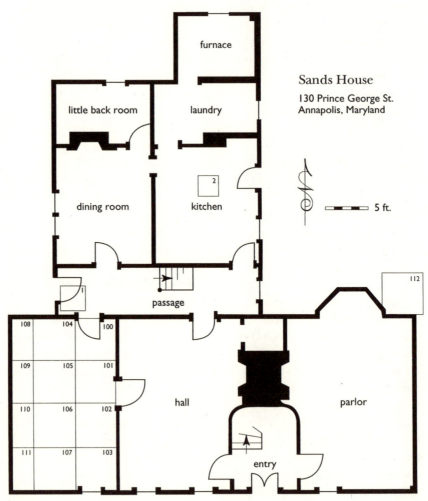

Fig. 5.1 Floor plan of the Sands House with original core and later addi-tions

uncovered underneath the west wing floor (fig. 5.2). Several features which were contemporaneous were perpendicular and parallel to the main house and street plan. They were spaced about six feet apart and were probably the remains of a shed, an addition, or a porch related to the Sands House, or maybe even the remains of an earlier structure. These features were not simple post holes and molds, but rather consisted of at least two holes, indicating that the

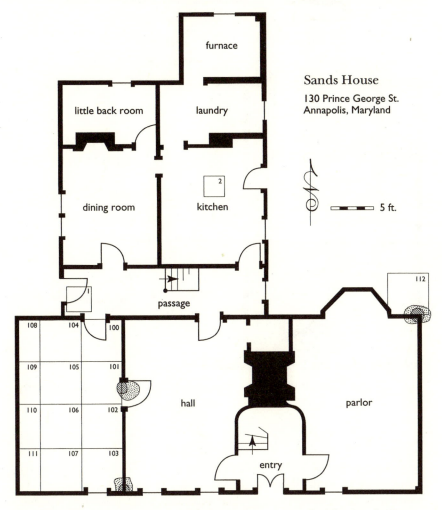

Fig. 5.2. Floor plan showing post holes in the west yard of the Sands House beneath the late-eighteenth-century addition.

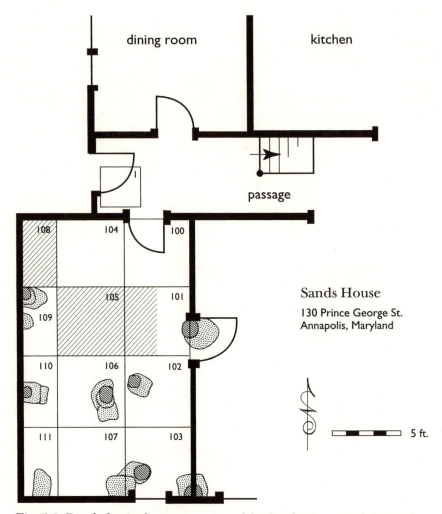

Fig. 5.3. Post holes in the west portion of the Sands House and the northeast corner that supported a block foundation.

post holes were redug and rotted posts were replaced, probably by a carpenter or other person knowledgeable in such matters. If this was the case, the residents of the Sands House may have participated in a maintenance relationship. Evan Jones required the short term but periodic services of a laborer with whom he may not otherwise have come into close contact. No firm date can be assigned to these features, because no artifacts were found within them.

However, the post holes underlaid a thin plow zone with numerous shovel scars, the remains of a kitchen garden. The stratigraphic layer overlying the post holes had a ceramic *terminus post quem (TPQ)* of 1650 and a mean ceramic date of 1713. Pipe stem diameters found in this layer yielded a manufacturing date that ranged between 1680 and 1710 (n = 15). Consequently, the garden layer probably was deposited between the last decade of the seventeenth century and the first decade of the eighteenth century; the post holes probably predate the early 1700s and must be earlier than about 1710.

The exposed western exterior of the hall wall indicates the displacement of studs for an additional doorway. Architects date the door design and molding to the 1720s.[27] A midden with a *TPQ* of 1720 was found adjacent to and north of the doorway within the west wing excavations. Therefore, the midden probably dates to the doorway construction that was placed in the hall to lead to house's west yard. The shed or the porch that produced the post holes under the west wing also may have been dismantled before or during this time, well in advance of construction of the house's westernmost addition.

The west wall of the eighteenth-century core is currently supported by brick piers. This feature allowed archaeologists to excavate under the structure as well as examine several architectural features. The original house sills were replaced during the nineteenth century, so clues to the original sill/stud and sill/post articulation with the frame were lost. The nineteenth-century brick piers overlaid a two-course fieldstone foundation. At first, it appeared that the fieldstone foundation was part of the original construction of the house. However, when the fieldstones were removed and excavations proceeded underneath them, at least two post holes were found directly underneath the sill of the westernmost part of the original structure (fig. 5.3). One was located in the southern corner underlying the raised corner post, the other was nine feet to the north in the center of the sill. The third post, expected in the northern corner, had been greatly disturbed by rodents, and was unfortunately destroyed.

To determine the function of the posts, an additional unit to the exterior of the northeastern corner of the main structure was excavated (fig. 5.3). Another post hole was found directly beneath the northeast corner. All the post holes relating to the main structure were originally dug to differing depths, varying as much as one foot. Therefore, from the limited excavations it is likely that the Sands House originally rested on hole-set blocks.

The Sands House was made "more permanent" when it was underpinned with fieldstone during some of the earlier eighteenth-century renovations, with at least one block pulled and its hole filled with stone. Diagnostic artifacts were recovered from underneath the fieldstone and in a post hole in the northeast corner of the building. These artifacts had a *TPQ* of 1700 and a mean manufacturing date of 1738. The underpinning of the structure probably occurred some time around 1725, with the work probably dating to the same time as the renovations in the hall and the placement of the door in the 1720s. These renovations occurred at the same time that most of Annapolis was increasingly participating in a consumer society.

Although a substantial number of pipe stems and ceramics were found in the yard area underneath the house's west wing, trampling and fragmentation of the assemblage left few identifiable ceramic forms. Those recognizable from the early eighteenth century include mostly coarse earthenwares and stonewares such as Westerwald, which was generally used as utilitarian vessels. One porcelain fragment from a tea cup and part of a tin-glazed plate were also found. The very low occurrence of refined wares suggests that the early Sands House residents were not integrated into the new consumer culture.

Grant McCracken's work shows that lineage and patina are the main vehicles for displaying status in preconsumer western society. Older objects that have been with a family for many generations tend to have more value than newer objects. The lack of fashionable consumer goods at the Sands House is probably indicative of the resident's perception of status and place in preindustrial society.[28]

The Main Street Site and the Advent of Consumerism in Annapolis

Documenting the original 1700 construction at the Main Street site is difficult and uncertain. The lot is within one block of both the State House and the Anglican Church, in lot 48 of Annapolis's 1718 Stoddert survey and was owned by Philemon Lloyd. No formal transactions have been discovered that detail the lease and construction of buildings on the lot. A 1748 deed of sale noted the presence of several structures on the lot, but it is uncertain if these structures refer to the remains found at the site. Lloyd probably entered into an informal lease agreement with entrepreneurs. These businessmen probably contracted with masons, carpenters, and other craftsmen to build domestic and business structures. Archaeological evidence indicates the construction of a building with a stone foundation on the lot early in the first quarter of the eighteenth century, maybe as early as 1700. Nancy Baker's analysis of the town's development indicates that by the 1710s and definitely by the 1720s a tavern and a luxury craftsman operated on the property. The tavern continued to operate for most of the first half of the eighteenth century.[29]

Architectural and Archaeological Evidence

The 1700 foundation associated with the Main Street site consisted of a one-course-thick fieldstone foundation with yellowish, shell-tempered mortar. No evidence of earthfast structures or other earlier buildings was found on the site. Associated with the foundation were early-eighteenth-century ceramics that had a *TPQ* of 1700 and a mean ceramic date of 1715. Only a portion of its western wall survived subsequent construction on the lot. What can be detected from the partial remains is that the building's western wall was perpendicular to Main Street and was about sixteen feet in length and the northern end stood immediately adjacent to the current sidewalk.

Material evidence from the first half of the eighteenth century produced a comparatively larger quantity of vessel forms than the Sands House Site and included utilitarian as well as formal teawares. A minimum vessel analysis revealed at least one set (n = 4) of 3-inch Chinese Porcelain tea cups and 6-inch saucers as well as one 2 1/2-inch and one 4-inch tea cup. Also included in the assemblage of teawares were three 6-inch porcelain bowls that may have been slop bowls and a white salt-glazed teaware pot. The assemblage also included several white, salt-glazed stoneware serving vessels, including a plate, a twiffler, and a mug. Three other coarse earthenware mugs were also recovered. The remainder of the vessels were coarse utilitarian wares that included jugs, storage vessels, bowls, chamber pots, and a slipware plate.

Apparently, the household and tavern keepers at the Main Street site acquired goods that were becoming easily available in the new consumer society. They owned some of the most fashionable mass-produced objects of the time and acquired matched sets of teawares and dinner plates. While pewter and wooden dishes were replaced by new and fashionable ceramic plates, the occupants at the Main Street site also participated in the tea ceremony.[30] In the early eighteenth century the tea ceremony was a rather exclusive social event because of the elaborate assemblage needed (i.e., tea table, tea caddy, silverware, tea cups, and saucers, tea pots, etc.), and few could afford all of the accoutrements. Taking tea also meant that the participants had leisure time and could afford time out from their daily activities.

Meanings of Material Culture and the Built Environment

The meanings of consumer goods can be controlled by interest groups, such as those influenced by class, gender, or ethnicity, in order to support their position in society. One way of achieving this domination is by making artificial phenomena and their meaning appear to be part of the natural order of things. Another strategy is to historicize the meaning, making it appear that historical precedent exists and that its meaning is inevitable. Interest groups at the center of control establish meanings for the purpose of domination over others.[31] These asymmetrical social relationships found in everyday power relations are continually being established and negotiated. Hodder, expanding on both Foucault and Miller and Tilley, explains that "[o]ne can argue that there is an unceasing struggle in which power relations are transformed, strengthened and sometimes reversed by the manipulation of symbolic and material capital. . . ."[32]

Even if there is equal access to the physical means of production, people tend to create groups and control specific types of information. Competition to acquire these goods will produce boundaries to exclude outsiders. Those within a group will synchronize their consumption activities with other members of the group who are being guided by similar circumstances. The consumption of goods allows for the classification of persons and events, and these meanings and classifications are continually defined and redefined. As information becomes finely tuned by members of the group their behavior becomes standardized within groups. Standardization usually occurs at the center of a competitive system while the underclass is more likely to subvert dominant symbolism of material culture.[33]

Intentions of mobility or permanency based on economic success and shifting from tobacco to grain crops, as suggested by Carson et al., are also recognized as factors in the development of permanent architecture.[34] The archaeology at the Sands House places this transition in the context of maintenance relationships. The building began its existence as an earthfast structure. Evan Jones, who originally owned and occupied the structure from at least the turn of the eighteenth century, relied on community-based maintenance relationships for the first several decades of the eighteenth century. The early archaeological assemblage also indicates that the occupants relied upon premodern customs and did not integrate mass-produced consumer goods into their daily routines. By the 1720s residents began to reject community-based relationships. Most noticeable is the shift from impermanent, maintenance-reliant architecture to that which needed little architectural maintenance. The change from an earthfast construction technique, which lasted an average of ten years without upkeep, to a more permanent, maintenance-free architecture can also be understood as an ideological decision. By building a more permanent structure, the residents became more independent and opted out of one noticeable segment of a strong community relationship, i.e., the maintenance relationship. The restructuring of social relations through explicit uses of material culture occurred in Annapolis during the 1720s, at a time of social and economic realignment. Just as colonial craftsmen received a small percentage of their income from maintenance relationships, so did Evan Jones, urban entrepreneur and resident of an earthfast structure, by being involved in his community as innkeeper and public servant. The type of structure in which he resided and archaeological evidence of replaced earthfast blocks indicate that he was probably involved in a maintenance relationship, possibly including other members of the community, such as carpenters. Sometime during the 1720s, the owner of the house broke somewhat from this community network and remodeled the house to make it "more permanent." These changes included the replacement of the wood blocks upon which the house was originally framed with a permanent and maintenance-free foundation made of fieldstone.

The early 1700s tavern at the Main Street site is indicative of the development of many other crafts and small industries in the city. The tavern keeper, or tavern keepers, at the Main Street site was an unknown businessmen who participated in a lease hold system. While an intensely committed community-based entrepreneur of the Sands House site owned his own means of production (i.e., his inn), the entrepreneur at the Main Street site did not. The Main Street tavern was established when four landowners began to monopolize the lands within the municipality, and by the 1720s those landowners held over half of the city's real estate. We know much about Evan Jones, owner of the Sands House, and his commitment to community relations, but little is known about who operated the tavern at the Main Street site. By not owning the land and the means of production, since the tavern was legally owned by the leaser, the tavern keepers (assuming there was more than one over a period of time) probably felt little commitment to the community and were therefore less inclined to partici-pate in community activities, such as maintenance relationships. One way of decreasing their dependence upon other laborers and craftspeople for their daily survival was to build a permanent structure with a fieldstone foundation, a low-maintenance architectural feature.

The tavern keepers at the Main Street site were also committed to more intense consumption at a comparatively earlier date. While the social relations of the town changed dramatically during the 1720s in Annapo-lis, the tavern occupants purchased and used mass-produced consumer goods. The ceramic assemblage contrasted noticeably with the utilitarian-dominated assemblage found at the Sands House. Jones, at the Sands House, actively participated in maintenance relationships and may have consciously or unconsciously neglected to participate in the new economic order associated with consumerism. Sets of objects, such as plates and tea cups found at the Main Street site, replaced the few communal objects found in preindustrial society. One plate or one cup for one person reflects a new individuality associated with the development of the consumer revo-lution and changing social relations in western society. In a developing consumer society, labor and craft no longer created people's own identity. People increasingly used material consumption to define themselves out-side the workplace. Work and consumption became polarized experiences where very different identities were constructed, and consumption became progressively more important.

Probate inventory analyses of the entire city also indicate the shift to-ward modern consumerism and the development of new individual iden-tities. These data indicate that from the 1710s consumption changed dras-tically among Annapolitans, although this phenomenon was not universal. At this time the wealthy acquired new consumer goods that differentiated the elite from lower groups. While a small portion of the poorer segments of the population also purchased these goods, members of the elite adopted new behaviors and meanings that were exclusively known to their group.[35] The new consumer material, such as matched sets of plates and teaware, found at the Main Street site might indicate that tavern patrons partici-pated in this new excluding behavior often found mostly among the elite in modern consumer societies. In contrast the early owners and clientele of the Sands House participated in a preindustrial tradition.

Early Annapolitans faced conflicting views of community relationships:

the communality and maintenance relationships of the preindustrial world versus the new ideals of consumerism in modern society. Both taverns performed similar basic functions but participated in the town's economy and social relations in very different ways. Both architectural and material remains reflect the contrasting worldviews of both tavern operators as well as the expectations of the their clientele.

Archaeology at Main Street and the Sands House is an example of diachronic documentation of the changing social relations in a community using archaeological and architectural materials. This analysis joins the growing literature that explains changing forms of architectural and everyday material culture to social, economic, and political phenomenon.[36] In this study, a trend is noted at the Sands House that is representative of the social relations of the rest of the city's residents. Specifically, there is a decrease through time in maintenance relationships and community involvement. From the 1720s urban entrepreneurs in Annapolis built substantial structures with permanent foundations and brick walls. It appears that only after some social and economic fluctuations in the city in the 1720s did a growing number of citizens participate in new mass consumer activities. Through the course of the eighteenth century, consumption and meanings of goods became more specialized and deeply rooted in a class structure based on negative reciprocity rather than balanced reciprocity found in the form of maintenance relationships.

Notes

To thank all of those involved to make this analysis possible would be an enormous task. Many volunteers, staff members, and University of Maryland, College Park, field school students participated in both excavations and the processing of artifacts. I an grateful to all of those involved, especially for their dedication and hard work. Mr. Paul Person allowed the Archaeology in Annapolis project to excavate at the Main Street parking lot while it was still in use. While I supervised the excavations in the first season, Dorothy Humph and Eileen Williams directed the work in the second and third seasons. Mrs. Dowsett, proprietor of the Sands House, allowed Archaeology in Annapolis to excavate in the Sands House during renovations. Stephen P. Austin assisted with the excavations throughout the entire project. All of the artifacts were processed at the University of Maryland, College Park, laboratory. Terry Churchill, Barbara Little, Liz Kryder-Reid, Paul Mullins, and Lynn Jones were all responsible for directing the processing of portions of these assemblages. Julia King, Barbara Little,

Henry Miller, Paul Mullins, and Mark Warner all provided helpful comments on this manuscript.

1. Kathleen Bragdon, Edward Chappell, William Graham, "A Scant Urbanity: Jamestown in the 17th Century," in *The Archaeology of 17th-Century Virginia,* ed. Theodore R. Reinhart and Dennis Pogue (Richmond: Archeological Society of Virginia, 1993), 223–49.

2. Cary Carson, Norman F. Barka, William M. Kelso, Gary Wheeler Stone, and Dell Upton, "Impermanent Architecture in the Southern American Colonies," *Winterthur Portfolio* 16 (2/3) (1981): 135–96; see also Fraser D. Neiman, "Domestic Architecture at the Clifts Plantation: The Social Context of early Virginia Building," *Northern Neck of Virginia Historical Magazine* 28 (1978): 3096–3128; some of the earlier studies of impermanent architecture include Ivor Noël Hume, "Matthews Manor," *Antiques Magazine* 40 (1966): 832–36; William T. Buchanan and Edward F. Heite, "The Hallowes Site: A Seventeenth-Century Yeoman's Cottage in Virginia," *Historical Archaeology* 5 (1971): 38–48.

3. Fraser D. Neiman, "Field Archaeology of the Clifts Plantation Site, Westmoreland County, Virginia," The Robert E. Lee Memorial Association (1980): 1–163; Carson et al., "Impermanent Architecture in the Southern American Colonies"; William M. Kelso, *Kingsmill Plantation, 1619–1800: Archaeology of Country Life in Colonial Virginia* (New York: Academic Press, 1984).

4. Andrew C. Edwards, William E. Pittman, Gregory J. Brown, Mary Ellen Hodges, Marley Brown II, and Eric Voigt, *Hampton University Archaeological Project: A Report on the Findings* (Williamsburg, Va.: Dept. of Archaeology, Colonial Williamsburg Foundation, 1989); Neiman, "Field Archaeology of the Clifts Plantation Site"; Louis Berger and Associates, Inc., "The Compton Site Circa 1651–1684: Calvert County, Maryland, 18CV279," East Orange, N.J.: Louis Berger & Associates, Inc., 1989; Alain Charles Outlaw, *Governor's Land: Archaeology of Early Seventeenth-Century Virginia Settlements* (Charlottesville: Univ. Press of Virginia, 1990); Henry Miller, *Discovering Maryland's First City* (St. Mary's City, Md.: St. Mary's City Archaeology Series No. 2, 1986); Kelso, *Kingsmill Plantation.*

5. Outlaw, *Governor's Land.*

6. Lorena Walsh, "Community Networks in Early Chesapeake," in *Colonial Chesapeake Society,* ed. Lois Green Carr, Philip D. Morgan, and Jean Russo (Chapel Hill: Univ. of North Carolina Press, 1988), 206; Blair St. George, "Maintenance Relationships and the Erotics of Property in Historical Thought," paper presented at the American Historical Association meetings, Philadelphia, 1983; Henry Glassie, "Vernacular Architecture and Society," in *Mirror and Metaphor: Material and Social Constructions of Reality,* ed. Daniel Ingersoll and Gordon Bronitsky (Lanham, Md.: Univ. Press of America, 1987), 229–45.

7. St. George, "Maintenance Relationships," 2.

8. Ibid.

9. Glassie, "Vernacular Architecture and Society," 237.

10. Henry Glassie, *Passing Time in Ballymore: Culture and History of an Ulster Com-*

munity (Philadelphia: Univ. of Pennsylvania Press, 1982); Paul A. Shackel, "Town Plans and Everyday Material Culture: An Archaeology of Social Relations in Colonial Maryland's Capital Cities," in *Historical Archaeology of the Chesapeake*, ed. Paul A. Shackel and Barbara J. Little (Washington, D.C.: Smithsonian Institution Press, 1994), 91–93.

11. Nancy Baker, "Annapolis, Maryland, 1695–1730," *Maryland Historical Magazine* 81 (1986): 200; see also Barbara J. Little, *Ideology and Media: Historical Archaeology of Printing in Eighteenth-Century Annapolis, Maryland* (Ann Arbor, Mich.: Univ. Microfilms International, 1987).

12. Edward C. Papenfuse, *In Pursuit of Profit: The Annapolis Merchants in the Era of the American Revolution, 1763–1805* (Baltimore: Johns Hopkins Univ. Press, 1975).

13. *Archives of Maryland* cited in Baker, "Annapolis, Maryland, 1695–1730," 201.

14. Nancy Baker, "Land Development in Annapolis, Maryland, 1670–1776," in "Annapolis and Anne Arundel County, Maryland: A Study of Urban Development in a Tobacco Economy, 1649–1776," ed. Lorena S. Walsh, 1983, N.E.H. Grant RS-20199-81-1955, Maryland Hall of Records, Annapolis, 5, 9.

15. Baker, "Annapolis, Maryland, 1695–1730," 19–21; Jean Russo, "Economy of Anne Arundel County," in Walsh, ed., "Annapolis and Anne Arundel County, Maryland," 3; Paul A. Shackel, *Personal Discipline and Material Culture: An Archaeology of Annapolis, Maryland, 1695–1870* (Knoxville: Univ. of Tennessee Press, 1993); Mark P. Leone and Paul A. Shackel, "The Georgian Order in Annapolis, Maryland," in New Perspectives on Maryland Archaeology, issue ed. Richard J. Dent and Barbara J. Little, *Maryland Archaeologist* 26 (1 and 2) (1990): 69–84; Mark P. Leone and Paul A. Shackel, "Forks, Clocks and Power," in *Mirror and Metaphor*, ed. Ingersoll and Bronitsky, 45–62.

16. See, for instance, James Scott, *Weapons of the Weak: Everyday Forms of Peasant Resistance* (New Haven: Yale Univ. Press, 1985); Scott, *Domination and the Arts of Resistance: Hidden Transcripts* (New Haven: Yale Univ. Press, 1990).

17. Baker, "Annapolis, Maryland, 1695–1730," 201–2.

18. Shackel, *Personal Discipline and Material Culture*; Shackel, "Town Plans."

19. Pierre Bourdieu, *Outline of a Theory of Practice* (Cambridge: Cambridge Univ. Press, 1977); Daniel Miller, *Material Culture and Mass Consumption* (New York: Basil Blackwell, 1987).

20. Miller, *Material Culture and Mass Consumption*; Shackel, *Personal Discipline and Material Culture*.

21. Shackel, *Personal Discipline and Material Culture*.

22. Inventories, 1720, vol. 4, pp. 197–207, Maryland Hall of Records, Annapolis; Inventories, 1727, vol. 12, pp. 71–91, Maryland Hall of Records, Annapolis; see also Shackel, "Town Plans," 90–92.

23. Anne Arundel County Court Land Records, 1706, WT 2, p. 402, Maryland Hall of Records, Annapolis.

24. Little, *Ideology and Media*, 115; Jane McWilliams, "The Sands House—130 Prince George Street: Historical Summary," Historic Annapolis Foundation, Annapolis, 1970, 1; Jane McWilliams and Edward Papenfuse, eds., *Final Re-*

port: *Appendix F Lot Histories and Maps,* 1971, N.E.H. Grant Number H69-0-178, Maryland Hall of Records, Annapolis.

25. Fraser D. Neiman, "Temporal Patterning in House Plans from the 17th-Century Chesapeake," in *The Archaeology of 17th-Century Virginia,* ed. Theodore R. Reinhart and Dennis Pogue (Richmond: Archeological Society of Virginia, 1993), 251–83.

26. Sarah Filkins, "Notes on the Sands House, 130 Prince George Street," Historic Annapolis Foundation, Annapolis, 1988.

27. Ibid.

28. Grant McCracken, *Culture and Consumption: New Approaches to the Symbolic Character of Consumer Goods and Activities* (Bloomington: Indiana Univ. Press, 1988).

29. McWilliams and Papenfuse, *Final Report*; Anne Arundel County Court Land Records, 1748, RB 3, Maryland Hall of Records, Annapolis, 6; Paul A. Shackel, *Archaeological Testing at the 193 Main Street Site, 18AP44, Annapolis Maryland* (Annapolis: Historic Annapolis Foundation, 1986), 17–54; Baker, "Annapolis, Maryland; 1670–1776," appendix.

30. See, for instance, Ann Smart Martin, "The Role of Pewter as Missing Artifact: Consumer Attitudes Toward Tablewares in Late 18th Century Virginia," *Historical Archaeology* 23 (2) (1989): 1–27.

31. Colin Campbell, *The Romantic Ethic and the Spirit of Modern Consumerism* (New York: Basil Blackwell, 1987), 17–226; Randall H. McGuire, "Dialogues with the Dead: Ideology and the Cemetery," in *The Recovery of Meaning: Historical Archaeology in the Eastern United States,* ed. Mark P. Leone and Parker B. Potter Jr. (Washington, D.C.: Smithsonian Institution Press, 1988), 375–406; Ian Hodder, *Reading the Past: Current Approaches to Interpretation in Archaeology* (Cambridge: Cambridge Univ. Press, 1986), 150.

32. Hodder, *Reading the Past,* 66; Michel Foucault, *Discipline and Punish: The Birth of the Prison* (New York: Vintage Books, 1979); Daniel Miller and Christopher Tilley, "Ideology, Power, and Prehistory: An Introduction," in *Ideology, Power, and Prehistory,* ed. Daniel Miller and Christopher Tilley (Cambridge: Cambridge Univ. Press, 1984), 1–15.

33. Mary Douglas and Baron Isherwood, *The World of Goods* (New York: Basic Books Inc., 1979), 118, 144.

34. Carson et al., "Impermanent Architecture in the Southern American Colonies."

35. Shackel, *Personal Discipline and Material Culture.*

36. Carson et al. "Impermanent Architecture in the Southern American Colonies," 135–96; Neiman, "Domestic Architecture at the Clifts Plantation," 3096–3128; Bernard Herman, *Architecture and Rural Life in Delaware, 1700–1900* (Knoxville: Univ. of Tennessee Press, 1987); Robert B. St. George, "'Set Thine House in Order': The Domestication of the Yeomanry in Seventeenth-Century New England," in *New England Begins,* ed. Jonathan L. Fairbanks and Robert F. Trent, 3 vols. (Boston: Museum of Fine Arts, 1982), 2: 159–88; J. Ritchie Garrison, *Landscape and Material Life in Franklin County, Massachusetts, 1770–1860* (Knoxville: Univ. of Tennessee Press, 1991).

6 Zooarchaeology and Social Relations in Annapolis, Maryland

Justin S. E. Lev-Tov

Many zooarchaeological studies in historical archaeology have focused on determining the socioeconomic status of various groups, such as slaves, planters, and merchants.[1] Analyses which have attempted to address this question have frequently concluded that socioeconomic status is not readily discernible in the patterning of many faunal assemblages.[2] Additionally, several other analyses have observed similarities and differences between compared assemblages, but such patterns have frequently been attributed to preservational factors instead of human behavior.[3] However, several other historic zooarchaeological studies have concluded that faunal remains did show differences attributable to status.[4]

The dichotomy evident in these results is interesting since it seems logical that zooarchaeological studies would reflect differences in socioeconomic statuses. In a market economy the diet (and therefore archaeologically recovered faunal remains) should vary according to the capital people could afford to invest in food. Due to the relationship between income level and variable food prices, faunal remains, among other things, may indicate a family's economic position in society. Lyman has postulated that meat purchases should closely correlate with purchasing power as dictated by income level.[5] This principle would have the effect of producing varying levels of cost-efficiency in meat purchases, minimizing cost per yield.

But people do not eat purely according to what they can afford to purchase. No doubt cost is a limiting factor, yet it is one with much room for variation at any monetary level. In fact, the food people eat is embedded with meanings that transcend pure economics. Diet is influenced by rules of etiquette, ethnicity, and even social relations or "power."[6] In fact scores of historians and sociologists have authored studies demonstrating that there is no clear or direct correlation of diet with income, contrary to what Lyman's model suggests.[7] Given the fact that food is so deeply embedded with meaning, some authors have urged scholars to sort out the various factors that may have influenced the production, distribution, acquisition, exchange, and use of food and other material goods.[8] Earlier zooarchaeological and other types of artifact studies have focused on a compound, simplified, variable—socioeconomic status—to address such themes.

More recently, however, socioeconomic status analyses have come under heavy criticism from researchers such as Orser and Howson.[9] These and other authors have critiqued mainly the rigidity inherent in the term "status." In both living and past societies social relationships were usually more complex and fluid than the castelike term status implies. Further, status varies too much from person to person to effectively apply to entire groups.[10] Any one person may hold a number of different statuses depending upon whom the individual interacts with. Orser and Howson both wish to replace status with "social relations" or "power" relationships.[11] Such studies focus on how groups, usually a dominant one and a subordinate one, structured their interactions with each other. One of the long-standing examples of such a perspective is in Annapolis, where research has centered on how politically influential and economically powerful people attempted to control the less powerful and wealthy groups.[12]

This study applies some of the general recommendations that Howson espoused in her commentary on plantation archaeology to urban archaeology in Annapolis.[13] By examining differences in the distribution (who got or sought particular animals or meat cuts), the related context of acquisition (how consumed species were attained), and use of food (how meat may have been used for goals beyond nutritional intake) through faunal remains, I hope to show how Annapolis's elite and middle classes structured their social interaction. Howson favors studying the context of production (the goals of livestock raising and markets for livestock products) in addition to the latter areas.[14]

Zooarchaeologists have spent considerable time studying patterns of meat distribution; the results are frequently presented in terms of people's use of meat according to various nutritional indices.[15] Faunal remains have been used to answer questions about distribution by looking at relative frequencies of various skeletal elements.[16] In urban settings, such studies have commonly employed this technique, sometimes successfully identifying differences, and sometimes not. Schulz and Gust, for example, found that the diet of late-nineteenth-century Sacramento residents did in fact differ due to socioeconomics, as revealed by their price-indexing system for ranking costs of various identified cuts of beef.[17] Bowen has also found some unexpected differences in element distributions between different status sites.[18] A low-status site contrasted with a high-status one showed a greater amount of high-quality meat cuts than poor-quality ones. Further, the relative frequencies of anatomical parts were similar overall at the two sites.[19]

Acquisition methods are also visible in faunal remains. Few historic zooarchaeological studies have specifically addressed this question, but relevant information has been found by studying peoples' use of wild versus domestic species. For instance, Miller observed some variation over time in the amounts and types of meat consumed by farmers of different economic standing.[20] In the seventeenth-century Chesapeake tenant and small-scale farmers as well as wealthy planters hunted deer. In the second half of the eighteenth century diets diverged, perhaps due to environmental degradation (causing wild species to be rarer and harder to get) or land shortages resulting from population growth. A number of other factors probably also contributed to the divergence, most notably an increase in the monetary and material gap separating the poor from the wealthy.[21]

It is also possible that the differences observed are the product of social inequality rather than economic inequality. The effects on diet of social stratification might be most visible in the context of use. The uses and meanings of food beyond filling nutritional requirements has seldom been examined using faunal remains. One notable exception is Yentsch's discussion of the role blacks played in the Chesapeake fishing industry.[22] In that essay, fish species identified from a number of archaeological sites around the Chesapeake region were used as evidence that African Americans participated heavily in the region's food economy. Because the English were apparently afraid of the water, it was up to slaves and free blacks to supply masters and markets with fish. As a result of African and African American traditions like fishing, whites were at times able to eat a greater variety of fish than would otherwise have been available.[23]

In the latter instance food in the form of various fish species conveyed the ethnic traditions of blacks in one context, but may have meant something quite different once placed upon a white person's table. So diversity in faunal remains may be the best context to examine the role of food in structuring social relations. Goody has pointed out a number of criteria that might differentiate an elite diet, including a wide variety of spices, exotic food, complex cooking techniques, and recipes, etc.[24] Only variety in the form of species diversity is addressable with animal bones. Great variety in diet was something actively sought after by both the elite from Medieval and Renaissance times onward into the seventeenth and eighteenth centuries.[25] Diversity in foodways, beyond being recognized as merely a static marker of social divisions, might also be considered an active force in structuring social relations. Research in cultural anthropology identifies foodways in general as helping to mark "existing social boundaries and . . . inclusion within or exclusion from a group. Any part of the pattern of eating may operate in this manner."[26] Reitz has recently identified zooarchaeological evidence for this phenomenon among eighteenth-century residents of St. Augustine.[27]

To examine whether social relationships did in fact influence the diets adopted by urban residents, a faunal assemblage deposited by residents of somewhat ambiguous social standing was contrasted with assemblages from a household whose social position was well known. The study utilized two faunal assemblages excavated in the city of Annapolis, one from the Calvert House and one from the Jonas Green House. Although a "socioeconomic status" view of Annapolis society was adopted in earlier versions of this chapter, it eventually became clear that this view was too rigid to account for the complexity of eighteenth-century Annapolis's social structure.[28] In fact, contemporary colonial views of social and economic class structure were complex and intertwined with one another. Prestige was combined with race, wealth, and occupation as the defining variables for classes. Eighteenth-century Americans most commonly divided Anglo-Americans into either two divisions, made up of the "better" and "common" groups, or three, labeled "better," "middling," and "common."[29]

The point is that social relations even at this time were quite complex and structured by several factors. But it is necessary to examine how individuals within this society used their positions and manipulated material goods to either increase their level of influence on other social groups or resist such attempts. The eighteenth-century was a time of social upheaval, where members of the merchant class increasingly challenged the right of the gentry to rule over them.[30] How did different classes use their positions to structure social relations to their own advantage, and how can we recognize the effects of this process using zooarchaeological material? The utility of using animal bones to address this issue will be demonstrated in the discussion to follow.

Site Backgrounds

The Jonas Green site was excavated first by Constance A. Crosby and later by Barbara J. Little, both of Archaeology in Annapolis. The print shop cellar deposit from which this faunal assemblage was recovered has been dated to the period 1765–80.[31] (map 6.1) All excavated dirt was screened through quarter-inch mesh, a method of recovery fine enough to capture hundreds of fish bones and scales.[32]

The Green family interacted in a number of contrasting social spheres, and therefore its position within Annapolis society is difficult to assess. According to historian Carl Bridenbaugh, printers in colonial society were considered artisans and thus members of the middle class.[33] Probate inventories for Jonas and Anne Catherine Green also demonstrate their middle-class income level. So, in terms of income and occupation, the Greens fit in between the high- and low-income strata of Annapolis's population. Although the Greens were in some ways members of the middle class, other aspects of their lives brought them into contact with people whose occupations and incomes placed them elsewhere in Annapolis society. Members of the Green family seem to have actively sought prominent social positions in various important private and public organizations, such as Jonas's membership in the exclusive Tuesday Club social society.[34]

Excavations at another Annapolis site, the Calvert House, were initiated in 1985 by Anne Yentsch of Archaeology in Annapolis (map 6.1). The faunal assemblage was taken from a brick-lined well and a hypocaust. The fill excavated from both features dates primarily to the mid-eighteenth-century.[35] The Calvert family's standing in Annapolis is quite clear com-

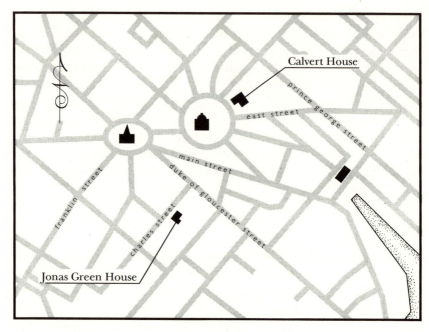

Map 6.1. Jonas Green House and the Calvert House, Annapolis.

pared with the Greens'. The family had occupied the "apex of the social pyramid" in England and prospered here as well. Family members were among the founders and early political leaders of Maryland. In addition to political power, they also owned great expanses of land, many slaves, and of course were quite wealthy.[36]

Methods and Materials

The faunal material from the Jonas Green site was analyzed using the comparative collections at the Smithsonian Institution's National Museum of Natural History in 1989. Data about the Calvert House was extracted from zooarchaeological reports on the two sites. Elizabeth Reitz analyzed the faunal material from the Calvert House.[37]

Within the field of zooarchaeology there is considerable controversy as to which of several methods commonly used to quantify faunal assemblages best represents the actual number of animals or amount of meat once present at a site.[38] Before choosing between various methods of quantification, it is often necessary to determine the types of sites involved in the study, since certain categories of sites lend themselves better to particular methods. It is also necessary to consider the potential impact of biasing effects from the use of particular methods. Calculation of the Minimum Number of Individuals (MNI) has long been a standard way to quantify faunal assemblages. The most prominent alternative method are simple bone counts, commonly known as Number of Identified Specimens (NISP's). Both methods have their shortcomings; MNI exaggerates the importance of rare species, while NISP can be severely affected by various taphonomic agents.[39] NISP was employed here to calculate relative abundance and forms attritional processes. MNI was also calculated, and complete lists of both these figures and NISP's are presented in tables 6.1 and 6.2.[40]

Table 6.1
Jonas Green House Species List

Animal	Count of Bones	MNI
Unidentified Mammal	3,176	
Unidentified Large Mammal	998	
Unidentified Medium Mammal	1,550	
Unidentified Small Mammal	40	
Sheep/Goat	97	8
Sheep	18	3
Pig	116	4
Cow	64	6
Unidentified Bird	1,031	
Ruffed Grouse	1	1
Ring-Necked Pheasant	5	2
Blue-Winged Teal	1	1
Duck Family	2	2
Mallard Duck	9	3
Chicken	43	6
Turkey	84	7
Goose	14	2
Unidentified Fish	737	
Unidentified Reptile	13	
Unidentified Crustacean	8	
General Unidentified	87	
Totals	8,134	45

Table 6.2
Calvert House Species List

Animal	Count of Bones	MNI
Unidentified Mammal	5,021	
Unidentified Large Mammal	1,535	
Unidentified Small Mammal	89	
Opossum	15	1
Wild Rabbit	44	4
Unidentified Rodent	30	
Grey Squirrel	17	2
Rat	367	32
Norway Rat	23	
Roof Rat	27	
Dog	6	1
Raccoon	2	1
Cat	1	1
Horse	1	1
Even-toed Ruminant	88	
Pig	143	6
White-tailed Deer	1	1
Cow	261	10
Sheep/Goat	60	4
Goat	2	
Sheep	11	
Unidentified Bird	1,155	
possible Duck	2	
Duck family	99	
dabbling Duck	65	6
Mallard Duck	2	1
Scaup, species unknown	65	7
Canada Goose	90	8
fowl family	121	
Bobwhite	5	1
Chicken	110	15
Turkey	168	15
possible Ring-Necked Pheasant	15	4
possible Peafowl	1	1
Common Snipe	1	1
Robin	2	1
Snapping Turtle	2	1
poisonous snake	1	1
Unidentified Fish	741	
Gar	1,334	2

Animal	Count of Bones	MNI
Pickerel	25	8
Toadfish	1	1
Catfish family	9	
Bullhead Catfish	12	3
Hardhead Catfish	11	2
Gafftopsail Catfish	2	2
temperate bass family	6	4
temperate bass, species unknown	87	1
Sunfishes	11	1
Yellow Perch	9	3
Jack	1	1
Snapper	11	2
Porgy family	3	1
Sea Trout, species unknown	5	1
Black Drum	2	1
Totals	12,086	173

SOURCE: Adapted from Reitz 1987c.

Epiphyseal fusion sequences were used by me to age domestic mammal bones at the Jonas Green site and by Elizabeth Reitz at the Calvert House site.[41] This data forms the basis for kill-off patterns discussed below. Calvert age data was not available for sheep and goats, so that no comparison for caprine kill-off patterns was possible. Age curves constructed for the Jonas Green data utilized limb bone fusion tables published by Silver.[42]

The Structure of Foodways Contexts in Annapolis

Production Context

The context of production in foodways has long been a subject of interest in zooarchaeology, but is usually discussed with respect to the process of domestication and the formation of early state societies in the Near East.[43] Recently, Bowen examined dairy production using faunal remains from historic contexts in both the New England and Chesapeake areas.[44] Wapnish and Hesse have outlined an approach to production which examines that aspect of urbanization that separates consumers from producers of domestic animal products.[45] The product itself can be milk, meat, or wool, or all of these together.

Generally speaking, no matter what the product, an animal-production economy can assume three broad forms. These forms are: 1) the self-contained production/consumption economy, 2) the consuming economy, and 3) the producing economy.[46] The type of economy present is examined by estimating ages at death for domestic mammals.[47] Each of the three economic orientations ideally produce distinct mortality profiles. The self-contained production/consumption economy profile should show "all of the mortality present in a population's mortality experienced by a herd." In other words, "all age present in a population," so that all age categories for each domestic species should be well represented; no one age category should predominate.[48]

In a consuming economy animals are acquired from specialized producers or markets, so that market-aged animals should dominate the profile. Market age for unimproved breeds of cattle would have been at three to four years, sheep and goats at about one and a half years, and hogs between two and three years.[49] Finally, a producing economy should show animals above and below market age, but few at the prime slaughtering age. In this type of economy, market-aged animals would be sold off to consumers rather than kept for local consumption.[50]

The mortality profiles constructed for cattle at the Calvert and Jonas Green sites (fig. 6.1) differ in the distribution of animals between the various age classes. The Calverts got their beef almost exclusively from animals culled at around two years of age. The Greens, however, got their beef from a wider age range of animals, mostly two years and older. The Calverts could have eaten prime beef every day of the week if they had wanted to. Their diet was more varied than this, but it's clear that when they did eat beef, it was usually from choice animals. The Calvert beef-mortality profile resembles a consuming economy. This may mean that they relied on town markets rather than bringing beef cattle in on the hoof directly from their plantations. In contrast, the Greens' cattle mortality profile looks more like a self-contained production/consumption economy. The problem with such a conclusion is that the Greens were neither landowners nor farmers and so would have had little opportunity to engage in livestock production. As Bowen has pointed out, kill-off patterns are not by themselves reliable enough to interpret herding strategies.[51] More likely, the Greens sometimes bought less desirable beef from old animals.

The mortality profiles for pigs at both sites were strongly similar (fig. 6.2). Both the Calverts and Greens ate pork almost exclusively from prime-aged animals. The focus at both sites is on market-aged animals, so the economic orientation is that of a consuming economy. Caprid kill-off patterning seen

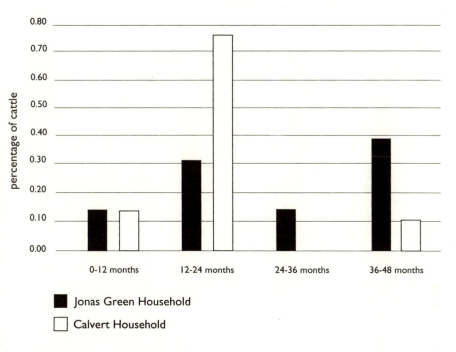

Fig. 6.1. Cattle kill-off patterns by age in months at death at the Jonas Green and Calvert households.

in the Green site assemblage closely resembled the pig mortality patterning (fig. 6.3).

What do the mortality patterns suggest about the relationship between the elite of Annapolis and that of the middling class? Both apparently were equally dependent upon the market for their source of meat. There were few differences in the domestic animal exploitation patterns so far reviewed. The sole difference was the Calverts' concentration on eating prime beef, as opposed to the Greens' less focused exploitation pattern. This is perhaps the only area in which differences due to purchasing power can be separated out from differences due to social influences.

Distribution and Acquisition Contexts

Once cattle, sheep, goats, and pigs were brought into the city's markets, how were they butchered? How were the cuts of meat valued—who purchased,

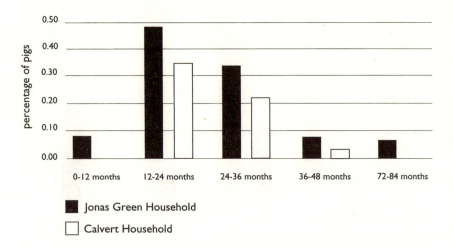

Fig. 6.2. Pig kill-off patterns by age in months at death at the Jonas Green and Calvert households.

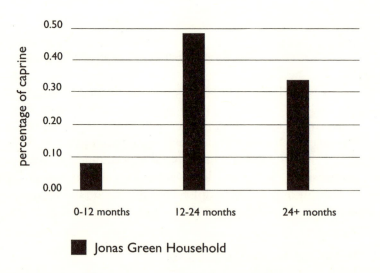

Fig. 6.3. Caprine kill-off patterns by age in months at death at the Jonas Green and Calvert households.

or was able to purchase, which parts of the carcasses? In order to address these questions, I compared the NISP values for individual butchering units between the Jonas Green and Calvert House sites.

The cattle butchering unit comparisons between the two sites did reveal divergent preferences for various meat portions (fig. 6.4). A chi-square test revealed differences at the p < .01 level of significance ($X^2 = 20,037$). The greatest areas of divergence were use of the head and of axial elements. The Calverts apparently favored dishes made with cattle heads; 33 percent of the bones were from this unit. The Greens evidently avoided such meat cuts; this butchering unit made up less than 1 percent of the sample. The Green family used mainly axial cuts from ribs and vertebrae.

The Calverts got a much greater proportion of their beef from the fore and hindquarters sections than did the Greens. While the percentages for these butchering units (4 and 2 percent, respectively) are probably depressed due to the overwhelming amount of rib and vertebral material, the differences appear to be real. The Calvert family dined not only on head meats, but also on fine steaks and roasts. The Green family, by contrast, either did not choose or could not afford to eat the same types of meat. Foot bones were present at both sites in small proportions. The distribution patterns of cattle elements between the two households appear to diverge mostly in the emphasis on head elements at the one house, and axial cuts at the other.

The distribution of pork butchering patterns between the Green and Calvert households continued some of the trends observed earlier (fig. 6.5). A chi-square test revealed significant differences in the distribution of pork butchering units between the two sites ($X^2 = 62.5$, p < .01). Once again, the Calverts made greater use of head meats, perhaps things like jowls, tongue, ears, and brains. These elements accounted for 45 percent of the pig bones identified at the Calvert site, compared to only 14 percent at Jonas Green's house. At the same time, the Greens favored pig's feet; foot bones made up almost 60 percent of that sample, but only 26 percent of the Calvert one. Rib and vertebral cuts were not used in this comparison since these elements are notoriously difficult to assign to species. Similar proportions of "meaty" cuts of pork from the fore and hindquarters units were identified at both sites. Fore and hindquarters butchering units accounted for 13 and 14 percent, respectively, at the Jonas Green site, and 9 and 10 percent at the Calvert site.

Significant differences in consumption of meat cuts from sheep and goats were also identified using a chi-square test ($X^2 = 87$, p < .01). The

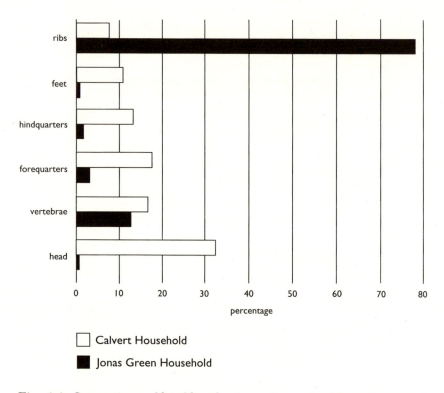

Fig. 6.4. Comparison of beef butchering units at the Jonas Green and Calvert households.

same butchering units that made up most of the differences between the two sites for other types of meat formed the major divergence points once again. Nearly 20 percent of the Calverts' mutton came from the animals' heads, compared to only 2 percent at the Green household. Feet were also somewhat more common at the Calvert House. Mutton from fore and hind-quarters were the most common ones at the Green household, but slightly less so at the Calvert home (fig. 6.6).

The distribution of butchering units between the two sites showed some unexpected patterning. The traditional view in zooarchaeology has been that the "meatiest" cuts, those having the highest muscle to bone ratio, will usually be the most expensive ones.[52] Therefore, high-status or up-per-class households' diets should contain mostly such meat cuts, Low-status households should have a minority of such cuts. Their diet might

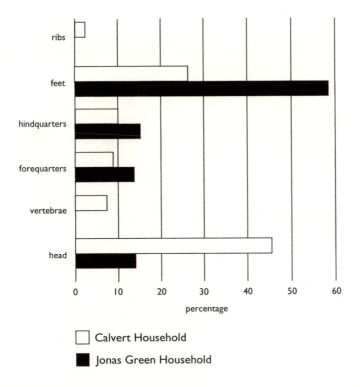

Fig. 6.5. Comparison of pork butchering units at the Jonas Green and Calvert households.

include "less-meaty" cuts as well as parts like heads and feet. Yet, in many cases such patterns have been either unclear or entirely absent in faunal assemblages from a variety of earlier time periods and places.[53]

Because of the inconsistency of the "meaty" pattern, zooarchaeologists have increasingly called into question the assumptions we have used in ranking cuts of meat. Bowen advocates that zooarchaeologists base status assessments on qualitative analyses of different meat cuts' relative importance.[54] Calf's head, hog's head, lamb's head, as well as a variety of other offal-based dishes were once popular menu items among the elite of early America.[55] Rankings of meat cuts at any one point or place in history have probably depended more upon fashion and taste than on strict estimates of nutritional return.[56] In the case at hand, it seems that animal heads, far from being reviled by the wealthy, were actually common fare for them.

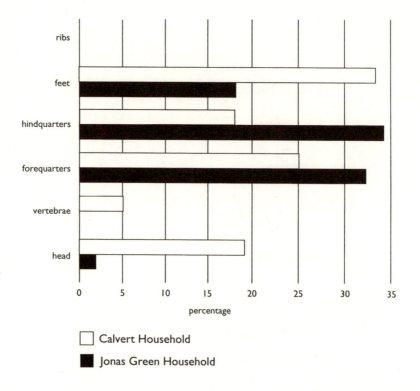

Fig. 6.6. Comparison of mutton/kid butchering units at the Jonas Green and Calvert households.

The relative abundance of these cuts at the Calvert House, and their relative absence at the Jonas Green House, suggests that such dishes may have been an item solely eaten by the gentry. With the exception of pigs' feet, the Greens' diet did not contain much offal. But the abundant similarities in the distribution of butchering units between the two assemblages are just as interesting as the differences. Other than offal as well as fore and hindquarters cuts of beef, the Green and Calvert assemblages are remarkably similar.

Bowen has suggested that quantitative analyses of meat cut distributions often fail to pick up differences because our expectations about what high- and poor-quality cuts consist of are based on contemporary rather than period views.[57] But the similarities may be real, which may mean that the Green household actively sought to emulate gentry like the Calverts, and therefore put on sumptuous meals for important dinner guests. This hypothesis can be evaluated using data from the other foodways contexts.

Acquisition Context

The degree of access urban households had to wild game from markets or from hunting and fishing activities in the environs surrounding cities during this time is unknown. Public markets carried a certain amount and variety of game and fish, at least in New York City.[58] Wealthy planters and urban gentry sometimes employed slaves to supply the master's table with a variety of fish and other game.[59] All of Annapolis's urban residents could have had access to wild game if it was carried at local markets. Perhaps only the gentry would have had the resources to acquire such foods if game was not readily available in markets. Eighteenth-century meat price lists from Annapolis make no mention of wild game.[60]

Studying the acquisition contexts of the food that the Green and Calvert families consumed may reveal differences due to the families' positions in the early American social hierarchy. Acquisition differences will perhaps be most visible in consumption of domestic versus wild animals. Because food can be used as a tool of inclusion or exclusion, it seems reasonable to suggest that factors such as effort expended in creating a household's dietary pattern may relate to attempts at social differentiation or imitation; by examining the distance, time, and capture technology necessary to procure wild species, some estimate of effort expended can be deduced.

Differences in patterns of species acquisition by the two households were measured by breaking down the assemblages according to habitat, taxonomic class, and then according to whether the taxon was wild or domestic. Degree of divergence between the two sites was assessed using statistical tests, percentage comparisons, and qualitative assessments of habitat distance from Annapolis.

Statistical tests run on data from the Jonas Green and Calvert House sites all revealed significant differences. A chi-square test ($X^2 = 1582$, $p < .01$) revealed a basic divergence point in the two households' dietary strategies. The Greens relied much more on terrestrial animals than did the Calverts, who made more extensive use of aquatic fauna. In keeping with this pattern, the Greens incorporated significantly more domestic mammals into their diet, while the Calverts consumed an array of wild

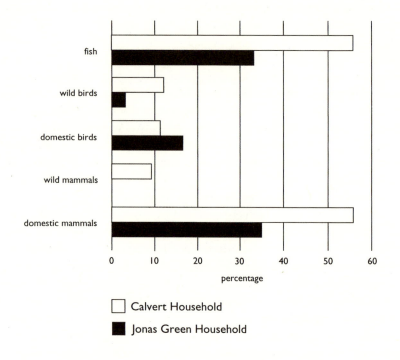

Fig. 6.7. Comparative summary of animal classes at the Jonas Green and Calvert households. The percentages were derived by dividing total NISP for each animal class by the individual category.

mammals (X^2 = 148, p < .01). In fact, no wild mammals were identified in the Green assemblage, but 14 percent of the identifiable mammalian fragments in the Calvert assemblage were wild species (fig. 6.7). Most of the wild mammals present in the Calverts' diet could have been easily trapped in areas immediately surrounding (or within) Annapolis.

Dietary emphasis on birds showed the same pattern as the mammals had at the two sites. The Calvert family ate a significantly higher amount of wild birds than did the Greens (X^2 = 148, p < .01), who instead concentrated on domestic species. In fact, 83 percent of the identifiable bird bones in the Green faunal assemblage were domestic taxa. By contrast, only 47 percent of the identifiable bird bones in the Calvert House assemblage were from barnyard fowl. The Calvert household clearly put a premium on having a variety of birds at their table since over half of the avian assemblage was from wild species.

The species of wild birds that appeared on the Calverts' table likely came from a variety of environments around the Bay, not just the local creeks and the Severn River. Canada geese, scaups, mallards, bobwhites, and a snipe were some of the wild species eaten by the Calverts. Mallards and Canada geese would have been common in the water and fields immediately surrounding Annapolis, whereas bobwhites prefer upland forests and fields.[61] Scaups, on the other hand, prefer more open, brackish waters and so might be found in larger embayments or away from shore in the Chesapeake itself.[62]

A considerable number of econiches were exploited to supply the Calvert household with a variety of game birds for their meals. This characteristic is also obvious when the species of fish present at the two sites are considered. Although a large number of fish bones were recovered at both sites, the number of species identified was quite divergent. At the Jonas Green site three species were identified (see table 6.1). By contrast, Reitz identified at least twelve species in the Calvert assemblage.[63]

All of the fish species consumed by the Green family inhabit shallow fresh or brackish waters and can easily be taken by hook and line. Some of the species that the Calverts consumed, such as gar, bullhead catfish, basses, sunfish, perch, and pickerel fit into this category as well.[64] In contrast, several of the species identified in the Calvert assemblage are exclusive residents of the deep and salty waters of the lower bay and ocean. Jacks and Porgies are denizens of this niche as, generally, are sea trout.[65] One notable group of fish present in the Calvert species array are snappers. The presence of these fish is particularly interesting since they usually do not occur in the Chesapeake at all, being restricted to the Atlantic Ocean.[66]

The differences between the Greens' and Calverts' diets are perhaps most striking in their use of fish and other nondomestic fauna. The Greens relied very heavily on domestic mammals and birds as well as shallow water–dwelling fish. But the Calverts followed a completely different path, they incorporated into their diet everything and exploited every econiche that the Greens utilized, and then went well beyond these constraints. They took game from locally abundant marshes, creeks, and embayments, but also were able to exploit upland woods and deep, open bay waters in addition to the ocean itself.

How did the Calvert household exploit so great a variety of species and econiches to form their diet, and why didn't the Green family's diet also feature this variety? If the town's public market sold such fish and birds, then residents should have had essentially equal access to these species. But perhaps the markets did not carry such a variety of game and fish. If this was in fact the case, then the Calvert family would have had a distinct advantage that allowed and encouraged them to exploit so great a variety of niches.

The great variety of fish in the diet of the Calverts could have been a consequence of the black watermen industry.[67] They were large slaveholders and so could have gotten their slaves to directly or indirectly procure fish for their meals. In fact few white families other than wealthy planters had the necessary tools to fish.[68] So, even though the Greens also had slaves, they probably could not have mustered the same access to the Bay's rich fauna.

Use Context

The most direct way to study consumption, or use of food, would be to examine the individual meals the families ate. Unfortunately, recovery of seasonings and sauces is beyond the realm of zooarchaeology. Further, the deposition of faunal material is such that one meal's worth of food remains can't be differentiated from one year's accumulation. Diversity analysis of faunal assemblages can provide some idea about the overall dietary patterns by demonstrating how the families utilized the market or surrounding environments to assemble their meals.

The diversity of the Calvert House and Jonas Green House assemblages was calculated using the Shannon-Weaver information statistic. This statistic has two components: diversity (or richness), which measures the number of species used at a site, and equability (or evenness), which estimates the frequency with which species are consumed.[69] In this index, richness may have a value anywhere from 0 to 4.99, where the higher the number is, the more diverse an assemblage is. The evenness figure is represented by a number between 0 and 1.0, with higher numbers indicating equal use of most species.

Comparison of diversity statistics calculated for the two assemblages revealed some expected and some surprising results. As hinted at by the analysis of acquisition context, the Green family did not pursue a dietary strategy that focused on diversity. The richness statistic for the latter assemblage was 1.723. Contrastingly, the richness score for the Calvert faunal assemblage measured 3.979, indicating that this household pursued a diverse dietary strategy.

The evenness scores derived from the faunal assemblages followed the latter patterns. Reitz and Scarry suggest that equability scores approaching 1.0 indicate a "normal" dietary pattern.[70] That is, such a score reflects a diet where there are a few abundant, some common, and many rare species. The evenness statistic for the Calvert House was slightly over 1.0. The evenness statistic for the Jonas Green House assemblage was 0.74. This evenness score is a middle equability value, a diet where a relatively small number of species are eaten, but most of these are heavily exploited.

The diversity analysis results follow from differences first observed in the context of acquisition. Clearly, the Greens relied heavily on domestic species and local wild species, meats that the most minimal of public markets would have carried. But the Calvert family took a different dietary course. To be sure, they also consumed the various domestic mammals in addition to pheasants, chickens, turkeys, freshwater fish, and local birds. But they also procured birds and fish that inhabited areas well away from Annapolis, access perhaps afforded them by their slaves. Why did the Calvert family go to the trouble and perhaps expense to construct a diet that virtually epitomized diversity?

The answer to the latter question and the possible meaning behind the observed diversity patterning lies in the context of use. Many cultures in different times and different places have used food and feasting as tools of social exclusion.[71] Bowen has pointed out that in both Medieval Europe and Enlightenment America, such banquets utilized not only sheer amount and variety of meats to impress guests, but also the presentation of spectacular dishes—whole animals, severed heads, and even birds cooked and then sewn back into their feathered skins.[72] Contemporary rules of etiquette even specified the precise number of dishes necessary for a given number of diners.[73] The Calvert family would have been expected to host such meals by their peers. But such functions no doubt served purposes other than to simply amuse Annapolis's pretentious wealthy families. Just as Leone has argued that formal gardens, clocks, and scientific instruments were used by the wealthy to enforce the existing social hierarchy, so too were meals and banquets visually forceful ways to repress the social unrest that threatened their power.[74]

• • •

The zooarchaeological evidence examined here paints Annapolis as a city with residents having divergent dietary adaptations. What is the meaning of the many dietary differences as well as the similarities with respect to the structuring of social relations between Annapolis's gentry and artisan class? I believe that many aspects of the Green and Calvert families' diets can be understood within the larger context of social relations in an uncertain political climate. The differences and similarities previously observed in the material culture contexts of production, distribution, acquisition, and use each help to paint a broader picture of social relations as they affected diet.

Most of the differences observable between the two assemblages at one level reflect the economic differences between the two families. Market-regulated access to meat helped to create dietary distinctions between classes by restricting consumers' access to the highest-quality meat. Thus, the Calverts' beef came only from prime-aged animals, while the Greens' beef selection was more eclectic. The most dramatic difference, in terms of meat cuts, was the Calverts' consumption of offal. According to a price list, heads were priced higher than many meats.[75]

I suggest that not only did the two households' diets differ along economic lines, but also, at another level, along social lines. The broad Calvert diet was evidently fueled by nonmarket sources who brought wild game to their table for the sort of grandiose meals common among their class at the time. Feasting behavior—a form of social display—is the key to understanding many of the differences displayed by this analysis. Heady drama at the table may be one reason why the Calvert family favored offal and sought a tremendously varied diet.[76]

The Calverts actively constructed a diverse diet by incorporating a variety of wild fauna into it, possibly created visually impressive table displays of both these species and the heads of others, and, in the midst of all the variety of cuts and animals, served up only the choicest beef, pork, and mutton. Why did they desire such a diet? While variety may be the spice of life to us, to the upper class, variety may helped them maintain power. By putting on sumptuous meals and conspicuous feasts, the Calvert household was drawing a line between themselves and merchants like the Greens. The middle-class merchants in this era were becoming increasingly dissatisfied with their lack of political clout. At times they were vocal in their discontent, and in some cities they even burned wealthy families' homes.[77] Amidst the chaos, the Calverts were forced to prove their right to rule. Leone has shown how other members of Annapolis's gentry maintained their power by building formal gardens and acquiring clocks, musical instruments, and scientific items.[78] The preceding analysis suggests that we can add foodways to that list.

But what about the Greens—shouldn't they have been clamoring for change? Emulation of the wealthy would have been one social advancement strategy for the Greens and other middle wealth people to pursue.[79] Yet, it is clear from the points of divergence between the two faunal assemblages that the Greens did not choose, or were not able to pursue, such a strategy. Alternatively, the Greens could have chosen to side with the middle class. In fact, their newspaper became increasingly supportive of the revolution over time.[80] Perhaps they consciously took the blander dietary path in order to be identified with Annapolis's middle class, despite their increasing wealth and prominent social position. Although the exact reasons for why the two families ate the diets they did are not clear, what is evident is that the differences are not simply attributable to economics.

In the last fifteen years, Archaeology in Annapolis has focused on the material manifestations of social conflict. This chapter demonstrates that foodways in the form of animal bones are a valuable but largely untapped source of such information about social relations. Integration of material culture contexts with zooarchaeological data has, I believe, produced a more precise study than possible with the more common "socioeconomic status" approach. With this new approach I was able to sort out the possible social versus economic reasons upon which the families based their dietary choices. Beyond shedding light on Annapolis's past, this study also represents another step toward fully integrating zooarchaeological research into the complex, theoretical research at the forefront of historical archaeology.

Notes

There are many people who helped me design, implement, and refine this study since it was first begun in 1989. Without the technical advice and guidance of Melinda Zeder and her patient assistant Susan Arter, the identification and quantification of the Jonas Green site faunal assemblage would have been impossible. Barbara Little and Mark Leone also provided guidance and comments on much earlier versions of this essay. Many thanks are offered to both the editors of this volume and fellow UT students Amy Young and Hank McKelway, all of whom offered helpful discussions about and criticisms of this chapter.

1. John Solomon Otto, *Status Differences and the Archaeological Record—A Com-*

parison of Planter, Overseer, and Slave Sites from Cannon's Point Plantation (1794–1861), St. Simon's Island, Georgia (Ann Arbor, Mich.: Univ. Microfilms International, 1975); Elizabeth J. Reitz, Appendix I: Vertebrate Fauna from McCrady's Tavern and Longroom, South Carolina (Zooarchaeology Laboratory, Univ. of Georgia, 1982); Peter D. Schulz and Sherri M. Gust, "Faunal Remains and Social Status in 19th Century Sacramento," Historical Archaeology 17 (1) (1983): 44–53.

2. Elizabeth J. Reitz, Taphonomy and Socioeconomic Status from Faunal Assemblages (Zooarchaeology Laboratory, Univ. of Georgia, 1987); Reitz, "Vertebrate Fauna and Socioeconomic Status," in Consumer Choice in Historical Archaeology, ed. Suzanne Spencer-Wood (New York: Plenum Press, 1987): 101–19; Reitz, Preliminary Analysis of Vertebrate Remains from Features 5 and 121, at the Calvert House, Annapolis, Maryland (Annapolis: Historic Annapolis Foundation, 1987); Henry M. Miller, "Pettus and Utopia: A Comparison of the Faunal Remains from Two Late Seventeenth Century Virginia Households," Conference on Historic Site Archaeology Papers 13 (1979): 158–79.

3. See, for instance Reitz, Vertebrate Fauna.

4. Karen Mudar, "The Effect of Socio-Cultural Variables on Food Preferences in Early 19th Century Detroit," Conference on Historic Site Archaeology Papers 12 (1978): 323–91; Schulz and Gust, "Faunal Remains"; Diana C. Crader, "The Zooarchaeology of the Storehouse and Dry Well at Monticello," American Antiquity 49 (3) (1984): 542–58.

5. R. Lee Lyman, "On Zooarchaeological Measures of Socioeconomic Position and Cost-Efficient Meat Purchases," Historical Archaeology 21 (1) (1987): 58–66.

6. Jean E. Howson, "Social Relations and Material Culture: A Critique of the Archaeology of Plantation Slavery," Historical Archaeology 24 (4) (1990): 70–78; Susan Kalčik, "Ethnic Foodways in America: Symbol and the Performance of Identity," in Ethnic and Regional Foodways in the United States, ed. Linda Keller Brown and Kay Mussell (Knoxville: Univ. of Tennessee Press, 1984): 37–65.

7. Brown and Mussell, "Introduction," in Ethnic and Regional Foodways, 3–15; Marvin Harris, The Sacred Cow and the Abominable Pig; Riddles of Food and Culture (New York: Simon and Schuster, 1985); Sidney W. Mintz, Sweetness and Power: The Place of Sugar in Modern History (New York: Penguin Books, 1985); Lyman, "Zooarchaeological Measures."

8. Jack Goody, Cooking, Cuisine, and Class: A Study in Comparative Sociology (Cambridge: Cambridge Univ. Press, 1982), 37; Howson, "Social Relations," 84.

9. Charles E. Orser Jr., "The Archaeological Analysis of Plantation Society: Replacing Status and Caste with Economics and Power," American Antiquity 53 (4) (1988): 735–51; Orser, "Toward a Theory of Power for Historical Archaeology: Plantations and Space," in The Recovery of Meaning, ed. Mark P. Leone and Parker B. Potter Jr. (Washington, D.C.: Smithsonian Institution Press, 1988), 313–44; Howson, "Social Relations."

10. Orser, "Archaeological Analysis," 738.

11. Ibid.; Howson, "Social Relations."

12. See, for instance, Paul A. Shackel, "Town Plans and Everyday Material Culture:

An Archaeology of Social Relations in Colonial Maryland's Capital Cities," in *Historical Archaeology of the Chesapeake*, ed. Paul A. Shackel and Barbara J. Little (Washington, D.C.: Smithsonian Institution Press), 85–96.

13. Howson, "Social Relations."
14. Ibid.
15. Lewis R. Binford, *Nunamiut Ethnoarchaeology* (New York: Academic Press, 1978).
16. Joanne Bowen, "Faunal Remains and Urban Household Subsistence in New England," in *The Art and Mystery of Historical Archaeology, Essays in Honor of James Deetz*, ed. Anne E. Yentsch and Mary C. Beaudry (Boca Raton: CRC Press, 1992): 267–81; Lyman, "Zooarchaeological Measures"; Schulz and Gust, "Faunal Remains."
17. Schulz and Gust, "Faunal Remains."
18. Bowen, "Urban Household Subsistence," 269–70.
19. Ibid., 270–73.
20. Henry M. Miller, "An Archaeological Perspective on the Evolution of Diet in the Colonial Chesapeake 1620–1745," in *Colonial Chesapeake Society*, ed. Lois Green Carr, Phillip D. Morgan, and Jean B. Russo (Chapel Hill: Univ. of North Carolina Press, 1988), 176–99.
21. Ibid., 186–87, 192–93.
22. Anne E. Yentsch, "Gudgeons, Mullet, and Proud Pigs: Historicity, Black Fishing, and Southern Myth," in *The Art and Mystery of Historical Archaeology*, 283–314.
23. Ibid., 307.
24. Goody, *Cooking, Cuisine, and Class*, 138–39, 191.
25. Elizabeth J. Reitz and C. Margaret Scarry, *Reconstructing Historic Subsistence with an Example from Sixteenth-Century Florida*, Special Publications Series No. 3 (Society for Historical Archaeology, 1985). Lewis R. Andrews and J. Reaney Kelly, *The Hammond-Harwood House Cookbook* (Annapolis, Md.: The Hammond-Harwood House Association, 1963), 339; Bowen, "Urban Household Subsistence," 275–276; Reitz, *Appendix I*, 65.
26. Kalčik, "Ethnic Foodways," 48.
27. Elizabeth J. Reitz, "Zooarchaeological Analysis of a Free African Community: Gracia Real de Santa Teresa de Mose," *Historical Archaeology* 28 (1) (1994): 23–40.
28. Justin S. E. Lev-Tov, "Intersite Faunal Analysis and Socioeconomic Status in Annapolis, Maryland," paper presented at the Society for Historical and Underwater Archaeology Meetings, Richmond, Va., 1991.
29. Jackson Turner Main, *The Social Structure of Revolutionary America* (Princeton: Princeton Univ. Press, 1965), 232.
30 Gary B. Nash, *The Urban Crucible: The Northern Seaports and the Origins of the American Revolution* (Cambridge: Harvard Univ. Press, 1979).
31. Barbara J. Little, *Ideology and Media: Historical Archaeology of Printing in Eighteenth-Century Annapolis, Maryland* (Ann Arbor, Mich.: Univ. Microfilms International, 1987).

32. Ibid., 187.
33. Carl Bridenbaugh, *The Colonial Craftsman* (New York: New York Univ. Press, 1950), 165.
34. Little, *Ideology and Media*, 124.
35. Anne E. Yentsch, "The Symbolic Divisions of Pottery: Sex-Related Attributes of English and Anglo-American Household Pots," in *The Archaeology of Inequality*, ed. Randall H. McGuire and Robert Paynter (Cambridge: Basil Blackwell, 1991), 192–230.
36. Gary B. Nash, *Red, White, and Black: The Peoples of Early America* (Englewood Cliffs, N.J.: Prentice-Hall, 1974), 215.
37. Reitz, *Preliminary Analysis*.
38. Donald K. Grayson, "Minimum Numbers and Sample Size in Vertebrate Faunal Analysis," *American Antiquity* 43 (1) (1978): 53–65; Theodore E. White, "A Method of Calculating the Dietary Percentage of Various Animals Utilized by Aboriginal Peoples," *American Antiquity* 18 (4) (1953): 396–99; Richard G. Klein and Kathryn Cruz-Uribe, *The Analysis of Animal Bones from Archaeological Sites* (Chicago: Univ. of Chicago Press, 1984).
39. Grayson, "Minimum Numbers"; Klein and Cruz-Uribe, *Analysis of Animal Bones*.
40. I do wish to acknowledge that there are many other analytical procedures available; indeed, there is considerable debate amongst zooarchaeologists about the most accurate quantitative methods. See, for example, R. Lee Lyman, "Quantitative Units and Terminology in Zooarchaeology," *American Antiquity* 59 (1) (1994): 36–71; and H. Edwin Jackson, "The Trouble with Transformations: Effects of Sample Size and Sample Composition on Meat Weight Estimates Based on Skeletal Mass Allometry," *Journal of Archaeological Science* 16 (1989): 601–10. However, I believe that for the purposes of this essay the inclusion of additional analytical methods, such as biomass, ultimately results in the introduction of another suite of methodological problems which detracts from rather than enhances the arguments being presented here.
41. Reitz, *Preliminary Analysis*.
42. I. A. Silver, "The Ageing of Domestic Animals," in *Science in Archaeology*, ed. Don Brothwell and Eric Higgs (New York: Basic Books, 1969), 250–68.
43. See, for instance, Melinda A. Zeder, *Feeding Cities: Specialized Animal Economy in the Near East* (Washington, D.C.: Smithsonian Institution Press, 1991).
44. Joanne Bowen, "A Comparative Analysis of the New England and Chesapeake Herding Systems," in *Historical Archaeology of the Chesapeake*, 155–67.
45. Paula Wapnish and Brian Hesse, "Urbanization and the Organization of Animal Production at Tell Jemmeh in the Middle Bronze Age Levant," *Journal of Near Eastern Studies* 47 (2) (1988): 81–94.
46. Ibid., 84.
47. Silver, "Ageing of Domestic Animals."
48. Wapnish and Hesse, "Animal Production at Tell Jemmeh," 84.
49. Rudolph Clemen, *The American Livestock and Meat Industry* (New York: Ronald Press, 1923); Wapnish and Hesse, "Animal Production at Tell Jemmeh"; Zeder, *Feeding Cities*.
50. Wapnish and Hesse, "Animal Production at Tell Jemmeh."

51. Bowen, "Comparative Analysis of Herding Systems," 161.
52. See, for instance, R. Lee Lyman, "Bone Density and Differential Survivorship of Fossil Classes," *Journal of Anthropological Archaeology* 3 (4) (1984): 221–36.
53. Lyman, "Zooarchaeological Measures"; Miller, "Pettus and Utopia"; Reitz, "Vertebrate Fauna and Socioeconomic Status."
54. See Bowen, "Urban Household Subsistence"; Miller, "Pettus and Utopia"; Reitz, "Vertebrate Fauna and Socioeconomic Status"; Elizabeth J. Reitz and Martha A. Zierden, "Cattle Bones and Status from Charleston, South Carolina," in *Beamers, Bobwhites, and Blue-Points, Tributes to the Career of Paul W. Parmalee*, ed. James R. Purdue, Walter E. Klippel, and Bonnie W. Styles (Springfield: Illinois State Museum, 1991).
55. Bowen, "Urban Household Subsistence," 274.
56. Ibid., 275.
57. Ibid.
58. Nan A. Rothschild, *New York City Neighborhoods: The 18th Century* (New York: Academic Press, 1990).
59. Yentsch, "Gudgeons, Mullet," 289–92.
60. Anne E. Yentsch, *A Chesapeake Family and Their Slaves* (Cambridge: Cambridge Univ. Press, 1994).
61. Brooke Meanley, *Birds and Marshes of the Chesapeake Bay Country* (Centreville, Md.: Tidewater Publishers, 1975); Roger Tory Peterson, *A Field Guide to the Birds of Eastern and Central North America* (Boston: Houghton Mifflin, 1980).
62. Peterson, *A Field Guide*; Christopher P. White, *Chesapeake Bay, Nature of the Estuary: A Field Guide* (Centreville, Md.: Tidewater Publishers, 1989).
63. Reitz, *Preliminary Analysis*.
64. Alice Jane Lippson and Robert L. Lippson, *Life in the Chesapeake Bay* (Baltimore: Johns Hopkins Univ. Press, 1984).
65. Ibid., 190–91, 217.
66. Richard C. Robbins and G. Carleton Ray, *A Field Guide to Atlantic Coast Fishes, North America* (Boston: Houghton Mifflin Company, 1986).
67. Yentsch, "Gudgeons, Mullet."
68. Ibid., 286–87, 296.
69. Reitz and Scarry, *Reconstructing Historic Subsistence*.
70. Ibid.
71. Mary Douglas, "Standard Social Uses of Food: Introduction," in *Food in the Social Order: Studies of Food and Festivities in Three American Communities*, ed. Mary Douglas (New York: Russell Sage Foundation), 1–39.
72. Bowen, "Urban Household Subsistence," 274–76.
73. Reitz, *Appendix I*, 65.
74. Yentsch, *A Chesapeake Family*, 228.
75. Mark P. Leone, "The Georgian Order as the Order of Merchant Capitalism in Annapolis, Maryland," in *The Recovery of Meaning*, 235–61.
76. Bowen, "Urban Household Subsistence."
77. Nash, *The Urban Crucible*.

78. Elaine Breslaw, "The Chronicle as Satire: Dr. Hamilton's 'History of the Tuesday Club,'" *Maryland Historical Magazine* 70 (2): 129–48, cited in Leone, "The Georgian Order," 249.
79. Leone, "The Georgian Order," 249.
80. Little, *Ideology and Media.*

7 Shifting Land Use, Shifting Values, and the Reinvention of Annapolis

Julie H. Ernstein

It is far better to realize the past has always been altered than to pretend it has always been the same. Advocates of preservation who adjure us to save things unchanged fight a losing battle, since even to appreciate the past is to transform it.

—David Lowenthal, *The Past Is a Foreign Country*

The 22 West Street backlot in Annapolis, Maryland, saw intensive use and alteration over the course of the last two centuries. This essay provides a reconstructed chronology of land use and a framework for considering the accompanying renegotiation of social and monetary values associated with the site and its surrounding neighborhood. Several issues of land use are addressed, and localized strategies for their resolution are identified. The specific resolutions achieved at the 22 West Street backlot do not, however, appear unique: a comparison with findings from a backlot investigation conducted by the author in the Fells Point National Historic District of Baltimore City reflects similar strategies.

The land-use comparison underscores a link between Annapolis and Baltimore which is sometimes explicit but always implicit in many versions of Annapolis's (and, indeed, Archaeology in Annapolis's) own creation myth.[1] The two sites and cities from which they hail prove interesting foils for each other on several levels. Comparing and contrasting them afford the opportunity to observe the relative fortune of Annapolis vis-à-vis that of Baltimore as well as each site's link to broader themes in urbanization, industrialization, and working-class history.

The Politics of Land Use and the Reinvention of Annapolis

A useful construct for framing this discussion is that of the politics of changing land use. Clearly, twentieth-century desires mediate our recovery of the ways historic sites were used in earlier decades of the current century and previous centuries. In many ways the very research designs that we construct serve to define many sites and issues as "unimportant" or "less important" than the very contexts which they privilege. White working-class history in Annapolis may well be antithetical to current research emphases on recovering subordinated histories of, for instance, enslaved Africans and African Americans; emancipated African Americans; landscape studies; economic development of crafts and businesses; and the structuring and restructuring of wealth in society. This need not be the case. The component that I propose to add to the many layers of Annapolis's pasts (to reinvent, if you will) is the insertion of a white working class that has been eclipsed by the tall shadow cast by other "elements of identity" packaged for tourists, visitors, and students who regularly visit our state's capital.[2]

A Context for Examining Shifts in Land Use in Annapolis

Several contexts or approaches exist for examining shifting land use in Annapolis and interpreting its possible meanings. One approach is that of the archaeology of the house lot.[3] Numerous excellent Chesapeake-specific house lot studies exist.[4] Among the issues commonly addressed in the archaeological study of the historical house lot are the separation between work and domestic space; changes in household structure over time; changes in individual house lots; the relationship between public and private space; increasing urbanization as manifest in more intensively occupied urban lands; and a host of other relationships directly observable via historical and archaeological inquiry. While I cannot hope to do justice to each and every one of these topics, I would like to discuss a few of the more salient points discovered in the course of excavation and interpretation of the West Street backlot and its Baltimore foil.

Admittedly, household membership on these two lots has been somewhat more transitory than might be wished for; it would be ideal to have more stable membership for a study of the developmental cycle of the households. In light of the disparity between documented owners and the less well-documented occupiers of the two lots, such an undertaking could not expect to meet with a great deal of success. Instead, I have opted to focus on the relationship between people's changing attitudes toward home and work place, public and private space, as well as attempts to privatize space in light of increasing commercialism and urbanization of the immediate area. Specifically, I consider the relationship between the past occupants of these two sites and their attempts to control the lots they occupied—not so much as a means for relating it to specifics of household composition or a study of changing family/household/houseful structure. Instead, my goal is to relate the changes to attitudes about domestic space. Lastly, one of the goals is to make the ever-widening move from observations of the house lot to that of the surrounding neighborhood, the city as a whole, and the Chesapeake region as a means for putting our studies of individual sites in broader, multiple comparative perspectives.

Change as Process and Not Simply Result

The reconfigurations and attendant intensification of land use on these two urban backlots is an urban process worthy of study in and of itself; it is not background "noise" to be cleared away in order to depict static moments or episodes in Annapolis's past. Ironically, the failure to consider this process of urbanization as "having a story to tell" may well be an instance of the interlocutor/interpreter's exclusion of stories antithetical to other bolder themes. Both qualitative and quantitative methods exist in historical archaeology to document the reconfiguration of urban spaces in light of the intensification of land use, and it is expected that this essay will contribute to the former.[5]

The 22 West Street Backlot

During the early days of Annapolis's history, buildings along the West Street corridor were used by craftspeople, innkeepers, and tradespeople of many types, clustered near the city gates just inside the palisade line protecting the small city of Annapolis. Study of the West Street corridor was initiated as a means for historically and archaeologically documenting a portion of the city that had received little previous attention in the course of several decades of historical and archaeological inquiry by both professional scholars and individuals with an avocational interest in the city's past.[6]

The 22 West Street backlot, located along the West Street corridor, lies along the westernmost edge of the city's historic district, toward the center of the block bounded by Calvert, Northwest, and West Streets (map 7.1). This portion of town was developed and occupied since the first quarter of the eighteenth century, and it has seen comparatively less archaeological investigation than have other portions of the historic district. The site underwent intensive salvage excavation at a point when construction of a multistory parking facility seemed imminent.[7] Many of the features recovered were architectural, ranging in date from the eighteenth through the late twentieth centuries, and they represent a long continuum of historic-era occupation and use of the lot as both domestic site and work space.[8]

Background History of the 22 West Street Backlot

Over the course of the last two centuries, this property has been known by several different street addresses and the numbering system has been entirely reordered.[9] The area currently encompassing the 22 West Street backlot was originally surveyed for townsman John Slaughter and comprises the westernmost portion of Lot 71 on the 1718 Stoddert survey of Annapolis (map 7.2). The parcel has seen use as both domestic and work space for an innholder, a silversmith, a blacksmith, a state politician, a hotel, a boarding house, and a duplex private residence. Substantial documentation addresses lot manipulation through the inclusion of outbuildings, workshops, garage space, a warehouse, fences, and a rear dividing wall, as well as improvements for the paved bed of West Street and the presence of sidewalks, telegraph, telephone, and electric light poles.[10] One notes dramatic maximization of land use throughout the entire historic period, but especially in the early twentieth century, when the lot sees simultaneous use by a barber, two insurance salesmen, three lawyers, a Montgomery Ward orders office, and an auto repair shop.[11]

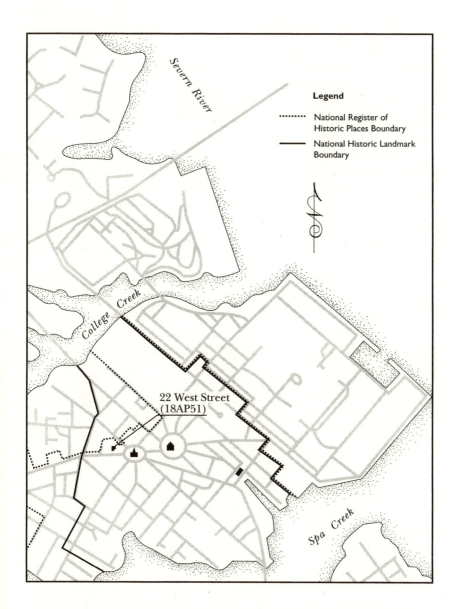

Map 7.1. The 22 West Street site in relation to NHL and NHRP boundaries, Annapolis.

By the mid-twentieth century, secondary accounts indicate that only half of the duplex then occupying the site remained in use, the other half having fallen into disrepair: "Lot No. 71 of old Annapolis today presents little semblance to its appearance in years long gone by. The fourteen-room brick residence once owned and occupied by Jonathan Pinkney and some years later by Chancellor Johnson is obscured by buildings erected in its former front yard. Half of it is owned and occupied by the family of Luigi Calabrese, a thrifty barber, while the other half is vacant and sadly in need of repair."[12] By the 1970s the duplex had experienced substantial fire damage, it was razed, and ownership of the lot was transferred to King and Cornwall Real Estate (sponsors of the excavation). By the time archaeology was initiated in the late 1980s, very little remained above ground to indicate that a substantial three-story brick structure, a rear garden and partition wall, and various outbuildings ever had stood on the lot.

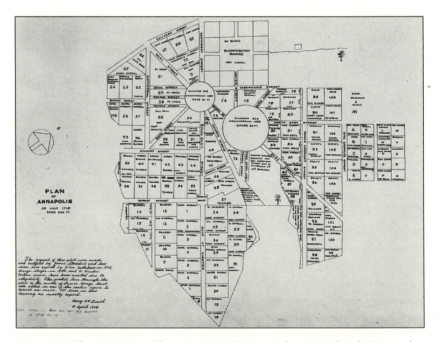

Map 7.2. The 1718 Stoddert Survey of Annapolis, Maryland. Site is located on a portion of Lot 71. Courtesy Maryland State Archives, MSA SC-1427-4.

Archaeology of the 22 West Street Backlot

Excavations conducted at the 22 West Street backlot revealed a great deal about the evolution of an intensively occupied Annapolis backlot. They also indicated that while the integrity of portions of an urban site might well have been entirely compromised, other areas might still retain intact, undisturbed deposits. In the early- to mid-1980s the property underwent three additional modifications with implications for our excavation of the lot. First, an unregistered "site" consisting of a portion of a brick wall was recovered in the course of digging out a basement or cellar hole for a structure moved immediately east of the 22 West Street backlot.[13] Then, archaeological testing of a site registered as the Quynn site (18AP35) was conducted in 1983.[14] Finally, an unprovenienced collection of artifacts was amassed in the course of reseating the structure moved to 20 West Street from elsewhere in the city. This moving of a structure from another portion of the city transpired about five years prior to our investigation of the property, but subsequent to the archaeological testing undertaken on the Quynn site.[15]

Each of these discoveries and events attested to the fact that, despite substantial filling and regrading to a large portion of the site and the razing of the duplex structure formerly identified as 20–22 West Street, portions of the site remained intact and informative about life and land use in this little-studied portion of Annapolis. This site's occupational and depositional history resembles that of complex urban backlots familiar to archaeologists working at sites outside of Annapolis. From the outset, the archaeological investigation of intensive occupation and use on this urban site was framed specifically with reference to the use, manipulation, and renegotiation of space.

Strata

The several centuries of occupation and land use on historic Lot 71 saw several modifications and alterations to the arrangement and use of space on the backlot. Of these modifications, several were documented with below-ground evidence recovered in the course of archaeological excavation. Fifteen separate soil strata were recovered, attesting to the intensive occupation and alteration of the lot. These strata spanned sterile subsoil deposits, to the earliest eighteenth-century cultural layers, through the late-twentieth-century destruction and fill episodes, and concluding with the modern ground surface. Construction and destruction episodes were documented, as were filling episodes, disturbances, and capping.

Archaeological Features

A total of 53 buried features were recovered from the 22 West Street backlot: 41 were cultural, 7 were natural (e.g., plant stains, root balls, and rodent burrows), and 5 were indeterminate. Of the cultural features, a generalized breakdown by type reveals that 29 were architectural (e.g., building foundations, supports, interior partitions, brick floors); 6 were midden, trash, or fireplace debris deposits; 1 was the result of previous archaeological investigation; and 5 were utility related (e.g., pipe trenches, repair trenches, or drains). One of the earliest features uncovered was an unmortared brick floor, laid in a herringbone pattern. This feature had a *terminus post quem* of 1762 and was present in 9 of the 18 units excavated.

Artifacts

The bulk of the material culture recovered from the site was classified as domestic/household refuse in the form of ceramic tablewares, serving dishes, glassware, and utilitarian food-preparation bowls. The other classes of materials recovered, such as metals, are likewise attributable to household use (e.g., door hardware, nails, straight pins, and a possible fireplace crane). In addition, a large amount of faunal materials (especially animal bones and egg shells) were recovered. A minimum vessel count has been completed for the ceramic assemblage, and 167 vessels were identified. A considerable lateral expanse of ground was uncovered in the course of excavations, and the 174 bags of artifacts recovered will permit interpretation and reinterpretation of this complex site for some time to come.

The Dynamics of Land Use at the 22 West Street Backlot

Marked renegotiations of land use occurred over the course of the eighteenth, nineteenth, and twentieth centuries. For brevity's sake, I have isolated four site-specific land use categories: domestic and work space, public versus private space, intensification of land use, and changing attitudes about domestic space.

Domestic and Work Space

The separation of home and work space has received considerable attention since the publication of Thompson's pivotal essay in 1967.[16] The archaeological manifestation of this separation has received careful consideration within the confines of Annapolis, as well as within urban historical archaeology as a whole.[17] Historical and cartographic documentation indicates that the total separation of domestic and work space within the confines of the 22 West Street backlot, while never totally complete, was cyclical. That is, there was heavy mixing of home and work space in the eighteenth and twentieth centuries, and in the intervening nineteenth century the large brick structure on the site was, first, the residence of a prominent local citizen and, subsequently, a mixture of temporary housing and support services.

For much of its history, mixed commercial/residential land use was the rule. Multiple sub-parcels and owners throughout the early eighteenth century attest to the presence of the homes and work spaces of a variety of craftspeople and their families (e.g., innholder, carpenter, and silversmith). By the latter half of the eighteenth century, innholder John Ball was operating what was for him a place of business as well as a temporary residence for travelers. During the third quarter of the eighteenth century, the lot was home to a silversmith, a tenement house, and an assortment of outbuildings. Within the first two decades of the nineteenth century a blacksmith shop was added to the lot's holdings.

Attitudinal insight can be gained when noting that in 1831 the lot was enough of a "prestige address" that the Hon. John Johnson Jr., the last chancellor of Maryland, made his home here. After his death, his daughter and her husband occupied the house and property for several decades. The character of the neighborhood underwent a decline during the second half of the nineteenth century, by which time the former Johnson family house had been transformed into a boarding house known as the National Hotel. By the last decade of the nineteenth century the major structure occupying the lot had been divided into a duplex residence, and this portion of West Street was repaved with oyster shells. The early twentieth century saw a high degree of mixed rental residential occupation and business/support services (e.g., barber shop, lunch counter, law offices, etc.). This intensively occupied, mixed land use continued through the middle of the twentieth century, when portions of the former Pinkney-Harris-Johnson house had fallen into an advanced state of disrepair. By the 1970s the structure was razed, effectively ceasing residential occupation of the lot. After this point, only businesses sat on and immediately adjacent to the backlot.

Public Versus Private Space

An interesting extension of the theme of separation of home and work space is the fact that several attempts to privatize lingering residential portions of the site were visible in the face of ever-increasing commercialism and urbanization. One example of an attempt to privatize remaining domestic space on the 22 West Street backlot came in the case of a rear or garden wall uncovered in the course of excavation. This mortared brick wall aligned north-south through the center of the duplex structure occupied the site in the nineteenth and first half of the twentieth centuries. Constructed in about 1894, the wall coincides with the construction of a six-foot-high brick wall separating the project area from the property immediately adjacent to its west.

Another archaeological manifestation of an increased desire for privacy in the face of intensive occupation is the construction of a six-foot-high brick wall separating the Lot 71 backlot from the Lot 70 property immediately to the west. Interestingly, the construction of these two walls was accomplished at the same date.

One final example of an archaeologically recovered feature that may well have served to lend some degree of privacy to the remaining late-nineteenth-century domestic portions of the 22 West Street backlot was the construction of a brick alley or walkway between the 22 West Street backlot and its western neighbor. This alley or walkway was uncovered in the course of backhoe stripping. For safety reasons, it was not possible to uncover or further explore the feature, because it underlaid an extant brick rear partition wall between our site and an adjoining business.

It is likely that more ephemeral materials, such as trees and shrubbery, may also have served screening purposes and separated public and private space on the 22 West Street backlot. The few twentieth-century planting features uncovered were limited to the northernmost portion of the lot. The only eighteenth-century planting feature encountered was an isolated find. This observation, therefore, is merely speculative, since the late-twentieth-century earth-moving activity on site may well have obliterated evidence for nineteenth-century separations of the rear yard areas from surrounding workshops, sheds, and other outbuildings.

Intensification of Land Use

The historic occupation of this backlot demonstrates a trend of intensification of land use through increasing commercialism and urbanization since

1718. By 1739, one landholder had reassembled the various components of historic Lot 71 into a single larger—and therefore more valuable—holding. In the intervening years between 1739 and the 1770s, the land records indicate a series of construction episodes and improvements to the lot. Even as early as 1778, neighboring landowner and silversmith Allan Quynn found it profitable to expand his landholdings eastward from Lot 70, where he maintained his residence and place of business. As is often the case, the language of these records is full of formulaic constructions such as "buildings and appurtenances" to the degree that one cannot be certain whether outbuildings, improvements, and the construction of ancillary structures are the product of building activity or flowery language by the recorder.

As the 22 West Street backlot comprises only a portion of historic Lot 71, it is occasionally difficult to determine which of the buildings described in the early land records sat on the parcel under investigation. Archaeological deposits attesting to improvements made to and on the lot in the eighteenth century include: architectural foundations of a substantial brick structure occupying the lot from as early as the 1770s through the late twentieth century; a portion of a faced and mortared iron-laden sandstone cellar hole; brick paving surfaces for an outbuilding or office; and a firebox and a hearth. Additional eighteenth-century features were present in the form of two discrete trash middens, a localized filling episode, a thick mortar layer serving as a capping episode for a mid-eighteenth-century yard surface, a possible planting stain, and a large rodent burrow. The interpretation of a squarish postmold-like feature was hindered by the intrusion of a complex of rodent burrows. While uncompleted, faunal analysis will most likely support the presence of rodents and burrowing animals on this lot, as attested to by burrows beginning in earnest in the late eighteenth century. This development may well be a function of the increasingly dense occupation of the neighborhood by that time.

Evidence for intensification of land use in the nineteenth century consisted of a series of rear additions to the substantial brick structure that occupied the lot; a doorway to same; and paving/flooring for these additions, with occasional mortar layers serving to cap filled in or reworked floors. Additionally, by the late nineteenth century it was necessary to pave an alleyway to facilitate pedestrian traffic through the backlot to West Street. Several nineteenth-century rodent burrows were encountered as well.

Moving into the current century, material evidence for the intensification of land use was manifest in the form of trash deposits associated with commercial ventures; destruction episodes; flooring/paving surfaces for assorted warehouses behind the 20-22 West Street duplex; utility trenches and repair trenches; and a brick downspout catchment into which a fragment of copper-clad gasket, a spark plug, copper alloy rivets and washers, a portion of an automobile valve stem, and other debris from a garage or automotive repair shop had been discarded.

Documentary evidence supports this claim to increasing density and intensity of occupation throughout the course of the nineteenth and twentieth centuries. The interpretation of cartographic evidence, particularly information culled from the Sanborn Fire Insurance maps for the nineteenth and twentieth centuries, supports and quite literally illustrates this contention. Further, as excavations could not focus on the front yard area of the duplex (a Christian Science Reading Room currently stands on that portion of the property), the documentary evidence permitted generalization about use of the lot for portions of the property that are not accessible to archaeological study. Clearly, it is the combination of approaches, historical and archaeological, that permits the fullest perspective.

Some of the most compelling evidence for intensification of land use and maximization of frontage onto the West Street thoroughfare comes from twentieth-century land use. By 1921, for instance, retail businesses literally set up shop in the former front yard of the western half of the duplex and located a warehouse in its back yard. By 1930, one notes the presence of two stores in the front yard area of the eastern half of the duplex. By 1951, the stores remained in the front of the duplex, the warehouse remained behind, and the western half of the duplex had fallen into disrepair. Architecturally, the lot remained densely occupied or cluttered until fire consumed the duplex and it became necessary to demolish the structure. Ironically, shortly thereafter the slow re-maximization of the lot and adjacent properties began. The structure which was relocated to the property adjacent to the now-abandoned backlot marked the reclaiming of otherwise unoccupied property. Subsequent to construction of the Gott's Court parking facility, the 22 West Street backlot was redesigned, and it currently is used as a small urban park. While nowhere near as intensively occupied as in its past, it is interesting to note that the backlot stood empty for less than twenty years before being reclaimed for another purpose.

In summary, one notes a diachronic pattern of maximizing land use on the 22 West Street backlot so as to generate revenue from shop and business sales and rental housing and maximize use of West Street frontage.

The last quarter of the twentieth century has witnessed the reclaiming of the lot for purposes of profit—the lot maximizes consumers' access to the commercial enterprises along West Street via a newly constructed parking facility and a park that links the parking garage with a public walkway to shops and businesses. Finally, this researcher found it ironic that the very motivation for documenting historic land use and occupation of this urban backlot was imminent redevelopment (read: reintensification and restructuring of land use yet again).

Changing Attitudes about Domestic Space

What becomes apparent in considering the renegotiation of the use of space on this lot is the fact that the property underwent redefinition as more profitable uses and combinations of uses were identified and as the situations which dictated profit and possibility were themselves redefined. A diachronic approach to changing land use on this lot demonstrates that for all of its history its use was never solely that of residential property. Until recently, however, some portion of the lot saw use as domestic space. It is particularly intriguing, I think, to consider why it is that over time the domestic component of the site became increasingly less visible, whether screened or crowded out by shops and businesses or rendered less visible in the long run by taking on a largely transitory nature.

The transformation of this lot from something of a "prestige address" to a less desirable part of a commercial neighborhood is a process that began in the second half of the eighteenth century and increased steadily over the course of the nineteenth and twentieth centuries. The relative fortunes of this lot must be seen in light of the ebb and tide of the town's history. In light of this, it seems likely that, while much of Annapolis's business and trade relocated to the port of Baltimore in the late eighteenth and nineteenth centuries, the neighborhood surrounding the 22 West Street backlot took on much of the boarding and rooming house character of many of the properties lining Calvert, West, and Northwest Streets.

Interestingly, as preservation and tourism continue to redirect attention to Annapolis once again, this is beginning to change. Several of the shops and galleries that formerly lined Main Street have recently relocated to this section of West Street. As similar changes seemed inevitable in the early to mid-eighteenth century, these businesses are being gradually incorporated into the feel of the historic district, instead of sitting on what is perceived as the edge of the district. It remains to be seen, of course, whether or not this trend will be realized. What can and should be addressed at this time, however, is how the processes of renegotiating meaning on the 22 West Street backlot accord with trends experienced, for example, on an urban backlot in Baltimore. Before considering such a comparison, let us briefly outline the rationale or basis for such a comparison.

A Baltimore Comparison

Discoveries made during archaeological investigation of an urban backlot along the Fells Point waterfront in Baltimore provide an interesting counterpoint to the trends noted at the West Street backlot.[18] Limited archaeological reconnaissance at 1609–1611 Thames Street (18BC99), completed under contract with the Baltimore City Life Museums, revealed that general trends noted at the West Street backlot also occurred in its Baltimore counterpart. As was true of the Annapolis site, the Thames Street backlot saw intensive residential, commercial, and industrial use over the course of the eighteenth through twentieth centuries. While some of the particulars of land use and development differ, the general outline of intensification of land use over time and strategies of land use follow a common pattern. Also of note is the fact that the latter half of the twentieth century saw political mobilization and the inclusion of this site within a nationally recognized historic district.

Archaeology at 1609–1611 Thames Street

Detailed archival analysis of a half-block area was conducted to assess the research potential, historic interest, and likely integrity of below-ground remains for historic Lots 61, 62, and 63 in Fells Point (map 7.3). Upon careful consideration of significant post-depositional modifications made to the lots (especially the construction and subsequent razing of a 1.3-acre brick and steel construction building on much of Lots 61 and 62), the easternmost portion of Lot 63 was selected for archaeological testing. The following summary provides a synopsis of development of the lots in question (see map 7.4):

> As became apparent after completing lot-specific land use histories, each of the three parcels was seen to have been directly linked to maritime trade in particular, contributing to the growth of Baltimore

city as a major shipping center. Among the themes for developments common to each of the lots was the reclaiming of "made land" and the extension of wharves out into the Patapsco River. This development was a common undertaking by the late eighteenth century, as attested by documentation of shoreline modifications specified above. In addition, the current project area served as home to local seagoing men, such as sailors and ship's captains, sailmakers, coopers, and others who worked in shipping-related trades. In retrospect, ownerships of the three lots was maintained in common until 1779, with development and occupation of the parcels having occurred at least by the 1780s. Later still, the Northern Central Railway gained inroads, and the rearmost portions of the three parcels were once again consolidated in the hands of a single owner. Throughout the late

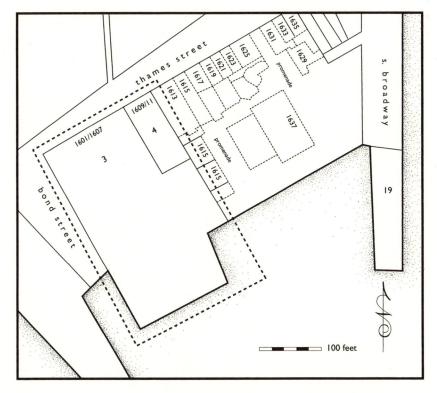

Map 7.3. The 1601–1611 Thames Street Project Area, Baltimore, Maryland.

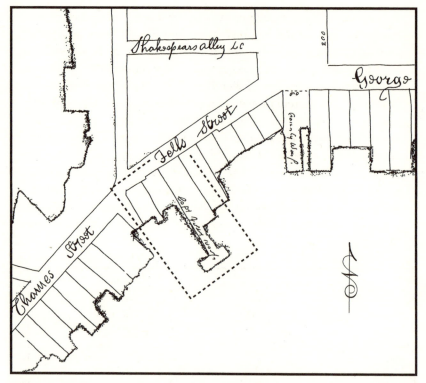

Map 7.4. Section of Presbury's 1787 map of Baltimore showing 1601–1611 Thames Street project area. Courtesy Baltimore City Archives.

eighteenth century and into the late twentieth century, the project area was an intensively used and occupied area that bore witness to the transition from a modest town with deep harbors to a large urban center and from the site of cottage industries to larger commercial and ultimately full-scale industrial ventures.[19]

Six five-foot units were excavated on historic Lot 63 (modern 1609–1611 Thames Street) to document the different phases of past land use for residential, commercial, and industrial (i.e., foundry and machine shop) purposes. Each of these types of land use was represented and documented archaeologically. Excavations resulted in the recovery and identification of six features, eighty-five bags of artifacts, and the reconstruction of seven discrete soil strata.

Residential land use was attested to by the presence of architectural features (brick foundation walls and decayed wooden sills), a substantial trash midden (containing large amounts of animal bones), and copious amounts of broken and whole glass bottles and ceramic sherds. Commercial land use was present in the form of kiln furniture and cobble remains from one of the two alleyways that traversed the parcel and served as access to the Patapsco River waterfront. In addition, a metal bale seal recovered on site was most likely from one of the many bales stored at the Cotton Press Storage Warehouses located on the western lot adjoining the site. Evidence for industrial land use was present in the form of a circa ten-foot-diameter, wood-lined ash pit associated with the Engel and Kirchheiner brass foundry and coppersmith business at 1609–1611 Thames Street. The foundry stood at that address from 1891 until all structures fronting onto Thames Street between the Terminal Building (1601–1605) and Brown's Wharf (1613–1617 Thames Street) were demolished (fig. 7.1). Many machine parts, copper and other metal scraps, fragments of rag mops, and a wide variety of strips of cloth (e.g., chamois, burlap sacking material) were recovered.

Fig. 7.1. Terminal warehouse building, Baltimore, Maryland. View is from the southwest. Courtesy of the Center for Urban Archaeology, Baltimore City Life Museums.

For much of the latter half of the twentieth century, the 1609–1611 Thames Street backlot has served as an asphalt parking lot providing commercial parking and access to the businesses, shops, and offices located in the immediate area. It is particularly interesting that, as was the case with the 22 West Street backlot, an awareness of preservation concerns and sensitivity toward the area's history has resulted in the re-landscaping and establishment of small urban parks within each of the project areas. Perhaps these are simply interim uses during a period of slow real estate development, or, better yet, perhaps such land use reflects the desire for nondisruptive, adaptive reuses for urban lots into green spaces.

Comparative Politics of Change

In both the Annapolis and Fells Point backlot investigations, one notes changes in land use from domestic to mixed residential/commercial and, in the case of the Fells Point site, subsequent entry into the industrial realm. While both the Annapolis and Fells Point lots experienced a diachronic intensification of commercialism and urbanization, the particulars of development occurred at slightly different times. Land speculation was initiated on the Annapolis lot within the first two decades of the eighteenth century, whereas these forces did not come into play on the Baltimore site until the last decades of the eighteenth century. The timing of these and subsequent events are very much a product of trends in the local histories and the relative prosperity of each at different points over the course of the last three centuries.

With the exception of Chancellor Johnson at the West Street site, it is worth noting that the past occupants of both sites were not, until recently, actively engaged in shaping local politics. Instead they were engaging in craft, commerce, and a shifting local logic. Just as meaning in Annapolis is generated in relation to and against other urban areas, it is worth considering Annapolis as controlled experiment and Baltimore as actualization; i.e., where industrialization gets worked out or realized on a large scale. The two differ, therefore, in terms of scale.

The fact that large pockets of modern Baltimore celebrate their working-class heritage and identity is no doubt attributable to the fact that such locales grew up around the industries and plants that spawned them and survived intact well into the twentieth century. Whereas Fells Point and other East Baltimore neighborhoods are increasingly framing their historically white working-class identities as worthy of scholarly attention, this is not yet the case in Annapolis.[20] To date, archaeologists in Annapolis have made great strides to move away from perpetuating the image of "an elegant, genteel past of aristocratic, bewigged gentlemen, men of power and property" to addressing the lives of its marginalized and largely invisible communities.[21] There appears to be a gaping middle ground, occupied by those we think of in nineteenth- and twentieth-century terms as the working class, many of whom were of European and European American descent and are as much a part of the missing picture as disfranchised African Americans and other muted groups. Working-class identity is a theme worthy of further investigation and may well prove equally liberating in terms of rendering an ever-fuller picture of Annapolis and its multiple pasts.

• • •

The recasting of identities in both Annapolis and Fells Point is an increasingly political one. Both communities are experiencing processes of gentrification and are the current battlegrounds of contested pasts and contested presents. By privileging isolated frozen moments of the historical past we deny the historical importance of sites and their occupants' lives in which strategies of accommodating increased commercialization, density of occupation, and a spate of other urban processes are the rule and not the exception. If such pasts are to be recovered, interpreted, and, in the process, reinvented, one must focus aggressively on change as well as the static moments it punctuates.

Notes

Several individuals were instrumental to realizing the fieldwork that is summarized in this essay, especially Louise E. Akerson, archaeological curator and project manager at the Baltimore Center for Urban Archaeology, Baltimore City Life Museums; Kent Johnson of Constellation Real Estate, Inc., sponsors of the 1609–1611 Thames Street (18BC99) excavations and the archival study that preceded it; Stewart Knower of King and Cornwall Real Estate, sponsors of the 22 West Street backlot (18AP51) investigation; Mark P. Leone, director of Archaeology in Annapolis; Barbara J. Little and Paul A. Shackel, Archaeology in Annapolis principal investigators; and Robert Trescott of Annapolis. Both Historic Annapolis Foundation and the Baltimore City Life Museums provided logistical and research support which is heartily acknowledged. And, finally, thanks are extended to Abdul Mustapha for discussion of the continuous and discontinuous relationships between Baltimore and Annapolis and to the editors for the opportunity to contribute to this volume.

1. This Annapolis–Baltimore link has been incorporated into the public program at almost every Annapolis site interpreted to the public. Tours have acknowledged that Annapolis experienced an economic decline at the end of the eighteenth century which continued into the nineteenth century as the importance of the Port of Baltimore increased.

2. Compare Parker B. Potter Jr., *Public Archaeology in Annapolis: A Critical Approach to History in Maryland's Ancient City* (Washington, D.C.: Smithsonian Institution Press, 1994).

3. For Annapolis house lot analyses, compare Julie H. Ernstein, *Continuity and Change on an Urban Houselot: Archaeological Excavation at the 22 West Street Backlot (18AP51) of the Annapolis National Historic District, Anne Arundel County* (Annapolis: Historic Annapolis Foundation, 1994); Barbara J. Little, *Ideology and Media: Historical Archaeology of Printing in Eighteenth-Century Annapolis, Maryland* (Ann Arbor, Mich.: Univ. Microfilms International, 1987); Paul R. Mullins and Mark S. Warner, *Final Archaeological Investigations at the Maynard-Burgess House (18AP64): An 1850–1980 African-American Household in Annapolis, Maryland* (Annapolis: Historic Annapolis Foundation, 1993); Paul A. Shackel, *Archaeological Testing at the 193 Main Street Site, 18AP44, Annapolis, Maryland* (Annapolis: Historic Annapolis Foundation, 1986); Warner, *Test Excavations at Gott's Court Annapolis, Maryland 18AP52* (Annapolis: Historic Annapolis Foundation, 1992); Warner and Mullins, *Phase I–II Archaeological Investigations on the Courthouse Site (18AP63): An Historic African-American Neighborhood in Annapolis, Maryland* (Annapolis: Historic Annapolis Foundation, 1993); and Anne E. Yentsch and Larry McKee, "Footprints of Buildings in 18th Century Annapolis," *American Archeology* 6 (1) (1987): 40–51.

4. On Chesapeake house lot archaeology, compare Charles D. Cheek and Amy Friedlander, "Pottery and Pig's Feet: Space, Ethnicity, and Neighborhood in Washington, D.C., 1880–1940," *Historical Archaeology* 24 (2) (1990): 34–60; Terrence W. Epperson, "Race and the Disciplines of the Plantation," *Historical Archaeology* 24 (4) (1990): 29–36; James G. Gibb and Julia A. King, "Gender, Activity Areas, and Homelots in the 17th-Century Chesapeake Region," *Historical Archaeology* 25 (4) (1991): 109–31; Robert W. Keeler, *The Homelot on the Seventeenth-Century Chesapeake Tidewater Frontier* (Ann Arbor, Mich.: Univ. Microfilms International, 1977); and Garry Wheeler Stone, Henry Miller, Alexander H. Morrison II, and Emily Kutler, *The Clocker's Fancy Site, 18 ST1-65, on St. Andrew's Freehold: An Archaeological Survey* (St. Mary's City, Md.: St. Mary's City Commission, 1987).

5. Compare Rothschild and Rockman's quantitative measures for assessing the degree of urbanization in Nan A. Rothschild and Diana DiZerega Rockman, "Method in Urban Archaeology," in *Archaeology of Urban America: The Search for Pattern and Process,* ed. Roy S. Dickens Jr. (New York: Academic Press, 1982), 3–18.

6. Much of the documentary research for the 22 West Street site was compiled by Jean Russo, director of research for Historic Annapolis Foundation.

7. Archaeology in Annapolis researchers were particularly interested in Gott's Court, a series of connected frame houses within the interior of this block and occupied by African American residents in the twentieth century. Compare R. Christopher Goodwin, *Phase II/III Archeological Investigations of the Gott's Court Parking Facility, Annapolis, Maryland* (Annapolis: Maryland Historic Trust, 1993); and Warner, *Test Excavations.*

8. Ernstein, *Continuity and Change.*

9. Ibid.

10. For a detailed study of Annapolis's paving history, see Jean B. Russo, "The Public Thoroughfares of Annapolis," *Maryland Historical Magazine* 86 (1) (1991): 66–76.

11. *Polk's Annapolis Directory,* 1939 (New York: R. L. Polk & Co., Inc., 1939).

12. Ruby R. Duval, "Lot Number 71, Annapolis: A Brief Historical Sketch," *Maryland Historical Magazine* 54 (1) (1959): 111.

13. Notes and a sketch resulting from a field visit by archaeologist Jody Hopkins documented the presence of an extant brick wall, recovered below-grade when relocating the structure currently identified as 20 West Street. Conversations with Robert Trescott were instrumental in establishing a chronology for some of the later twentieth-century alterations to the lot.

14. Archaeological testing at 18AP35 was conducted under the direction of Anne E. Yentsch. A final site report was not produced; however, surviving field notes are on file with Historic Annapolis Foundation.

15. While these materials are unfortunately unprovenienced, they do attest to the presence of eighteenth-century deposits on the site.

16. E. P. Thompson, "Time, Work-Discipline, and Industrial Capitalism," *Past and Present* 38 (1967): 56–97.

17. See, for example, Wall, "The Separation of the Home and Workplace in Early Nineteenth-Century New York City," *American Archeology* 5 (3) (1985): 185–89.

18. Funding for an archival study as well as subsequent limited archaeological investigation was provided by Constellation Real Estate, Inc., of Columbia, Maryland. Compare Ernstein, *Historic Land Use and Cultural Development of 1601–1611 Thames Street: Block 1827 (Lots 61, 62, and 63) of the Fells Point National Historic District, Baltimore Maryland* (Baltimore: Baltimore Center for Urban Archaeology, 1992); and Ernstein, *Archaeological Reconnaissance at 18BC99, The 1609–1611 Thames Street Backlot, Block 1827 (Lot 63B and 63C) of the Fells Point National Historic District, Baltimore, Maryland* (Baltimore: Baltimore Center for Urban Archaeology, 1997).

19. Ernstein, *Historic Land Use,* 62.

20. Scholarship on working-class neighborhoods in Baltimore includes Daniel Randall Beirne, *Steadfast Americans: Residential Stability Among Workers in Baltimore, 1880-1930* (Ann Arbor, Mich.: Univ. Microfilms International, 1976); Gary Browne, *Baltimore in the Nation, 1789–1861* (Chapel Hill: Univ. of North Carolina Press, 1980); Elaine Eff, director, *The Screen Painters* (Los Angeles: Direct Cinema, 1989); Elizabeth Fee, Linda Shopes, and Linda Zeidman, eds., *The Baltimore Book: New Views of Local History* (Philadelphia: Temple Univ. Press, 1991); Roland L. Free-

man, *The Arabbers of Baltimore* (Centreville, Md.: Tidewater Publishers, 1989); Edward K. Muller and Paul A. Groves, "The Emergence of Industrial Districts in Mid-Nineteenth Century Baltimore," *Geographical Review* 69 (1) (1979): 159–78; Leslie Rehbein and Kate E. Peterson, eds., *Beyond the White Marble Steps: A Look at Baltimore Neighborhoods* (Baltimore: Citizens Planning and Housing Commission, 1979); Linda G. Rich, Joan Clark Netherwood, and Elinor B. Cahn, *Neighborhood, A State of Mind: Photographs and Interviews from the East Baltimore Documentary Photography Project* (Baltimore: Johns Hopkins Univ. Press, 1981); Norman G. Rukert, *The Fells Point Story* (Baltimore: Bodine and Associates, Inc., 1976); and Gilbert Sandler, *The Neighborhood: The Story of Baltimore's Little Italy* (Baltimore: Bodine and Associates, Inc., 1974).

21. Brian Fagan, *Time Detectives: How Archeologists Use Technology to Recapture the Past* (New York: Simon and Schuster, 1995), 244.

8

Societal Change on the Household Level: A Quantitative Spatial Analysis of the Green Family Print Shop Site

Laura June Galke

The household is recognized as one of the basic organizing units of a culture.[1] Activities which occur at the household level provide information about the way in which a particular society is organized, and how it changes through time. Socially acceptable disposal practices, spatial organization, and activities are negotiated daily by site inhabitants and may be reflected in the archaeological record. Using historical documents and archaeologically-recovered materials, I consider how broad cultural changes in society are reflected and imposed at the household level at one colonial household.

Technological changes in production and modernization resulted in societal changes which are detectable at the household level.[2] Archaeologically recoverable evidence will be sought and examined for its potential to document the transformation from a mercantile economy to an industrial economy at the Green family print shop site (18AP29) (map 8.1). Whallon's unconstrained clustering technique using pure locational clustering is applied to select eighteenth- and nineteenth-century strata from the Green family print shop.[3]

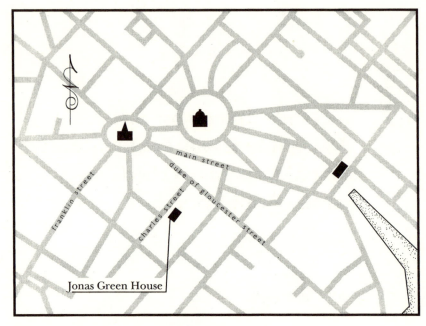

Map 8.1. The Jonas Green Site, Annapolis.

The Green Family Household

The socioeconomic relationship between the members of the Green family and the activities in which they engaged changed dramatically in response to factors within the wider socioeconomic environment.[4] This transformation in turn affected the way in which the Greens spatially organized their domestic and craft activities. During the eighteenth century, craft and domestic activities occurred at the Green family house and yard, while in the nineteenth century their craft, a print shop, was moved to another location within the city, separating the craft shop from the domestic household (map 8.2). This intrasite analysis is an attempt to discover activity areas which reflect a gradual, eighteenth-century separation between craft activity areas and domestic activity areas.

The Greens first came to Annapolis in 1738. Jonas Green, the third generation of Green family printers in America, moved to the state capital in response to a request for a state printer.[5] The *Maryland Gazette,* a weekly newspaper, was being printed at their home on Charles Street by

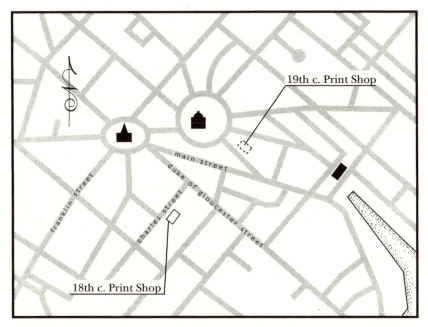

Map 8.2. The eighteenth- and nineteenth-century Green family print shops, Annapolis.

1745. Their home also served as the post office, as was often the case at printing houses during this time.[6]

During the middle of the eighteenth century, the Green family household was similar to many households of its time, in that it was the locus of both craft and domestic life; i.e., it was both a home and the location of the family's print shop.[7] The Green family print shop was composed of Jonas and Anne Catharine Green, their fourteen children, their slaves, employees, and apprentices. The Green family and their employees at the print shop all shared the same household and yard space. This living arrangement was normal for the period, in which the master craftsman was expected to provide housing for his employees.[8]

Frederick Green, son of Anne Catharine and Jonas, moved the print shop and post office to Francis Street in 1786 (map 8.2). This move created a physical break between the activities of craft and home.[9] This was a trend of the time, part of the shift toward industrial capitalism in which the relationship between employer and employee became characterized by contractual obligations, not familial responsibilities.

Investigating the Green Family Print Shop Site

The artifact assemblage at the Green family print shop has long since left its systemic context. Through investigations of the artifact deposits, a reasonable inference can be made regarding the processes responsible for patterning within the archaeological context. The archaeological record is not a static representation of the deposits from past behavior, but rather a result of formation processes upon those deposits. Formation processes not only cause deposits and their associated artifacts to deteriorate, but are also capable of creating patterning of their own, unrelated to the original human behaviors that deposited artifacts.[10]

The objective of any analysis of the assemblage at the Green family print shop is to discriminate between the cultural and natural formation processes which are responsible for the artifact patterns observed. I am assuming that noncultural formation processes acted equally on all the deposits within a given stratum.

The nineteenth-century strata (strata 5 and 4) were affected by two cultural formation processes: refuse removal and gardening. Refuse removal was a significant formation process in the nineteenth century. At this time, especially in cities, refuse management was an important issue for concerned social reformers. The removal of refuse from the site affects the amount and kind of artifacts found at many historic sites in the United States. Late-twentieth-century gardening at the site appears to have compromised the vertical integrity of the nineteenth-century deposits. This will be discussed in more detail later.

"Activity area" refers to an area in space which served a specific, single function. Such areas often have been assumed to be associated with a specific gender, though this assumption has been challenged by a number of feminist critiques.[11] Activity areas are identified by a concentration of functionally related or activity-related artifacts which occur in discrete locations. Because activity areas represent locations of discrete or specific use created by a site's inhabitants, they provide information concerning how activities were organized and how these activities changed over time. The duration of the activities, and the number of people who participate in them, affect the visibility of the activities archaeologically.

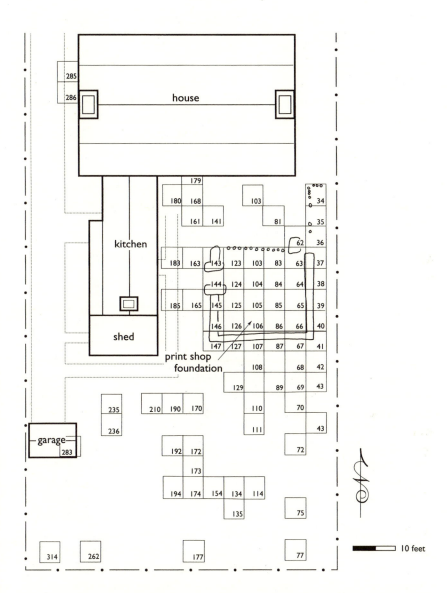

Fig. 8.1. Green family print shop with excavated units labeled. Except for the print shop and associated stone piers, these structures are extant. Adapted from Barbara J. Little, *Ideology and Media: Historical Archaeology of Printing in Eighteenth-Century Annapolis* (1987).

Data Recovery at the Green Family Print Shop Site

The Green family print shop was excavated during the summers of 1983 through 1986 by Archaeology in Annapolis. A 5-by-5-foot excavation grid was established over the site (fig. 8.1). Controlled excavation, via trowel and shovel, was guided by natural stratigraphy. Out of 234 possible units, 36, or 15 percent, were excavated to subsoil. An additional 20 units were excavated partially, but did not reach subsoil. The field-recovery strategy was judgmental, with excavations focusing on the print shop once its foundations were uncovered.[12]

Excavated soil layers were divided into analytical units designated as strata. Ten major strata were identified ranging in age from the first quarter of the eighteenth century through the twentieth century. In this chapter, select strata are analyzed, dating from the second quarter of the eighteenth century (stratum 8) to the second quarter of the nineteenth century (stratum 4).

Artifact classes were chosen which reflect domestic and craft activities. Domestic artifacts were diverse at the Green family print shop. Among the artifacts chosen for analysis were ceramics, which were divided into utilitarian wares (coarse earthenwares and stonewares), refined ceramics (refined earthenwares and stonewares), and porcelain. Glass was separated into container glass (e.g., bottles) and tableware (e.g., wine glasses and tumblers). Faunal remains were included in the analysis due both to their prevalence at this site and their use in determining refuse areas. It is assumed that areas high in faunal material will represent refuse disposal. Tobacco pipes were selected as a measure of personal recreation, but they occur in such small quantities at this site that their presence made little impact on the cluster compositions or subsequent interpretations. Architectural material was excluded from analysis, as were items such as buttons and nails. These items were not considered diagnostic toward illustrating specific domestic- or craft-use areas.

Printer's type was chosen for its obvious utility in identifying craft activity areas due its restricted and functionally specific characteristic. It enters the archaeological record through loss or discard. Craft activity areas will be identified by the presence of large amounts of printer's type. It is not expected that craft activity areas will be composed exclusively of printer's type; doubtless, other materials are associated with printing activities, including evidence for eating, drinking, or smoking. In general, areas with high printer's type content are assumed to reflect printing activities, or printing disposal activities. The identification of an area as specifically for craft use was distinguished by both the presence of large amounts of printer's type and the absence, or paucity of, domestic activity artifacts.

Unconstrained Clustering and Analysis of the Data Set

A number of intrasite analyses focusing on the delineation of activity areas have been conducted during the past decade in Maryland.[13] These and other studies show that most artifacts in use at colonial era sites end up as dispersed surface deposits, or sheet refuse. Often, trash seems to have been merely tossed out the door.[14] An effective visual interpretation of artifact patterning at the seventeenth-century Van Sweringen site revealed preserved middens despite plow zone disturbance.[15] Using the computer program SYMAP, artifact distributions at this site were plotted. The patterns found exhibited a proclivity for inhabitants to dispose of refuse in public areas such as roads. A more recent application using SYMAP is offered by Henry Miller.[16] In this study, Miller used functional artifact classes to interpret activity areas by visually analyzing patterns. His analysis demonstrated spatial segregation of activities and the presence of special-purpose areas at a seventeenth-century dwelling.

These visual examinations are an important initial step in examining artifact patterning within a site, even when using unconstrained clustering. Statistical approaches such as unconstrained clustering strengthen interpretations by recognizing relationships among artifact classes which are not readily discernible through a visual analysis alone. Developed by Robert Whallon, unconstrained clustering is a flexible procedure and can be applied to both point provenience and grid count data, an advantage lacking in many analytical techniques.[17] It does not require 100 percent excavation of a site, but the larger a sample of the site retrieved the more accurately it will reflect past activities.

Whallon's development of unconstrained clustering was inspired in part by his dissatisfaction with the ability of existing intrasite spatial techniques to describe archaeological distributions in culturally meaningful terms. Whallon noted that most spatial analysis techniques describe an artifact distribution's size, shape, density, composition, and patterns of association as factors held constant. However, ethnoarchaeological observations demonstrate that these factors are variable.

Ethnoarchaeological studies have shown that "particular constellations of items (tools, raw materials, and by-products) in various given proportions seem to be characteristic of particular activities."[18] However, some activities may be dominated by a single artifact type. Ethnoarchaeological research shows that the relative quantities of artifact types within activity areas and across a site are relatively stable and seem to reflect activities more directly than absolute quantities.[19]

Unconstrained clustering is based upon categories, or groupings, of artifacts. Craft and domestic artifact classes can therefore be analyzed as groups rather than as discrete artifact types. The percentages of these artifact groupings within specific excavation (grid) units are utilized in my analysis. In this application, counts of each artifact class (printer's type, container glass, bone, etc.) were calculated for each grid unit within a stratum. These counts were then converted to percentages. Unlike raw count data, the percentages of artifact classes are not strongly influenced by the size or density of the individual artifacts themselves.[20] One serious problem with the use of percentage data in a grid-based analysis such as this one is the effect of low artifact densities. A wide variety of artifact classes combined with a low artifact density compounds the problem. A simple solution to this problem is to eliminate from analysis any units with a grid count below a certain quantity. For the Green family print shop data, a minimum grid count of ten items was chosen; therefore, no single artifact can count for more than 10 percent of the assemblage.

Summary of Unconstrained Analysis

Unconstrained clustering analysis was applied to each stratum under investigation (strata 8, 7, 6, 5, and 4). First, the absolute density of each class of artifact for each grid unit was calculated. These absolute densities were converted into relative densities. The resulting relative densities were used to assign the grid unit to a particular cluster using the pure locational clustering technique.[21]

Through pure locational clustering, all the grid units are initially assigned to a single cluster. Then, those units farthest from the center of this cluster are split off to form new clusters. The new clusters are formed from units which are closer to the new cluster's center than to the old cluster's center. This processes continues until the maximum number of clusters is reached. In this analysis, a ten cluster level was chosen *a priori* and is felt to represent the maximum culturally meaningful number of clusters which could exist for a particular stratum at a given time.

Once the cluster analysis is complete, the clusters are plotted on a grid map of the site, with the assigned cluster number printed within each contributing grid unit. The clusters are not necessarily spatially contiguous, but are formed from units possessing the same relative densities and classes of artifacts, therefore representing similar activities occurring within these various portions of the site.

The results of the pure locational clustering analysis indicated which of the ten cluster levels were significantly clustered. A stratum can have more than one significant cluster level; that is, a stratum may exhibit statistically significant clustering at three clusters and five clusters. However, space limitations prevent full analysis of all significant cluster levels within each stratum. Instead, one cluster level was chosen for discussion for each stratum analyzed.[22]

Stratum 8 (ca. 1725–49) dates to a period when the Green family household served as the center for craft and domestic activities. Stratum 8 exhibited distinct domestic and craft activity areas as demonstrated at the four cluster level of analysis (fig. 8.2, table 8.1). While the material present within this stratum is scant, unconstrained clustering analysis of the data does reflect a dual craft and domestic use. Clusters 1–3 represent secondary deposits of refuse disposal, while cluster 4 is a craft activity area.

Cluster 1 occurs to the south of the print shop and represents craft-related refuse disposal (fig. 8.2). It is dominated by printer's type, a craft artifact, which accounts for 48.5 percent of the cluster (table 8.1). Also present in significant percentages are refuse disposal indicators such as faunal remains (21.4 percent) and refined ceramics (15.2 percent).

Cluster 2, located along the southern edge of the print shop, gives evidence of domestic refuse disposal (fig. 8.2). It is composed almost entirely of container glass, at 92.9 percent, followed by a single fragment of refined ceramics, at 7.1 percent (table 8.1). These materials are potentially dangerous and represent a high hindrance potential.[23] The location of these artifacts indicates that they were discarded in an area out of foot traffic.

Cluster 3, occurring in 2 units to the east and north of the print shop is composed of 54.6 percent bone, 33.8 percent refined ceramics, and 10.4 percent porcelain (table 8.1). Of all the refuse disposal clusters described above, cluster 3 seems to best represent general domestic refuse disposal, because it is dominated by faunal remains and significant amounts of refined

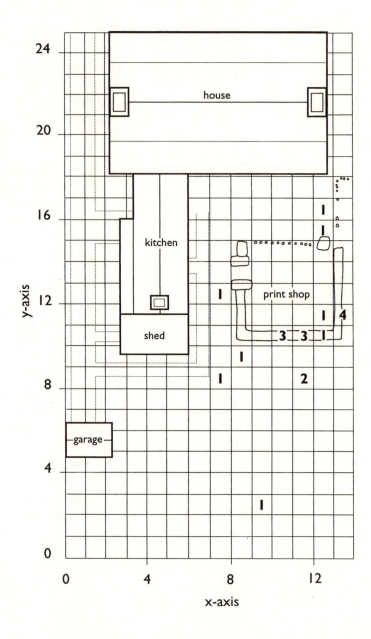

Fig. 8.2. Four cluster level for Stratum 8 of the Green family print shop site.

Table 8.1
Stratum 8 (ca. 1725–1749), Four Cluster Level

| Clus | No. | Ceramics | | | | % Bone | % Type | Glass | |
		% Util	% Ref.	% Porc.	% Pipe			% Cont.	% Table
1	2	0.0	15.2	3.6	4.3	21.4	48.5	6.3	0.8
2	1	0.0	7.1	0.0	0.0	0.0	0.0	92.9	0.0
3	2	0.0	33.8	10.4	0.0	54.6	0.0	0.0	1.2
4	2	3.0	3.2	2.6	0.4	3.2	84.7	2.8	0.0

ceramics and porcelain. With so few excavation units containing preserved deposits dating to this time period, it is not possible to designate this cluster as an example of a midden or as sheet refuse.

Cluster 4 is located to the south of the print shop and appears to represent a craft activity area, since it is composed overwhelmingly of printer's type (84.7 percent), followed by small percentages of refined ceramics (3.2 percent) and faunal remains (3.2 percent) (fig. 8.2, table 8.1). This area previously has been interpreted as a craft refuse area for the print shop.[24] While this cluster may not represent a primary deposit, "it is sometimes helpful to broaden the concept of primary refuse to include instances where artifacts are discarded at activity-related locations but not locations of use. Such cases fall within the spirit of . . . primary refuse."[25] Cluster 4 fits well with this notion of primary refuse. Cluster 4 has the density of material and the percentage of printer's type which demonstrates that this is a craft activity area.

Clusters 1, 2, and 4 are associated spatially and behaviorally. Clusters 1 and 2 apparently reflect food-consumption refuse areas which complemented the craft activities (cluster 4) occurring along the south side of the print shop. The presence of 21 percent faunal remains in cluster 1 and 93 percent container glass in cluster 2 suggest that food and beverage consumption occurred alongside composing activities during the early to mid-eighteenth century.

During the third quarter of the eighteenth century (stratum 7, ca. 1750–74), craft and domestic pursuits continued to occupy the Green family. Only five units contained material dating to this period. Analysis indicates that significant clustering is not present within this stratum. Unconstrained cluster analysis was not applied to this stratum of unclustered material.

The last quarter of the eighteenth century (stratum 6, ca. 1775–99) witnessed several important events at the site. In 1780 the backyard print shop burned to the ground. Between 1780 and 1786 it is not clear whether the print shop was reconstructed, but the margin of the *Maryland Gazette* stated that printing continued at Charles Street. Frederick Green moved the print shop to Francis Street in 1786.[26]

The domestic and craft activities of Stratum 6 were best represented at the three cluster level (fig. 8.3, table 8.2). Clusters 1 and 2 indicate domestic refuse disposal, with cluster 1 composed of faunal remains and container glass (46.81 percent and 25.08 percent, respectively) and cluster 2 composed entirely of refined ceramics (table 8.2). The dispersal of cluster 1 and its composition is characteristic of a sheet midden. The location of cluster 2 is more discrete, and its composition suggests a midden deposit or perhaps even a potbreak.

Cluster 3 represents a craft activity area, evident by the presence of 64.8 percent printer's type followed by a smaller amount of bone, at 11.6 percent (table 8.2). This cluster reveals that craft activities, perhaps composition, continued to occur along the south edge of the print shop (fig. 8.3). An additional area of craft activity or craft activity disposal is approximately 30 feet to the south of the print shop, within adjacent units 134 and 135 (fig. 8.3). Documentary evidence indicates that printing continued to occur at this site even after the print shop burned in 1780, but the condition of the print shop itself is unclear. The presence of faunal materials within cluster 3 may indicate that food consumption occurred alongside craft production. It may also indicate that this is a refuse area where both craft and domestic items were disposed.

Stratum 5 (ca. 1800–1824) was from a period in which the location of the print shop was moved from the backyard at Charles Street to another location in the city, on Francis Street. The three cluster level best illustrates the activities occurring at this time (fig. 8.4). At this level, one cluster represents

Table 8.2
Stratum 6 (ca. 1775–1799), Three Cluster Level

Clus	No.	Ceramics				% Bone	% Type	Glass	
		% Util	% Ref.	% Porc.	% Pipe			% Cont.	% Table
1	8	2.7	16.5	2.3	3.6	46.8	1.6	25.1	1.5
2	2	0.0	100.0	0.0	0.0	0.0	0.0	0.0	0.0
3	6	2.9	6.8	2.5	2.1	11.6	64.8	9.4	0.0

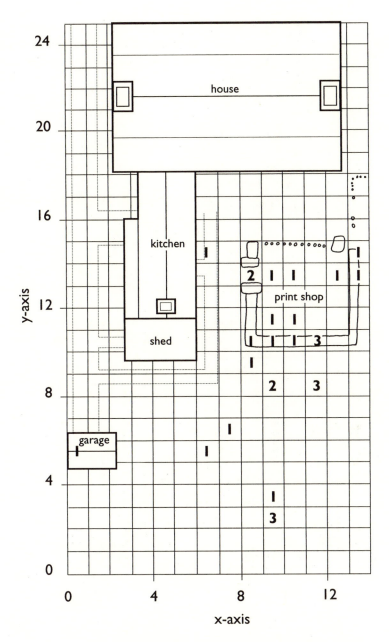

Fig. 8.3. Three cluster level for Stratum 6 of the Green family print shop site.

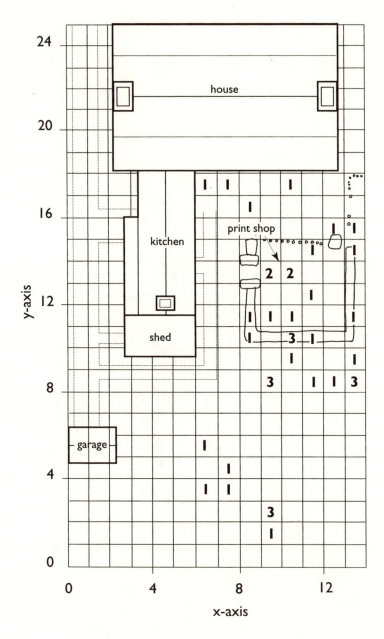

Fig. 8.4. Three cluster level for Stratum 5 of the Green family print shop site.

craft activities (cluster 1) and two clusters reflect domestic activities (clusters 2 and 3). Cluster 1 is a craft activity area, composed of 53.5 percent printer's type (table 8.3). This cluster is associated with the exterior, south side of the former print shop, an area which has proven in previous strata to be related to craft activities. However, cluster 1 is more scattered than the spatially discrete craft activity areas represented by clusters 1 and 4 of stratum 8 (fig. 8.2) and by cluster 3 of stratum 6 (fig. 8.3).

Two possibilities exist which would account for the presence of this craft activity during a time when craft activities should no longer be a part of the occupations at this site. First, and most likely, subsequent formation processes such as twentieth-century gardening have affected the archaeological record, bringing material from eighteenth-century, craft-activity deposits toward the surface. This also would help account for the horizontal dispersion of this cluster, which is not as spatially discrete as previous craft activity areas in this portion of the site have been. Another explanation is that the documentary record is incomplete, and that some printing activity continued at the site during the nineteenth century.

Cluster 2 is a domestic refuse deposit which, while spatially dispersed, tends to occur in potentially low foot traffic areas. Units which make up cluster 2 occur within the defunct print shop, along the northeast exterior corner of the defunct print shop, and against the southern wall of the house. The composition of cluster 2, 56.5 percent refined ceramics followed by 16.2 percent container glass, indicates a high hindrance potential deposit, as broken ceramics and glass produce sharp edges.[27] Cluster 2 seems to represent a deliberate propensity to dispose of potentially dangerous material in areas subjected to less foot traffic.

Cluster 3 is widely dispersed. Its composition is dominated by faunal material (41.2 percent), refined ceramics (19.9 percent), and container

Table 8.3

Stratum 5 (ca. 1800–1824), Three Cluster Level

Clus	No.	% Util	Ceramics			% Bone	% Type	Glass	
			% Ref.	% Porc.	% Pipe			% Cont.	% Table
1	5	4.1	11.7	1.8	1.6	16.5	53.5	9.7	1.0
2	7	5.1	56.5	2.2	2.5	10.1	4.0	16.2	3.4
3	15	4.1	19.9	2.9	3.3	41.2	7.9	18.4	2.4

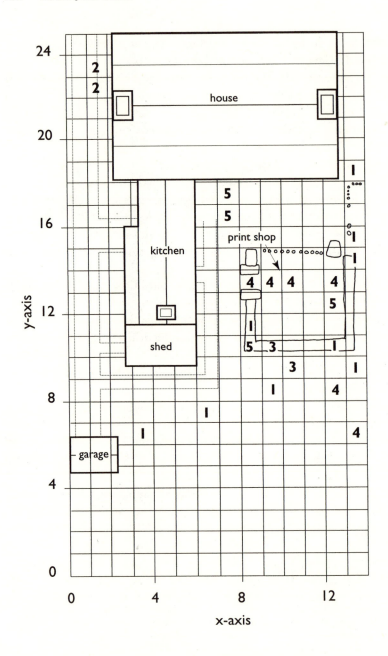

Fig. 8.5. Five cluster level for Stratum 4 of the Green family print shop site.

Table 8.4

Stratum 4 (ca. 1825–1849), Five Cluster Level

Clus	No.	Ceramics				% Bone	% Type	Glass	
		% Util	% Ref.	% Porc.	% Pipe			% Cont.	% Table
1	9	15.4	26.0	2.7	1.0	21.9	12.4	16.6	3.8
2	2	1.9	0.0	8.8	1.9	12.7	0.0	74.6	0.0
3	2	1.1	17.7	0.0	0.0	9.0	65.4	6.7	0.0
4	6	3.7	12.2	2.7	0.4	61.6	6.6	12.0	0.8
5	4	1.6	69.6	9.5	0.8	3.7	3.1	5.1	6.6

glass (18.4 percent), all indicative of domestic refuse. This wide dispersal suggests that the deposit represents a sheet midden.

Dating to the early to mid-nineteenth century, stratum 4 (ca. 1825–49) demonstrates the continuing domestic-oriented use of the yard. Financial difficulties saw the demise of the *Maryland Gazette* in 1839.[28] However, at the five cluster level, evidence for craft activities continues to be seen (cluster 3). Cluster 3 is found within two excavations units, both associated with the south wall of the print shop (fig. 8.5) and contains 65.4 percent printer's type and 17.7 percent refined ceramics (table 8.4). As with stratum 5, twentieth-century gardening is likely responsible for bringing eighteenth-century craft activity deposits into stratum 4.

The artifacts which compose clusters 1 and 5 and the spatial dispersion of these clusters together suggest that both clusters represent sheet refuse. Cluster 1 is composed of comparable amounts of refined ceramics (26.0 percent) and faunal material (21.9 percent). Cluster 5 is dominated by reined ceramics (69.9 percent) and porcelain (9.5 percent).

A discrete, high hindrance deposit (cluster 2) dominated by container glass occurs along the northwestern edge of the domestic structure. Cluster 4 represents a midden deposit and demonstrates the use of the defunct print shop as a place for waste disposal.[29] The assemblage of cluster 4 is dominated by faunal material (61.6 percent), followed by refined ceramics (12.2 percent) and container glass (12.0 percent).

• • •

Generations of the Green family lived and worked at their home on Charles Street in Annapolis. This continuity of family and craft provided an opportunity to study the effects of the Industrial Revolution with factors such as site function and ethnicity held constant. For most of the eighteenth century, the household and print shop were spatially and conceptually close. However, in 1786 the print shop was moved to a different location from the domestic unit—a physical statement reflecting the social values of the time.

Whallon's unconstrained clustering technique delineated distinct domestic and craft clusters related to the changing use of the Green family print shop over time. The analysis was particularly successful in identifying activity areas related to domestic refuse disposal activities. In general, two distinct types of domestic refuse disposal were clearly identified by this analysis. The first type was sheet refuse or yard scatter characterized by spatially scattered units composed of diverse domestic artifacts (e.g., cluster 1, stratum 6). Evidence for this behavior was found within each stratum. The second type of domestic refuse management consisted of conscious, discrete episodes of disposal or middens (e.g., cluster 2, stratum 6). This was evidenced by discrete areas of diverse and dense material, usually dominated by faunal remains and/or refined ceramics. This dichotomy of domestic disposal (sheet refuse and middens) is best represented by the three cluster configuration of stratum 6 (ca. 1775–99).

Domestic activities were distinct and separate from craft activities throughout the eighteenth and nineteenth centuries. Once the print shop was relocated, the number of clusters which contain printer's type, and the amount of printer's type within the clusters, decrease. This reflected the changing society of which the Green family was a part, in which the corporate, public nature of the household was becoming increasingly private.[30] Eventually, these domestic and craft activities became completely segmented as the role of employee and employer under capitalism was defined. By the mid-nineteenth century, craft activities took place in a different location from the domestic unit altogether, as the print shop was located in a different portion of the city. This trend, observed on the household level, is indicative of what was occurring on the societal level.

Evidence for craft activities, defined by high concentrations of printer's type, were present in the eighteenth-century strata (strata 8, 7, and 6). Printer's type continues to be present within the nineteenth-century strata (strata 5, 4, and 3). The effects of twentieth-century gardening provides a plausible reason for the continuing presence of printer's type during the nineteenth century. A characteristic of gardening seems to be the vertical displacement of material and, to a lesser extent, the lateral movement of material.

Other than refuse disposal, no evidence for specific domestic activities was identified by this analysis. I conclude from this that many domestic activities occurred within the household, rather than in the backyard.

Two kinds of craft activity areas were visible, including craft secondary refuse areas and craft primary refuse areas. These are distinguished from one another by the varying percentages of material present. A cluster dominated by printer's type but with substantial percentages of domestic artifacts was deemed a craft secondary refuse area (e.g., cluster 1, stratum 8), while those clusters which contained markedly greater concentrations of printers' type with little to no other kinds of domestic refuse were deemed primary craft activity areas (e.g., cluster 4, stratum 8).

While it is clear that the analysis identified two distinct kinds of craft activity, an alternative interpretation of these craft refuse areas is possible. It could be equally well argued that clusters with high percentages of printer's type and substantial percentages of domestic artifacts are not secondary refuse areas, but are actually the craft activity areas. The clusters dominated by printer's type with little or no domestic material may represent secondary deposits of craft refuse disposal.

The transformation at the Green family print shop is of greater significance than simply the separation of a business from the household's backyard. Instead, it is indicative of a transformation in social attitude which occurred on a greater regional scale as well. This change indicates that the concept of the appropriate use of the household changed. Changes in the domestic realm throughout the eighteenth and nineteenth centuries in America are the result of economic variables and can be traced to a shift from an agrarian, household-centered society to an industrial, factory-based society.[31]

Notes

1. James Deetz, "Households: A Structural Key to Archaeological Explanation," *American Behavioral Scientist* 25 (6) (1982): 717–24. See also Susan Kent, *Analyzing Activity Areas* (Albuquerque: Univ. of New Mexico Press, 1984).
2. Mary C. Beaudry, "Archaeology and the Historical Household," *Man in the Northeast* 28 (1984): 27–38; Beaudry, "The Archaeology of Historical Land Use in Massachusetts," *Historical Archaeology* 20 (2) (1986): 38–46. See also James Deetz, *In Small Things Forgotten: The Archaeology of Early American Life* (Garden City, N.Y.: Anchor Books, 1977); and Henry Glassie, *Folk Housing in Middle Virginia* (Knoxville: Univ. of Tennessee Press, 1975).

3. Robert Whallon, "Unconstrained Clustering for the Analysis of Spatial Distributions in Archaeology," in *Intrasite Spatial Analysis in Archaeology,* ed. Harold Hietala (Cambridge: Cambridge Univ. Press, 1984): 242–77; and Keith Kintigh and A. Ammerman, "Heuristic Approaches to Spatial Analysis in Archaeology," *American Antiquity* 47 (1) (1982): 31–63. For further details, see Laura J. Galke, *A Quantitative Analysis of the Green Family Print Shop Site in Annapolis, Maryland* (Ann Arbor, Mich.: Univ. Microfilms International, 1995).

4. Kent, "A Cross-Cultural Study of Segmentation, Architecture, and the Use of Space," in *Domestic Architecture and the Use of Space: An Interdisciplinary Cross-Cultural Study,* ed. Susan Kent (Cambridge: Cambridge Univ. Press, 1990), 127; Stephen Mrozowski, "Exploring New England's Evolving Urban Landscape," in *Living in Cities: Current Research in Urban Archaeology,* ed. Edward Staski (Historical Archaeology Special Publication No. 5, 1987), 7; Dana Beth Oswald, "The Organization of Space in Residential Buildings: A Cross-Cultural Perspective," in *Method and Theory for Activity Area Research: An Ethnoarchaeological Approach,* ed. Susan Kent (New York: Columbia Univ. Press, 1987), 300; and Edward Shorter, *Work and Community in the West* (New York: Harper and Row, 1973), 2.

5. Barbara Little, *Ideology and Media: Historical Archaeology of Printing in Eighteenth-Century Annapolis, Maryland* (Ann Arbor, Mich.: Univ. Microfilms International, 1987), 120.

6. L. Febvre and H. Martin, *The Coming of the Book: The Impact of Printing 1450–1800* (London: Atlantic Highlands Humanities Press, 1976), 210; Little, *Ideology and Media,* 170.

7. Little, *Ideology and Media,* 125–28.

8. Fernand Braudel, *The Structures of Everyday Life: Civilization and Capitalism 15th–18th Century, Vol. I* (New York: Harper and Row, 1979); Stephen Innes, ed., *Work and Labor in Early America* (Chapel Hill: Univ. of North Carolina Press, 1988), 155; and W. J. Rorabaugh, *The Craft Apprentice: From Franklin to the Machine Age in America* (New York: Oxford Univ. Press, 1986), 7.

9. Little, *Ideology and Media,* 171.

10. Michael B. Schiffer, *Formation Processes of the Archaeological Record* (Albuquerque: Univ. of New Mexico Press, 1987), 4, 7; Lewis Binford, "Dimensional Analysis of Behavior and Site Structure: Learning from an Eskimo Hunting Stand," *American Antiquity* 43 (3) (1978): 330–61; Schiffer, *Behavioral Archeology* (New York: Academic Press, 1976); Richard Wilke and Schiffer, "The Archaeology of Vacant Lots in Tucson, Arizona," *American Antiquity* 44 (3) (1979): 530–36; and W. Raymond Wood and Donald L. Johnson, "A Survey of Disturbance Processes in Archaeological Site Formation," in *Advances in Archaeological Method and Theory, Vol. 1,* ed. Michael B. Schiffer (New York: Academic Press, 1978): 315–81.

11. Kent, *Analyzing Activity Areas,* 2, 8.

12. Little, *Ideology and Media,* 187–88.

13. Julia A. King, "A Comparative Midden Analysis of a Household and Inn in St. Mary's City, Maryland," *Historical Archaeology* 22 (2) (1988): 17–39; King, *An*

Intrasite Spatial Analysis of the Van Sweringen Site, St. Mary's City, Maryland (Ann Arbor, Mich.: Univ. Microfilms International, 1990); King and Henry M. Miller, "The View from the Midden: An Analysis of Midden Distribution and Composition at the Van Sweringen Site, St. Mary's City, Maryland," *Historical Archaeology* 21 (2) (1987): 37–59; Miller, *Discovering Maryland's First City: A Summary Report on the 1981–1984 Archaeological Excavations in St. Mary's City, Maryland* (St. Mary's City, Md.: St. Mary's City Commission, 1986); and Miller, "The Country's House Site: An Archaeological Study of a Seventeenth-Century Landscape," in *Historical Archaeology of the Chesapeake*, ed. Paul A. Shackel and Barbara J. Little (Washington, D.C.: Smithsonian Institution Press, 1994).

14. King and Miller, "The View from the Midden"; and Miller, *Discovering Maryland's First City.*
15. King and Miller, "The View from the Midden," 52.
16. Miller, "The Country's House Site."
17. Whallon, "Unconstrained Clustering," 243–45.
18. Ibid., 246.
19. Ibid.
20. Kintigh, "Intrasite Spatial Analysis: A Commentary on Major Methods," in Mathematics and Information Science in Archaeology: A Flexible Framework, issue ed. A. Voorrips, *Studies in Modern Archaeology* (Bonn: Holos) 3 (1990): 165–200.
21. Ibid., 184–90.
22. For discussion of all significant clusters, see Galke, *A Quantitative Analysis.*
23. B. Hayden and A. Cannon, "Where the Garbage Goes: Refuse Disposal in the Mayan Highlands," *Journal of Anthropological Archaeology* 2 (1983): 117–63.
24. Mark P. Leone and Barbara J. Little, "Seeds of Sedition," *Archaeology* 43 (3) (1990): 36–40.
25. Schiffer, *Formation Processes*, 58–59.
26. Little, *Ideology and Media*, 181, 186, 159.
27. Hayden and Cannon, "Where the Garbage Goes," 120.
28. Little, *Ideology and Media*, 169.
29. Ibid., 186.
30. Deetz, "Households"; and Deetz, *In Small Things Forgotten.*
31. Mary C. Beaudry, "The Lowell Boott Mills Complex and its Housing: Material Expressions of Corporate Ideology," *Historical Archaeology* 23 (1) (1989): 19–32; P. Faler, *Mechanics and Manufacture in the Early Industrial Revolution: Lynn, Massachusetts, 1780–1860* (Albany: State Univ. of New York Press, 1981); Jack Goody, "The Evolution of the Family," in *Household and Family in Past Time*, ed. P. Laslett and R. Wall (London: Cambridge Univ. Press, 1972), 103–24; Innes, *Work and Labor*; Kent, *A Cross–Cultural Study*; and W. Ogburn and M. F. Nimkoff, *Technology and the Changing Family* (Boston: Houghton Mifflin Company, 1955).

9 "The Best There Is of Us": Ceramics and Status in African American Annapolis

Mark S. Warner

One of the important issues which is often overlooked or muted in the archaeologies of African America is the internal complexities of the groups who are commonly described as the "African American Community." The apparent uniformity of a homogeneous African America highlights the problem (for some) of an unwillingness or an inability to recognize diversity among people of color. African America clearly is and has been as economically, culturally, and socially heterogeneous as all other social groups. Indeed, W. E. B. Du Bois commented on the range of African American diversity in 1908: "Few modern groups show a greater internal differentiation of social conditions than the Negro American, and the failure to realize this is the cause of much confusion. . . . The forward movement of a social group is not the compact march of an army, where the distance covered is practically the same for all, but is rather the straggling of a crowd, where some of whom hasten, some linger, some turn back; some reach far-off goals before others even start, and yet the crowd moves on."[1]

Over the last two decades historians have been quite active in exploring and ultimately confirming Du Bois's insight. A substantial amount of time and effort has been dedicated to exploring both the diversity and commonality of experiences among people of color. Unfortunately, archaeology has been substantially slower in following this trend. To be sure, a good deal of work has been done recently which problematizes issues of race, class, and ethnicity. However, a substantial amount of archaeological work continues to refer, however implicitly, to an undifferentiated African American community where comparisons of assemblages are made primarily on the basis of skin color rather than issues of geographic, temporal, or economic comparability. As a discipline it is imperative to address this dilemma. While historical archaeologists have explored the differing influences of Dutch, French, Jewish, Spanish, and English settlement in the Americas, many continue to overlook the heterogeneity of African America and freely compare artifact assemblages from sites which had nothing in common except the color of the skin of the people who occupied the site.[2]

Without question, this tendency toward homogenization of peoples is not just an issue in the explorations of African America. Archaeologists have commonly tended to lump geographically, temporally, or culturally diverse groups together for analysis. Comparisons between groups are certainly invaluable to archaeologists in understanding past lifeways (e.g., urban versus rural comparisons). However, comparisons become spurious when one does not recognize and attempt to limit the scope of the comparison. The point of this is that considerable attention *must* be given to recognizing the diversity and complexities of people's lives. This complexity has been faithfully documented in exploring the histories of Anglo America yet has been considerably less faithfully documented in the exploration of various minority groups.

This chapter presents a small example of the heterogeneity that historically has existed in African America. Specifically, I will explore how consumer choice in the acquisition and use of particular ceramic types was utilized by African American Annapolitans to delineate social and/or economic distinctions *within* African American Annapolis. By comparing ceramic and glass assemblages from two African American–occupied sites and a third white-occupied site, I hope to show how African Americans created and maintained social differences within African American Annapolis and simultaneously defined differences with white Annapolis.

The Sites

The materials analyzed in this essay were recovered from three sites in Annapolis. Two were occupied by African Americans and one by whites; all three sites are located within a few city blocks of each other. The white-occupied site was the Main Street site (18AP44), a single-family dwelling located on Main Street just off State Circle (map 9.1). The site was continuously occupied by white Annapolitans from the early eighteenth century until the twentieth century. The materials analyzed in this chapter were recovered from a privy dating from the late nineteenth to early twentieth century, when the property was owned and occupied by physician Frank Thompson and his family.[3]

The two African American–occupied sites to be discussed are Gott's Court (18AP52) and the Maynard-Burgess House (18AP64). Gott's Court was a series of twenty-five connected frame houses constructed in on a block interior off Church Circle between West and Northwest Streets (map 9.1). Throughout its existence as a residential area (from 1907 to the early

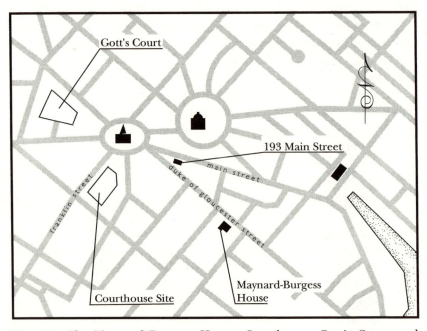

Map 9.1. The Maynard-Burgess House, Courthouse, Gott's Court, and Main Street excavations, Annapolis.

1950s), Gott's Court was owned by white Annapolitans and occupied by African American renters. The occupants of the court were primarily employed as laborers or in various service-related positions, such as laundresses, waiters, domestics, and porters. In 1910, for instance, the four most frequently reported occupations for court residents were laborer, laundress, cook, and houseworker. The materials recovered were from three and a half weeks of test excavations by Archaeology in Annapolis during the summer of 1989, prior to the construction of a parking garage which was completed in 1993.[4]

The third site, the Maynard-Burgess House (18AP64), was a single-family dwelling built by the free black household of John and Maria Maynard in the 1850s. The house was occupied continuously by the Maynards and their relatives the Burgesses until the early 1980s. The assemblage discussed here was recovered from a cellar with an external bulkhead entryway which was located near the home's central hearth. The feature measured roughly five by eight feet and was approximately three and a half feet deep. The date of the cellar's construction is uncertain, but it was filled after 1889. The feature's 1889 *terminus post quem* was taken from an 1889–1907 Bromo-Seltzer bottle recovered at the base of the feature.[5] The cellar apparently was filled with a mixture of coal ash and household debris over a brief period of time after 1889.[6]

Statistical Analysis

This assemblage analysis compares the percentages of specific artifact categories from each of the three sites. For instance, if wine bottles made up 35 percent of the Gott's Court glass assemblage, and 25 percent of the Main Street glass assemblage, is that difference meaningful? To compare the percentages of artifact types and the artifact classes, a Z-test of proportions at a 95 percent confidence interval was used to identify statistically meaningful similarities and differences.[7] This test allows comparison of the percentages between two categories to establish whether differences between percentages are statistically significant—i.e., that either there was no meaningful difference between the two categories, or, if there was, there was less than a 5 percent chance that the identified difference occurred simply through chance.

Only larger groupings of artifacts were compared because of the nature of the Z-test and the relatively small sample size of some of the materials recovered. Comparisons between artifact classes which accounted for less than 10 percent of the assemblage would not be particularly reliable. In all cases the percentages that were used for comparison were based on minimum vessel counts.

For the three bottle assemblages only two comparisons were performed because of the particularly small vessel assemblages recovered from Main Street and Gott's Court (tables 9.1, 9.2, 9.3). The two comparisons of bottle assemblages were made between the cumulative percentage of bottles containing alcohol and the largest single type of bottle recovered on all three sites, which was pharmaceutical bottles. In both cases no significant differences were identified between any of the three sites.

The similarity in the three glass assemblages is a distinct contrast from

Table 9.1

Bottle Glass Assemblage from Gott's Court

Bottle Type	Number	Percentage
Pharmaceutical	16	38.1
Liquor	4	9.52
Fresh	7	16.67
Beer	2	4.76
Food	2	4.76
Wine	7	16.67
Personal	3	7.14
Milk	1	2.38
Total	42	100.00

Table 9.2

Bottle Glass Assemblage from Maynard-Burgess, Feature 71

Bottle Type	Number	Percentage
Pharmaceutical	22	27.85
Liquor/Whisky	18	22.78
Fresh	6	7.59
Food	15	18.99
Wine/Champagne	5	6.33
Preserving Jars	2	2.53
Unknown Form	11	13.92
Total	79	99.99

Table 9.3

Bottle Glass Assemblage from Main Street, Feature 12

Bottle Type	Number	Percentage
Pharmaceutical	17	44.74
Liquor	1	2.63
Beer	3	7.89
Food	5	13.16
Soda	3	7.89
Unknown Alcohol	1	2.63
Ink	5	13.16
Personal	3	7.89
Total	38	99.99

the ceramic consumption tendencies which will be discussed later in this chapter. The uniformity of consumption in bottled goods and variation in ceramic consumption across class and racial lines highlights the fact that particular classes of goods will be responded to by people in differing ways. Instead of there being wholesale differences between assemblages, the ceramic and glass comparisons demonstrate very specific and distinct responses to particular goods. In this case, the bottle glass comparison demonstrates that the uniformity in consumption of bottled goods, particularly alcohol-related products, was consistent across a fairly broad spectrum of the Annapolis population.

For the first test of the total percentage of alcohol-containing bottles, the bottle types which were combined for the calculations included beer, wine, liquor, and pharmaceutical bottles. Pharmaceutical bottles were included in the calculations of alcohol-containing bottles because of the nebulous Victorian boundary between medication and intoxication. Although they were marketed as medicines, the alcohol content of pharmaceuticals generally ranged from 17 to 44 percent, a percentage of alcohol which is roughly equivalent to that of contemporary whiskeys.[8] As a result, pharmaceuticals frequently were purchased and consumed as much for their alcohol content as they were for their supposed healing properties.[9]

Bottles that contained some form of alcohol made up the vast majority of the bottles recovered from each of the three sites, much as they would on most contemporary sites. On Gott's Court, 69 percent of all the bottles recovered contained some form of alcohol; on Main Street the percentage was 58 percent; and at the Maynard-Burgess House it was 57 percent. Individually, pharmaceutical bottles were the most prevalent type identified in each of the three assemblages: the percentage of pharmaceuticals ranged from a high of 45 percent of the total bottle assemblage at Main Street to a low of 28 percent at the Maynard-Burgess House. In none of the cases were the differences in percentages found to be statistically significant. The relatively uniform consumption of alcohol between differing classes clearly contradicts the common misperception that the amount of alcohol consumed by minorities and/or the poor typically was far greater than the quantities consumed by other groups.[10]

While the bottle glass assemblages did not reveal any meaningful differences between the three assemblages, the comparisons of the ceramic assemblages revealed a notable contrast in the frequency of particular vessel forms. The specific contrast noted was the differing frequencies of teawares from each of the three sites (tables 9.4, 9.5, 9.6).[11] On the Main Street site, teawares comprised 47 of the 121 vessels in the assemblage, accounting for almost 39 percent of the total vessel assemblage. At the

Table 9.4
Ceramic Vessel Forms from Gott's Court

Vessel Form	Number	Percentage
Tea Pot	1	1.30
Cup	3	3.90
Saucer	6	7.79
Unknown Teaware	2	2.60
Bowl	1	1.30
Tankard	3	3.90
Bottle	2	2.60
Unknown Lid	1	1.30
Jar	5	6.49
Jar Lid	1	1.30
Holloware	14	18.18
Plate	14	18.18
Flatware	9	11.69
Chamber Pot	1	1.30
Handle	1	1.30
Flower Pot	6	7.79
Unknown	7	9.09
Total	77	100.01

Table 9.5
Ceramic Vessel Forms from Main Street

Vessel Form	Number	Percentage
Teaware	47	38.84
Plates	28	23.14
Bowls	7	5.79
Other	39	32.23
Total	121	100.00

Table 9.6
Ceramic Vessel Forms from the Maynard-Burgess House

Vessel Form	Number	Percentage
Cup	5	11.90
Tea Pot	1	2.38
Deep Saucer	5	11.90
Coffee Cup	1	2.38
Saucer	2	4.76
Possible Spout	1	2.38
Twiffler	2	4.76
Plate	6	14.29
Spittoon	1	2.38
Bowl	1	2.38
Holloware	8	19.05
Basin	1	2.38
Flower Pot	2	4.76
Crock	1	2.38
Match Holder	1	2.38
Flatware	2	4.76
Figurine	1	2.38
Egg Cup	1	2.38
Total	42	99.98

Maynard-Burgess House 15 of the 42 vessels were teawares, making up approximately 36 percent of the assemblage. In contrast, only 12 of the 77 vessels (16 percent) recovered from Gott's Court were teawares.

Before discussing the implications of these results I would like to interject a note of caution in reading the similarities and differences identified through the statistical evaluations of these three data sets. If a comparison is found to be statistically meaningful, it is not necessarily also substantively meaningful.[12] The benefit of using a test such as the Z-test of proportions is that it can help to identify similarities and differences in the assemblages. The test *is not* designed to identify an undifferentiated pattern of consumer behavior or provide any self-evident conclusions; rather, it simply highlights particular similarities and differences between assemblages. To explore some of the social implications that the data represents, I will examine how other sources of information on people of color in Annapolis can illuminate the social significance that the differences in teawares may have had for various segments of the city's population.

"The African American Community"

Despite a tendency of historical archaeology to assume that there exists a culturally homogenous and undifferentiated African American community, it is possible to explore diversity within that "community" through archaeology. The comparisons of the bottle and ceramic assemblages provide a point of departure to explore social differences among African American Annapolitans.

The similarity of the bottle assemblages between the three sites is suggestive of some degree of unanimity in the acquisition and consumption of bottled products. Given the similarities of the percentages of pharmaceutical bottles as the largest category of bottles and a similar uniformity in the consistently large volume of alcohol-containing bottles, it appears that these African Americans and whites shared similar alcohol-consumption habits.

Some scholars have noted that despite the pervasive influence of Jim Crow laws (which, among many other things, constrained access to some goods by African Americans), people of color were in selected aspects extremely dedicated consumers of particular commercial products. For instance, Paul Edwards's 1932 study of African American consumption found that, for the most part, people of color made very deliberate choices in the marketplace. In grocery purchases they expressed specific preferences for the selection of brand-name goods rather than discount or less well-known brands. In contrast, relatively few individuals placed emphasis on brand names in the selections that were made in their clothing purchases.[13]

More recently, Paul Mullins has explored this question in a discussion of the bottle assemblages which were recovered from several sites in

Annapolis, including the Maynard-Burgess House, Gott's Court, and Main Street. In his analysis of the bottles recovered from these three sites, he has argued that the bottles from Maynard-Burgess illustrate the consumer habits noted in Edwards's 1932 study, where national brands and canned goods are loyally purchased at the expense of local brands or the home preservation of goods.[14] However, he also argues that, while some patterns of brand-name consumption were apparently quite similar between whites and people of color, the strategies underlying them were potentially quite different. Mullins argues that the superficial similarity of consumer habits illustrated through material remains is substantially more complicated once one begins to examine those same objects within the broader contexts surrounding their acquisition.

The initial image of homogeneity of consumer habits is also contradicted by the statistical comparisons of ceramic remains from the three sites. As mentioned earlier, significantly lower percentages of teawares were recovered from Gott's Court than either the Maynard-Burgess or Main Street assemblages. I would like to suggest that the 24 and 27 percent differences in the frequency of teawares between Gott's Court and the Maynard-Burgess and Main Street sites illustrate social class differences between the occupants of Gott's Court and the other two sites in this comparison.

Tea, Coffee, and Society

The formal or semiformal act of serving tea (or more recently the serving of coffee) has a long history dating back to at least the mid-seventeenth century.[15] Initially, tea consumption was primarily a product of the European aristocracy, but in little more than a century it became an occasion for eating, drinking, and socializing across all economic groups. Further, the taking of tea came to have diverse social meanings ranging from that of a formal social event to an informal family gathering or meal.[16] Although the social importance of tea and coffee serving waned as the twentieth century progressed, there is no question that the significance of serving tea or coffee as a social function was an important part of Annapolis society and continued into at least the early twentieth century.

In Annapolis there is ample evidence that the formal serving of tea as a social event was a frequent occurrence among both white Annapolitans and people of color. Among the most unequivocal evidence is a photograph of a midshipmen's tea dated to about 1893 (fig. 9.1). In the African American press, such as Baltimore's *Afro-American Ledger* and Washington's *Bee,* there were repeated references to African American teas throughout the 1890s and early 1900s. Typical of the notes that would be found in the paper was the *Afro-American Ledger*'s January 6, 1906, notice that "Mrs. W. H. Bates gave a tea in honor of a number of her friends from Washington, D.C. It was quite a fine affair."[17] A year later the paper reported that "[t]he Martha Washington Tea Party will be celebrated Friday night, under the auspices of the A.C.E. League. Mr. J. W. Woodhouse of Baltimore will speak on that occasion."[18]

Much like the society columns in today's newspapers and magazines, the social events among African Americans in Annapolis were regularly reported in the *Afro-American Ledger* and the *Bee.* A detailed reading of those reports indicates that a very specific social circle was being reported on in the paper. Members of the Bates household, for instance, were regularly mentioned in the *Afro-American Ledger*'s columns on Annapolis's social news. Wiley

Fig. 9.1. Tea being served in the home of the Naval Academy superintendent, circa 1893. Courtesy of the Maryland State Archives, Merrick Collection, MSA SC 1477–4038.

Bates was clearly a leader of Annapolis's African American community, and contemporary accounts indicate that he was one of the wealthiest men in Annapolis. On January 9, 1897, Bates was the subject of a large front-page article in the *Bee* which read in part:

> Thirteen years ago the house of W. H. Bates started business in Annapolis, and has been largely successful in the venture, and the establishment takes rank among the leading grocery houses of the city. . . . Mr. Bates is able to offer advantages to his customers which can hardly be duplicated elsewhere in the city. His range embraces many of the leading families of the city and surrounding districts. Goods are delivered to any address in the city limits, and no effort is spared to meet the wants of his customers, who can always rely on receiving fair and honorable treatment at his house. Mr. Bates is an active, energetic and enterprising business man, who is achieving a well-merited success.[19]

In addition to his business success, Bates served as an alderman, a trustee of the black school, a loyal member of the church, and a Mason. Annapolis's African American high school eventually was named after him.[20] His activism within Annapolis was quite evident in the repeated references to him as a participant in a variety of events where he was variously identified as the host of events, the presenter of awards, and a principal speaker.[21] The centrality of his position was more dramatically presented in a 1910 editorial in the *Afro-American Ledger* that included him among the members of a suggested statewide committee to fight the erosion of African Americans' rights. The editorial noted that he and the other members of the proposed committee "represent the best there is of us, and if we cannot have confidence in them we cannot have confidence in anyone."[22]

Two conclusions can be drawn from the preceding discussion of Wiley Bates and the newspaper and photographic accounts of African American Annapolis. The first is that having a tea was clearly an important form of entertaining in portions of the African American community of Annapolis, and this form of entertainment continued well into the twentieth century. The second point which requires more amplification is that there clearly were distinct social circles within the city's African American population. Furthermore, it appears that individuals such as Wiley Bates and his wife, Annie, the Butler family, the Bishop family, and others repeatedly mentioned in newspapers' society columns constituted what could be considered a "black elite" within Annapolis.

On a nationwide level, the idea of class differences within African America has been explored in considerable detail in Willard Gatewood's recent study *Aristocrats of Color*.[23] Gatewood explores at length African American elites in several parts of the country, including Baltimore and Washington, examining how the so-called "upper ten" was perceived and defined by African America. Specifically, he addresses the various strategies employed by the elite to maintain themselves as members of a distinct African American "aristocracy" through, among many other things, upbringing, education, and parties, balls, and in-home receptions.[24] As one African American educator cited by Gatewood bluntly stated: "[t]here is no social equality among Negroes, notwithstanding the disposition of some whites to put all Negroes in one class. Culture, moral refinement and material possessions make a difference among colored people as they do among whites."[25]

While Gatewood's study is among the most recent—and certainly the most extensive—examinations of differentiation in African America, the idea of African American class distinctions was at least implicit in the works of many earlier scholars. For instance, a portion of Du Bois's study of African American families explored how class differences within African American communities are manifested in housing differences.[26] Distinctions within African America also were implied in Paul Edwards's study of African American consumers, and turn-of-the-century studies on various aspects of consumer habits examined numerous aspects of class difference.[27] Locally, class differences were discussed in Jeffrey Brackett's 1890 study of African Americans' social life in Maryland, where he commented that "there are small fashionable groups; [and] there are the large masses who are out of fashion."[28] In Annapolis specifically, Sallie Ives explored class differences in her examination of the shifting locations of African American residences in the city.[29] Ives concluded that there was a distinct element of social and economic stratification within the city's African American community, arguing that "[g]reater wealth accumulation, higher rates of residential persistence, and visible leadership activities characterized to some extent an upper class of blacks and distinguish them from a more frequently propertyless, mobile, and invisible majority composed of common laborers and domestic service personnel."[30]

Differences within the African American community in Annapolis also were noted in oral history interviews. In a series of interviews Hannah Jopling conducted with former residents of Gott's Court (see chapter 4, this volume), interviewees made clear that they had a very strong sense of community with other residents of "the Court." However, they also stressed in one particular interview that this sense of community on Gott's Court was based, in part, upon a perception that they were looked down upon by others:

Q: When you say you came from Gott's Court what was the reaction? What sort of reputation did Gott's Court have as a neighborhood or as a place to live?
A: When I go to different conventions, different meetings and people will say to me, where are you from? And I'll say "Gott's Court" they look at me like, you're from Gott's Court! People still look down on you when you say you are from Gott's Court until you let them know that you know . . . just as much, if not more about the world affairs as they know. . . .
Q: Do you think that Gotts Court was looked down upon at the time when you were in Gott's Court?
A: Oh yeah.
Q: Why was that?
A: . . . People thought that we was living in what people call slums. And . . . when we came out of Gott's Court we were all dressed, starched.[31]

Interviews conducted with residents of other parts of the city also expressed fairly specific senses of communities within a community.[32] For instance, interviews with former residents of the Franklin Street neighborhood recall regularly visiting with other residents on their street on both informal ventures—such as borrowing a cup of sugar—and on a somewhat more formal basis, such as when somebody would host a tea.[33]

There is no conclusive evidence to indicate specifically what the Maynards' social circles may have been, but there is considerable evidence which argues that the Maynards were part of a "middle class" of African Americans and were in the same social circle as people such as Wiley Bates. Ives has identified five longstanding African American neighborhoods in Annapolis, and one of these, the Market Street neighborhood, included the Maynard-Burgess House. In her brief discussion of the Market Street neighborhood, Ives notes that while it was one of the smaller neighborhoods it was also the location of some of the wealthier residents of color in Annapolis.[34]

A second point which argues that the Maynards were part of this group were the occasional references to household members participating in various social events that were reported in the *Afro-American Ledger*. One example is an account of an Annapolis dance which identified Louisa Maynard among the attendees.[35] Furthermore, a few years later several members of the Burgess family also consistently were mentioned in social accounts of the city, a period when social notes on Annapolis were more consistently reported in the *Afro-American Ledger*.[36] The significance of this point is that, as Gatewood has noted, African American social circles were fairly static.[37] In this case, the visibility of the families suggests that the Maynards and Burgesses were a fairly consistent part of the social milieu of families such as the Butlers and Bates, who clearly would have been considered the "elite" of African American Annapolis.[38]

Finally, the Maynard house inventory taken by William Butler and James C. Bishop at John Maynard's death in 1876 indicates a relatively high standard of comfort. The assessed value of his goods was $105.50, and the diversity of Victorian furnishings and decorative goods suggests a reasonably genteel existence.[39] Further, in tax assessments of 1849 the assessed value of John Maynard's possessions was $525; that total was greater than 53 percent of the African American households and 31 percent of the white households assessed in Annapolis.[40] All in all, it is reasonable to state that financially the Maynards were relatively well off and socially they were part of the most prominent social circles in the city.

Archaeology and Status in African American Annapolis

It is clear that there was a group of African Americans who formed a distinct social core within the African American community in Annapolis, and they were the focus of many, if not most, of the elaborate African American social events in the city. To a significant degree, "elite" social status of this group was paralleled by their economic status as the most affluent African Americans in the city. Furthermore, it also has been noted that the Maynards were to a significant extent a part of this group. They were homeowners, had lived in Annapolis since at least 1847, were prominent in the church, and were mentioned in the social news of Annapolis. Now I would like to return to the archaeological evidence and argue that one material correlate of their status in the African American community was the volume of teawares recovered from the Maynard excavations. I believe that the presence of significant amounts of teawares in quantities similar to those found on upper-middle-class white-occupied sites and in substantially larger quantities than those found on Gott's Court is in part a reflection of class differences within Annapolis's African American community.

Unquestionably the serving of tea and/or coffee was an important part of African American Annapolis's social fabric. However, two points should be stressed to qualify this argument. The first is that this chapter *is not* attempting to argue that the presence of significant percentages of teawares on African American-occupied sites is illustrative of a monolithic measure of status. All too frequently archaeologists exploring African American pasts have attempted to develop universal markers to identify sites which were occupied by African Americans. Instead of viewing high percentages of teawares as indicators of African American socioeconomic status, I would prefer a somewhat more narrowly defined argument. The statistically identified similarities and differences in teawares reflect strategies in which the Maynard household chose to signify and affirm their identity as part of Annapolis's African American elite. The combined archaeological data and documentary sources strongly suggest that serving tea and/or coffee was an important social function among the most financially and socially prominent segment of African American Annapolis.

In addition, it should be stressed that I am not intending to imply that the presence of teawares uniformly equates to economic and social prominence.[41] It is quite likely that some individuals who were part of the city's elite rejected particular status symbols or activities such as serving formal teas. Indeed, contemporary accounts often make note of this behavior of deliberate rejection of supposed elite status symbols, such as the avoidance of particular goods by the wealthy because they are seen as being "too showy." Conversely, it is also quite possible that individuals who were less financially secure devoted a disproportionate amount of time and resources to acquiring genteel goods or engaging in costly activities. In fact, in his biography Wiley Bates addressed this second point when he complained that people of color often spent their time and money on activities they could not afford.[42]

Another issue which should be addressed is the appropriateness of comparing the Maynard assemblage to the materials recovered from the white physician's household and the implications of comparison across racial lines. Several scholars have argued that many actions and behaviors which are created and utilized to reinforce class distinctions are generally the products of an elite who are attempting to maintain and reinforce their privileged position in society. Furthermore, these actions and behaviors are emulated by groups of less-prominent status as part of their attempts to elevate their position in society. The elite, in turn, develop other behaviors to maintain their social distance.[43] The net result of this is that class differences are replicated consistently.[44]

Returning specifically to teawares, Sidney Mintz has presented a compelling argument that the history of sugar consumption (and, through sugar consumption, tea) is illustrative of this process of emulation of consumption habits. Mintz noted that sugar initially was a perk of the elite in the seventeenth century, and over time it became a more commonly consumed good by the masses. By the nineteenth century, sugar's presence and access to it were nearly universal. To tie together the data from the Maynard-Burgess House with the argument presented by Mintz, it would be appropriate to ask what the implications are of the similarity in percentages of teawares between the Maynard household and the white physician's household on Main Street. Does the similarity in teawares simply reflect that consumer habits were driven by social emulation?; i.e., were the Maynards (who were comparatively disenfranchised through Jim Crow racism) simply emulating the status-affirming behaviors of the physician through their consumption of tea and/or coffee?

To begin to explore this question it is important to recognize the multiplicity of meanings that particular objects have for different individuals or groups. Daniel Miller has commented that "material culture often hides its polysemic nature, since specific configurations of objects may be differentially incorporated within competing systems of ideas, without necessarily changing themselves, and often a dominated group is better able to retain the appearance of conformity while maintaining its alternative perspective on the world."[45] His point that objects have different meanings to different people at different times has been demonstrated repeatedly.[46] However, it also should be stressed that this *does not* imply that material culture is open to an unbounded array of potential interpretations. The underlying meanings attributed to archaeological data are always constructed within a specific range of potentialities. As Alison Wylie has noted, the interpretive challenge of archaeology is that archaeological data is neither an absolute given nor is it "infinitely plastic," i.e., there is an interpretive middle ground.[47]

The relevance of Miller's argument to the discussion of teawares is that it provides an alternative explanation for the similarities between the Maynard and Main Street assemblages. Rather than arguing that the Maynards were simply emulating the behaviors of their Anglo counterparts, I believe that the use of teawares was somewhat more complex. The Maynards were using the same objects, but their presence had somewhat different meanings and implications for them than it did for the physician's household.

One of the significant critiques of class emulation as it has been articulated by McKendrick et al. is the work of Colin Campbell. Campbell argues that status definitions are often more complicated than simply one class of people copying the actions and behaviors of another class. In fact, Campbell argues that the symbols of social status often are contested and, indeed, rejected by the comparatively disenfranchised.[48]

Mullins also has addressed this issue in his discussion of ceramic decorative types recovered from several African American sites in Annapolis. While Victorian etiquette emphasized the acquisition of matched table settings, Mullins has noted that the decorative motifs on the ceramic assemblages from several African American–occupied sites are quite different from what standard etiquette practices dictate or, indeed, what archaeologists have identified as the expected norm. Mullins has noted that while the vessel forms are no different from those of other nineteenth-century sites, the decorative patterns are quite distinctive. Rather than having matched sets, the assemblages were characterized by several differing decorative styles. Mullins argues that the reason for the variability in decorative patterns is not simply one of poverty (i.e., people of color did not have the economic wherewithal to purchase matched sets of dishes); instead, he attributes this variability to African Americans consciously rejecting rapidly changing decorative tastes and curating ceramics for long periods of time. The result is that African Americans simultaneously were participating in the Victorian ideal by, on the one hand, acquiring teawares and serving tea, while, on the other hand, ignoring or rejecting elements of that ideal which dictated that the table should be set with matched sets of ceramics.[49] In short, African Americans were using the same material culture and many of the same activities, such as serving tea or coffee, as white Annapolis, but they were using them for very specific ends, specifically to help create and reinforce identities apart from white Annapolis.

Within African American Annapolis the acquisition of teawares and serving of tea or coffee among particular segments of the community served several somewhat contradictory purposes. First of all, the acquisition of teawares by the Maynards does suggest that, to some extent, the Maynards identified with a Victorian ideal of serving tea. Nevertheless, as I have argued, the intent of this practice was to serve as a way to create and maintain an African American elite in the city. This chapter has attempted to explore the similarities and differences in uses of material culture *within* an African American population. The use of quantitative comparisons of ceramic and glass assemblages has provided an initial point of departure to explore more general questions of social relations. The qualitative data such as newspapers, oral histories, and other scholarly works have provided the ethnographic content to elaborate upon the potential significance of the similarity and differences in the uses of bottles and ceramics. When utilized together the two sources of information provide some initial explorations of status differences within African American Annapolis. The differences in the percentages of teawares recovered from the three sites begin to materially illustrate social differences within African American Annapolis and apart from white Annapolis.

Notes

This work has undergone considerable transformations over the past few years. Of those who suffered through the earliest versions of this work and who provided much needed commentary, I would like to thank Jeff Hantman, Chuck Perdue, Richard Handler, Reginald Butler, and Fred Damon. More recently, I thank Paul Mullins, Paul Shackel, Amy Grey, and Mark Leone for further suggestions for revision. Steve Plog deserves particular thanks for his direction in the statistical analyses. On an institutional level I would like to acknowledge the support of the city of Annapolis for granting the initial access to test Gott's Court and Orlando Ridout IV and Port of Annapolis, Inc., for access to the Maynard-Burgess property as well as the University of Maryland and the Historic Annapolis Foundation for their continued support of Archaeology in Annapolis. Finally, I thank Amy Grey for her unflagging support of my work.

1. W. E. B. Du Bois, *The Negro American Family* (New York: Negro Universities Press, 1969), 127.
2. To cite just a few representative examples of works which have explored particular groups influences see Paul R. Huey, "The Dutch at Fort Orange," in *Historical Archaeology in Global Perspective*, ed. Lisa Falk (Washington, D.C.: Smithsonian Institution Press, 1991), 121–67; Donald P. Heldman, "Michigan's First Jewish Settlers: A View from the Solomon-Levy Trading House at Fort Michilimackinac, 1765–1781," *Journal of New World Archaeology* 6

(4) (1986): 21–33; Alaric Faulkner, "Maintenance and Fabrication at Fort Pentagoet 1635–1654: Products of an Acadian Armorer's Workshop," *Historical Archaeology* 20 (1) (1988): 63–94; Kathleen A. Deagan, *Spanish St. Augustine: The Archaeology of a Colonial Creole Community* (New York, Academic Press, 1983).

3. Paul Shackel, *Archaeological Testing at the 193 Main Street Site, 18AP44, Annapolis, Maryland* (Annapolis: Historic Annapolis Foundation, 1986); Paul R. Mullins, *Analysis of Feature 12 Ceramic Assemblage, Main Street Site (18AP44)* (Annapolis: Historic Annapolis Foundation, 1988); Michele Beavan, *Analysis of Bottle Glass Recovered from Feature 12, Main Street (18AP44)* (Annapolis: Historic Annapolis Foundation, 1988).

4. Mark S. Warner, *Test Excavations at Gott's Court, Annapolis, Maryland, 18AP52* (Annapolis: Historic Annapolis Foundation, 1992). Additional excavations were conducted on Gott's Court during the fall and winter of 1992–93 by R. Christopher Goodwin and Associates. See R. Christopher Goodwin, *Phase II/III Archeological Investigations of the Gott's Court Parking Facility, Annapolis, Maryland* (Annapolis: Maryland Historic Trust, 1993).

5. Paul R. Mullins and Mark S. Warner, *Final Archaeological Investigations at the Maynard-Burgess House (18AP64), An 1850–1980 African-American Household in Annapolis, Maryland, Volume I* (Annapolis: Historic Annapolis Foundation, 1993), 106.

6. Ibid., 99–121.

7. Wilfrid J. Dixon and Frank J. Massey, *Introduction to Statistical Analysis* (New York: McGraw-Hill, 1969), 249–50.

8. Ronald R. Switzer, *The Bertrand Bottles: A Study of 19th-Century Glass and Ceramic Containers* (Washington, D.C.: National Park Service, U.S. Dept. of the Interior, 1974).

9. Sarah H. Hill, "An Examination of Manufacture-Deposition Lag for Glass Bottles from Late Historic Sites," in *Archaeology of Urban America: The Search for Pattern and Process*, ed. Roy S. Dickens Jr. (New York: Academic Press, 1982), 321–22; Switzer, *The Bertrand Bottles*, 77.

10. For example, Jacob Riis comments that "[n]ext to idleness the tramp loves rum; next to rum stale beer, its equivalent of the gutter. And the first and last go best together." Jacob Riis, *How the Other Half Lives* (New York: Dover Publications, 1971), 64.

11. The vessels forms which constitute teawares in this analysis include tea cups and saucers as well as any other vessel forms which were obviously related to the serving of tea or coffee, such as tea pots.

12. David Hurst Thomas, *Refiguring Anthropology: First Principles of Probability and Statistics* (Prospect Heights, Ill.: Waveland Press, 1986), 461–63; Thomas, "The Awful Truth About Statistics in Archaeology," *American Antiquity* 43 (2) (1978): 233–35. It should also be noted that the rationale for using a Z-test rather than the more commonly utilized chi-square test is that it avoids the potential methodological problem of being influenced by differences in sample size.

13. Paul K. Edwards, *The Southern Urban Negro as a Consumer* (1932; reprint, New

York: Negro Universities Press, 1969), 151–66. See also Riis, *How the Other Half Lives*, 118–19; and Kelsey B. Gardner, *Consumer Habits and Preferences in the Purchase and Consumption of Meat*, Dept. Bulletin 1443, U.S. Dept. of Agriculture, Washington, D.C., 1926, 51. One of the findings in Gardner's study was that people of color were quite loyal in terms of whom they bought their meat from: roughly half of the sampled population had bought their meats from the same person for two years or longer.

14. Paul R. Mullins, "A Bold and Gorgeous Front: The Contradictions of African America and Consumer Culture, 1880–1930," paper presented at the School of American Research Advanced Seminar "The Historical Archaeology of Capitalism," Santa Fe, N.Mex., Oct. 2–6, 1993; Warner and Mullins, *Phase I–II Archaeological Investigations on the Courthouse Site (18AP63), An Historic African-American Neighborhood in Annapolis, Maryland* (Annapolis: Historic Annapolis Foundation, 1993), Mullins and Warner, *Final Archaeological Investigations*, 1993.

15. Sidney W. Mintz, *Sweetness and Power: The Place of Sugar in Modern History* (New York: Penguin Books, 1985), 117, 141. See also Rodris Roth, *Tea Drinking in 18th-Century America: Its Etiquette and Equipage* (Washington, D.C.: Smithsonian Institution Press, 1961); W. H. Ukers, *All About Tea* (New York: The Tea and Coffee Trade Journal Co., 1935).

16. Susan Williams, *Savory Suppers and Fashionable Feasts: Dining in Victorian America* (New York: Pantheon Books, 1985), 186–87. This point has also been suggested by Diana DiZerega Wall, "Sacred Dinners and Secular Teas: Constructing Domesticity in Mid-19th-Century New York," *Historical Archaeology* 25 (4) (1991): 79.

17. *Afro-American Ledger*, Jan. 6, 1906, 1.

18. *Afro-American Ledger*, Feb. 23, 1907, 1.

19. *The Bee*, Jan. 9, 1897, 1.

20. Ann Jensen, "Do You Know What I Have Been?" *Annapolitan* (1991): 36–37.

21. Compare *Afro-American Ledger*, Feb. 16, 1906, 4; May 26, 1906, 5; Sept. 28, 1907, 5; Aug. 28, 1908, 1; Feb. 20, 1909, 1; Nov. 26, 1910, 5.

22. *Afro-American Ledger*, Apr. 9, 1910, 4.

23. Willard B. Gatewood, *Aristocrats of Color: The Black Elite, 1880–1920* (Bloomington: Indiana Univ. Press, 1990).

24. Ibid., 182–209.

25. Ibid., 24.

26. Du Bois, *The Negro American Family*, 64–68.

27. Edwards, *The Southern Urban Negro*; Gardner, "Consumer Habits," 1926, H. B. Frissell and Isabel Bevier, *Dietary Studies of Negroes in Eastern Virginia in 1897 and 1898*, Bulletin No. 71, Office of Experiment Stations, U.S. Dept. of Agriculture, Washington, D.C., 1899.

28. Jeffrey R. Brackett, "Progress of the Colored People of Maryland since the War," in *History, Politics, and Education*, vol. 8, Johns Hopkins University Studies in Historical and Political Science, ed. Herbert B. Adams (Baltimore: Johns Hopkins Univ. Press, 1890), 403.

29. Sallie M. Ives, "Black Community Development in Annapolis, Maryland, 1870–1855," in *Geographical Perspectives on Maryland's Past*, ed. Robert D. Mitchell and Edward K. Muller, Occasional Papers in Geography No. 4, Dept. of Geography, Univ. of Maryland, College Park, 1979, 129–49.
30. Ibid., 148.
31. Hannah Jopling, unpublished oral history interview, Dept. of Anthropology, Univ. of Maryland, College Park, Feb. 1, 1992.
32. Compare Jopling, chap. 3, this volume.
33. Hannah Jopling, unpublished excerpts from interviews with the residents of the Franklin Street neighborhood, Dept. of Anthropology, Univ. of Maryland, College Park, Apr. 1, 1991.
34. Ives, "Black Community Development," 137.
35. *Afro-American Ledger*, Jan. 7, 1899, 1.
36. *Afro-American Ledger*, June 12, 1915, 3; Dec. 11. 1915, 6; Apr. 29, 1916, 3; July 29, 1916, 3; Mar. 17, 1917, 3.
37. Gatewood, *Aristocrats*, 26–27.
38. Two additional notes suggest a considerable degree of social prominence of the Maynards in Annapolis. First, one of the stained glass windows in Mt. Moriah A.M.E. Church was donated in the memory of John and Maria Maynard; see Jane McWilliams, "Maynard-Burgess House Research," Port of Annapolis, Inc., Feb. 1991. Second, the men who took Maynard's inventory, Butler and Bishop, were among the most prominent men of color in Annapolis during the late nineteenth century. Compare Gatewood, *Aristocrats*, 74; Clarence Marbury White Sr. and Evangeline Kaiser White, *The Years Between* (New York: Exposition Press, 1957): 86–87.
39. Mullins and Warner, *Final Archaeological Excavations*, appendix 1. See Daniel Horowitz, *The Morality of Spending* (Baltimore: Johns Hopkins Univ. Press, 1985), 54–55, on household items and economic status.
40. Jane McWilliams, "Maynard-Burgess House Research Report 3," Port of Annapolis, Inc., 1991.
41. I would like to acknowledge the recent works of Robin Ryder on this point. She has recently commented on the value of a more "fluid" or context-specific understanding of the use of material culture in the construction of African American identities where the archaeologist acknowledges the variability in the understandings of ethnic definitions. Robin L. Ryder, "Fluid Ethnicity: Archaeological Examinations of Diversity in Virginia from 1800–1900," paper presented to the Council of Virginia Archaeologists Symposium VII, 1993.
42. Wiley H. Bates, *Researches, Sayings and Life of Wiley H. Bates* (Annapolis: City Printing Co., 1928), 14.
43. See Neil McKendrick, John Brewer, and J. H. Plumb, *The Birth of Consumer Society* (Bloomington: Indiana Univ. Press, 1982); Paul A. Shackel, *Personal Discipline and Material Culture* (Knoxville: Univ. of Tennessee Press, 1993); Thorstein Veblen, *The Theory of the Leisure Class* (New York: Viking, 1935).
44. A further comment on the point of class differentiation is the recognition that class differences were clearly not color-blind. Whites may have recognized themselves

as being "working class," but part of their definition of the position was based upon their identification of themselves as "not black." See David R. Roediger *The Wages of Whiteness* (London: Verso, 1991), 13. The implication is that there was a clear recognition of racial differences between whites and blacks, so while one talks about a black "middle class," it is important to recognize that racial differences were of fundamental importance. See also Eric Lott, *Love & Theft: Blackface Minstrelsy and the American Working Class* (New York: Oxford Univ. Press, 1993).

45. Daniel Miller, "The Limits of Dominance," in *Domination and Resistance*, ed., Daniel Miller, Michael Rowlands, and Christopher Tilley (London: Unwin Hyman, 1989), 76.

46. Compare Ian Hodder, *The Present Past* (New York: Pica Press, 1982), 215–16; Charles E. Orser Jr., "Beneath the Material Surface of Things: Commodities, Artifacts and Slave Plantations," *Historical Archaeology* 26 (3) (1992): 94–104; Margaret Purser, "Consumption as Communication in Nineteenth-Century Paradise Valley, Nevada," *Historical Archaeology* 26 (3) (1992):105–16; Christopher Tilley, "Interpreting Material Culture," in *The Meaning of Things*, ed. Ian Hodder (London: Unwin Hyman, 1989), 185–94.

47. Alison Wylie, "The Interplay of Evidential Constraints and Political Interests: Recent Archaeological Research on Gender," *American Antiquity* 57 (1) (1992): 25.

48. Colin Campbell, *The Romantic Ethic and the Spirit of Modern Consumption* (Oxford: Basil Blackwell, 1987), 51–54.

49. Mullins, "A Bold and Gorgeous Front."

Part III

Landscapes and Architecture

Historic Landscapes

Since the 1970s landscape studies has developed into an important genre in analyzing historic material culture. Scholars increasingly recognize that landscapes are themselves artifacts which express and reinforce cultural ideals.[1] Approaches to historic landscapes range from particularistic concerns that document and reconstruct historic landforms to symbolic and ideological approaches that examine the meanings and uses of the cultural environment. Particularistic concerns appear to dominate the current funding agenda in the United States, but it is important to recognize that gardens and other landscape features are not solely ornamental. Indeed, colonial and historical American landscape features were also expressions of baroque and Renaissance ideals which reflected assertions of power over the natural environment. Those landscapes also served as a mechanism to display social, material, racial, gendered, and class control and reproduce established social hierarchies.

Some early landscape studies in historical archaeology concentrated on recovering functional patterns associated with the homelot and interpreting formal gardens.[2] During the 1980s the focus of landscape research expanded to include studying a variety of constructed landscapes and the manipulation of the natural environment. These inquiries include work on town plans, house lots, factories and boarding houses, rural landscapes, and gardens.[3] Recently the field has witnessed a growth of edited books and journal volumes dedicated to the exploration of a broadening variety of landscapes research topics.[4] This introduction reviews some of the work in historic landscape archaeology and positions Archaeology in Annapolis's landscape investigations within broader archaeological research on landscapes. Archaeologists' interest in landscapes has grown rapidly, so this section is intended to be representative rather than all-encompassing.

Houselot and Urban Development

An early analysis that discerned changing functional uses and organization of space of house lot landscapes is Robert Keeler's work on seventeenth-century frontier settlements. He examines features such as yards, fences, and outbuildings along with documentary and geochemical analysis to show changing functional uses of the house lot.[5] More recently, archaeologists have attempted to identify activities on the household level and assess the influence of gender relations in the development of the house lot. Henry Miller, for instance, has examined the landscape associated with the Country's House, the governor's domicile in St. Mary's City. The house was converted into public use in 1660s, a period when the town was transformed by the introduction of a modest baroque town plan. He discovered that as the town plan of St. Mary's became increasingly formalized, there was a corresponding change in the use of yard space where the use of particular portions of the yard became more functionally specific.[6]

Landscape architects recognize that fences can serve both utilitarian and symbolic functions; that is, fences are not only barriers, but they also create distinctive use areas and symbolic meanings for enclosed and excluded spaces. For example, Mark Leone's interpretation of the historic landscape in Salt Lake City provides an ideological analysis of Mormons' perceptions of themselves and the rest of the world. Fences, he argues, create a separation of their world from the outside.[7]

Other investigations in urban and industrial settings provide analyses of how industrial capitalists manipulated the cultural landscape to create and reinforce industrial discipline. Uniform architecture, grid-based town plans, and rules of behaviors helped to create the new industrial era in

Lowell, Massachusetts, as well as in many other industrializing American cities.[8] In Harpers Ferry, West Virginia, workers were confronted with a quite different scenario from that in Lowell. The lack of corporate paternalism and a structured built environment led to the persistence of craft ideology, despite the introduction of new industrial machinery. "Whimsical theories" of mass production were rejected by Harpers Ferry laborers, sometimes quite forcefully. It was not until the installation of military control that some form of factory discipline developed. This new work ethic went hand-in-hand with the development of uniform architecture and a grid-based town plan.[9]

While market forces contributed to urban development, some studies have discerned newly developed eighteenth- and nineteenth-century interrelationships between the urban population and its environment.[10] For instance, the manipulation of the natural environment in early-nineteenth-century industrializing centers played a significant role in creating and reinforcing an industrial ideology. The creation of gardenlike landscapes intentionally planted around industrial sites attempted to suggest a harmonious coexistence between nature and manufacturing.[11]

Ellen Savulis notes that Shaker landscapes reflect and mask the social order in a similar fashion to industrial landscapes. Shaker villages were seen by outsiders as a reflection of an egalitarian society, even though their internal structure was dominated by men. Men dominated community planning strategies and, in turn, legitimized the social order. Women's roles were confined to the domestic realm, and women had little input into overall community design. Placement of buildings in relationship to the center of town by those who had greater prestige was among the mechanisms which indicated the general influence of particular members.[12]

Formal Gardens

An early and influential landscape study is Mark Leone's analysis of the William Paca garden in Annapolis, Maryland. Leone examined the principles of plane geometry and the careful calculations used for terrace construction. Wealthy landowners manipulated the rules of geometry to create an illusion of augmented space, especially in relatively small urban lots. Between the 1760s and 1780s, formal garden builders in Annapolis claimed to understand the natural order, and they used rules of geometry within ostentatious formal gardens to legitimate their social predominance. An analysis of the Carroll garden in Annapolis demonstrates such gardens' planned geometric configuration. Landscape measurements, such as widths of terraces, are a multiple of a dimension of the house. Later, nineteenth- and twentieth-century occupants of the Carroll property changed and adopted the landscape to their own utilitarian and ideological needs. For instance, gardening for subsistence and the eventual placement of a cemetery in the midst of the terraced garden became more important than the maintenance of a formal landscape.[13]

Leone envisions two particular needs for the study of landscapes and gardens: typology and precise descriptions. Typology, of course, has always been an essential part of archaeology; it is our method for imposing a form of order onto the material world. Henry Glassie is well known for constructing grammars of vernacular architecture. While complete typologies do not yet exist in landscape archaeology, there is a growing literature of historic landscape descriptions.[14]

William Kelso and Rachel Most's *Earth Patterns: Essays in Landscape Archaeology* is a collection that contains a variety of approaches to landscape studies.[15] The volume includes essays on Virginia country gardens, urban landscapes, old world landscapes, and archaeobotanical studies. The plantation and formal landscape at Thomas Jefferson's Monticello is one of the most extensive archaeological landscape projects. Work has revealed fence lines, tiered garden walls, buildings, roadways, and earlier topography. Included in the reconstruction is a set of slave quarters, Mulberry Row, that has become part of Monticello's interpretation of the plantation's growth and its link to enslaved labor. Excavations at Bacon's Castle, one of Virginia's oldest and best-studied structures, has revealed an associated seventeenth-century formal garden. The Baltimore Center for Urban Archaeology gardens excavated Monte Claire in Baltimore, a mansion constructed by Declaration of Independence signer Charles Carroll of Carrollton. This work led to the reconstruction of Carroll's late-eighteenth-century garden. Other country landscape analyses include a study of the former lieutenant governor of Virginia's garden at Germanna, Robert "King" Carter's plantation, and urban gardens in Williamsburg, Virginia.[16]

The literature on landscape studies is growing at a tremendous rate. Rural landscapes and plantations studies have contributed significantly to this development. Landscape studies have increasingly used archaeobotanical research for reconstruction and interpretation. The analysis of pollen, phytolith, and macroflora data have made great contributions to historical landscape interpretation.[17]

The Essays

The essays in this section focus on the meanings and uses of landscapes. They focus on a variety of material culture, such as gardens, houses, and town plans, and demonstrate their interrelationship with landscape issues within the larger field of anthropology. While landscapes are often viewed for aesthetic purposes, these authors provide an alternative scenario which places their subjects in relations to power. Material goods in any form can be highly charged with ideological meanings, and their changing meanings may be masked in natural phenomena. For example, Barbara Little examines print culture and its relationship to industrialization and the metaphor of the garden and the machine. Elizabeth Kryder-Reid proposes that the Annapolis gentry embedded their power in laws of nature and used gardens as one means to express their position in the social hierarchy. Christopher Matthews examines the rise of Georgian architecture and the use of natural proportions which provided a means for the elite to establish a new cultural authority. Mark Leone, Jennifer Stabler, and Anna-Marie Burlaga demonstrate the construction of Annapolis's city plan and the conscious spatial strategies developed by its builders. In these case studies in Annapolis, Charles Carroll of Carrollton's garden, the Green family print shops, William Buckland's use of Georgian architecture, and the changing characteristics of State Circle, are all stories of power relations between people, groups, and institutions.

The context for Annapolis's dynamic material culture and landscape changes stems from changing power relations and competition for status. Christopher Matthews explains that during the early reign of King George III there was a radical departure in style and behavior. The king sponsored a circle of intellectuals to construct new styles based on the past glories of Britain and the concept of beauty derived from Classical and Renaissance ages. People grabbed for power and they expressed their views through a new order of politics, art, and social activities. Many of these new ideals were incorporated into everyday material culture.[18]

Matthews notes that new architectural design books helped to spread the new cultural ideals. Their publication increased dramatically in the 1720s, and such books were found mainly in the libraries of the elite. By the 1750s, the size of the books was half the size of the earlier editions, indicating that they were now in the pockets of artisans; consequently, theory was rapidly being integrated into practice. As Annapolis developed into a social and cultural center, architecture became an increasingly important form of social discourse. Matthews describes how the Annapolis elite used Georgian architecture once their power was challenged just prior to the American Revolution. As the town's population increased there was a new wealth and gentry members desired to boast their allegiance to the new cultural revolution.

During the 1770s boom, one of colonial America's well known craftsmen and architects, William Buckland, moved to Annapolis. His work on Annapolis's two most elegantly designed structures, the Hammond and Chase-Lloyd houses, demonstrates how he operated within the new cultural revolution found within the British world. While his design followed the principles of symmetry, he also made use of historical precedent and naturalized understanding of harmony and proportion. The new Georgian buildings provided the gentry a vehicle to signify their participation in new hierarchy. These style changes came at a time of social and political instability, and they helped to bolstered the claims of the Annapolis elite to an eroding position of political authority. These new ideals filtered throughout society and were incorporated into the design of other material culture forms. For instance, Elizabeth Kryder-Reid notes that Charles Carroll of Carrollton changed his landscape, from a yard that sloped to the Severn River to a terraced garden with strategically placed ornamentation. As Buckland had with his homes, Carroll used Renaissance ideals to construct his garden. Kryder-Reid shows how Carroll controlled the experience of the visitor in the garden through the manipulation of access and sight lines. The eye was drawn to strategic points in the landscape by the construction of monumental architecture or the exacting placement of vegetation. Terracing, for instance, created an illusion of depth. The water at the base of his property blurred the lines between his property and the landscape beyond.

Many of the landscape features relied upon classical design which allowed Chesapeake planters to root themselves in the past in an attempt to project their position as being long held and natural, thus unchallengeable. Kryder-Reid illustrates how Carroll's power and status as a legislator and signer of the Declaration of Independence was presented as natural because it was embedded in an agrarian, idyllic nature.

In a similar vein, printers relied upon expressions of nature when justifying their craft in industrializing society. Barbara Little explains that as the machine invaded the Annapolis garden, a different metaphor was created for organizing and comprehending daily life. Originally, the American landscape was perceived to be an unspoiled garden for the Old World. The pastoral ideal, however, eventually turned to explicit political uses. For instance, machines with natural ornamentation became a popular expression signifying the machine's place and status in America's industrializing society. Little also demonstrates that printers perceived their occupation as linked to nature and guided by supernatural guidance. Printing was promoted as natural and essential to the proper and just order of things.

Using a model from postmodern geographer Edward Soja, Little explores the importance of the use of space in human social life. In particular, she highlights the organization of Annapolis's town plan. The Anglican Church and the State House occupied Annapolis's highest topographic points, a positioning intended to emanate their power and authority. Little explains that "authority was vested in the great 'speaking books,' the Law (statehouse) and the Bible (church)." These books of authority allowed replicability and were central to the political and social structure of Annapolis, as well as any other town in the New World.

Little describes how the Green family of printers, who worked for nearly 100 years in this craft, moved closer to a source of power, the state government, soon after their power started to erode. In 1738, Jonas Green established his print shop on Charles Street, several blocks from State Circle. The Greens prospered as they monopolized printing for the colony and state and published the city's only newspaper. After the American Revolution, Frederick Green, Jonas's son, moved the printshop office to Main Street in clear view of the State House, and he moved again within a block of the capital in 1800. Frederick became known for his attacks on the ruling party, and when his son Jonas inherited the business the family lost their title as state printer. Jonas moved the business to State Circle, adjacent to the state's power, after he had lost power.

The creation of State Circle and the use of various geometric forms is considered by Mark Leone, Jennifer Stabler, and Anna-Marie Burlaga. Using historic maps and archaeological data, they defined and outlined the inner and outer perimeters of the circle. These data conclude that while State Circle may have been conceptualized as a circle, sometime in its early development it was transformed into a geometric-shaped egg.

Depending upon the placement of the structure, and despite the uneven terrain, this geometrically contrived perimeter road provides the illusion of a symmetrically located building. Depending upon the viewing section, the egg-shaped perimeter road also provides the appearance of being a circle. This geometric configuration harmonizes the natural topography with the built space and makes its positioning appear quite natural.

In the late nineteenth century, the front of the State House was terraced in the form of geometrically shaped egg. The egg lies directly under the dome and Leone, Stabler, and Burlaga explain that the purpose was to make the front door of the State House the focal point when viewed from the street.

Leone, Stabler, and Burlaga also review other techniques used to create the authority of the state. For instance, the width of the streets that enter State Circle either converge or diverge. Ignoring some of the basic principals of Baroque town planning, the converging street do not intersect at the circle's center. Instead, the Baroque principles were readjusted and designed to focus on the State House.

All of the articles in this section provide some insight into how individuals used landscapes as strategies of power. William Buckland helped Annapolitans create a modern landscape by crafting the newest Georgian architecture. This new architecture was a means to proclaim authority in the new social hierarchy. In a similar fashion Charles Carroll of Carrollton redesigned his landscape by creating a terraced garden with monumental features, adjacent to the water. Carroll used mathematical proportions to create illusions of space which also gave him the opportunity to express his power as being embedded in an agrarian, idyllic nature. The Green family printing business prospered and remained in a residential area until the end of the American Revolution. The movement of the printshop demonstrates shifting power relations. As the family increasingly lost business and the title as the state's printer the enterprise moved closer to the state house. Annapolis's town plan incorporates various forms of baroque planning to helped create a symbol of authority. While the State House's meanings and uses changed, so too did the road system around it. It appears that the geometric egg was used to provide an illusion that the State House was centered in the town plan. In all of these case studies the landscape is infused with value and it provides a symbolic medium for social interaction. The Annapolis landscapes is dynamic and its meanings are continually negotiated.

Notes

1. See, for instance, Edward T. Linenthal, *Sacred Ground: Americans and Their Battlefields* (Chicago and Urbana: Univ. of Illinois Press, 1993); J. Ritchie Garrison, *Landscape and Material Life in Franklin County, Massachusetts, 1770–1860* (Knoxville: Univ. of Tennessee Press, 1991), Bernard L. Herman, *Architecture and Rural Life in Central Delaware, 1700–1900* (Knoxville: Univ. of Tennessee Press, 1987); Herman, "Fences," in *After Ratification: Material Life in Delaware, 1789–1820*, ed. J. Ritchie Garrison, Bernard L. Herman, and Barbara McLean Ward (Newark: Museum Studies Program, Univ. of Delaware, 1988), 7–20; John R. Stilgoe, *Common Landscape in America, 1580–1845* (New Haven: Yale Univ. Press, 1982); Ary J. Lamme III, *America's Historic Landscapes: Community Power and the Preservation of Four National Historic Sites* (Knoxville: Univ. of Tennessee Press, 1989); Richard Westmacott, *African-American Gardens and Yards in the Rural South* (Knoxville: Univ. of Tennessee Press, 1992).

2. Robert Keeler, "The Homelot on the Seventeenth-Century Chesapeake Frontier" (Ph.D. diss., Univ. of Pennsylvania, 1977); Mark P. Leone, "Interpreting Ideology in Historical Archaeology: Using the Rules of Perspective in the William Paca Garden in Annapolis, Maryland," in *Ideology, Power, and Prehistory*, ed. Daniel Miller and Christopher Tilley (Cambridge: Cambridge Univ. Press, 1984), 25–35.

3. Mark P. Leone, Julie Ernstein, Elizabeth Kryder-Reid, and Paul A. Shackel, "Power Gardens in Annapolis," *Archaeology* 12 (2) (1989): 34–39; Henry Miller, "Baroque Cities in the Wilderness: Archaeology and Urban Development in the Colonial Chesapeake," *Historical Archaeology* 22 (2) (1988): 57–73; The Archaeological Use of Landscape Treatments in Social, Economic, and Ideological Analyses, issue ed. Faith Harrington, *Historical Archaeology* 23 (1) (1989); Henry Miller, "The Country's House Site: An Archaeological Study of a Seventeenth-Century Domestic Landscape," in *Historical Archaeology of the Chesapeake*, ed. Paul A. Shackel and Barbara J. Little (Washington, D.C.: Smithsonian Institution Press, 1994), 65–83; Mary C. Beaudry, "The Lowell Boott Mills Complex and Its Housing: Material Expressions of Corporate Ideology," *Historical Archaeology* 23 (1) (1989): 19–33; Adrian Praetzellis and Mary Praetzellis, "'Utility and Beauty Should Be One': The Landscape of Jack London's Ranch of Good Intentions," *Historical Archaeology* 23 (1) (1989): 33–45; Julia King, "Rural Landscape in the Mid-Nineteenth-Century Chesapeake," in *Historical Archaeology of the Chesapeake*, 283–99; Leone, "Interpreting Ideology in Historical Archaeology"; Leone, "Rule by Ostentation: The Relationship Between Space and Sight in Eighteenth-Century Landscape Architecture in the Chesapeake Region of Maryland," in *Method and Theory for Activity Area Research: An Ethnoarchaeological Approach*, ed. Susan Kent (New York: Columbia Univ. Press, 1987), 604–33.

4. See, for instance, Harrington, "The Archaeological Use of Landscape Treatments"; Barbara Sarudy, "Eighteenth-Century Gardens of the Chesapeake,"

Journal of Garden History 9 (3) (1989): 104–59; William Kelso and Rachel Most, eds., *Earth Patterns: Essays in Landscape Archaeology* (Charlottesville: Univ. of Virginia Press, 1990); Peter Martin, *Pleasure Gardens of Virginia* (Princeton: Princeton Univ. Press, 1991); D. Fairchild Ruggles and Elizabeth Kryder-Reid, eds., *Journal of Garden History* 14 (1) (1994); Rebecca Yamin and Karen Bescherer Metheny, eds., *Landscape Archaeology: Reading and Interpreting the American Historical Landscape* (Knoxville: Univ. of Tennessee Press, 1996).

5. Keeler, *The Homelot.*

6. Mary C. Beaudry, "Archaeology and the Historic Household," *Man in the Northeast* 28 (1984): 27–38; James G. Gibb and Julia A. King. "Gender, Activity Areas, and Homelots in the 17th-Century Chesapeake Region," *Historical Archaeology* 25 (4) (1991): 109–31; Miller, "The Country's House Site."

7. John B. Jackson, "A New Kind of Space," *Landscape* 18 (1969): 33–35; Mark P. Leone, "Archaeology as the Science of Technology: Mormon Town Plans and Fences," in *Research and Theory in Current Archaeology*, ed. Charles Redman (New York: John Wiley and Sons, Inc., 1973), 125–50.

8. See Mary C. Beaudry, "The Archaeology of Historical Land Use in Massachusetts," *Historical Archaeology* 20 (2) (1986): 38–46; Mary C. Beaudry and Stephen Mrozowski, "The Archeology of Work and Homelife in Lowell, Massachusetts: An Interdisciplinary Study of the Boott Cotton Mills Corporation," *IA: The Journal of the Society for Industrial Archeology* 14 (2) (1988): 1–22.

9. Paul A. Shackel, "Interdisciplinary Approaches to the Meanings and Uses of Material Goods in Lower Town, Harpers Ferry," in An Archaeology of Harpers Ferry's Commercial and Residential District, issue ed. Paul A. Shackel and Susan E. Winter, *Historical Archaeology* 28 (4) (1994).

10. See Stephen L. Mrozowski, "Exploring New England's Evolving Urban Landscape," in Living in Cities: Current Research in Urban Archaeology, ed. Edward Staski, Special Publication Series No. 5, Society for Historical Archaeology, 1987, 10–18.

11. Paul A. Shackel, "Archaeology of an Industrial Town: Harpers Ferry and the New Order of Manufacturing," *CRM* 17 (1) (1994): 16–19.

12. Ellen-Rose Savulis, "Alternative Visions and Landscapes: Archaeology of the Shaker Social Order," in *Text-Aided Archaeology*, ed. Barbara J. Little (Boca Raton: CRC Press, 1992), 195–203.

13. Leone, "Interpreting Ideology in Historical Archaeology"; see also Barbara Paca Steele with St. Claire Wright, "The Mathematics of an Eighteenth-Century Wilderness Garden," *Journal of Garden History* 6 (4) (1986): 299–320; Elizabeth Kryder-Reid, "The Archaeology of Vision in Eighteenth-Century Chesapeake Gardens," in *Journal of Garden History*, issue ed. D. Fairchild Ruggles and Elizabeth Kryder-Reid, 14 (1) (1994): 42–54; Leone, "Rule by Ostentation"; Mark P. Leone and Paul A. Shackel, "Plane and Solid Geometry in Colonial Gardens in Annapolis, Maryland," in *Earth Patterns*, 153–68; Elizabeth Kryder-Reid, "'As Is the Gardener, So Is the Garden': The Archaeology of Landscape as Myth," in *Historical Archaeology of the Chesapeake*, 131–48.

14. Mark P. Leone, "The Relationship Between Archaeological Data and the Docu-

mentary Record: 18th-Century Gardens in Annapolis, Maryland," *Historical Archaeology* 23 (1) (1989): 29–35; Henry Glassie, *Folk Housing in Middle Virginia: A Structural Analysis of Historic Artifacts* (Knoxville: Univ. of Tennessee Press, 1975).

15. Kelso and Most, eds., *Earth Patterns.*

16. William Kelso, "Landscape Archaeology: A Key to Virginia's Cultivated Past," in *British and American Gardens in the Eighteenth Century: Eighteen Illustrated Essays on Garden History,* ed. R. P. Maccubbin and P. M. Partin (Williamsburg: Colonial Williamsburg Foundation, 1984), 159–69; William Kelso, "Landscape Archaeology at Thomas Jefferson's Monticello," in *Earth Patterns,* 7–22; Nicholas Luccketti, "Archaeological Excavations at Bacon's Castle, Surry County, Virginia," in *Earth Patterns,* 23–42; Elizabeth Anderson and Christine Stevens, "Mount Clare: Introducing Baltimore to 18th-Century Splendor," in New Perspectives on Maryland Historical Archaeology, issue ed. Richard J. Dent and Barbara J. Little, *Maryland Archaeology* 26 (1 & 2) (1990): 86–94; Douglas Sanford, "The Gardens at Germanna, Virginia," in *Earth Patterns,* 43–58; Carter L. Hudgins, "Robert 'King' Carter and the Landscape of Tidewater Virginia in the Eighteenth Century," in *Earth Patterns,* 59–70; Marley R. Brown and Patricia M. Samford, "Recent Evidence of Eighteenth-Century Gardening in Williamsburg, Virginia," in *Earth Patterns,* 103–22.

17. For discussions on rural and plantation landscapes, see Adrian Praetzellis and Mary Praetzellis, "'Utility and Beauty Should Be One': The Landscape of Jack London's Ranch of Good Intentions," *Historical Archaeology* 23 (1) (1989): 33–45; Dell Upton, "White and Black Landscapes in Eighteenth-Century Virginia," in *Material Culture in America, 1600–1860,* ed. Robert Blair St. George (Boston: Northeastern Univ. Press, 1988), 357–69; Upton, "Imagining the Early Virginia Landscape," in *Earth Patterns,* 71–86; Julia King, "Rural Landscape in the Mid-Nineteenth-Century Chesapeake," in *Historical Archaeology of the Chesapeake,* 283–99; Terrence W. Epperson, "Race and the Disciplines of the Plantation," in Historical Archaeology on Southern Plantations and Farms, issue ed. Charles E. Orser Jr., *Historical Archaeology* 24 (4) (1990): 29–36. For discussions of microfloral and macroflora analyses, see Cheryl A. Holt and Louise A. Ackerson, "Mount Clare Orchard Planting Pattern," unpublished MS on file at the Baltimore Center for Urban Archaeology, 1986; V. M. Bryant and R. G. Holloway, "The Role of Palynology in Archaeology," in *Advances in Archaeological Method and Theory,* vol. 6, ed. Michael B. Schiffer (New York: Academic Press, 1983), 191–224; James Schoenwetter, "A Method for the Application of Pollen Analysis in Landscape Archaeology," in *Earth Patterns,* 277–96; Gerald Kelso and Mary Beaudry, "Pollen Analysis and Urban Land Use: The Environs of Scottow's Dock in 17th, 18th, and Early 19th Century Boston," *Historical Archaeology* 24 (1) (1990): 61–81; Mrozowski, "Exploring New England's Evolving Urban Landscape"; Linda Scott Cummings, "Diet and Prehistoric Landscape During the 19th and Early 20th Centuries at Harpers Ferry, West Virginia: A View from the Old Master Armorer's Complex," in An Archaeology of Harpers Ferry's Commercial and Residential District, issue ed. Paul A. Shackel and Susan

E. Winter, *Historical Archaeology* 28 (4) (1994); Gerald Kelso, "Pollen-Record Formation Processes, Interdisciplinary Archaeology, and Land Use by Mill Workers and Managers: The Boott Mills Corporation, Lowell, Massachusetts, 1836–1942," *Historical Archaeology* 27 (1) (1993): 70–94; Irwin Rovner, "Fine-Tuning Floral History with Plant Opal Phytolith Analysis," in *Earth Patterns*, 23–42; Rovner, "Fine-Tuning Floral History with Plant Opal Phytolith Analysis," in *Earth Patterns*, 23–42; Rovner, "Macro- and Micro-ecological Reconstruction Using Plant Opal Phytolith Data from Archaeological Sediments," *Geoarchaeology* 3 (1988): 155–63; Anne E. Yentsch, Naomi F. Miller, Barbara Paca, and Dolores Piperno, "Archaeologically Defining the Earlier Garden Landscapes at Morven: Preliminary Results," *Northeast Historical Archaeology* 16 (1987): 1–29; William F. Fisher and Gerald K. Kelso, "The Use of Opal Phytolith Analysis in a Comprehensive Environmental Study: An Example from Lowell, Massachusetts," *Northeast Historical Archaeology* 16 (1987): 30–48; Rovner, "Floral History by the Back Door: A Test of Phytolith Analysis in Residential Yards at Harpers Ferry," in An Archaeology of Harpers Ferry's Commercial and Residential District, issue ed. Paul A. Shackel and Susan E. Winter, *Historical Archaeology* 28 (4) (1994): 37–48.

18. See, for instance, Paul A. Shackel, *Personal Discipline and Material Culture: An Archaeology of Annapolis, Maryland, 1695–1870* (Knoxville: Univ. of Tennessee Press, 1987).

10 Cultural Landscapes of Printers and the "Heav'n-Taught Art" in Annapolis, Maryland

Barbara J. Little

My purpose in this chapter is to begin to address how people maintain and change their understandings, interpretations, and images within a changing world. Both textual and nontextual material culture are things that people use to create settings in which to structure their lives. The time is the eighteenth and nineteenth century. The place is Annapolis, Maryland, in the New World of the Americas. The social identity and form of expression is printers and print culture. My organizing thoughts are of two types: metaphor and spatiality. To typical anthropological discussions of metaphor, I wish to add and emphasize that it is not only language which is expressive of culture, but also things. To the "unbudgeably hegemonic historicism" of which postmodern geographer Edward Soja complains, I would add the archaeologist's confirmation that it is not only time but space which matters to human social life.[1]

Taking cues from landscape studies in historical archaeology and postmodern geography, I address culturally bound understandings of the world tied to particular locales from broad to narrow. The three settings for these locales include overarching metaphors for understanding both the New World and the place of the printing craft in the order of things, regional power shifts in the Chesapeake, and the politics of landscape in Annapolis. An explanation from Anthony Giddens should make some of the terminology clear:

> Locales refer to the use of space to provide the *settings* of interaction, the settings of interaction in turn being essential to specifying its *contextuality*. . . . Locales may range from a room in a house, a street corner, the shop floor of a factory, towns and cities, to the territorially demarcated areas occupied by nation-states . . . the features of settings are also used . . . to constitute the meaningful content of interaction. . . . Context thus connects the most intimate and detailed components of interaction to much broader properties of the institutionalization of social life.[2]

Locales, then, are spatially defined places, while settings are more complex physical, social, and ideological places of human interaction. Settings are related to the idea of spatiality, which is socially produced space, with a link to human action and motivation.[3] Emphasizing that the constitution of society is both spatial and temporal, Soja writes that "spatiality is socially produced and, like society itself, exists in both substantial forms (concrete spatialities) and as a set of relations between individuals and groups, an 'embodiment and medium of social life itself.'"[4]

In the eighteenth and nineteenth centuries, American lives were changing drastically in social, political, economic, and technological ways. All of these changes had to be placed within temporal, spatial, and conceptual settings of interaction that made sense—that made the changes sensible, rational, and comprehensible. This essay uses different scales of locale to explore one aspect of those far-reaching changes. I use the craft of printing to exemplify some of the changes wrought by the "machine in the garden" as culture changed in the industrializing society. The machine that invades the Annapolis garden is not just printing, or any technology, but a wholly different metaphor for organizing and comprehending daily life. To understand such change requires paying attention to all of the forms of material and textual expression that eighteenth- and nineteenth-century people used. Therefore, I refer to disparate cultural expressions: metaphorical and actual gardens, press design, printers' poetry, regional political and economic changes, a city plan, the great "speaking books," and changing locations of a business office.

The issue of appropriate spatial scale of analysis, or choice of locale, is an important methodological concern in historical archaeology, but it is difficult to treat programmatically and it has been afforded very little explicit attention.[5] Perhaps prescriptions for defining proper scales of analysis should not be much more detailed than Deetz's suggestion that we can use more coarsely grained data to address larger scale questions, even if the data is too coarse to use for more local or detailed analysis.[6] Artifacts collected from a town dump, for example, cannot shed light on household consumption, but they can contain information on the broader community. This methodological insight does not mean that only the global scale of analysis is important. While different sorts of data may be useful for different sorts of interpretation, it is important to avoid assigning *a priori* authority. It is also important to avoid the needless limitation of assigning particular scales of questions to any level of data. Artifacts, for instance, are not to be confined to addressing questions at the individual behavioral level. Nor are changes in the world economy and concomitant cultural changes to be ignored at the level of individual behavior. The integration of scales and of questions will suggest questions about the integration of culture; therefore, it is essential to take advantage of the insights that can be gained by shifting and comparing scales of analysis. Otherwise we are left with both partial conclusions and partial questions and restrict our insights to a compartmentalized view of culture.

I would like to note that appropriate temporal scale is also an important consideration. For example, Braudel's scales of short- to long-term history, comprised of individual or event time, social time, and the *longue durée*, have been used to organize archaeological interpretation.[7] Lack of attention to temporal or historical scale in this article does not imply that considering space and time are methodologically mutually exclusive, a conclusion that would be archaeologically absurd. Soja is sensitive to the critique leveled at geography and is careful to avoid an anti-history label. He writes:

[T]his spatialization of critical thought does not have to project a simplistic anti-history. As with Foucault, the reassertion of space in critical social theory does not demand an antagonistic subordination of time and history, a facile substitution and replacement. It is instead a call for an appropriate interpretive balance between space, time and social being, or what may now more explicitly be termed the creation of human geographies, the making of history, and the constitution of society. . . . It is the dominance of a historicism of critical thought that is being challenged, not the importance of history.[8]

In some respect, all scales of data make different contributions to understanding a particular time period or phenomenon. Printing and print culture lend themselves to examining different spatial scales because of the simultaneous broad influence and detailed nature of printing. Different scales of printing-related data create in their own way cultural settings for human comprehension. Such settings are created by the imagery of language as well as by the design and placement of cities, buildings, and objects. Both documents and other objects are used by people to create their surroundings and perceptions. Although some may argue that we don't need more neologisms, I like the idea of "printscape" to suggest settings that are created through the medium of print or through the influences of print culture as printing and print culture create and influence nontextual material culture. As the cultural landscapes of print culture, printscapes may provide a way of conceptualizing relationships between abstract and concrete things.

Questions and Locales

Interpretation of setting and locale must consider landscapes, gardens, cityscapes, and house lots. It is instructive to think about the two-dimensional and three-dimensional use of space and about interrelationships among scales in the use of space: Is the New World a garden for the Old? Is the Annapolis city plan a garden for the capital? Are lots designed as settings for their houses? Are facades designed to harmonize with the geometry of their gardens? Do floor plans echo the organization of social life? Do activities and products create a social setting? Do artifacts create settings for social, economic, and cultural understandings? Can the layout of a newspaper or the design of a book echo or create the two-dimensional and three-dimensional conceptions of space that guide the design of gardens, house lots, cities, and continents?

In many areas printing was central to the settlement of the New World, including navigation, discovery, colonization, and "advertising" for settlement in the New World. Print culture made available to the reading and listening public the conflicting opinions about the New World, about Nature and the Garden. In some ways, print culture created much of the setting for exploration and exploitation of the New World and its people.[9] Printing provided a new medium for the expression of Renaissance ideas, which were also stimulated through discovery and exploration. "The Age of Discovery . . . was not so much a break with the past and a new departure, but rather a quickening of pace, a stimulus to nascent ideas. The New World provided, as it were, a gigantic laboratory in which the speculations of Renaissance man could be tested modified and developed."[10]

In thinking about *setting* at any scale it is useful to return to Leo Marx's influential book *The Machine in the Garden,* written a generation ago.[11] In it he explores technology and the pastoral ideal, both literary and political, in American culture. Such an exploration of categories, of explicit values and concepts about what Americans considered proper and desirable settings, can and must illuminate the changes we are able to trace in the archaeological and documentary records. The availability of such information allows historical archaeology to broaden into historical anthropology.

The opposition between art or culture and nature is a long-lived theme in European culture. With the discovery of the New World the conflict took on a new reality. Here was a landscape perceived to be unspoiled suddenly invaded by a dynamic and purposeful civilization. The conflict engendered ambiguity. Was America a paradise? America as garden was a powerful controlling metaphor. America could be seen as the site for a new Golden Age. Here, then, is a vision of Nature as Garden, an idealized, benign, and orderly Nature.[12] Robert Beverly, writing in 1705, referred to Virginia as a land that "did still seem to retain the Virgin Purity and Plenty of the First Creation, and the People their Primitive Innocence."[13] There was the New World as garden and promise for the Old World. On the other extreme was an idea about Nature that saw it not as a garden but as a hideous, threatening wilderness that demanded constant action and mastery of Nature.

Marx traces an important, but he thinks unexpressed, pastoral ideal from Elizabethan times through the eighteenth century.[14] He sees the pastoral ideal turned to explicit political uses with Thomas Jefferson's *Notes on Virginia,* published in 1785. However, there are politicized uses of landscape and garden before this time. For example, the political meanings of gardens in Annapolis have been described for an eighteenth-century society that understood the meanings of cultivated and ordered Nature very clearly.[15] William Paca and Charles Carroll of Carrollton, both signers of the Declaration of Independence, were wealthy men in Annapolis who, along with others of their class, created formal gardens in which they used rules of perspective to direct sight and demonstrate their control over nature through both their management of the viewers and of the plants. Because society was understood to be a phenomenon of nature during the "Age of Reason," part of the "argument" of the Revolutionary era gardens in Annapolis was that their designer-owners also had the requisite knowledge and right to rule society.[16]

The uses of gardens in Annapolis demonstrate broad themes that concern every scale of material culture. These themes center on power, on nature, and on ideology. Legitimation of power through naturalization (i.e., through exploiting the perceived inevitability of nature) is a central phenomenon in hegemonic ideology. It is therefore apparent at many scales of interpretation.

If the garden was a root metaphor during the eighteenth century in America, it took relatively little time for the machine to infiltrate and become a dominant cultural symbol. A new vocabulary was coming into use in the 1780s and 1790s as the machine became incorporated into the garden and then replaced it. In the early 1800s a new aesthetic developed as artistic expression became attached to the machine. John Kasson notes that ornamentation of machines was an attempt to assimilate the machine and signify its place and status in American society.[17] Such decoration satisfied the national passion for both beauty and utility. Iconography was often entirely clear. Printers were capable of being explicit in their imagery both in words and in the things they designed. The Columbian printing press, first produced in 1813, evoked these words from a British observer, a printer, in 1825:

> If the merits of a machine were to be appreciated wholly by its ornamental appearance, certainly no other press could enter into competition with "The Columbian." No British-made machinery was ever so lavishly embellished. We have a somewhat highly-sounding title to begin with; and then, which way soever our eyes are turned, from head to foot, or foot to head, some extraordinary features present themselves—on each pillar of the staple a caduceus of the universal messenger, Hermes—alligators, and other draconic serpents, emblematize, on the levers, the power of wisdom—then, for *the balance of power* (we rude

barbarians of the old world make mere cast-iron *lumps* serve to inforce our notions of the *balance of power*) we see, surmounting the Columbian press, the American eagle with extended wings, and grasping in his talons Jove's thunderbolts, combined with the olive-branch of Peace and cornucopia of Plenty, all handsomely bronzed and gilt *resisting and bearing down* ALL OTHER POWER![18]

The metaphor of machine and of nature coexisted in printing, which is perhaps fitting, given the somewhat ambiguous nature of this craft that was nearly industry. For centuries printing was the craft that used interchangeable parts and employed division of labor and yet did not become mechanized to any extent until the 1830s, when many other crafts also were.

From printers' own hands comes other explicit imagery in the form of various analogies between printing and nature and printing and the supernatural. A long poem by a printer published in Edinburgh in 1713 is titled "Contemplation upon the mystery of Man's regeneration, [an] Allusion to the Mystery of Printing." Therein is laid out an elaborate analogy of God as the Master Printer. One hundred and thirty years later in 1850 there is the same sort of analogy but printing becomes likened to nature. Here is the endnote to a book of printers' poems:

> Here ends the work,—the last sheet of the heap
> Has been thrown off,—the form is washed, and laid
> Upon the board, stripped of its furniture,
> To be forthwith distributed, and then
> The type composed anew:—The Press is thus
> Analogous with Nature, as she wheels
> The changing seasons, and renews herself
> In thousand varying forms, from that first font
> Cast in the matrix of Almighty power,
> By HIM the glorious ARCHETYPE of all.[19]

An "Ode to Printing" written in 1730 included this verse in its praise for the establishment of William Park's press in Virginia:

> Happy the Art, by which we learn
> The Gloss of Errors to detect,
> The Vice of Habits to correct,
> And sacred Truths from Falsehood to discern!
> By which we take a far-stretch'd View,

> And learn our Fathers Vertues to pursue,
> Their Follies to exchew.[20]

There are many such examples of printers' poetry. A printers' toast from 1868 continues in the same vein:

> The Press—all lands shall sing,
> The Press, the Press, we bring,
> All lands to bless.
> O pallid want ! O labor stark !
> Behold we bring the second ark—
> The Press, the Press.[21]

Strong nationalism also becomes apparent, as indicated in the following.

> Why is it that the progress of modern nations in every branch of useful knowledge is so inconceivably rapid, compared with the slow growth of ancient Europe in the arts of civilization? The answer is simple and satisfactory. The art of printing, and the habit of reading, have done all. Here we have the talismanic wand which as by enchantment, lays forests prostrate, throws splendid arches over rivers that impeded man in his labours, builds great cities, raises the fanes of religion, and the palaces of justice, and the abodes of science in every part of the country. It is this that makes the farmer capable of doubling and quadrupling the production of his lands, and the manufacturer of supplying the most useful, ornamental, abundant and cheap fabrics for every purpose of domestic and social life. It is this that lends wings to commerce that she may fly to the ends of the earth. The proprietors of this work, humbly offer their services to the public to promote these great national objects.[22]

Printing was understood, by printers, as the "Art of all Arts." As a "heav'n-taught art" it enjoyed supernatural guidance.[23] It was a natural art; it had political and social power as it preserved "Law, Liberty, Love, Order, Knowledge, Religion!"[24] Supernatural, natural, and national power imbued the press with real authority.

Printers, of course, had much more to say about their craft. In the American colonies, ideas about the appropriateness of neutrality or partisanship changed through the eighteenth century, particularly during the Revolutionary era.[25] During unionization and industrialization, printers were articulate about both their craft and their own place in society.[26] Further elaboration on printers' written views, however, would be beyond the scope of this chapter. It will suffice to understand broadly the way that printers saw their craft and the place of their craft in the grand scheme of things: in supernatural, natural, political, and practical settings. Printing, a clearly artificial invention that could support wide-ranging intentions, was promoted as "natural" and essential to the proper and just order of things.

At a broad scale, then, is the European New World and controlling cultural metaphor. The garden as metaphor gives way, at least partially, to the machine by the late eighteenth century. Naturalizing ideology remains an essential element of cultural hegemony, however, and can be identified in printers' own broad perceptions of their craft. The same naturalizing ideology becomes apparent at other scales of analysis, even as the machine itself becomes naturalized.

Narrowing the scale of analysis from the New World and the changing cultural metaphors of garden and machine leads to the levels of colony (or state) and city. Other scales could be added. On the regional and interregional scales, for example, printers' networks for news and employment and booksellers' networks would provide sources for examining print culture.

Within the region, the geographic placement of Maryland's capital was a strategy for power. When Governor Francis Nicholson moved the site of the capital of Maryland from St. Mary's City to Ann Arundel's town (renamed Annapolis) in 1694, he made less of an economic decision than a political one as he moved from a Catholic to a Protestant stronghold.[27] With the government came a printer and the craft that was essential to governmental bureaucracy.

Major economic changes occurred in the late eighteenth and nineteenth centuries. The shift in wealth which occurred during this time involved the restructuring of regional economics as Baltimore grew to eclipse its older neighbor. After 1800, Baltimore grew rapidly in population and industry and as a location of investment capital, becoming one of the major American industrial and cultural centers during the nineteenth century. Printing was no exception to the growth of craft and industry in Baltimore. The type foundry of Binney and Ronaldson began selling printers' type in 1796. Frederick Green, the official state printer in Annapolis, purchased large amounts of type from the foundry in 1798 and in 1800.[28] Annapolis would never have its own foundry. In Annapolis William Parks printed the colony's first newspaper, the *Maryland Gazette,* from 1727 until 1734, and the name was adopted by Jonas Green for his newspaper begun in 1745. By 1800, two other papers had been started in Annapolis. In contrast, there was no newspaper in Baltimore until 1773 but by 1800 nineteen papers had been started, a handful of which survived more than a few years. By 1820, Annapolis had two weekly papers while Baltimore had four daily papers and two weeklies. As the Annapolis pre-Revolution "Golden Age" faded, Baltimore flourished.

At the locale of colony and state, printing comes into play as evidence for the regional shift of economic and social power from Annapolis to Baltimore. Printing also had traveled with power when the capital was moved from St. Mary's City in southern Maryland to Annapolis in 1694.

The Annapolis city plan is composed of circles and radiating streets rather than a grid (map 10.1). The town plan has been analyzed extensively.[29] Designed as a seat of power in 1694 by Governor Nicholson, it is a baroque

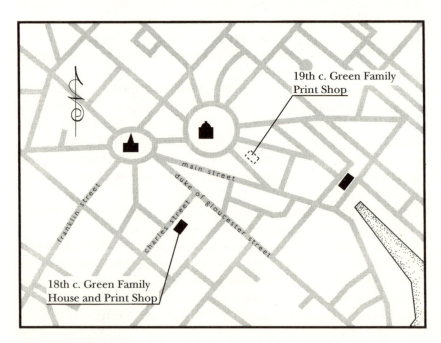

Map 10.1. The eighteenth- and nineteenth-century Green family print shops, Annapolis.

plan that uses two- and three-dimensional space to create vistas and statements about power. The two foci are circles that contain the Anglican church and the statehouse.

The powerful institutions of Church and State highlighted by the plan are hierarchical, with the parts being subordinated to the whole. Until the Revolution the effect was to focus the views of people upward to authority. However, with the acceptance of a state power based on the assumption of individual rights and responsibilities of citizenship, the opposite view—the view down from centers of authority—became equally and possibly more important.[30] Leone and Little argue that "the State House dome, built after the Revolution and in response to the triumph of the theory of individualism embodied in the Bill of Rights, is a panopticon, an all-seeing eye of the state watching and being watched by fellow citizens who are liberty-loving and liberty-endowed individuals."[31] This shift in the relations of power within the state is expressed in a shift in spatial metaphor for the nature of that power.

Initially, the town plan contained another expression of metaphorical understanding of authority. When this metaphor shifted the power of print had become firmly and broadly implanted throughout many settings. From the two circles of the baroque plan, it may be understood that both streets (paths to and from power) and authority emanated. Authority was vested in the great "speaking books," which are the Law (embodied in the statehouse) and the Bible (embodied in the church). These sources of authority carried great influence among the unlettered as well as among the learned.[32] The power of print culture and the permanence and replicability it enables were and are central to the organization of the political and social structure of the city and of the New World.[33]

The power of the "speaking books" as such was partly rooted in traditions of oral culture and concomitant respect for and dependence on experience and face-to-face learning. Print culture is democratizing and creates individuals who read silently. The speaking books became omnipotent in their silence, and they and other products of the press became permanent, deeply culturally embedded, and powerful, as all printers knew.

Within the city, the movement of print shops through the eighteenth century demonstrates shifting power relations. The locations of some of the earlier print shops is not entirely certain, although there are strong clues for some of them. The earliest printer in Annapolis was Dinah

Nuthead, widow of the government printer in St. Mary's City. The location of her shop or of any material relating to it are unknown. A public building near the city dock was apparently used by Thomas Reading perhaps as early as 1700, but certainly by 1709.[34] In the thirteen years following Reading's death in 1713 the city contracted three different people to do official government printing, but little if any actual printing was done inside the city limits. Two of these people almost certainly subcontracted work to printers working outside the city.[35] The other was John Peter Zenger, who later became well known in a "freedom of the press" trial in New York. Zenger apparently lived outside of the city of Annapolis, as Maryland Assembly proceedings report him as living in Kent County on the eastern shore of Maryland.[36] When William Parks came to Annapolis in 1726 he settled in "Newtown," an area of gridded lots designed for occupation by craftsmen.[37] In 1738 Jonas Green established his shop on the opposite side of town on Charles Street where he and his descendants printed exclusively for at least half a century and continued to use the print shop for several decades thereafter.[38] Each of these locations is away from the physical center of power, i.e., the Capitol at State Circle. After the American Revolution Frederick Green moved the print shop office to the main street of town to a location with a clear view of the statehouse.[39] He moved again no more than a block away in 1800.[40] Frederick Green became known for his attacks on the policies of the ruling party. When he died his son did not inherit the title of printer to the state. The man who was awarded the position defended the "cruelties of the democratic party"; cruel, it may be supposed, in denying support to the Green family that had served government for three generations.[41] Jehu Chandler wrote in the *Maryland Republican* in 1813, "Frederick Green, (late printer to the state,) was continued in office until the day of his death in 1811, by the democrats, notwithstanding he was the editor of a federal paper, and one of the most violent partizans in the federal ranks."[42] Frederick's son Jonas moved the shop up the hill to a location directly opposite the statehouse after the family lost the lucrative title of official printer to the state. This grandson of the founder of the *Maryland Gazette* moved his shop to a position of power just when he lost power and when his financial situation began its downslide to eventual bankruptcy.[43] Whether the final move can be interpreted as a challenge, a claim, an act of defiance, a plea, or something else remains to be judged.

Within Annapolis the printscape expressed in the town plan is related to shifting political theory and to the shift in authority from oral to print culture. The speaking books' religious and legal authority, rooted in the connection between oral and print culture, permeated every part of society. The changing locations of the print shops suggest some connections between spatial relations of power and the uses of space that let people relate to power in a spatial way.

Cultural Landscape/Cultural Metaphor

> A whole history remains to be written of *spaces*—which would be at the same time the history of *powers* (both of these terms in the plural)—from the great strategies of the geopolitics to the little tactics of the habitat.
>
> —Foucault, cited in Soja, *Postmodern Geographies*

Space is used to express or enforce power both regionally, in the movement of the capital to Annapolis, and within the city, through the design of the city plan and through the changing placement of printing offices relative to the symbolic and actual seat of power. The organization of space within the household may also be an expression of power. Elsewhere, I have analyzed rebuilding and the arrangement of artifacts in both home and print shop between 1767 and 1775 by Anne Catherine Green, a printer and widow of the printer, Jonas Green. I have suggested that, as an expression of a gender-based preference for a different cultural metaphor, she followed a domestic task orientation rather than the emergent wage-labor time orientation expressed by her husband and that her choice is visible in the archaeological record. She attached the printshop to the house and performed both printing and household tasks throughout the home.[44]

The use of space also helps illuminate changes that are occurring with the emerging culture of capitalism. Both the separation of home space from work space and the segmentation of the layout of the newspaper are markers of a changing cultural "common sense" that focuses on the individual rather than on community.[45]

Ideology that roots social constructs in nature is relatively common in eighteenth-century Annapolis. The power and inevitability of Nature are important cultural forces in Enlightenment thought. Nature and the idea of setting are closely interwoven, especially in an age that is not yet industrialized. Printers naturalize their own craft before, during, and after industrialization. Even after the machine displaces the garden as a primary cultural metaphor, printers continue to root their craft in the natural and even the supernatural world.

Marx explores the cultural metaphors of garden and machine within Anglo-American society.[46] Print culture can be served by both metaphors as printing is "naturalized" and the technology and products of the press are glorified. As the machine supplants the garden as controlling cultural metaphor, there is a concomitant shift in material expressions of culture. It should not be surprising that the shift may be connected to the many binary oppositions identified as characteristic of the shift in worldview in the eighteenth century: organic/mechanical; nature/culture; corporate/individual.[47] The culture change is pervasive as a wholly different metaphor for organizing and comprehending daily life.

Practitioners of cognitive semantics explain metaphor as a cognitive mapping from the source domain of the humanly experienced world to the abstract target domain of language.[48] George Lakoff finds the basis of metaphor in physical experience, in body-sense and body-image.[49] I suggest that, in addition, the understanding born of concrete experience is necessarily cultural, as the spatiality and material conditions and experiences of the body are culturally contextualized. Lakoff grounds metaphor in day-to-day bodily experience, but it is crucial to understand that such experience is not "natural" in any noncultural sense; nor is it expressed in language only. It is expressed, clarified, and worked out in material culture as well.

Setting at every spatial level shapes and is shaped by cultural perceptions. Objects, houses, yards, streets, cities, and continents represent scales for creating and then for understanding setting and sense of place. Culture that is active must include the material as well as the mythological, linguistic, and literary. Both textual and nontextual material culture are understood as the things that people use to create their settings and structure their lives.

The first of Soja's eight premises of postmodern geography provides a useful summary for archaeology which also continues to theorize human use and understanding of space: "Spatiality is a substantiated and recognizable social product, part of a 'second nature' which incorporates as it socializes and transforms both physical and psychological spaces."[50] In the case of Annapolis, the spatiality of the town plan influenced power relations and printers' choices for the locations of their offices.

Dell Upton has discussed both physical and psychological space. One of his goals is the conjunction of symbolism, ideology, and the psychology of perception of the physical world.[51] In discussing the cultural landscape of the city as a metaphorical system, he offers this premise: "The landscape articulates the individual and the social, as the self constructs and interprets the body-in-space, the self *in* its surroundings."[52]

Upton discusses the interaction of language and things: "Language filters our experience, but the language through which we interpret the landscape acquires specificity through the experience of specific mental configurations."[53] This thought begins the extension of a source domain for metaphor into the material, but Soja would argue that it just stops short, at mental configurations. One of Soja's complaints, in fact, is that the power of space is denied by the relegation of spatial organization to the mind. He regards this tendency as a misguided attempt to avoid the presumed dangers of spatial fetishism.[54]

The settings created by print culture and by the culture of capitalism were not, and are not, necessarily identical, but some of their overlap can be identified in the processes of exploration and colonization, of economic and social manipulation, of negotiations and revolutions of power, and of design, production, and consumption of objects. These locales—landscape, cityscape, printscape—are active. They may determine some actions; they influence, limit, and open up possibilities. This active nature of culture is an essential agent in Giddens's structuration and is essential for understanding the use and meanings of the settings we create.[55] From texts to gardens and city plans, these objects of everyday life provided a way for people to create "micro-settings," which incorporate changes occurring at all scales. Through the small scale of micro-setting, individuals could bring the macro-settings of a vastly changing world into perspective on a human scale.

Material culture, not just the human body, is a source domain for the target domain of language. Material culture may also be a target domain for creating expressions of cultural metaphors which are multilayered. Some of the major metaphorical changes seen here in material culture are those in the town plan as the structure of the state changed; in the language used to understand the metaphysical and political place of printing, an important technology of expression; in the changing metaphor of garden and industry; and in the shifting authority from oral to written and from the realm of experience to that of institutionalized education and the ideal of universal literacy.

Notes

1. Edward W. Soja, *Postmodern Geographies: The Reassertion of Space in Critical Social Theory* (New York: Verso, 1989).
2. Anthony Giddens, *The Constitution of Society: Outline of the Theory of Structuration* (Berkeley: Univ. of California Press, 1984), 118–19.
3. Soja, *Postmodern Geographies*, 80.
4. Ibid., 120.
5. See, however, James Deetz, "Scale in Historical Archaeology," paper presented at the Society for Historical Archaeology, 1986; and Marley Brown, "Some Issues of Scale in Historical Archaeology," paper presented at the Society for Historical Archaeology, 1987.
6. Deetz, "Scale in Historical Archaeology."
7. For example, Barbara J. Little and Paul A. Shackel, "Scales of Historical Anthropology: An Archaeology of Colonial Anglo-America," *Antiquity* 63 (1989): 495–509; and Shackel, *Personal Discipline and Material Culture: An Archaeology of Annapolis, Maryland, 1695–1870* (Knoxville: Univ. of Tennessee Press, 1993).
8. Soja, *Postmodern Geographies*, 23–24.
9. See, for example, Wayne Franklin, *Discoverers, Explorers, Settlers; The Diligent Writers of Early America* (Chicago: Univ. of Chicago Press, 1979).
10. Quoted in Gordon R. Willey and Jeremy Sabloff, *A History of American Archaeology*, 2d ed. (London: Thames and Hudson, 1980), 14.
11. Leo Marx, *The Machine in the Garden: Technology and the Pastoral Ideal in America* (Oxford: Oxford Univ. Press, 1964).
12. Ibid.
13. Quotation in ibid., 76.
14. Marx, *The Machine in the Garden*.
15. For example, Mark P. Leone, "Interpreting Ideology in Historical Archaeology: Using the Rules of Perspective in the William Paca Garden in Annapolis, Maryland," in *Ideology, Power and Prehistory*, ed. Daniel Miller and Christopher Tilley (Cambridge: Cambridge Univ. Press, 1984), 25–35; and Leone, "Rule by Ostentation: The Relationship between Space and Sight in Eighteenth-Century Landscape Architecture in the Chesapeake Region of Maryland," in *Method and Theory for Activity Area Research*, ed. Susan Kent (New York: Columbia Univ. Press, 1987), 604–33.
16. Ibid.; Leone and Shackel, "Archaeology of Town Planning in Annapolis, Maryland," report to the National Geographic Society, 1985; Leone and Shackel, "Forks, Clocks and Power," in *Mirror and Metaphor: Material and Social Constructions of Reality*, ed. Daniel W. Ingersoll and Gordon Bronitsky (Lanham, Md.: Univ. Press of America, 1987), 45–61; and Leone, Julie Ernstein, Elizabeth Kryder-Reid, and Shackel, "Power Gardens in Annapolis." *Archaeology* 42 (2) (1989): 34–39, 74–75.
17. John F. Kasson, *Civilizing the Machine: Technology and Republican Values in America, 1776–1900* (New York: Penguin Books, 1976).

18. Quotation in ibid., 254.
19. James J. Brenton, ed., *Voices of the Press: A Collection of Sketches, Essays, and Poems, by Practical Printers* (New York, 1850).
20. J. Markland, *Typographia, an Ode on Printing* (Williamsburg, Va., 1730).
21. Charles Munsell, ed., *A Collection of Songs of the American Press and Other Poems Relating to the Art of Printing* (Albany, N.Y., 1868).
22. Anonymous, "Internal Improvements," *Washington Quarterly Magazine* 1 (1) (1823): 2–7.
23. Robert S. Coffin, *The Printer and Several Other Poems* (Boston, 1817), 9.
24. William Burdick, *An Oration on the Nature and Effects of the Art of Printing* (Boston, 1802), 1.
25. See, for example, Stephen Botein, "'Meer mechanics' and an Open Press: The Business and Political Strategies of Colonial American Printers," in *Perspectives in American History*, vol. 9, ed. D. Fleming and B. Bailyn (Cambridge: Harvard Univ. Press, 1985), 127–225.
26. For example, William Pretzer, "Tramp Printers: Craft Culture, Trade Unions, and Technology," *Printing History* 6 (1984): 3–16.
27. Nancy Baker, "Annapolis, Maryland, 1695–1730," *Maryland Historical Magazine* 81 (3) (1986): 191–209; John W. Reps, *Tidewater Towns: City Planning in Colonial Virginia and Maryland* (Williamsburg, Va.: Colonial Williamsburg Foundation); see also Henry Miller, "Baroque Cities in the Wilderness: Archaeology and Urban Development in the Colonial Chesapeake," *Historical Archaeology* 22 (2) (1988): 57–73.
28. J. J. Cornigan, "Binney and Ronaldson's First Type," *Printing and Graphic Arts* 1 (1953): 27–35.
29. For example, Reps, *Tidewater Towns*; Mark P. Leone and Barbara J. Little, "Artifacts as Expressions of Society and Culture: Subversive Genealogy and the Value of History," in *History from Things: Essays on Material Culture*, ed. Steven Lubar and W. David Kingery (Washington, D.C.: Smithsonian Institution Press, 1993), 160–81; Leone and Shackel, *Archaeology of Town Planning*; Shackel, "Town Plans and Everyday Material Culture: An Archaeology of Social Relations in Colonial Maryland's Capital Cities," in *Historical Archaeology of the Chesapeake*, ed. Shackel and Little (Washington, D.C.: Smithsonian Institution Press, 1994): 85–96.
30. Leone and Little, "Artifacts as Expressions," 165–66.
31. Ibid., 161–62.
32. Rhys Isaac, "Books and the Social Authority of Learning: The Case of Mid-eighteenth century Virginia," in *Printing and Society in Early America*, ed. W. L. Joyce, D. D. Hall, R. D. Brown, and J. B. Hench (Worcester, Mass.: American Antiquarian Society, 1983), 228–49.
33. For example, Elizabeth Eisenstein, *The Printing Press as an Agent of Change: Communications and Cultural Transformation in Early Modern Europe* (Cambridge: Cambridge Univ. Press, 1979); Eisenstein, *The Printing Revolution in Early Modern Europe* (Cambridge: Cambridge Univ. Press, 1983).
34. *Proceedings and Acts of the General Assembly of Maryland* 26 (Sept. 1704–Apr.

1706), Archives of Maryland, Maryland State Archives, Annapolis, 129, 577; Lawrence C. Wroth, *The Colonial Printer* (Portland, Maine: Southworth-Anthoesen Press, 1938), 19.

35. *Proceedings and Acts,* vol. 33 (May 1717–Apr. 1720), 271; vol. 35 (Oct. 1724–July 1726), 99.

36. *Proceedings and Acts,* 33 (May 1717–Apr. 1720), 501; 34 (Oct. 1720–Oct. 1723), 19.

37. *Proceedings and Acts,* 35 (Oct. 1724–July 1726), 439; Provincial Court Deeds DD 4/522, Maryland State Archives, Annapolis.

38. Barbara J. Little, *Ideology and Media: Historical Archaeology of Printing in 18th-Century Annapolis, Maryland* (Ann Arbor, Mich.: Univ. Microfilms International, 1987).

39. *Maryland Gazette,* Feb. 9, 1786.

40. *Maryland Gazette,* Oct. 16, 1800.

41. Quotation in J. T. Wheeler, *A History of the Maryland Press, 1777–1790* (Baltimore: Maryland Historical Society, 1938), 70.

42. Ibid.

43. Little, *Ideology and Media.*

44. Barbara J. Little, "'She Was . . . An Example to Her Sex': Possibilities for a Feminist Historical Archaeology," in *Historical Archaeology of the Chesapeake,* 189–204.

45. Barbara J. Little, "Craft and Culture Change in the 18th-Century Chesapeake," in *The Recovery of Meaning: Historical Archaeology in the Eastern United States,* ed. Mark P. Leone and Parker B. Potter Jr. (Washington, D.C.: Smithsonian Institution Press, 1988), 263–92; and Barbara J. Little, "Explicit and Implicit Meanings in Material Culture and Print Culture," *Historical Archaeology* 26 (3) (1992): 85–94.

46. Marx, *The Machine in the Garden.*

47. Deetz, *In Small Things Forgotten: The Archaeology of Early American Life* (Garden City, N.Y.: Anchor Books, 1977).

48. For example, Mark Johnson, *The Body in the Mind: The Bodily Basis of Meaning, Imagination, and Reason* (Chicago: Univ. of Chicago Press, 1987); George Lakoff, *Women, Fire, and Dangerous Things: What Categories Reveal About the Mind* (Chicago: Univ. of Chicago Press, 1987); and Lakoff and Johnson, *Metaphors We Live By* (Chicago: Univ. of Chicago Press, 1980).

49. Naomi Quinn takes exception to what she regards as an overstatement that metaphors *create* understanding and instead considers that they are *partly* constitutive of understanding. Hoyt Alverson expresses this opinion as well, one shared by many anthropologists, that metaphors are irreducibly *cultural.* Alverson writes, "Let us approach the problem of image schemas . . . as Lakoff insists, from the 'experience of things.' Let us further suggest that fundamental lived-body experiences of spatiality are kinesthetically, visually, tactilely informed—but also that these can be linguistically/culturally elaborated or augmented" (112). By this Alverson implies that what is cultural is also linguistically expressible. See Alverson, "Metaphor and Experience: Looking Over the Notion of Image Schema," in *Beyond Metaphor: The*

Theory of Tropes in Anthropology, ed. James W. Fernandez (Stanford, Calif.: Stanford Univ. Press, 1991), 94–117; and Quinn, "The Cultural Basis of Metaphor," in *Beyond Metaphor*, 56–93.

50. Soja, *Postmodern Geographies*, 129.

51. Dell Upton, "Form and User: Style, Mode, Fashion, and the Artifact," in *Living in a Material World: Canadian and American Approaches to Material Culture*, ed. Gerald L. Pocius (St. John's, Newfoundland: Institute of Social and Economic Research, 1991), 156–69.

52. Upton, "The City as Material Culture," in *The Art and Mystery of Historical Archaeology: Essays in Honor of James Deetz*, ed. Anne E. Yentsch and Mary C. Beaudry (Boca Raton: CRC Press, 1992), 52.

53. Ibid., 53.

54. Soja, *Postmodern Geographies*, 77.

55. Giddens, *The Constitution of Society*.

11 Part of a "Polished Society": Style and Ideology in Annapolis's Georgian Architecture

Christopher N. Matthews

During the 1760s and 1770s over a dozen large brick houses either were constructed or altered in Annapolis, Maryland. Built by a group of mostly young and well-educated men, these houses displayed the wealth and taste of their builders to the city's inhabitants and visitors. All of the houses were built in the fashionable Georgian style and thus are rigidly symmetrical, harmonic, and sparsely ornamented. The use of this style served the group as it inspired the observation that Annapolis was the site of "several modern edifices which make a good appearance," and they encouraged the visitor to believe Annapolis was part of a "polished society."[1] Inasmuch as the effect of this architecture was to connect wealthy Annapolitans to the standards of taste dominant in the British empire, these houses can act as the impetus for an anthropological investigation of Annapolitan architecture before the American Revolution. This chapter is an interrogation of style which clearly relates the elements of Georgian architecture to a discourse over power found throughout the English world in the eighteenth century. By analyzing Georgian architecture in terms of design and implementation, it can be seen that it materializes an ideology which bolstered the claims of members of the

Annapolitan economic elite to the positions of political authority. Ultimately this ideology successfully underwrote their leadership in Maryland during and after the Revolution by making their authority seem obvious and legitimate.

Defining the Georgian Style: Eighteenth-Century Architectural Publications

The application of stylistic attributes to the objects of the material world imbues these objects with ideas taken to be appropriate and, perhaps, natural. However, these ideas often developed as part of the construction of a partisan political perspective, and thus are arbitrary. When this is the case, styles in material objects install, reproduce, and engrain ways of thinking about the world and society which promote and reproduce that perspective, thus acting as ideology.[2]

A Marxist analysis of Georgian architecture must consider the intended and hoped-for consequences of Georgian style by its builders. In mid-eighteenth-century Annapolis, the Georgian style was known to builders and prospective owners more because of published designs in pattern books and architectural treatises than because of worldly experience. The wealthy and educated were able to draw ideas from the great country houses in England as well as the unbuilt designs of the mother country's greatest architects, which were published in pattern books. Annapolitans were by no means alone; the use of pattern books was common throughout the colonies and the rest of the British empire during the eighteenth century.[3] These books, therefore, should provide a unique glimpse into the social practice of English architecture.

To understand the construction of the Georgian style and to assess its function as an ideology, I surveyed a sample of pattern books. Several physical and textual facets of the books were analyzed and the brief texts were examined for what they suggested about the style. The sample of 128 different volumes consisted of books known to be available in the American colonies prior to the American Revolution. This list was assembled by Helen Park in 1973 and draws from both the inventories of American colonial elites as well as booksellers' lists. Park identified 87 different volumes known by exact title and 19 known only by conjecture due to inaccuracies in the recording of book titles by inventory takers. I have added to that sample a variety of books published in England by some of the same authors read in the American colonies.

Several patterns emerged from this analysis. When they are tied to the political dynamics of the early Georgian era in England, these patterns demonstrate how an architectural style clearly can act as an agent of an ideology. Fig. 11.1 is a tabulation of the number of books published per year. The maximum is 14 for the year 1760, but perhaps more interesting is the apparent increase in publication of books in general immediately after 1720. The rise in publications coincides with the time of the coronation of George I and of the formation of a group known as the Rule of Taste. At that time in English history an unprecedented coalition between the monarchy and parliament was constructed. Although this was part of a principle established after the Glorious Revolution of 1688, it failed to be effective during the reigns of King William III and Queen Anne because of party politics. With the arrival of George III in 1718 things changed. King George's international interests drew him to the Whig platform, thus he supported Whig efforts and established a Whig cabinet. This was immediately followed by the rise of Robert Walpole to First Minister in 1722. Walpole was an effective leader and administrator who held on to his post for twenty years, an astonishing feat for the period. In that time he created and maintained a political stability, sometimes called a Whig oligarchy, which had significant impact on English society. The rise of the Whigs to the top of the social hierarchy forced a readjustment of the upper strata and opened room for elite social competition. Many

Fig. 11.1. Tabulation of the number of English architectural books published per year.

people tried to grab various forms of power ranging from political to artistic to social power. This competition drove elite factions to find ways to assert themselves and garner support for their agendas.

The Whig government, however, benefited its own kind. In the arts this was the Third Earl of Burlington, Richard Boyle, a Whig with a peerage, a patron of the arts, and the leader of the Rule of Taste group. The Rule of Taste expressed in print that the new King represented a radical departure from what came before and demanded a revolution in style. To do this, Burlington sponsored a circle of artists including architects, sculptors, painters, dramatists, writers, and musicians to construct the new style.[4] The group was guided by a supposed "Rule of Taste" and the desire of instituting a style based on the past glories of Britain and the concepts of beauty derived from the Classical and Renaissance ages. Architecture was Burlington's specialty and through his patronage of architects such as Colen Campbell, Giacomo Leoni, William Kent, and Isaac Ware, the Rule of Taste came to dominate British civic and high style domestic architecture in the 1720s and 1730s.[5] Significantly, the Rule of Taste made use of the printed media to propagate its style. This is what is recorded by the jump in publications after 1720.

Fig. 11.2 is a tabulation of the number of books sampled at certain heights. The height of a book was generally a function of its cost: the taller

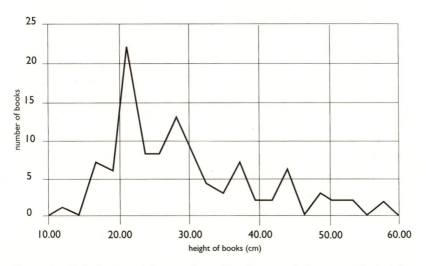

Fig. 11.2. Tabulation of the number of books sampled at specific heights.

the book, the more expensive it was. Along the horizontal axis are the actual heights of the books in centimeters and along the vertical axis is the quantity of books at a given height. The majority of books published are toward the smaller end of the scale. At first this is not surprising from the point of view of cost. However, the importance of this pattern derives from the fact that the contents of these smaller books are on the whole remarkably different from the contents of the taller ones. While the larger books were filled mostly with plates of facades, plans, and design elements, the smaller books were "companion" books which, according to their authors, were to be carried in the pockets and tool chests of the laborers and journeymen so they could be referenced on the site. Thus, the smaller books were aimed at builders, craftsmen, and workmen, and the larger books were aimed at the master craftsmen and prospective owners.

Another way to see the difference in these books is to compare those books that had a patron with those that were sold directly by the printers. Table 11.1 shows this distribution. Books with patrons were more often those with more designs than texts, and they tended to be taller and thus more expensive. This pattern suggests that these books were to be owned by the prospective owners of the buildings as evidence of their appreciation of the designs of the Rule of Taste group, or other architects at the time. The fact that lists of patrons were published in the front of the books only more clearly announced who was an active participant in the propagation of the Georgian style.

Fig. 11.3 shows the average height of all the books published within a given year of publication. Here the graph shows that the smaller books tend, on average, to be printed later than the taller volumes. In 1720 the average height was approaching 45 centimeters while in 1750 the average height was closer to 25 centimeters. This pattern suggests that when the Rule of Taste group first formed, the books were taller, possibly reflecting that the early books

Table 11.1

Comparison of the Mean Height of Books in the Sample with the Presence of a Patron

	Mean Height	Count
Books with Patron	31.49	25
Books w/o Patron	26.78	35

published were to be found in libraries of the wealthy rather than the pockets of the workmen. This makes sense since the conversion of the patrons of architects, the prospective house owners, was vital to the installation of a new style. Consequently, the craftsmen in the building trades would only need to be informed of the new style when they were called upon to build. This point is also supported by the data in Table 11.2, which provides a mean date for those books with a patron versus those without a patron. Books with a patron have a mean date almost a quarter of a century earlier than those without. This is a very significant difference, because it suggests a decreasing reliance on patronage by architectural writers.

It is clear from these patterns that there was a trend which saw the stepped-up publication of architectural books following the formation of the Rule of Taste. An initial review of the contents of these books also has noted that the majority of these books contributed to the construction and propagation of the principles of the Rule of Taste. To understand these principles, and their effect on the construction of the style as an ideology, it is necessary to more closely examine the elements of the Georgian style.

Perhaps the single most influential individual on the Rule of Taste architects and the Georgian style was the Renaissance Italian architect Andrea Palladio (1508–1580). Palladio drew significantly from the classical landscapes in and around Rome to develop the theoretical basis for his architecture. The study of the work of Vitruvius, whose *Ten Books of Architecture* was the only surviving architectural volume from classical

Fig. 11.3. Average height of all books in the sample published within a given year.

Table 11.2
Comparison of the Mean Dates of Publication of Books in the Sample
with the Presence of a Patron

	Mean Date	Count
Books with Patron	1721	28
Books w/o Patron	1745	38

Rome, guided much of Palladio's thought. Palladio was the author of *The Four Books of Architecture*, in which he laid out his principles for design and building. Much of this book was readily accepted as correct, and it began to be rapidly propagated throughout Europe. It reached England first in the seventeenth century through the work of the architect Inigo Jones, and then was revived by the Rule of Taste in the early eighteenth century.

To understand Palladio and Palladianism, then, is vital to understanding Georgian style. A. Placzek lays out the essential elements when he notes that "Palladiansim is the conviction, first of all, that a universally applicable vocabulary of architectural forms is both desirable and possible; secondly, that such a vocabulary had been developed by the Romans, . . . and thirdly, that a careful study and judicious use of these forms will result in Beauty. This Beauty, according to the Palladians, is therefore not only derived from ideal forms and harmony; it is also rooted in historical correctness."[6] Architecturally, Palladianism produced stark structures where ornamentation is subdued in favor of the expression of harmonic proportion. Emphasis was placed on symmetry and order, ultimately aiming at a beauty constructed using principles believed to be derived from nature. Throughout *The Four Books of Architecture*, the notions of the classics were ingested without critical appraisal, prominent among them harmony and the ratios it produced between elements. These ratios were believed by Palladio to be the result of natural phenomena, a belief first developed by Pythagoras in the sixth century B.C.[7]

Palladio's influence on the Rule of Taste is evident in the publication of Palladio's *The Four Books of Architecture*, translated into English first by Leoni in 1715–17 and then again by Ware in 1738.[8] It is also seen in the several trips made to Italy by Rule of Taste architects to observe and draw Palladio's work. Burlington, for example, made his own Italian pil-

Table 11.3

Comparison of the Mean Height of Books in the Sample with the
Presence of Palladio's Five Orders

	Mean Height	Count
Books with Five Orders	28.35	46
Books w/o Five Orders	28.41	28

Table 11.4

Comparison of the Mean Dates of Publication of Books in the Sample
with the Presence of Palladio's Five Orders

	Mean Date	Count
Books with Five Orders	1725	49
Books w/o Five Orders	1741	32

grimage in 1719, and in 1721 he bought Inigo Jones's previously collected
Palladian drawings.

To quantitatively assess the importance of Palladianism to the Rule of
Taste and the Georgian style, tables 11.3 and 11.4 relate the presence and
absence of at least a brief discussion of Palladio to book heights and dates
of publication.[9] Table 11.3 shows that there is no difference between the
inclusion of the orders and whether the book was small or large. This reflects a general acceptance of their validity, regardless of the books' prospective buyer. Table 11.4 shows that of the eighty-one books in the sample
which included the orders, those that made an explicit attempt to interpret the five orders had a mean publication date of 1725, and those that
did not had a mean date of 1741. This difference of sixteen years suggests
an early drive to include and explain the orders associated with the Rule
of Taste. Later in the century, there was apparently less interest in the
orders. Of course this does not mean the orders were forgotten. Rather,
this reflects a mid-century lull in enthusiasm for re-publishing the orders,
either as general information or in an improved form. It also indicates the
influence of opponents of the Rule of Taste who became more vocal after
the 1740s, as the Rule of Taste's English dominance ebbed.

The contents of these publications also were explored to interpret how early-eighteenth-century architectural publications helped to construct an ideology which the Whigs and the Rule of Taste faction used to achieve dominance. On the one hand, this was accomplished through the propagation of the Palladian-influenced Georgian style in line drawings of the great country houses of Britain's economic and social elite. These plates and figures made a clear statement of the inherent quality to the style, but what was especially important to the authors was the notion that these houses accurately demonstrated proportionality based on the rules of harmony handed down from the ancient Greeks. Such accuracy was believed to be achieved through the association of numbers, following the same principles of harmony and proportion devised by Pythagoras and translated into architecture by Palladio. The basis of harmonic proportion was the mathematical relationship of parts that derived from a unit, or module, which was the diameter of a column. Unfortunately, this system inspired a considerable amount of confusion in the successful reproduction of the style by architects and craftsmen working under varying conditions. Therefore, in many of the companion books published in the 1730s and afterward, attempts were made rationalize the construction of harmony. An example can be made of William Halfpenny's *Practical Architecture, or a Sure Guide to the True Working according to the Rules of that Science: Representing the Five Orders, etc.* (published in 1736). Several pages of this book are devoted to charts of numbers which provided a guide to proportionality based on the use of one or another module size. Essentially, an obsessive need to render harmony in architecture is portrayed. That such faith was placed in numbers is also a demonstration of the new architects' support of a rationalized, scientific approach to their trade. The arts were believed from the late seventeenth century in England to be tied to chaos, and if architecture was going to play an effective role it had to align itself with science and order and not with art and chaos.

This thought was expressed definitively in William Leybourne's 1678 dedication in *The Mirror of Architecture:* "To the Lovers of Architecture, Reader, as in all things order is to be observed that we may avoid confusion or else there will be a chaos, as the poet's fancy; so especially in this excellent art of architecture it is requisite that every part have its right order and proportion." Referring to charts such as those compiled by Halfpenny and others it is apparent that this advice was followed meticulously in the eighteenth century. This evidence is used here to show the acceptance of this building style by the craftsmen responsible for carrying out the plans issued by architects and owners. This acceptance may very well be evidence that the arts, like science, were considered a viable means to understand nature as long as the artistic work was done scientifically.

The Annapolitan Context of Georgian Architecture

Turning to the actual built forms of Georgian architecture in Annapolis, we can trace the acceptance and use of the ideas of the Rule of Taste group from published treatises to actual houses. Annapolis is the site of some of the finest examples of Georgian architecture. A social examination of the design and building of the Chase-Lloyd and Hammond-Harwood houses will demonstrate the practice of Georgian architecture in the American Colonies. Both were built in the last years prior to the American Revolution and were the products of one of the colonies' most renowned architects, William Buckland. However, through their architecture, they are also

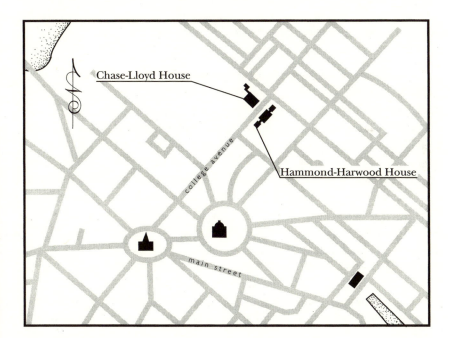

Map 11.1. The Hammond-Harwood House and Chase-Lloyd House, Annapolis.

informative examples of the efforts of the Annapolitan wealthy to incorporate the ideology of the Georgian style in their houses and, by extension, their lives. To more fully understand this argument these houses need to be tied to the contexts of their design and construction.

In the 1770s, Annapolis was the social and political center of Maryland, with a high-style winter social calendar associated with the legislative session. As recorded by William Eddis, a secretary to the proprietary Governor during the 1760s, these typically included:

> a heady round of balls, card parties, and fetes. . . . Horse races were held at the track outside the city gate and in Parole; the theater erected on West Street in 1771 produced the staples of the London stage; Annapolis society danced at the Assembly Rooms on Duke of Gloucester Street. Clubs proliferated: the Jockey Club, the Forensic Club, and the South River Club. . . . Under the editorship of Jonas [and Anne Catherine] Green, the Maryland Gazette kept Annapolitans up-to-date on politics, literature, and London tobacco prices. Annapolis society grew refined without losing touch with the countryside that supplied its wealth; the ability to judge good horse flesh remained as much a mark of a gentleman as the inclination to dispute on the number of Latin vowels.[10]

This extravagant social life was based on a notably expanding economy. The financial base of the city itself was limited throughout the eighteenth century because of the rural Chesapeake tobacco economy. In this system no central storage and distribution centers were necessary to move the commodity into the world economy. Rather, the typical planter moved his crop from his own waterfront along one of the many rivers that empty into the Chesapeake Bay. Towns in this system remained small centers where social interaction was defined more in terms of politics and religion than in terms of economics. Annapolis, as such, never developed a class of native and permanent urban elites. Instead, the town was developed into a social and cultural center by the wealthy, rural population, who brought to the provincial capital the facets of society and culture that distinguished the urban center from the surrounding countryside.

Of the resident population in Annapolis during the early eighteenth century, the majority were tied to the colonial government. In the period prior to the city's "Golden Age," Annapolis bureaucrats earned the majority of reported income in the city, and during the Golden Age the value of their income increased. Not surprisingly, groups of merchants, crafts-

men, and servants came to Annapolis in support of the full-time bureaucracy. Once there, they enjoyed a prosperous situation.[11]

This prosperity expanded in the 1760s because of dramatic developments associated with the enforcement of proprietary laws, especially
concerning taxation. The "rigorous enforcement of proprietary rights such
as quitrents, alienation fines, escheat, and title to vacant lands" drove up
the demand for lawyers in Annapolis after 1763.[12] Men such as William
Paca and Matthias Hammond were able to earn large incomes as their
training at the Inns of Court in London gave them an advantage in the
practice of law. As these and other men earned substantial incomes in law
(often combined with planting and merchant wealth), they subtly formed
a class of wealthy, well-educated, and publicly known individuals independent of the state. These men were responsible for the development of
the city into the social and cultural node it became for Maryland. In addition, these men also began to forcefully oppose the political practices
of the proprietary government because they were the city's first generation to hold significant wealth independent of the state. Not being *of* the
state, however, imposed a limit to the power that usually came with the
wealth they controlled. It was this contradiction that underwrote the political dimension of the Golden Age and the building campaign intimately
related to the period.

A boom in the building and luxury trades in Annapolis was initiated
by members of the social elite, who used their urban residences as performance stages which dramatized their wealth during the court and legislative seasons. Houses were filled with the finest in imported and locally
crafted ceramics, silver and gold, furniture, and fine art (especially por-
traiture), yet the houses themselves were very much part of the presentation. These architectural achievements are a highlight of Annapolis's
Golden Age. During this period impressions of Annapolis evolved rapidly.
In 1708, a traveler called Annapolis a "city situated on a plane, where
scarce a house will keep out the rain"; in 1762 the city was described as
the site of "several large buildings with Capacious Gardens," albeit without "any degree of elegance or Taste"; however, by 1770 the city was home
to "several modern edifices which make a good appearance."[13]

The stylistic character of Annapolis is in part related to the influence of
the carver/joiner/architect William Buckland. Buckland's rise to prominence
as an architect offers important insights about the practice of architecture in
Annapolis. Buckland had, through his own desires for success, acquired the

astute ability to translate not only the aesthetic wishes of his clients into buildings, but their political motivations as well.

Buckland was born in Oxford, England, in 1734, and in 1748 he became a building trades' apprentice to his uncle James Buckland, "citizen and Joiner of London."[14] This training came during a period of rich architectural growth in London: the population was expanding as a result of the rural enclosures, and the city was still recovering from the Great Fire of 1666. The efforts of the Rule of Taste and the foundations of the Georgian style also were openly discussed and practiced, so "probably at no time in the history of English architecture [had] there existed a more perfect knowledge of the technical arts of building."[15] London provided Buckland with an excellent situation in which his work would be thoroughly scrutinized by an active audience, and it also introduced him to published architectural discourses. It is highly probable that Buckland was particularly influenced by the surplus of architectural publications, because his uncle was the proprietor of a book shop in Pater Noster Row which specialized in the sale of architectural volumes.[16] This allowed Buckland to absorb the designs considered essential to the craft and to gain an appreciation of the use of books as guides in building. It is not surprising to learn, then, that Buckland owned seventeen books on architecture and related arts, which was at the time a large number of books to be owned by a craftsman, at his death in 1774.[17]

In 1755 Buckland was indentured to Thomas Mason of London. Buckland was sent overseas to Virginia to do the carving and joinery for Gunston Hall in Fairfax County, owned by George Mason, Thomas Mason's brother. Buckland's carving of interior adornments and his design of an octagonal porch entry brought him praise and started his rise to success. He took with him high accolades from George Mason to Richmond County, where he gained commissions to do work in other phases of construction beyond joinery. By 1762 he was able to take on projects from "plans to completion."[18] In this area of Virginia's Northern Neck, many men accumulated great wealth through tobacco planting and inheritance, and they emerged as local social leaders. Such men wanted to establish themselves on the landscape materially through stately manors and sponsored public works. Buckland's expertise and availability made this possible. Undoubtedly this work confirmed in his mind and practice the relationship between architecture and political motivations, and perhaps ideology. He was commissioned in the early 1760s, for instance, to complete John Tayloe's Mount Airy and then Landon Carter's Sabine Hall.

He then designed and built a prison, a workhouse, and the Glebe House for Lunenberg Parish between 1767 and 1769.

By the 1760s Buckland and his apprentices apparently were not working solely in southern Virginia, and they began to take commissions throughout the Chesapeake. In 1772 Buckland moved to Annapolis, because he saw there the opportunity to successfully attain the rank of Gentleman, something he openly desired.[19] The commissions of the Chase-Lloyd House and the Hammond House induced Buckland to move, but his work in Annapolis obviously opened his eyes to the local elites' competitive desire to affirm themselves through opulent architecture, providing Buckland a substantial market.[20]

In all of Buckland's work, from Gunston Hall through Mount Airy to the Hammond House (his last project), the influence of published Georgian architectural designs is clear. In Annapolis, Buckland's work seldom carried any deviation from the accepted formulas laid out in pattern books.[21] It is likely that Buckland's influence made the architecture of Annapolis's Golden Age appear more rigidly adherent to the pattern books. However, his implementation is not the work of a copyist; rather, I suggest, it is the one of a designer who understood the cultural significance of working with designs that make use of historical precedent and the naturalized understanding of harmony and proportion. It is this sophistication in design as well as his interpretation of a way of thinking (i.e., an ideology) that needs to be taken from Buckland when analyzing his work at the Chase-Lloyd and Hammond-Harwood houses.

The Chase-Lloyd House (figs. 11.4 and 11.5) and the Hammond-Harwood House (figs. 11.6 and 11.7) stand facing each other across Maryland Avenue at the corner of King George Street, creating a looming elite atmosphere that has lasted into the present. Both were built in the 1770s, and both were the product, at least in part, of William Buckland. However, they are very different in structure and express some of the variation possible in Georgian architecture. Further, the articulation of functional necessities and design have produced idiosyncrasies in these houses which will be highlighted.

The Chase-Lloyd House is a well-known landmark today because its first owner, Samuel Chase, was a signer of the Declaration of Independence. In Annapolis he was a regarded as a vigorous patriot who openly criticized the enforcement of Proprietary laws and the Stamp Act. By the time of the Revolution Chase had won the reputation of being "adept at

Fig. 11.4. The Chase-Lloyd House, built 1769–74. Christopher Matthews.

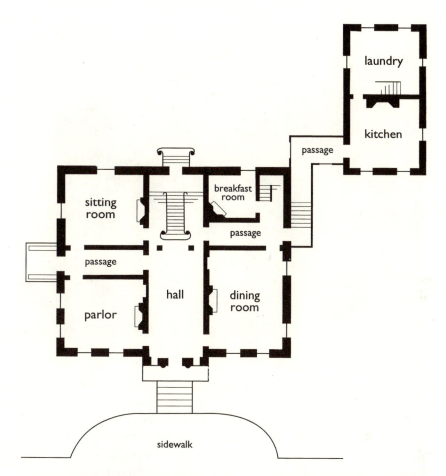

Fig. 11.5. Plan of the Chase-Lloyd House. Adapted from R. R. Bierne "The Chase House in Annapolis," *Maryland Historical Magazine* 44 (3) (1954).

raising a mob, a master of invective eloquence and too outspoken for his own good."[22] He did not come from a wealthy background, nor did he marry into one of the region's more prominent families. Instead, as the son of a clergyman, he was from a middling background. Chase was locally educated in law and rapidly established himself, and in 1765 the twenty-four-year-old was elected to the assembly. Once there, he apparently admired the recently built elite residences in the city, such as William Paca's (1763) and John Ridout's (1765) houses and formal terraced gardens. In

Fig. 11.6. The Hammond-Harwood House, built 1774. Christopher Matthews.

1769, Chase initiated the construction of his own town house. He sought to build a three-story structure, a height only known in Annapolis at the home of Charles Carroll of Carrollton, the wealthiest individual in the colony. Such plans appeared to suit Chase's extravagant personality and taste, but not his finances. In 1771, Chase was forced to abandon his project and sold the unfinished, unroofed shell.

The incomplete building was purchased by Edward Lloyd of Talbot County. Lloyd was from a long line of Maryland landowners who held plantations in Talbot and Queen Anne's Counties, as well on the Chesapeake's western shore. Lloyd's wealth tied him to the colonial authorities as a member of the Governor's Council for twenty-seven years. This connection found him in Annapolis every legislative season; yet, in 1771 he was elected to the assembly as a representative of Talbot County and transferred his allegiance away from the Proprietor. Upon winning this position he decided to seek a suitable home for his family to reside in during the winter months, and he resolved to finish what Samuel Chase had begun. Lloyd had married Elizabeth Tayloe, daughter of Col. John Tayloe

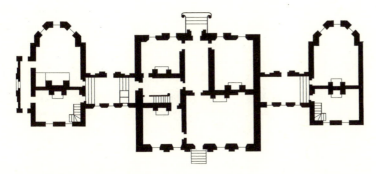

Fig. 11.7. Plan of The Hammond-Harwood House. Adapted from W. H. Pierson "The Hammond-Harwood House: A Colonial Masterpiece," *Antiques Magazine* 111 (1) (1977).

of Mount Airy, in Virginia in 1767. This marriage brought together Lloyd and his unfinished Annapolis house with William Buckland, who was Mount Airy's architect. The completion of the Chase-Lloyd House in 1771 and 1772 ultimately brought Buckland to Annapolis for the last three years of his life. Buckland completed the roof and flooring and is credited with a majority of the interior carving. Buckland was relieved of the final structural work on the property, such as the stable and the party wall, by William Noke when the Hammond house project began.[23]

The architecture of the Chase-Lloyd House demonstrates the principles of harmonic proportion found in Georgian architecture. From the facade to the plan of the main block to certain interior features, the orderly arrangement of parts rigidly follows both the rules of symmetry and harmony. The Maryland Avenue facade is perfectly balanced along a vertical axis running from the central doorway up through the point of the pediment, splicing the chimney stacks. The horizontal string courses draw the eye out from this line, enforcing the vertical balance of the form. The harmony of parts in the facade also is found in the declining elevations of the stories as they rise above the ground level. Though the first and second stories both make use of six-over-six windows, the second story is actually slightly shorter. The six-over-three windows in the third floor clearly show the reduced height of this story. The function of this reduction of scale is to emphasize height by using the rules of perspective well-known to builders in the eighteenth-century. Just as the varied widths and heights of terraces and falls in a formal garden serve to either make a space look larger or smaller than it really is, the systematic reduction of the elevations of the stories at the Chase-Lloyd House enhances the house's elevation by making the upper stories seem to be farther from the eye than they really are.[24]

The effects of these illusions, whether in landscapes or architecture, only work if they follow the rules of harmony as well as perspective. The ratios of intervals developed by Pythagoras and reproduced over the subsequent two-and-one-half millennia guided the spatial ordering of parts in Georgian architecture. Here the rows of window panes show that the ratio of the story elevations follow a systematic pattern in the reduction, following the well-known Pythagorean ratio of 3-4-5.

On the interior the organization of space is again rigidly symmetrical and harmonious. The plan shows the arrangement of rooms, with the exception of passages (which only partition larger spaces), to be strictly symmetrical along the central hall line. This interior central line is reinforced by the central stairway running up from the rear of the main hall to the second floor. This stair passage is set off from the main hall by two ionic columns. It is expected, though as yet untested, that the diameter or area of the base of these columns may serve as the unit of measure in this house plan. This would follow the precedent found in Palladio's work, where the proportion of room sizes, facades, and all of the features is determined by the unit established by the area of the column. It is not surprising that in a house such as Chase-Lloyd the symmetry of the house is accentuated on the garden facade by a Palladian window which lights the middle landing of the main stairway.

The orderly proportion of parts is ultimately expressed in this house in the first-floor front rooms. These two parlors are furnished with some of the finest carving in colonial American architecture, and the larger parlor is fitted with carved, paneled mahogany doors, which were truly rare and found only in the finest colonial houses.[25] Apart from the material of these doors and the accompanying carved door frames, chair rail, and baseboard, there are also three finished and ornamented mahogany doors which are false doors installed into the parlors simply to maintain the harmony of parts within the rooms; two of the three can be identified on the plan view along the walls of the main hall. The use of false doors demonstrates the importance of continuity in style regardless of function. Here the message is the importance of harmony as integral to the success of the design. It is also clear that the false doors serve to accentuate the potency and importance of harmony as part of the Georgian style. The emphasis on symmetry, proportion, and even perspective serves to associate Samuel Chase and Edward Lloyd with an interpretation of harmony developed by Pythagoras and elaborated on, and masked through time, in the Italian Renaissance and Georgian England. In each of these periods the ratio of numbers in terms of harmonic proportion guided thinking about the orderly arrangement of natural phenomena.[26] That harmony was integral to the design of the Chase-Lloyd House makes the house a clear expression and a materialization of the Georgian style as an ideology.

At the Hammond-Harwood House many of the same elements of this ideology are present. The house was built by William Buckland for Matthias Hammond in 1774, and it is considered one of the finest examples of Georgian architecture in the colonies. Like Chase, Paca, and other local elites, Matthias Hammond was a young, wealthy, and eager lawyer. Hammond became active in Maryland politics in the early 1770s, and by 1773 the twenty-five-year-old decided to build a house to suit his needs as a provincial assemblyman.[27] Hammond may have been engaged to be married and intended the house for his new family, but he never actually married by the time of his death at a young age. Some scholars even suggest he may have never lived in the house.[28]

The architectural details of the facade and plan follow the same principles of the ideology of Georgian design and harmony found in the Chase-Lloyd House. The facade has the same symmetry and proportion in the elevation. Here the bull's-eye windows in both the rear and front central pediments provide cross hairs which determine the vertical line of balance. Again, there is a string course which draws the eye out from the central bay to the extremities of the structure, enforcing the symmetry. The proportional relations between the stories also is identified by the windows. On the first floor they are nine-over-six, and on the second floor they are six-over-six. This provides the same ratio as the Chase-Lloyd house of 3-4-5, but here the "3" level is absent. Yet, what the building does—and presumably the architect planned for this—is assume that the viewer's gaze will fill in this gap to complete the harmonic relation.

At first glance, the floor plan of the Hammond House is quite asymmetrical. Some architectural historians believe this floor plan is precocious in its use of stylistic pattern more typical of the neoclassical era of the 1780s and 1790s.[29] However much this may or may not be the case, it is striking how the floor plan makes sense of the symmetry and proportion in a way not nearly so obvious as at Chase-Lloyd and many of the other central-hall houses in Annapolis. This is likely the result of Buckland's forward-looking taste as an experienced master architect, as well as his ability to read the political maneuvering of the Annapolitan elite on the eve of the Revolution. The use of a floor plan which conceals the stairs and segregates space to a much greater degree than known before in Annapolis made the significant entertaining rooms (that is, the dining and ball rooms) seem much larger. As such, the space of the interior was reorganized around the social stage of performance. In terms of the interior design, the emphasis shifts from a plan with perfect symmetry and visual order to a plan without symmetry, but which retains perfect harmonic proportion. Another untested expectation is that as part of the design a single element, perhaps the area or perimeter of the rear columns or the area of one of the front rooms, was the unit of harmonic proportion. The point, however, of this design was not to confuse the enlightened visitor, but to challenge and encourage the visitor to recognize that the use of harmony was intact. This again makes use of the Georgian style as an ideology in which harmony is integral.

The Hammond House also makes use of false doors to insure each individual room's coherence and symmetricality. But the house also has a jib door in the rear that highlights the efforts of the builder to keep the presentation of order and proportion intact. The enlarged dining room cuts into space where the central hall should divide the house into symmetrical left and right sides. In order to maintain external symmetry, however, the door to the garden should be in the central bay; for the sake of internal symmetry within the enlarged dining room, the doorway to the garden should be to the left of the central bay, with a window where the door actually is. In order to compensate for this, Buckland designed a door that from the interior looks like a window but functions as a door passage when the wainscoting is opened at the same time as the window's lower sash.

•   •   •

This chapter has been an attempt to understand architectural practice as part of the ongoing discourse of social relations within a society. It has made use of the notion of culture as the repertoire of practices that people use and create to make sense of, order, and manipulate the social world. In making a clear connection between the stylistic choices made by architects and house owners and the social contexts in which those choices were made, it was shown that the Georgian style worked in the eighteenth century because it grounded partisan and arbitrary political factions in history and nature. Georgian architectural style was not taken for face value in this study, but instead was treated as a problem. It was interrogated and interpreted as ideology. On one hand, that ideology made use of historical precedent in terms of the classical Western European heritage handed down and guarded over by the English nobility and, by extension, the Annapolitan elite. On the other hand, it appealed to the supposedly natural phenomenon of harmony. Harmony, however, was in effect placed into nature in terms of a constructed understanding of the relation among parts, and then apparently discovered as natural when those parts are found to make sense because they function harmonically. This kind of circular reasoning is how ideologies work, but I would also suggest it is how culture works in systems of inequality. A Marxist historical archaeology does not take the facets of a culture for granted, but instead make those facets problems to understand through the theoretical tools available from anthropology and political economy. My hope is that my effort has made at least initial steps toward that goal.

Notes

I wish to thank Hannah Jopling for an encouraging edit of an earlier draft and Dan Bluestone, Joan Vincent, Elaine Combs-Schilling, David Koester, and the editors of this volume for their thoughtful critiques and suggestions. I also express my gratitude to Mark Leone, Nan Rothschild, and Terry D'Altroy for their support throughout of this and other parts of my ongoing research in Annapolis.

1. Aubrey Land, ed., *Letters from America by William Eddis* (Cambridge: Harvard Univ. Press, 1967), 13.
2. Parker Potter makes a similar point in his discussion of the recursivity of material culture. See Parker B. Potter Jr., *Public Archaeology in Annapolis: A Critical Approach to History in Maryland's "Ancient City"* (Washington, D.C.: Smithsonian Institution Press, 1994).
3. M. di Valmarana, *Building By the Book* (Charlottesville: Univ. Press of Virginia, 1986).
4. Nonarchitects in this group included Alexander Pope, Jonathan Swift, and Georg Friedrich Handel.
5. Warren J. Cox, "Four Men, The Four Books, and the Five-Part House," in *Building By The Book*, 126–29.
6. Placzek, introduction to Andreas Palladio's *The Four Books of Architecture* (New York: Dover Publications, 1965), v–vi.
7. Rudolph Wittkower, *Architectural Principles in the Age of Humanism* (1962; reprint,

New York: W. W. Norton, 1971); Frederick V. Hunt, *Origins in Acoustics: The Science of Sound from Antiquity to the Age of Newton* (New Haven: Yale Univ. Press, 1978); Jamie James, *The Music of the Spheres: Music, Science, and the Natural Order of the Universe* (New York: Grove Press, 1993).

8. The Ware volume is dedicated to Burlington. See Palladio, *The Four Books of Architecture.*

9. Frequently Palladio and his pretenders were critiqued, such as in William Salmon's 1738 *Palladio Londonensis,* where in his preface Salmon states that he aims at improving on Palladio, Scamozzi, and Vitruvius by teaching how to draw the five orders in proportion for any height and applying rules to these methods, which improve on the ideas of Halfpenny and Langley.

10. Land, *Letters from America;* Elizabeth B. Anderson and Michael P. Parker, *Annapolis: A Walk through History* (Centreville, Md.: Tidewater Publishers, 1984), 17–18.

11. Edward C. Papenfuse, *In Pursuit of Profit: The Annapolis Merchants in Era of the American Revolution, 1763–1805* (Baltimore: Johns Hopkins Univ. Press, 1975), 12–15.

12. Ibid., 32.

13. E. Cooke (1708), cited in Paul A. Shackel, *Personal Discipline and Material Culture: An Archaeology of Annapolis, Maryland, 1695–1870* (Knoxville: Univ. of Tennessee Press, 1993), 61; Mifflin (1762), cited in Davis Deering, *Annapolis Houses, 1700–1775* (New York: Architectural Book Publishing, 1941), 21; Land, *Letters from America,* 13.

14. R. R. Bierne and J. H. Scarff, *William Buckland, 1734–1774: Architect of Virginia and Maryland* (Annapolis: Board of Regents of Gunston Hall and Hammond-Harwood House Association, 1958), 4. There are several other biographical sketches of Buckland. See, for example, Deering, *Annapolis Houses;* R. T. H. Halsey, "Matthias Hammond House, Part 2," in *Early Homes of New York and the Mid-Atlantic States* (1929; reprint, New York: The Early American Society, 1977), 209–23; Smith, "Annapolis, Maryland"; and Effingham C. Desmond, "Matthias Hammond House, Part 1," in *Early Homes of New York.* There are two specific volumes dedicated to Buckland exclusively: Board of Regents of Gunston Hall ed., *Buckland: Master Builder of the Eighteenth Century* (Annapolis: Board of Regents of Gunston Hall, 1977); and Bierne and Scarff, *William Buckland.*

15. Bierne and Scarff, *William Buckland,* 9.

16. Deering, *Annapolis Houses,* 19.

17. Bierne and Scarf, *William Buckland,* Appendix E.

18. Board of Regents, *Buckland: Master Builder,* 14.

19. Bierne and Scarff, *William Buckland,* 82.

20. It has been suggested, though not definitively confirmed, that Buckland had a hand or at least a major influence on the great majority of Golden Age constructions in Annapolis and Anne Arundel County. These houses (and their dates of construction) include Paca (1763), Ridout (1765), James Brice (1770), Hammond (1774), Chase-Lloyd (1769), Scott (1765), Tulip Hill (1760s), Ogle Hall's Rear

Addition (1760s), Whitehall (1769), Strawberry Hill (1760s), and the Old Governor's Mansion (1760s).

21. Bierne and Scarff, *William Buckland,* 70.
22. Bierne, "The Chase House in Annapolis," *Maryland Historical Magazine* 44 (3) (1954): 178.
23. The house remained in the Lloyd family until 1826 when Henry Harwood purchased it, and he lived there until he died in 1839. The house was then purchased by Hester Ann Chase and her nieces, descendants of Samuel Chase, in 1847. The last of the nieces died in 1886, and the house was bequeathed to the Episcopal Church. It is still owned by the church today and is a retirement home for women.
24. Mark Leone, "Interpreting Ideology in Historical Archaeology: Using the Rules of Perspective in the William Paca Garden, Annapolis, Maryland," in *Ideology, Power, and Prehistory,* ed. D. Miller and C. Tilley (Cambridge: Cambridge Univ. Press, 1984), 25–35.
25. George B. Tatum, "Great Houses from the Golden Age of Annapolis," *Antiques* 111 (1) (1977): 184, plate 11.
26. See Hunt, *Origins in Acoustics*; James, *The Music of the Spheres*; Wittkower, *Architectural Principles*; Erwin Panofsky, *Meaning in the Visual Arts* (Garden City, N.Y.: Anchor Books, 1955).
27. Charles Willson Peale painted Buckland's portrait in 1774 showing him posing with his plan for the Hammond house on the table he is leaning over.
28. After Hammond's death the house passed into a branch of the Chase family until 1857, when the house passed by marriage to William Harwood, great-grandson of William Buckland. The Harwood family owned and occupied the house until 1924. The house was then put up for auction, and St. John's College bought and opened the house as a museum in 1926. It is now owned and operated by the Hammond-Harwood House Association as a historic house museum.
29. For example, see William H. Pierson, *American Buildings and Their Architects, Volume 1* (Garden City, N.Y.: Doubleday and Co. 1971), 190–93.

12 The Archaeology of Vision in Eighteenth-Century Chesapeake Gardens

Elizabeth Kryder-Reid

During the eighteenth century, travelers throughout America's mid-Atlantic region often recorded in diaries and letters the scenery they observed on their journeys. As they rode inland along the river valleys or followed roads connecting coastal ports, these writers repeatedly used specific terms to capture their experience of sight in the landscape. This vocabulary of vision—view, vista, eminence, situation, prospect—appears in descriptions of both the natural landscape and the estates of the colonial planter-gentry. Describing Gov. John Howard's garden in Baltimore, Maryland, in 1794, Thomas Twining wrote, "Situated upon the verge of the descent upon which Baltimore stands, its grounds formed a beautiful slant towards the Chesapeak. . . . The spot thus indebted to Nature and judiciously embellished was as enchanting within its own proper limits as in the fine view which extended far beyond them. . . . Both perfections of the landscape, its near and distant scenery, were united in the view from the bow-window . . . with the desire, I believe, of gratifying me with this exquisite prospect."[1]

In 1791 another traveler, William Loughton Smith, reported of George

Fig. 12.1. George Ropes's 1806 painting of Mount Vernon and its view overlooking the Potomac River. Copyright Board of Trustees, National Gallery of Art, Washington.

Washington's Mount Vernon (fig. 12.1): "I hardly remember to have been so struck with a prospect. . . . the view extends up and down the river a considerable distance . . . embracing the magnificence of the river with the vessels sailing about; the verdant fields, woods, and parks."[2]

In addition to these descriptions, images of garden views and estate prospects abounded on painted furniture, and in portrait backgrounds, needlework samplers, and other objects in America during the late eighteenth and early nineteenth century. The predominance of such textual and visual depictions suggests that views in and out of the landscape were highly charged with meanings—conscious and unconscious, intended and received. The specific meanings of those views, however, are less apparent.

Vision as the physical phenomenon of optical sight is known only through culturally determined perception. Interpreting the social and symbolic significance of vision in the early American landscape, therefore, requires not only reconstructing *what* was seen, but understanding the *way* it was seen. This endeavor—interpreting the subjectivity of vision—forms the cornerstone of much contemporary writing and social commentary,[3] but it has long been a premise of anthropology, particularly since the pioneering work of linguists Edward Sapir and Benjamin Whorf in nonwestern languages. Demonstrating that languages such as Hopi and Navaho had radically different conceptualizations of time and space, Whorf challenged the assumption that since "every person has talked fluently since infancy . . . he has merely to consult a common substratum of logic or reason which he and everyone else are supposed to possess." Whorf argued against the view that thought depends "on laws of logic or reason which are supposed to be the same for all observers of the universe . . . whether they speak Chinese or Choctaw." Instead, Whorf asserted, the way we categorize time, space, motion, and objects—literally the way we "dissect nature"—is determined by our native languages. That which we hold to be "natural" and universal is instead the product of our culture.[4]

For garden historians, this concept of culturally constructed vision offers the opportunity to go beyond interpretations of aesthetics or style; it offers an avenue of inquiry into the ideology of another time as encoded in the organization of space. In the case of the American colonial landscape, the cultural embeddedness of vision requires the garden historian both to reconstruct what the gardens looked like and to investigate how they were perceived by their diverse audience. This essay discusses some of the interpretations of the meaning of sight in America's colonial gardens and then presents the results of excavations of a terraced garden built in Annapolis, Maryland, in the 1770s as a case study for this archaeology of vision.

Vision and View in Colonial America

The complexity of vision is not a modern scholarly problem. Noah Webster, author of America's first English language dictionary, was aware of the varied meanings of words such as prospect and view. He lists among the eleven connotations of "view" that which is seen ("prospect; sight; reach of the eye, the whole extent seen") and that which is the act of seeing, both physically and metaphorically ("the power of seeing"; "intellectual or mental sight"). Webster acknowledges several meanings for "prospect," including "that which is presented to the eye" and the "place which affords an extensive view," as well as the more metaphorical "view of things to come."[5]

In the Chesapeake region, landscape gardens built in the last half of the eighteenth century were crafted with a similar awareness of the complexity of the operation of vision.[6] Members of the elite planter-gentry, most of whom made their money growing tobacco for export to England, capitalized on the natural prominences and waterfront views along the Chesapeake Bay and its tributaries to locate their Georgian-style brick or frame country seats. In the few urban centers such as Williamsburg, Alexandria, Annapolis, and Baltimore, the limited topographic relief on smaller city lots often was enhanced by terracing. Garden buildings and ornaments, such as pavilions, temples, summerhouses, statuary, obelisks, and fountains, were used as focal points and viewing platforms. The ornamented exteriors of these generally neoclassical-style structures often belied their more practical functions in the plantation landscape. For instance, Thomas Jefferson designed an ice house for his friend James Madison in the form of a classical temple.[7] At His Lordship's Kindness, Henry Darnall's seat in Prince George's County, Maryland, one of a pair of neoclassical brick pavilions housed a five-hole privy.[8] Excavations of the William Paca garden in Annapolis, Maryland, discovered the foundations of matching spring and garden houses flanking the pavilion at the base of the terraced garden.[9] Charles Willson Peale painted a *trompe l'oeil* arch on the tool shed beside his fountain at Belfield and decorated it with nationalistic emblems celebrating the new republic.[10]

While the architecture, planting, and scale of even the most elaborate of colonial gardens would seem simplistic compared to the premier gardens of Europe, the emphasis on the creation of views in American landscape gardens was as sophisticated as the resources would allow. Moreau de St. Mery, born in Martinique of French parents, commented while traveling in the 1790s: "In America almost everything is sacrificed to the outside view."[11] Using pattern books and garden treatises as guides,[12] the creators of these Chesapeake landscape gardens used a variety of techniques to fashion eye-catching scenes within the garden, to enhance views of the house, and to create vistas to the surrounding countryside. For example, the governor's garden in Annapolis contained a mount which served as a focal point within the garden and a viewing platform for the landscape beyond. William Eddis described the scene in 1769: "The garden is not extensive, but it is disposed to the utmost advantage; the center walk is terminated by a small green mount, close to which the Severn approaches: this elevation commands an extensive view of the bay and the adjacent country. . . there are but few mansions in the most rich and cultivated parts of England which are adorned with such splendid romantic scenery."[13]

The energies of plantation owners were not lost on their many visitors as this 1793 account of David Meade's estate in Virginia attests:

> These grounds contain about twelve acres, laid out on the banks of the James river in a most beautiful and enchanting manner. Forest and fruit trees are here arranged as if nature and art had conspired together to strike the eye most agreeably. Beautiful vistas, which open as many pleasing views of the river; the land thrown into many artificial hollows or gentle swellings, with the pleasing verdure of the turf; and the complete order in which the whole is preserved, altogether tend to form it one of the most delightful rural seats that is to be met with in the United States, and do honour to the taste and skill of the proprietor, who is also the architect.[14]

This discussion began by noting that knowing what people saw in these gardens was only the beginning of understanding the way in which the landscapes were seen. For instance, the description of the Meade garden is, at first, seemingly transparent: Meade's garden was enchanting because it had beautiful and pleasing vistas. Yet, beneath this observation lies another subtext—the landscape is worthy of praise; David Meade made it and owns it, therefore David Meade is worthy of praise. But even this syllogistic implication which brings "honour to the skill and taste of the proprietor" is complex and requires spectators (and garden historians) to bring certain assumptions to the scene. Understanding the audiences of these gardens and the assumptions they brought to them is critical if we are to assess how colonial American gardens were read and how perspectives operated within them.

Spectators of Chesapeake gardens were a diverse audience and their opportunities for views of a garden differed markedly depending on whether they sailed past it, peeked at it over the garden wall, processed around it, or gazed upon it from the "great house." Unfortunately, history generally records only the reactions of those landowners or invited guests who had access to the privileged viewing spots. Rarely do we hear the voice of the slave who weeded the garden or the child who peered through the fence. Yet, the potential audiences of a garden become evident as we begin to reconstruct the garden's form: the height of fences or walls, the locations of apertures (windows or gates) in those visual screens, prominent landmarks in the garden and the landscape beyond, sight lines through alleys of boxwood or avenues of trees, the relationship of house and garden.

Interpretations by archaeologists, historians, and cultural geographers have tried to explain the meanings of such garden views and vantage points. In general, views looking into the garden have been seen as attempts by their owners to enhance their status by displays of wealth, expertise, and taste. For instance, Mark Leone has postulated that the peak of garden construction on the eve of America's break with England may be explained as attempts to shore up an eroding power base through the ostentatious display of resources.[15] Views looking out of the garden have been regarded as claims to a relationship with the outer world by linking the private landscape with distant landmarks or broad vistas.[16]

Views within the landscape may—through the iconography of statuary, the symbolism of objects such as sundials or arches, or the connotations of spaces such as groves—make claims to a mythical past[17] or to "natural" and therefore inevitable forces such as time, geometry, or astronomy.[18] In the long tradition of landowners, the Chesapeake planters rooted themselves in the past in an attempt to project their positions into the future and placed themselves in nature in such a way as to make those positions appear natural and beyond challenge.[19] Views within the landscape have also been seen as attempts to control the experience of the visitor through manipulation of access and sight lines in the garden. For example, Dell Upton has presented an interesting analysis of late-eighteenth-century American gardens as a series of social barriers. He argues that, like the hierarchical arrangement of public and private spaces within the plantation house, the landscape presented obstacles to the white visitor in the form of trees, terraces, and dependencies which had to be passed in order to reach the central seat of the planter. The extent of one's access was an index of one's status. Upton further observes that this formal pattern of movement was constantly circumvented by the black slaves upon whose labor the plantations were dependent. While slaves were not subject to the social posturing of the gentry, in part because their subservience was ensured by force, the freedom to transgress the processional landscape of the planters allowed the slaves one means of forming a private landscape with meanings distinct to their own community and their own social relations.[20]

The Archaeology of Vision in the Charles Carroll Garden

Given the importance of the control of optical sight in these eighteenth-century gardens, the recovery of garden perspectives is essential to the interpretation of these spaces. But how, two hundred years later, can one reconstruct the views and vistas which figured so prominently in their visitors' descriptions? One method is to locate the garden in three-dimensional space using visual, textual, and, most significantly, archaeological evidence. The latter is of course constrained by the preservation of the colonial landscape remains and by the costs of archaeological investigation. Excavations are time consuming (and therefore expensive), and the scale of landscape archaeology generally requires dealing with large areas and often vast amounts of earth moving. Furthermore, archaeology is destructive; once the soil layers of a garden's stratigraphy are excavated, they are lost.[21] Garden archaeology justifies its costs and intrusiveness in cases where recovering the physical evidence of a garden provides information that is not recorded in any other way. These finds include plant remains in the form of pollen, phytoliths, or seeds;[22] ephemeral soil features such as planting beds, tree holes, and ramps which are rarely recorded on deed records, insurance maps or other plan-views; circulation routes such as avenues, stairs, walks; and evidence of garden architecture such as walls, grottos, and pavilions.

Of particular importance for the reconstruction of perspective is that garden archaeology not only identifies these features, but it locates them in three-dimensional space. Much as measured architectural drawings record a standing structure, systematic excavations allow one to plot the exact positions of buried garden features. Two-dimensional representations such as plat maps or insurance records provide evidence of a site's plane geometry, but only the three-dimensional reconstruction of garden elements provides the evidence needed for reading the solid geometry of a garden.[23] Furthermore, archaeology reveals what was actually built, as opposed to what was planned in presentation drawings or imagined in artist renderings.[24]

The Charles Carroll site in Annapolis, Maryland, provides an example of the use of archaeologically recovered evidence for reconstructing and interpreting vision.[25] The site dates to the late seventeenth century when the property was purchased by Charles Carroll the Settler at the same time as the capital of the colony was moved from St. Mary's City to Annapolis.[26] The site's most famous inhabitant, however, was the Settler's grandson, Charles Carroll of Carrollton, who was born there in 1737 and made it his chief residence after returning in 1765 from sixteen years of education in France and England. By the time of his death at the age of ninety-five, Carroll of Carrollton was known primarily as "the last living signer" of the Declaration of Independence, but today he is recognized for his role in the formation of the new American nation. Carroll served as a commissioner in negotiations for a French Canadian alliance in 1776; he argued a view of the constitution in the widely read "First Citizen Debates" which challenged British authority and supported local autonomy;[27] he was the only Roman Catholic to sign the Declaration of Independence; and he served in the Continental Congress and both state and federal legislatures. Carroll's participation in the political process is all the more significant because, in the colonial government prior to 1776, his Catholicism denied him the right to vote and access to elected office.

It was during the time of his early political activities in the 1770s that Carroll embarked on an ambitious program of architectural and landscape improvements at his Annapolis seat. Of particular interest for this discussion was the construction of a terraced garden to the east of the house in the triangular plot created by Carroll Creek (now Spa Creek), Duke of Gloucester Street, and the house (map 12.1). The garden consisted of a series of slopes and terraces falling to the waterfront below and connected

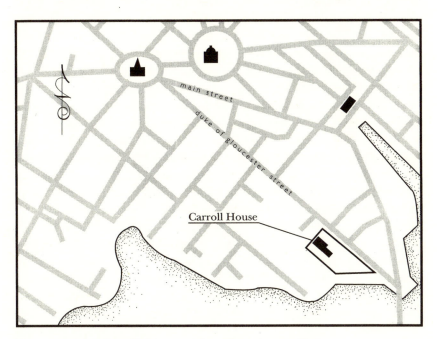

Map 12.1. The Carroll House and garden, Annapolis.

by turfed ramps. The dimensions of the garden were based on the core of the brick house adjoining the garden, and the sides of the right triangles created by the intersecting ramps and terraces were in 3-4-5 proportions.[28]

This Carroll site was excavated over the course of five field seasons (1987–91) by Archaeology in Annapolis.[29] Investigations focused on the garden and the house, including a wing demolished in the mid-nineteenth century. The strategy for the garden excavations was determined in part by clues from the existing topography, in part by documentary evidence, and in part by practical constraints of funding and access. The techniques used to recover perspectives in the garden can be summarized as follows. The first step was to make a topographic map of the existing surface of the garden which was remarkably intact given its location in the heart of Annapolis's Historic District. A remote sensing survey was then conducted which combined the nondestructive techniques of ground-penetrating radar, soil resistivity, and magnetometer readings to locate below-ground anomalies. Each of these techniques—whether reading reflected sound waves, differences in the conductivity of electrical currents, or different measurements of density—identified anomalies below ground; further, the identification of features such as buried paths, areas of fill dirt, or utility lines relied on interpreting the shape of the feature (fig. 12.2). Such identifications were therefore tentative and undated.

To corroborate and clarify the findings of remote sensing, the next stage of investigation was to begin digging, which complemented the site history known from documentary and visual sources. At the Carroll site, we combined two complementary types of testing: coring and excavations. The coring provided a limited view of a wide area while the excavations provided a detailed view of a small area. Cores were taken by driving a metal tube into the ground and retrieving soil samples from a depth of up to eight feet (figs. 12.2 and 12.3). These samples provided a picture of the stratigraphy or soil layers and told the story of the garden's construction by cutting and filling the natural slope of the hillside. Excavation squares (five feet by five feet) were placed in areas of particular interest identified by the remote sensing, by documentary sources, or by the coring samples. For instance, the only evidence of intact planting beds in the garden were found on the top terrace where cores indicated the least nineteenth- and twentieth-century disturbance. In another example, testing of the "deep feature" to the south of the house identified by remote sensing revealed a late-eighteenth-century refuse pit.

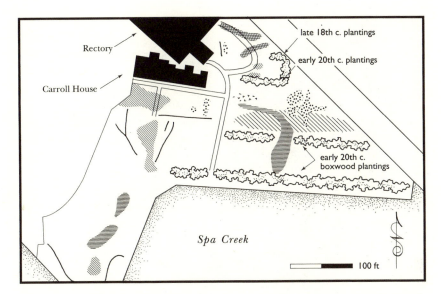

Fig. 12.2. Summary of findings from remote sensing survey of the Carroll garden by Bruce Bevan in 1987 using ground-penetrating radar, soil resistivity, and magnetometer sensing.

The Meaning of Vision in the Charles Carroll Garden

While the function of perspective in Carroll's garden is certainly not unique among landscape gardens or even among post-medieval visual arts,[30] the excavations provided a basis for reconstructing and interpreting the particular operation of vision at this site (fig. 12.4). Identifying the views into and out of Carroll's garden gives us an idea of how it was intended to be seen by a variety of audiences and therefore what meanings may have been encoded in the space. The problem remains of accounting for spectators such as the laborers in the garden who interacted with the space in very different ways from the invited guest or even passing public. But reconstructing the intended views and circulation routes is the first step in understanding the effectiveness or ineffectiveness of garden perspectives from different locations. The audiences of Carroll's garden had the potential for three distinct sets of vantage points which will each be explored in more detail below: views from outside the garden looking in, views within the garden, and views from the house.

Fig. 12.3. Soil core sample being taken from the Carroll garden.

The principal views of the garden from the outside were from the waterfront because the garden wall effectively screened the garden from view to street traffic. Any passing boat rounding Carroll's point and heading up the well-traveled creek had a view of the house with the garden in the foreground. As the traveler journeyed upstream, the oblique relation of the garden and house resolved into a full frontal perspective with views straight up the ramps. As noted above, a common function of Chesapeake landscape gardens was to enhance the view of the house. The Carroll garden was no exception, and the archaeology of the garden revealed several ways that Carroll made his house appear larger and therefore more impressive to the water traffic along the creek. Leone and Paul Shackel have reported

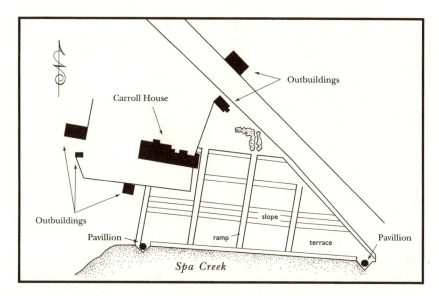

Fig. 12.4. Reconstructed plan of the terraces, walks, and ramps in the Carroll garden based on archaeological, documentary, and photographic evidence.

how the varying widths of the terraces made it difficult for the observer at the base of the garden to estimate the distance to the house and therefore made the house appear larger than it was.[31] Carroll also emphasized the height of the Georgian-style brick structure by building a terrace with a stone retaining wall on the waterfront side of his house. From the base of the garden the lower portion of the ground floor is hidden by this wall, making it difficult to determine the number of floors or to judge the height of the house. In addition to its role as a visual screen, the terrace's sunken, rectangular shape suggests it may have served as a bowling green, although there is no documentary reference to its function.

A second aspect of the view presented to spectators outside the garden helps to explain the unusual oblique relation of the house and garden. It has been noted that the relation of Carroll's house and his triangular garden is unique in the American colonies, and one explanation for the peculiar shape and location of the triangular garden to the east of the house has been that they were determined by the existing parameters of the street and creek.[32] While there are English precedents for the

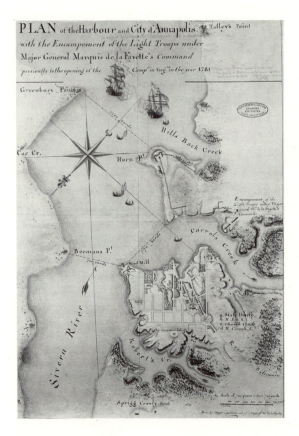

Map 12.2. A plan of the harbor and city of Annapolis, 1781, known as the Frenchman's map. The Carroll property is on the peninsula in the upper right of the town indicated by "d" on the map. Courtesy of the Maryland State Archives, Special Collections, Marion E. Warren Collection, MSA SC 1890–3502.

symbolic association of triangular shapes and the number three with Catholicism,[33] Carroll never explicitly linked the shape of his garden to his religious faith. Instead, the orientation of house and garden may have been an intentional arrangement to associate Carroll's urban seat with a prominent symbol of power. From the water, the house aligns with the statehouse, the highest landmark in the city. The state capitol building was situated on a hill and conscribed by a circle with radiating streets by Gov. Francis Nicholson, creator of Annapolis's baroque town plan of 1695.[34] Its visibility is evidenced by the Frenchman's map of 1781 which lists only four landmarks in its key, two of which are the statehouse (a) and the Carroll house (d) (map 12.2). Both the buildings were standing when Carroll began construction of his garden in 1770, and he appears to have taken advantage of this existing relationship. As a late-nineteenth-century photograph taken

Fig. 12.5. Redemptorist students, Annapolis, Maryland, 1864. This earliest known photograph of the St. Mary's site shows the Carroll House flanked by the Redemptorists' rectory (1858) and the statehouse dome in the background. Courtesy of St. Mary's Parish Archives.

from the water view demonstrates, the foreground of the garden served as a frame for the house and the apparently adjacent domed tower of the capitol, symbol of Maryland's provincial government and the single most recognizable element of Annapolis's colonial skyline (fig. 12.5).

Carroll also enhanced the views of the house from outside the garden by placing his most elaborate architectural elements on prominent locations for public view. For example, he constructed his two brick pavilions, described by Peale as an octagonal temple and a summerhouse, overhanging the water at each end of the stone seawall at the base of the garden.[35] Carroll also constructed a gatehouse at the street entrance of the garden which would have been visible from the north side of the promontory. The public visibility of these structures is particularly notable given that there appears to have been no obvious architectural focal points within the garden such as along axial vistas of the terraces or at the top of the garden in line with the central ramp and alley. This emphasis on the view of the garden from without, rather than the experience of the visitor within, again demonstrates the outward focus of Carroll's garden design.

The second set of vantage points, those within the garden, include views looking at the house, at the vista beyond the garden, and at focal points within the garden. These views were available to the Carroll family and invited guests, as well as any laborers or slaves. Arriving via the waterfront entrance,[36] visitors were led by a series of ramps and terraces

Fig. 12.6. Detail of the Carroll Mansion from Sachse's Birdseye View of Annapolis, 1858. Courtesy of the Maryland State Archives, Special Collections, Joseph Bonaparte Girault Collection, MSA SC 1195.

upward toward the highest terrace where they were presented with a striking view of a rolling, verdant lawn in the foreground,[37] Carroll Creek in the middle ground, and the woods and meadows of the opposite bank receding in the distance. Carroll framed this expansive view with a pavilion at each end of the garden seawall and, using the varying widths of the terraces and the foreshortening effect of the slopes to "bring in the country," created the impression that the water at the base of the garden was closer than it actually was. In doing so, Carroll blurred the line between "his" property and the landscape beyond and made a visual claim that reinforced his political and social aspirations.

The third set of vantage points operated from the various windows and viewing platforms of the house itself, particularly from the porch on the east end of the now demolished eastern "frame house" visible in the Sachse view of 1858 (fig. 12.6). As proposed above, Carroll manipulated lines of sight in the first two sets of vantage points to create optical illusions which

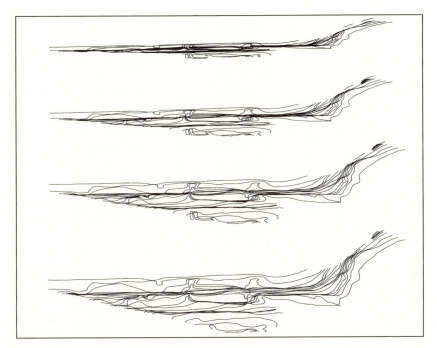

Fig. 12.7. A series of computer-assisted drawings using topographic lines to create perspectival views. The vantage point looks south from the top of the Carroll garden toward the creek below. The viewer of the drawings is in the same position as the viewer at the top of the garden. The viewer's eye is shown at four elevations (10, 15, 20, and 25 degrees), representing positions at increasing heights above the garden. The views demonstrate that the higher the viewer, the less the effect of the foreshortening illusion created by the terraces and slopes of a falling garden.

affected viewers both within and without the garden. But for the third audience—those within the house—Carroll presented an opportunity to "see through" the illusions. Clearly Carroll realized that the illusionistic aspects of the garden are most effective when viewed from the eye level of a person standing in the garden. For instance, the foreshortening effect is minimized as one's height above the garden increases (fig. 12.7). It would seem calculated, therefore, that the principal articulation of the house and garden was from a porch on the first floor (i.e., one floor above ground level) off the eastern end of the house. Because of the elevated position of the windows, doors, and porticos, viewers from the house were not subject to the same manipulations of perspective as those in the garden or looking up from the water level of the creek. Visitors privileged enough to be admitted into the private sanctuary of the house were not only exempted from the managed perspectives, they were also given the ideal vantage point to observe the patterns of the parterre plantings and the plane geometry of the garden's triangular layout of ramps and terraces.

Using archaeological, architectural, and documentary evidence, it has been possible to assemble a picture of the garden Charles Carroll of Carrollton crafted in the 1770s. The reconstructed plan of this three-dimensional space then allowed us to decipher the creation of views from within and from without the garden. This evidence of the manipulation of perspective in turn suggested the positions of spectators of Carroll's landscaping efforts. But the question remains: what did these views mean to the garden's viewers? In his book on the psychology of perspective, Michael Kubovy argues that perspective in Renaissance painting had several uses: the "structural" rationalization of the representation of space, the "illusionistic" appearance of depth, the "narrative" effect of drawing the spectator's eye to a key figure or action, and the symbolic effect of providing artists with a new code for concealing allusion and meaning in their work. The manipulation of perspective in Carroll's garden, I would argue, served all the same functions. It presented its owner as a master of the allied arts of geometry, botany, and architecture. It enhanced or negated the illusion of depth depending on the position of the spectator. It drew attention to the Carroll's architectural signature—his massive brick house. Finally, the garden's 3-4-5 proportions encoded a knowledge of geometry and classical harmonic proportions.

The positions of spectators provide further clues for interpreting the meaning of vision in Carroll's garden. The emphasis on the external views of the garden suggests that Carroll was concerned with displaying his holdings to the full spectrum of Annapolis society. To this audience, the garden was a display of wealth in a medium that was timeless and natural and therefore immune to challenge. Carroll's position was presented as "natural" because it was embedded in an agrarian, idyllic nature: a man with the resources and the right to own them. It can be argued that for those admitted into the garden, the vista from the top terrace embracing the landscape beyond was an act of incorporation—Carroll's visual claim on the world beyond his walls. Finally, the most select audience (the family and visitors to the house) was given an elevated view which not only gave them the best prospect for appreciating the plane geometry of parterres and garden plan, but also exempted them from the foreshortening illusions of the terracing. This display of the manipulation of the rules of perspective, the propagation of plants, and the tenets of classical architecture suggests that Carroll's message to his privileged guests was of a select and sophisticated variety. To those more fluent in the intricacies of the Enlightenment arts, the garden bespoke the skills of a natural legislator and the right to practice them.[38] In sum, the perspectives of the garden presented Carroll as a man with all the qualifications for governing—money, the knowledge to use it, and the right to have it. And the perspectives were designed so that optical illusions enhanced Carroll's position before a broad audience while the ability to create illusions was demonstrated to a smaller but more empowered audience.

• • •

The manipulation of sight lines for different viewers suggests some of the meanings Carroll inscribed in his landscape, but it also raises the problem of how those meanings were read by a disparate audience. Each of the interpretations relies on the same supposition as the author of the description of Meade's garden presented above: each assumes a link between the property seen by the spectator and the property's owner. They assume, too, that attempts to naturalize one's position through the medium of the garden relied on a shared concept of what was "natural." But did all the spectators of Carroll's garden participate in the same notions of property, time, space, nature, and natural rights?

The Renaissance has been examined as a time of pivotal change in the relation between the subject and the object or the viewer and the viewed. The argument is that for the first time in painting—and it would follow in landscape design—the centrality of the spectator is paramount. A picture (and a garden) is organized "in terms of the point of view of a particular individual who observes from a particular point of view at a particular moment."[39] This "one-point perspective" relies on a perception of space as continuous, infinite, homogeneous, and quantifiable, as well as on a humanist notion of the spectator as an individual. One such writer, Leonard Goldstein, suggests that this transformation of vision is linked to the economic structure which marked the shift to a post-medieval world, namely the new form of private property in commodity production which is today called capitalism. He concludes, "All this means that the individual property owner, generalized in Renaissance philosophy as Man, becomes indeed the center of action and of interest, the measure of all things, for it is indeed man who more and more comes to control the world around him and to determine its nature. The increasing control of man over himself and nature is a product of man as entrepreneur, as active, rational organizer of commodity production."[40]

Grounding perspective in the economic means of production would simplify interpretations of vision in the garden, but it also raises a number of questions with which I close. If vision is culturally constructed, can we assume that the audiences of these colonial landscape gardens shared a common understanding of what they saw? Certainly slaves and planters participated in the emerging American economy in very different ways. Did they, in Whorf's words, "consult a common substratum of logic or reason," or were their cultural vocabularies different enough that the gardens served as a means of communication only among a small group of elites with similar landscaping tastes and political ambitions? Furthermore, is capitalism a precondition for the connection of vision and property? Can we make similar connections between elevated position and status, between the display of resources and claims of power in the gardens of Islamic palaces and Roman theaters, to say nothing of prehistoric landscape architecture such as Andean mountain terracing or Pueblo villages?[41] In short, is there any aspect of vision in the garden which is universal, or is the relativity implied by the subjectivity of vision uncompromising?

Notes

This essay is reprinted in slightly edited form with permission from "Site and Sight in the Garden," an issue of the *Journal of Garden History* 14 (1) (1994): 42–54, guest-edited by Elizabeth Kryder-Reid and D. Fairchild Ruggles. The work reported here is indebted to the Archaeology in Annapolis field crews and colleagues who excavated the St. Mary's site under the auspices of the University of Maryland at College Park and Historic Annapolis Foundation. I am especially grateful to Mark Leone for his intellectual guidance and to Barbara Little, Paul Shackel, and Parker Potter for making my entry into the project such an easy one. I wish also to thank Robert Worden for his generous assistance in navigating the St. Mary's Parish Archives, the editors of the Carroll Papers for their help with that material, John Dixon Hunt for the opportunity to present the collection in which this essay originally appeared, and Therese O'Malley for her insightful comments and invaluable support. I wish to thank Dede Ruggles for her enthusiasm and camaraderie in our similar pursuits. Finally, I offer thanks to the editors of this volume for tackling the monumental task of assembling and making sense of the work that has been Archaeology in Annapolis.

1. Thomas Twining, *Travels in America 100 Years Ago* (New York: Harper and Brothers, 1894), 115–16.
2. William Loughton Smith, *Journal of William Loughton Smith, 1790–1791*, ed. Albert Matthews (Cambridge, Mass.: The Univ. Press, 1917), 63.
3. One of the most influential writers on the construction of vision and its operation as an exercise of power has been Michel Foucault, *Discipline and Punish: The Birth of the Prison* (New York: Vintage Books, 1979). See also John Rajchman, "Foucault's Art of Seeing," *October* 14 (1988): 89–119; Jonathan Crary, *Techniques of the Observer: On Vision and Modernity in the Nineteenth Century* (Cambridge: MIT Press, 1990); and the collection of essays in Hal Foster, ed. *Vision and Visuality*, Dia Art Foundation, Discussions in Contemporary Culture, no. 2 (Seattle: Bay Press, 1988).
4. Benjamin Lee Whorf, "Science and Linguistics," in *Language, Thought, and Reality*, ed. John B. Carroll (Cambridge: MIT Press, 1956), 207–19.
5. Noah Webster, *A Compendious Dictionary of the English Language* (Hartford: Sidney's Press, 1806).
6. Among the growing corpus of American garden history, see Peter Martin, *Pleasure Gardens of Virginia* (Princeton: Princeton Univ. Press, 1991), for a description of Virginia's colonial gardens. Barbara Sarudy, "Eighteenth-Century Gardens of the Chesapeake," *Journal of Garden History* 9 (3) (1989): 104–59, provides a detailed view of a cross-section of Maryland gardens from the craftsman's town garden of William Faris to the private estates and public gardens of Baltimore.
7. Frederick Doveton Nichols and Ralph E. Griswold, *Thomas Jefferson, Landscape Architect* (Charlottesville: Univ. Press of Virginia, 1978), 117.
8. Julie Ernstein, personal communication, 1993.
9. Stanley South, "The Paca House, Annapolis, Maryland" (Annapolis: Historic Annapolis Foundation, 1967). For an analysis of the geometry of the Paca garden, see Barbara Paca-Steele with St. Clair Wright, "The Mathematics of an Eighteenth-Century Wilderness Garden," *Journal of Garden History* 6 (4) (1986): 299–320.
10. Therese O'Malley, "Charles Willson Peale's Belfield: Its Place in American Garden History," in *New Perspectives on Charles Willson Peale*, ed. Lillian B. Miller and David C. Ward (Pittsburgh: Univ. of Pittsburgh Press, 1991), 273.
11. Moreau de St. Mery, *American Journey, 1793–1798*, ed. Kenneth Roberts and Anna Roberts (Garden City, N.Y.: Doubleday, 1947), 121.
12. For a discussion of early American garden literature, see Sarudy, "Eighteenth-Century Gardens"; O'Malley, "Appropriation and Adaptation: Early Gardening Literature in America," *The Huntington Library Quarterly* 55 (3) (1992): 401–31; and Brenda Bullion, "Early American Farming and Gardening Literature: 'Adapted to the Climates and Seasons of the United States,'" *Journal of Garden History* 12 (1) (1992): 29–51.

13. Aubrey Land, ed., *Letters from America by William Eddis* (Cambridge: Harvard Univ. Press, 1969), 12.

14. Rev. John Spooner's 1723 description of Maycox in Prince George's County, Virginia, as quoted in Fiske Kimball, "A Landscape Garden on the James in 1723," *Landscape Architecture* 14 (2) (Jan. 1924): 123.

15. Mark P. Leone, "Rule by Ostentation: The Relationship Between Space and Sight in Eighteenth-Century Landscape Architecture in the Chesapeake Region of Maryland," in *Method and Theory for Activity Area Research: an Ethnoarchaeological Approach*, ed. Susan Kent (New York: Columbia Univ. Press, 1987), 604–33.

16. For example, the views created at Monticello are interpreted by Walter L. Creese, "Jefferson's Charlottesville," in *The Crowning of the American Landscape: Eight Great Spaces and Their Buildings* (Princeton: Princeton Univ. Press, 1985), 34–37, and by Dell Upton, *Holy Things and Profane: Anglican Parish Churches in Colonial Virginia* (Cambridge: MIT Press, 1986), 215–16.

17. For example, O'Malley has noted the classicizing allusions in Charles Willson Peale's garden at Belfield near Philadelphia, particularly his obelisk possibly referencing an obelisk dedicated to Ptolemy Philadelphus. See O'Malley, "Peale's Belfield," 271–72.

18. Mark P. Leone and Paul A. Shackel, "Forks, Clocks and Power," in *Mirror and Metaphor: Material and Social Constructions of Reality*, ed. Daniel W. Ingersoll and Gordon Bronitsky (Lanham, Md.: Univ. Press of America, 1987), 46–61.

19. Raymond Williams traces the links between changing power structures and landownership in England. See Raymond Williams, *Problems in Materialism and Culture* (London: Verso, 1980), and *The Country and the City* (London: The Hogarth Press, 1985). Rhys Isaac incorporates a similar argument for eighteenth-century Virginia in *The Transformation of Virginia, 1740–1790* (Chapel Hill: Univ. of North Carolina Press, 1982). For a case study using archaeological evidence from Annapolis see Leone, "Interpreting Ideology in Historical Archaeology: Using the Rules of Perspective in the William Paca Garden in Annapolis, Maryland," in *Ideology, Representation, and Power in Prehistory*, ed. Daniel Miller and Christopher Tilley (Cambridge: Univ. of Cambridge Press, 1984), 25–35.

20. Upton, "White and Black Landscapes in Eighteenth-Century Virginia," in *Material Life in America, 1600–1860*, ed. Robert Blair St. George (Boston: Northeastern Univ. Press, 1988), 357–69; and Terrence W. Epperson, "Race and the Disciplines of the Plantation," *Historical Archaeology* 24 (4) (1990): 29–36.

21. William Kelso notes an additional potential drawback of garden excavations. At Bacon's Castle in Virginia, the combination of the impact of heavy machinery used to remove the topsoil and two years of exposed subsoil created severe drainage problems in the subsequently reconstructed garden. See William M. Kelso, "Landscape Archaeology and Garden History Research: Success and Promise at Bacon's Castle, Monticello, and Poplar Forest, Virginia," in *Garden History: Issues, Approaches, Methods*, ed. John Dixon Hunt (Washington, D.C.: Dumbarton Oaks, 1992), 35.

22. Peter Murphy and Robert G. Scaife, "The Environmental Archaeology of Gardens," in *Garden Archaeology*, ed. A. E. Brown, Council of British Archaeology Research Report, 78. (London: Council of British Archaeology, 1991), 83–99.
23. Mark P. Leone and Paul A. Shackel, "Plane and Solid Geometry in Colonial Gardens in Annapolis, Maryland," in *Earth Patterns: Essays in Landscape Archaeology*, ed. William M. Kelso and Rachel Most (Charlottesville: Univ. Press of Virginia, 1990), 153–67.
24. For excellent discussions of the problematics of landscape and architectural representations, see Robin Evans, "Translations from Drawing to Building," *AA Files* 12 (1986): 13–18, and James Corner, "Representation and Landscape: Drawing and Making in the Landscape Medium," *Word & Image* 8 (3) (1992): 243–75.
25. The Carroll site is officially known as the St. Mary's site (18AP45), taking its name from St. Mary's Catholic Church which presently occupies the property. The property is owned by the Congregation of the Most Holy Redeemer *(Congregationis Sanctissimi Redemptoris)* whose generous hospitality made these archaeological investigations possible.
26. The rise and fall of Carroll the Settler's political fortunes including his emigration from Ireland, alliance with Cecil Calvert (Lord Baltimore, Proprietor of Maryland), and career as attorney general have been traced by Ronald Hoffman, "'Marylando-Hibernus': Charles Carroll the Settler, 1660–1720," *William and Mary Quarterly* 3d ser., 45 (2) (1988): 207–36.
27. Peter S. Onuf, ed. *Maryland and the Empire, 1773: the Antilon-First Citizen Letters* (Baltimore: Johns Hopkins Univ. Press, 1974).
28. Leone and Shackel, "Plane and Solid Geometry," 159–62. Revisions to their geometric analysis which detail the deviations from this ideal geometry in the executed garden design are presented in Elizabeth Kryder-Reid, *Landscape as Myth: the Contextual Archaeology of an Annapolis Landscape* (Ann Arbor, Mich.: Univ. Microfilms International, 1991), 182–86. For instance, the angle of the "right" triangle is actually 84 degrees and the proportions of the triangle's sides are never exactly 3-4-5.
29. Archaeology in Annapolis is jointly sponsored by the Historic Annapolis Foundation (a private, nonprofit preservation organization) and the University of Maryland at College Park. Throughout the excavations, a public program presented the archaeological findings and interpretations to the public. The Carroll house, currently undergoing restoration by Charles Carroll House of Annapolis, Inc., is open for tours which include interpretations of the garden. A site report for the 1987–90 excavations is in progress. The principal findings from the garden are described in Kryder-Reid, *Landscape as Myth*. The 1991 excavations of the interior of the Carroll House are reported in George C. Logan et al., *1991 Archaeological Excavations at the Charles Carroll House in Annapolis, Maryland (18AP45)* (Annapolis: Historic Annapolis Foundation, 1992).
30. Michael Kubovy, *The Psychology of Perspective and Renaissance Art* (Cambridge: Cambridge Univ. Press, 1986).
31. Leone and Shackel, "Plane and Solid Geometry," 163.
32. Kryder-Reid, "'As Is the Gardener, So Is the Garden': the Archaeology of Land-

scape as Myth," in *Historical Archaeology of the Chesapeake*, ed. Paul A. Shackel and Barbara J. Little (Washington, D.C.: Smithsonian Institution Press, 1994), 131–48.

33. Although Carroll traveled extensively in England, particularly in the southwest region of the country, it is not known whether he was familiar with architecture such as the Triangular Lodge at Rushton Hall (1593–95), which incorporated Catholic symbolism into its architectural and decorative program. See Nikolaus Pevsner, *Northamptonshire*, Buildings of England Series (Middlesex: Penguin Books, 1961), 399.

34. John W. Reps, *The Making of Urban America: A History of City Planning in the United States* (Princeton: Princeton Univ. Press, 1965), 103–8.

35. Charles Willson Peale, *Diary*, (B:P31-2), Philadelphia: American Philosophical Society). Peale's description of the Carroll garden is found in vol. 20: 52–54.

36. The location of the water entrance to the garden is not known, but a likely place is in the center of the seawall where the central ramp meets the water or near the western pavilion.

37. Charles Wilson Peale's description indicates that, at least in 1804, some of the terraces contained parterres planted as kitchen gardens. The only other evidence of planting arrangements comes from beds recovered archaeologically on the upper terrace and from a letter discussing planting privet in a quincunx pattern (Charles Carroll of Annapolis to Charles Carroll of Carrollton, Mar. 27, 1777, Carroll Papers Ms. 206, no. 383 [736], Baltimore: Maryland Historical Society).

38. Mark P. Leone et al., "Power Gardens of Annapolis," *Archaeology* (Mar./April 1989): 34–39, 74–75; Kryder-Reid, "As Is the Gardener."

39. Leonard Goldstein, *The Social and Cultural Roots of Linear Perspective* (Minneapolis: MEP Publications, 1988), 78.

40. Ibid., 82.

41. Cheryl Nickel, "The Semiotics of Andean Terracing," *Art Journal* 42 (3) (1982): 200–203; and John Fritz, "Chaco Canyon and Vijayanagara: Proposing Spatial Meaning in Two Societies," in *Mirror and Metaphor*, 313–49.

13 A Street Plan for Hierarchy in Annapolis: An Analysis of State Circle as a Geometric Form

Mark P. Leone, Jennifer Stabler,
Anna-Marie Burlaga

Annapolis, Maryland, has an important place in the history of urban planning in America. Annapolis falls within the class of cities deliberately planned as centers of administration and power. John Reps, the major historian and interpreter of historic American cities, considers Annapolis an important baroque plan whose pleasing effects are still available to be experienced today. Thus, our understanding of the city comes from the fields of cultural geography, represented by Reps, and from historic preservation. Historic Annapolis Foundation, the sponsor of the research here, is responsible for resuscitating the impact of the baroque city.

Reps uses Francis Nicholson's history as colonial administrator and well-informed citizen to connect the designs of Annapolis and Williamsburg to English and French landscape and urban design. Nicholson designed both cities when he was royal governor of Maryland and Virginia, respectively. Reps makes a secure case that the design of these two capitals was not delegated to some lesser official but was done by Nicholson himself, who considered the layout of a new or redesigned city as central to assuming his duty as chief local politician.

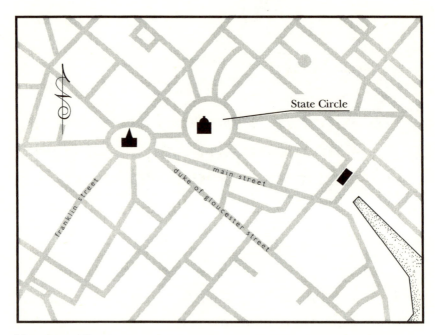

Map 13.1. The Center of Annapolis showing Church and State Circle, Annapolis.

Nicholson had seen Paris and, probably more important, Versailles. He was in London when Wren and Evelyn were redesigning that city after the fire of 1666. He could have known Evelyn through their joint membership in the Royal Society. Moreover, Reps argues, Nicholson owned books on baroque landscape and planning that he brought with him to the American colonies.

With all these historical citations as a base, Reps argues that Nicholson experimented with partial success at a baroque layout for Annapolis. The success consisted of two great circles, a great square (now gone), and a series of streets radiating into them as diagonals aimed at buildings; the buildings closed the ends of the axis formed by each diagonal. The two circles can circumscribe the square and fit within it respectively, showing that Nicholson understood how to use mathematical proportions to achieve harmonious spatial relationships. These, in turn, achieved order which was intended to produce a sense of equilibrium for the viewer.

Reps sees Williamsburg as Nicholson's greatest achievement in urban planning. It is simpler, more harmonious, equally intimate, yet contains no serious mistakes. Annapolis, while both original and intimate, contains a series of diagonals that do not intersect at a vista closed off by a public building. This mistake, according to Reps, was common to Evelyn's plans of London as well, and is attributed by Reps to the incomplete skills at urban planning on the part of these two individuals.[1] Here we will show that Reps is incorrect and that a true evaluation of Nicholson's abilities can be achieved by using maps made in the field and reconstructions of original areas of the plan available through archaeology. We will show that Nicholson was a far more effective urban designer than he has been made out to be.

Our long-term goal, however, is not the rehabilitation of Gov. Francis Nicholson's reputation as an urban designer. It is, rather, to understand why Nicholson designed a baroque city for Annapolis in the first place. Unlike most scholars until recently, Nicholson would have known that Maryland's first capital, St. Mary's City, was a baroque setting. Henry Miller has demonstrated that the systematic use of axes with public buildings closing off vistas is the composition used to plan and build that town.[2] Nicholson would have been operating within a baroque tradition which included rules for size of front yard, angle of facade, height of building, and other devices for controlling the vista formed by an axis. Reps indicates that Nicholson was guided by the use of axes, squares, and the "stimuli of space consciousness."[3]

Zucker, as a representative of scholars who interpret urban design, makes an important distinction between Italian baroque and French classicist concepts of external space and expands on what Nicholson would likely have been reading. Zucker makes it fairly clear that Nicholson was acting on French and English monarchical principles, not those of the Italian baroque, which emanated from the Renaissance. A summary of Zucker's argument allows for an understanding of what Nicholson used in order to achieve his successful plans for two capital cities. Both Italian baroque tradition and French classicist tradition used axes to organize how space is perceived. The Italian tradition tends to arrest sight by shifting it from space to space, using the nearer to define the relationship to the farther.[4] The search is for the unexpected, acceleration of sight, and continuous shifting of it. This is achieved without leaving unity aside by using clearly related proportions. This last principle was derived from the Renaissance, and, when used then, it strove to produce balance and quiet harmony. But in the Italian baroque visual movement and illusion were connected to producing tension.

The French planners aimed at the reverse. As one planner argued, "Order in planning, reflecting the centralistic, nay, absolutistic, tendencies of the state, does not allow any spatial deviation, nor any play with infinite vistas. The legitimacy of the reasonably expected takes the place of the surprise of unexpected vistas, the finite takes the place of the infinite of Roman provenance. . . . The equilibrium is . . . stressed by conscious, regular design based mostly on geometric figuration, a rectangle, a square, or a circle."[5]

Nicholson entered a Maryland colony which recently had been taken away from its proprietor by the king, leaving the colony's residents split over their loyalties. He understood centralized authority and had seen its architecture in England and France, and he knew that the built environment had an impact on the spectator. He put all these understandings to work in Annapolis and created closed vistas and squares or rondels as final stops for the monumental buildings that, when built, were to arrest "visual flight."[6] His rondels are called circles in Annapolis, and we have discovered that the bigger one, and the more important politically, was designed and built as an egg.

We know from Batty Langley and John Evelyn that an egg-shape, sometimes called an egg-oval, was used in landscape and urban planning.[7] Langley showed how to build one in his direction book of 1728: "To describe a figure, called an Egg Oval, equal to any breadth given, as $h\ n$. . . . make $a\ c$ equal to $h\ n$, and bisect $a\ c$ in b; whereon, with the distance $a\ b$, describe [draw] the semicircle $a\ d\ c$; on a, with the interval $a\ c$, describe the arch $c\ e$, and with the same opening on c, the arch $a\ f$, crossing the former in g, completing the oval required."[8]

These directions were accompanied by the figure of an egg with the parts lettered consecutively so that these directions are illustrated as in a geometry textbook. Langley knew that, although this is a feasible way to produce an egg, the result is not a geometrically true egg, although it is visually. He then goes on to describe the more complicated maneuvers needed to produce an oval; that is, one continuous arc with no angles.

Langley also described the purpose of building an egg: "The circle, ellipsis, octagon, and mixed figures composed of geometrical squares, parallelograms, and arches of circles [eggs], makes very beautiful figures for water [in the middle of them]. . . . But of them all, the circle is the most grand and beautiful."[9]

From this description it is clear that an egg is to be built by drawing half a circle first and that it is a figure like all the others and that all such figures are built to provide visual interest. Nicholson not only built an egg, he built it on a steep slope. Langley indicates that when a landscape is to include a slope, the slope must be preserved by treating it in particular ways. This is important because State Circle is on a mount with varying slopes: "When very large hills of great perpendicular heights are to be cut into slopes and terraces, then we may justly endeavor to imitate those grand structures . . . grand amphitheatrical buildings, used by the ancients . . . (whereon their gladiators exercised) by cutting concave or convex, etc."[10]

Langley was not describing urban planning, and he wrote after Nicholson's urban designs, but all the landscapes of the nobility he describes had been built by Nicholson's time; consequently, the principles would have been known to the royal governor. Further, Langley's whole effort was to improve the use of the optical principles employed in English gardens since the seventeenth century.

No matter whether one cites Langley or the earlier mainstream landscape designers he criticizes, it is clear that a hillside which had to be enclosed in a planned landscape was to have its slope shaped either by cutting into it or extending it, creating the illusion that is was smooth and extensive (like the interior slope of an amphitheater). To do so required combinations of arcs.

This background highlights the large space Nicholson planned for the center of Annapolis, the location for Maryland's statehouse. He called his design for this sloping hillside Public Circle, and we have discovered that he used an egg to control that space and link the eight converging entries, terminating them all at the statehouse building. The point of the rest of our analysis is to show how we discovered what Nicholson built, how long it has been in existence, and how it has been misunderstood. No recent scholar has given Nicholson credit for such novel planning in Annapolis, and no historian has recognized the sophistication of the plan and its existence through today.

In 1990, Archaeology in Annapolis, which is sponsored jointly by the Historic Annapolis Foundation and the University of Maryland, College Park, undertook a major excavation of State Circle prior to its rebuilding. The State of Maryland granted money to the City of Annapolis to rebuild the street that edges the circle. The road was to be rebuilt and all the below-ground utility lines were to be replaced and those overhead were to be placed underground. This construction was preceded by an extensive archaeological excavation which placed twenty-two pits, called units, at strategic locations around the circle in order to discover earlier boundaries. Eighteenth- and nineteenth-century artifacts in intact features were found in a number of locations on the inner and outer perimeters of State Circle, thus allowing the possibility of describing the shape of the circle at times in the past. The subsequent report concluded that the perimeters of State Circle had not been stable and had shifted over the years; indeed, the whole circle had tended to shift from south to north.[11] It was also concluded that if the circle had ever been truly circular, there was no archaeological evidence of it. If anything, the configuration of the land needed to be seen as dynamic, not stable. By the end of the report writing phase, we concluded that State Circle had never been a circle and we could not tell why its current shape was so amorphous.

Then the search began for an explanation of the odd shape. In 1990 an accurate map of the circle made with a laser theodolite had been commissioned by the City of Annapolis. Inspection of this map lead Leone to suggest that the circle was actually an egg. Stabler learned how to draw an egg and superimposed one on the 1990 map. An egg can be drawn by linking four intersecting arcs of circles drawn from four centers, with three of the centers arranged as a triangle and the fourth center being a mid or center point in the base. The fit between the egg and the perimeter of the 1990 circle is very close, as illustrated in map 13.2.

Eggs have several important characteristics. They begin with two back-to-back triangles (compare map 13.2). If the triangles are Pythagorean, the base of the triangle will divide an even number of times into the perimeter of the egg.[12] Langley showed that the base measure can be taken from an element of the monument to be the focus of attention, which he said provides a sense of harmonious union of building and landscape, especially if the perimeter were a function of some element of the building. In addition, an egg would allow a focal point like the statehouse or church to be a center of attention from many points of view, or while in motion around the monument. It would unify the view from many points on an irregular periphery. An egg also would take a steep slope and give it the appearance of unity like the curve of an amphitheater, viewed either from inside or outside.

Once we realized that State Circle is an egg and not an amorphous circular form, we wanted to know how long it had been one. The answer could be provided by historic maps and our own excavations. To discover how long State Circle had been an egg, a true geometric egg was imposed on

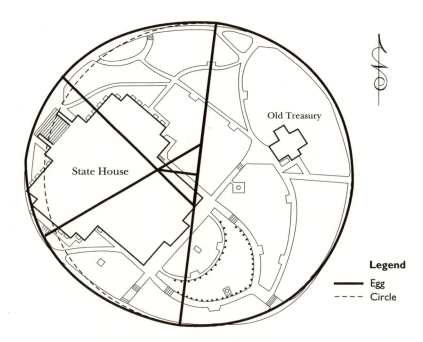

Map 13.2. Survey drawn in 1990 of outline, topography, and buildings on State Circle. Superimposed is an egg construction (note its back-to-back triangles) projected by using AutoCAD. Drawing by Amy Grey adapted from AutoCAD plot by Ann-Marie Burlaga.

maps of it from the 1885 Sanborn Fire Insurance map (map 13.3), and the Stoddert map of 1718 (map 13.4) and the relative error for both an egg and a circle was calculated for each by Leone and Burlaga.[13] A historic map must be entered into a database by tracing it, but then an egg can be superimposed on it quite easily. But even with a digitizing program like AutoCAD, the egg must begin with twin triangles whose location is a matter of judgment.

An egg was superimposed on the 1882 plan for changing the statehouse grounds. Visual inspection of the State Circle on this map shows that it is likely to be an egg. The digitally superimposed egg and the calculations for the fit shows that this hunch was accurate.

Burlaga, who did all the digitizing for this study, discovered two significant additions. Terracing was added to the land immediately outside

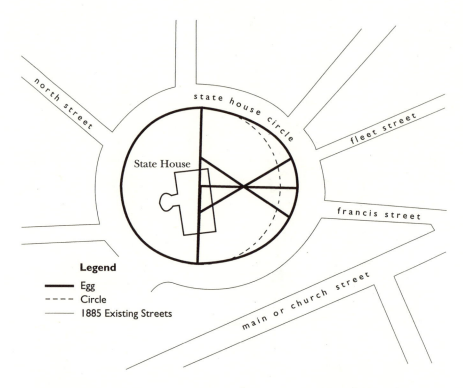

Map 13.3. An 1885 Sanborn Fire Insurance map. This illustration demonstrates the fit of an egg on State Circle versus the fit of a circle. The egg is the closer fit. Drawing by Amy Grey adapted from AutoCAD plot by Ann-Marie Burlaga.

the east, or original front, of the statehouse in 1882. The plateau on top, which serves as an extension of the porch of the statehouse, contains the semicircular arc of an egg. Map 13.5 shows the plateau, which still exists. It is the base of an egg. In built reality, the top of the plateau is an amphitheater, although flat. Its side, which shapes the hillside or slope is convex and accentuates the slope of the hill when viewed from the entry street below. The apex, or the top of the geometric egg, lies directly under the center of the dome in the statehouse. Second, the lines of the triangles needed to produce this arrangement are still visible on the original map. Thus, we know that, at least in the 1880s, the purpose of using an egg as the basis of monumental urban buildings and landscapes was either still understood or had been rediscovered. The purpose of using an egg to form this upper terrace was probably to accentuate the front door and porch of the statehouse as the focal point when standing on the hill below. Burlaga also noticed that the finial on the peak of the slate house, original to the eighteenth century, is an egg.

Archaeological data compose an important alternate source of information, especially when maps do not exist or were too inaccurate for AutoCAD use. The stratigraphy on the eastern two-thirds of State Circle, from Maryland Avenue to the State House Inn, was largely intact. Of the eleven five-foot units dug in these locations, all contained levels which could be dated accurately. Of these pits (units), seven contained features that we interpret as either the inner or (more frequently) the outer edge of State Circle. These features include two public wells, walkways, fence posts for paling, and post holes for

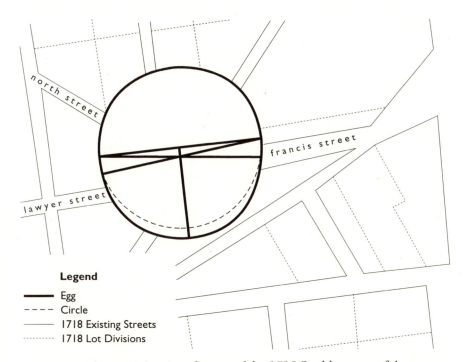

Map 13.4. The 1743 (unsigned) copy of the 1718 Stoddert map of Annapolis. This picture shows the fit of an egg and a circle on what is, supposedly, a true circle. Drawing by Amy Grey adapted from AutoCAD plot by Ann-Marie Burlaga.

lanterns or signs. These were all entered as points in AutoCAD. Those dating 1800–30 make up one set. The computer program generated arcs and twin triangles that could connect these pits. Map 13.6 shows the result, and the fit is poor. There is much tolerance in these lines and some pits are excluded in this trial connection of locations. AutoCAD can approximate the shape desired to link the archaeological locations, and the needed triangle is reshaped as well; thus, there is little certainty of the shape of the circle in 1800–30.

Nonetheless, it is the eighteenth century and earlier, when the circle was planned and created, that comments on Nicholson and his abilities. No one doubts Nicholson's knowledge of baroque town planning, and thus the question is: could he have been sophisticated enough to have employed the known principles of building an egg to unify a space that included a hill top for his statehouse and the surrounding uneven slopes? Could he have used an egg to create a monument visible from all sides, when the

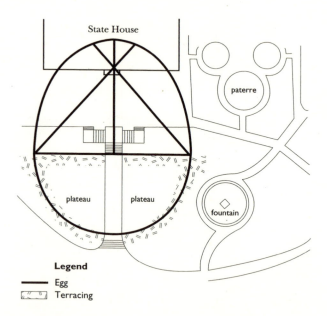

Map 13.5. A fragment of George Gray's plan for renovating State Circle in 1882. This portion shows the semicircular plateau in front of the Maryland Statehouse as the base of an egg whose tip falls directly under the top of the dome. Drawing by Amy Grey adapted from AutoCAD plot by Ann-Marie Burlaga.

Table 13.1
Relative Error for the Fit of an Egg and a Circle

Maps	Circle	Egg
Stoddert (1743)	1.0%	0.6%
1700s: test units	1.6%	0.5%
1800s: test units	0.5%	no fit for an egg
1885 Sanborn	2.0%	0.4%
1990 topographic map	1.8%	0.6%

hilltop was in no way symmetrical but rather fell off with varying degrees of steepness?

To answer this question, arcs were made to link locations which date archaeologically from 1720 to 1800, admittedly a broad period. The divergence between the shape created using AutoCAD and a true egg appears in map 13.7. It appears that State Circle is egg-shaped. This leaves a problem with the 1718 Stoddert Plan, which is the earliest surviving plan of the city

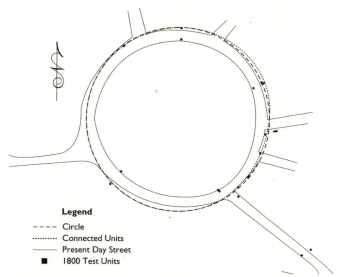

Legend
- - - - Circle
·········· Connected Units
——— Present Day Street
■ 1800 Test Units

Map 13.6. Archaeological test units (represented on the map as small rectangles) containing edges of State Circle dated 1800–1830. They are connected with arcs calculated to link as many units as possible. Superimposed is a circle (the egg construction did not fit). Drawing by Amy Grey adapted from AutoCAD plot by Ann-Marie Burlaga.

and which shows both State and Church Circles named as true circles. Once there is the possibility that the main circle never was truly circular, Stoddert's work is problematic. Was a circle planned and never executed? Was Stoddert simply an incompetent surveyor? Was a circle planned and the execution inept? After all our other work was done, Stoddert's plan was digitized and turned out to be an egg. With this discovery we feel confident that Nicholson planned and built an egg. He probably intended the result to look like a circle because of the harmony attributed to that shape, and an egg created the appearance he sought.

An egg, like any of the other shapes mentioned by Langley, unifies a view, but the view is itself created by the axes to it. The eight streets and alleys that Nicholson used as vistas up to the statehouse are an important

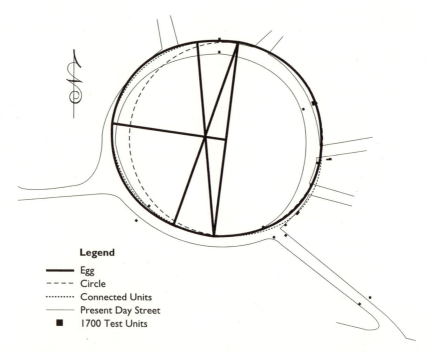

Legend

—— Egg
---- Circle
········· Connected Units
—— Present Day Street
■ 1700 Test Units

Map 13.7. Archaeological test units containing edges of State Circle dated 1720–90. They are connected with arcs calculated to link as many of the units as possible. Superimposed are an egg and a circle (note the egg is the closer fit). Drawing by Amy Grey adapted from AutoCAD plot by Ann-Marie Burlaga.

and central part of his plan. They help demonstrate that the governor's comprehension of baroque design was thorough, even novel.

One curious detail is in the diagonal streets. Those leading into the State House Circle have a pinwheel alignment with not one directly on axis with the center of the circle. It is hard to believe that this was accidental, but the motives are unclear. It may well have been that Nicholson did not fully comprehend one of the aims of baroque design; that is, to create as many terminal vistas as possible by ending diagonal streets at some great public building or monument, with the center line of the street precisely on axis with the center of the structure.[14]

And again:

One feature seen rather quickly is that if the center lines of all the streets entering the two great circles are prolonged, they do not intersect at the center of the open spaces or at any other common point. Tabernacle Street and North Street are decidedly off center. The geometry is even more confused in this respect at State House Circle. It seems strange, moreover, that School Street, the short connection between the two circles, does not have quite the same bearing as East Street, which extends outward to the town boundaries from a point almost opposite. . . .

Why does the Annapolis plan, therefore, show so many instances where the principle of multiaxial planning is violated? It seems doubtful that surveying or drafting errors are responsible. The exceptions are simply too numerous and great. It is also difficult to believe that they may have resulted from subtle adjustments to topography, though it is just conceivable that this may have been the case.[15]

Burlaga points out that the street lines around the circle converge on the statehouse itself (map 13.8). Reps seems to have thought that State Circle was an open space. The statehouse does fill it visually, but the building is in fact very far off true center, although it does not appear to be. Thus, Reps was either fooled by Nicholson's work or never visited Annapolis to see the location of the statehouse. Nicholson created a harmonious ensemble out of awkward elements, including eight entry points which converge directly on the monumental building. Further, in 1990 the archaeological team surveyed the eight entries leading into the circle to discover if their sides were parallel. The five with the longest vistas have sides which diverge as they approach the statehouse, thus making the distant object appear bigger and closer than it was. The two shortest streets have sides which converge on the statehouse, thus making a near object appear more distant than it is, giving the appearance of more space between spectator and object. One street has parallel sides. For the most part, these relationships held when measured on the 1885 Sanborn Insurance Company Map. These measurements show Nicholson using a principle of baroque planning not reported by Reps, but well known in late-seventeenth- and eighteenth-century English books on landscape design. The idea was to make an object appear farther away than it is in a small space by making the sight lines converge and to make an object appear closer

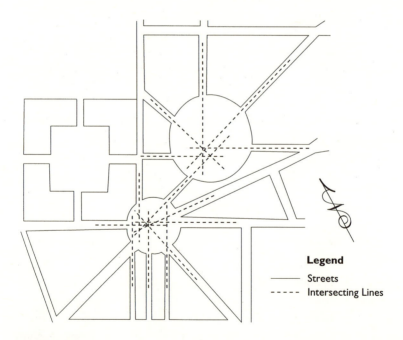

Map 13.8. Reps's hand-drawn rendition of the 1718 Stoddert plan digitized by Ann-Marie Burlaga. This illustration displays the center lines of the streets intersecting on State Circle, where the statehouse is the locus of the intersection of the center lines. Drawing by Amy Grey.

in a large space by making the sight lines diverge on the object. Reps understood that the center line of the street was important when enhancing the importance of a public monument, but he seems to have misunderstood what baroque planners assumed: plans are executed as volumes and the sides of the vista, not just the bottom plane, need to be managed, too. Nicholson must have understood that he was working in three dimensions for the purpose of enabling his design for a center of power.

We have concluded that the plane geometry of an egg, plus the ideas of baroque town planning, which included the use of principles of perspective, were used to plan, build, and change State Circle over the last three hundred years. This conclusion is tempered by not being sure of the circle's shape in the early nineteenth century, and by not knowing how many different times the circle subsequently has been renovated using an egg as a design. As a result of these observations, we conclude that the plane geometry of an egg plus the ideas of baroque axial planning which included the use of closed perspectives were used to plan and build State Circle.

Like Reps, we conclude that Nicholson drew heavily from landscape design, which was already a mature field, when he became governor of Maryland and then of Virginia. Our conclusion depends on the fact that he visited Versailles and witnessed the rebuilding of London. From historical inferences, analysis of maps, and archaeological discoveries, we conclude that Nicholson utilized many principles of baroque landscape and architectural design to shape a park as his city, with the monumental buildings acting as fermata (i.e., points of visual closure) for the vistas or axes that ended in the squares he made for buildings housing the centers of power.

We conclude that Nicholson probably did not make the errors Reps attributes to him. Although we can agree that Williamsburg may be his greater success, it is a success because he situated it on flat ground, which was much easier to handle. Annapolis, located on a series of ridges and already extant as a town, was much more difficult to manage and constitutes a greater technical achievement. We can also see that in the 1760s and up to the Revolution, eighty years after Nicholson's design, the baroque gardens of Annapolis were not novelties at all, but followed the rules for baroque landscape design drawn on by Nicholson. Paca, Ridout, Carroll, Chase, Hammond, Scott, Dulany, and all the other Annapolitans who built great houses with terraced, rectangular gardens used Nicholson's model to create their own visually spectacular properties. They made statements about the necessity of their places in hierarchical authority and used the built environment to proclaim them. This is Zucker's point about the absolutistic tendencies of contemporary French and British states. The only addition we make to this analysis is to say that baroque planners and artists knew they were working with illusions which created images of a reality that was not there. Sometimes they used illusion to copy reality; sometimes they used it to see what reality was. They wanted to see if harmony could be made. Nicholson and his successors in Annapolis did create a permanent harmonious environment. And it has been permanently connected to hierarchy for three hundred years. Unlike Reps's explicit conclusions about Nicholson's competence in designing Annapolis, yet in accordance with Reps's own deepest suspicions, Annapolis is a very successful town for the establishment of centralized power.

Notes

1. John Reps, *Tidewater Towns: City Planning in Colonial Virginia and Maryland* (Williamsburg, Va.: Colonial Williamsburg Foundation, 1972), 127.
2. Henry Miller, "Baroque Cities in the Wilderness: Archaeology and Urban Development in the Colonial Chesapeake," *Historical Archaeology* 22 (2) (1988): 57–73.
3. Paul Zucker, *Town and Square, From the Agora to the Village Green* (New York: Columbia Univ. Press, 1959), 234.
4. Ibid., 233.
5. Ibid., 234.
6. Ibid., 235.
7. Batty Langley, *New Principles of Gardening: Or the Laying Out and Planning of Parterres, Groves, Wildernesses, Labyrinths, Avenues, Parks, etc.* (1728; reprint, England: Gregg International Publishers, Ltd., 1971).
8. Ibid., 17, plate I.
9. Ibid., 202.
10. Ibid., vii.
11. Esther Doyle-Read, Mark P. Leone, Barbara J. Little, Jean B. Russo, George C. Logan, and Brett Burk, *Archaeological Investigations Around State Circle in Annapolis, Maryland* (Annapolis: Historic Annapolis Foundation, 1990).
12. Alexander Thom, *Megalithic Remains in Britain and Brittany* (London: Oxford Univ. Press, 1978).
13. A measurement point along the true periphery of State Circle (taken from the maps) was recorded every ten degrees. The distance between the point and the model egg/circle was computed and entered into a formula to determine the relative error of each. The distance is a positive number measured along a line perpendicular to the egg/circle that passes through the data point.
14. Reps, *The Making of Urban America* (Princeton: Princeton Univ. Press, 1965), 108.
15. Reps, *Tidewater Towns*, 123–24.

E pilogue: From Georgian Order to Social Relations at Annapolis and Beyond

Charles E. Orser Jr.

Observers unaware of the subtle nuances of academic scholarship may believe that all is quiet in American historical archaeology. Their reasons for thinking so would appear well founded. After all, numerous skilled excavators have worked diligently to make historical archaeology a respectable pursuit both to the professional archaeological community and to the general public at large. Signs of historical archaeology's success are particularly encouraging outside the profession. For example, newspaper editors—though still especially enamored with articles proclaiming the discovery of new finds in ancient Egypt, the Middle East, and the Valley of Mexico—regularly find space for pieces about the archaeology of more recently occupied sites. In addition, every summer scores of eager archaeo-tourists stroll around sites excavated by historical archaeologists and peer through exhibition glass at tiny pieces of history excavated from post-Columbian sites. On the funding side, the federal government includes historical archaeology within the purview of its cultural resource management concerns, and numerous granting agencies have finally decided that historical archaeology really is archaeology (though a few tenacious holdouts unfortunately still exist). In light of this expanding exposure, no one can seriously question the permanence of historical archaeology in archaeology's future. Historical archaeology has finally come of age, and the many archaeologists of Annapolis, a number of whom are represented in this volume, have done much to help the discipline mature.

Though we may well conclude that historical archaeology is secure as a scholarly endeavor, we would be wrong to imagine that historical archaeologists have decided upon only one theoretical perspective or that there are no major issues still to be resolved in the field. On the contrary, historical archaeologists have only now begun to scratch the surface of understanding the post-1492 world, and many intellectual debates still rage in the discipline. Like all scholars of antiquity, historical archaeologists are still searching for the most appropriate ways to study the past. In keeping with this intellectual quest, a quiet struggle is raging in today's historical archaeology. This struggle, because it involves a transformation of thought—a veritable shift in perspective—has the ability to change the discipline in a deeply significant way.

No better place than the American Chesapeake exists to consider this intellectual tussle in American historical archaeology. Within this large and historically significant region, archaeologists have settled upon one of its most prominent hubs, Annapolis, as a particularly fertile locale for theoretical exploration and interpretive exposition. In an important sense, and as the present volume demonstrates, Annapolis has become a testing ground for serious, theoretically rooted historical archaeology. Its quiet lanes and stately buildings, its green backyards and gray basements have become places to take intellectual chances, laboratories to test new ideas about old things. As Brian Fagan observed, the archaeological research at Annapolis has "revolutionized our perceptions of Annapolis' past."[1] We could easily expand Fagan's assessment to say that research at Annapolis has helped to revolutionize the entire field of historical archaeology.

As is true of any struggle—intellectual or otherwise—at least two sides must be represented. In historical archaeology, the factions are often difficult to discern with absolute clarity. On one side of the debate, though, are archaeologists who generally adhere to the cherished idea that archaeology provides a pathway to learn about past culture. Understanding culture, of course, forms the core of American anthropology, and American archaeologists are comfortable taking part in the culturalist exercise. It is, after all, what American archaeologists are supposed to do. As a group,

American archaeologists view culture as nothing less than the "dominant factor in determining social behavior" and as "the primary means by which human societies adapt to their environment."[2] Non-American archaeologists—who usually have not been formally trained as anthropologists—make the tie between archaeology and the study of culture much less explicit, and often they do not make it at all.[3] Though some archaeologists outside the United States have recently discovered the part anthropology can play in their research, this discovery has not been required in American archaeology since its association with anthropology is many decades old. American historical archaeology, though its association with anthropology was once a matter of considerable debate, is now a full-fledged partner in anthropology's pursuit of cultural knowledge.

The study of culture by American historical archaeologists has followed many tracks, but perhaps its best and most well-conceptualized example is embodied in the Georgian Order. The close association between the archaeological study of culture and the Georgian Order has been particularly strong at Annapolis.

Recently, however, some excavators have decided to draw away from the Georgian Order's overt culturalist stance. Instead, they have decided to focus on the social interactions and exchanges of everyday life. Their attention is drawn to the ways in which past men and women interacted to maintain families, to keep food in the household, and to purchase material things; in short, everything necessary to create daily life and to make history. A key element of this perspective is that men and women live in ways that we may label "cultural" if we wish, but that as living actors, people in the past performed their daily chores—including all those things that leave archaeological traces—within constantly changing networks of social interaction. In this mutualist perspective, people are more concerned with the daily give and take of their social associations than with some vague notion of culture they may not even be able to conceptualize.

For many years, the culturalist perspective has held sway at Annapolis. But as the chapters in this volume show, many historical archaeologists there may now be ready to abandon the culturalist framework for a more sociological approach. This shift in perspective is significant for two important reasons. First, it appears in Annapolis, a site of steady leadership in archaeological theory. Historical archaeologists throughout America listen to the research at Annapolis because of the cadre of highly skilled, thoughtful excavators who work there. The interpretations that come from this colonial city matter to the discipline. Second, many of the connections that bound together men and women in the past still exist today, linking us directly to the past we study as historical archaeologists.[4] An overt mutualist perspective allows us to link present and past with little intellectual angst. But to understand the significance of the shift from Georgian Order to social relations, we must begin with the Georgian Order.

The Georgian Order

The idea of the Georgian Order, first termed the Georgian worldview, was invented by James Deetz to explain the changes he perceived in the material creations of eighteenth-century Anglo Americans. Using Levi-Straussian structuralism by way of folklorist Henry Glassie, Deetz explained the changes in Anglo American material culture by arguing that they reflected a larger transformation of thought in the British world. Deetz's archaeological work showed discernible shifts, from the late medieval to the early modern ages, from asymmetrical to symmetrical house plans, from unmatched to neatly matching table settings, and from widely scattered burials to interments arranged in neat, evenly spaced rows. Deetz proposed a unique and inventive answer to explain these rather radical changes: he said that they constituted the visible evidence of an alteration in the people's thought processes.[5] For him, these material changes, though seemingly unassociated, were actually the material expressions of a new way of looking at the world, a world in which imposed order and neatness were intended to replace natural (that is, unplanned) chaos and disorder. The Georgian worldview was culture at its best because it allowed men and women to adapt to the new circumstances of a rapidly changing, early modern world.

Deetz used the notion of the Georgian worldview to explain the material transformation of Yankee America and to provide an understanding of why New Englanders had transformed themselves from sloppy medievalists to neat moderns. But for many decades New England has served as a convenient metaphor for all of America,[6] and archaeologists in other regions—particularly in the Chesapeake, including at Annapolis—eagerly accepted the idea of the Georgian worldview. Renaming it the Georgian Order, Annapolitan archaeologists responded positively to Deetz's culturalist view. Most not only liked "the charisma of Deetz," but many believed that the Georgian Order allowed them to link observable patterns of material culture to long-dead patterns of thought.[7] It appeared to many that an understanding of the Georgian Order would provide a way to get into the heads of early British colonists in America. For archaeologists, what could be better than to understand the way past people thought? Thus, the central question for the most prominent archaeologists at Annapolis became not whether the Georgian Order ever actually existed—they eagerly accepted that it did—but rather to show how it would be possible "to apply adequately the idea of the Georgian Order to areas beyond New England." The key issues for archaeologists at Annapolis became "Why the Georgian worldview? What gave rise to it? How, precisely did it emerge? and What did the emergence look like, at a fine-grained level of analysis?"[8]

Having accepted the Georgian Order as a historical fact, archaeologists at Annapolis set about to refine it. Taking one tack, they extended its material expressions to include keeping time, reading novels, playing music, dividing space, and painting—in other words, to activities seldom studied by archaeologists. But this expansion of the Order's purview was not enough, and archaeologists at Annapolis wanted more from it: they wished to know *why* it existed. It was with this inquiry into the root causes of the Georgian Order, then, that the archaeologists of Annapolis made their greatest contribution to its study, for lurking within it they found the face of capitalism. Their realization that capitalism was somehow connected to the Georgian Order suggested that something other than just the structure of the human mind controlled the new way English men and women looked at the world.

At first, this new version of the Georgian Order seemed like a bold step away from Deetz's culturalist view.[9] After all, at its core, capitalism consists of a complex set of interwoven social relations that are played out and manipulated in various ways by conscious human actors. Capitalism cannot be considered as either natural or part of a universal human psyche. Nonetheless, even after having discovered capitalism, Annapolitan archaeologists could not make a serious break with Deetz's culturalist position. To resolve the knotty problem of refining the Georgian Order without offending its creator, Annapolitan archaeologists chose to define capitalism as a "culture" in order "to avoid violating the coherence of a cognitive and structuralist interpretation of material culture so fruitfully created by Glassie and Deetz." So, just as they were on the brink of making the leap to the full-blown study of Annapolitan social relations—and abandoning the confining culturalism of the Georgian Order—the archaeologists of

Annapolis had as their goal "to demonstrate what Glassie and Deetz may contribute to an understanding of capitalism."[10] The stated objective of their research, then, was to make capitalism conform to Deetz's culturalist perspective, not to study capitalism as a historically occurring phenomena. Capitalism thus became a culture: people in the past grew up with it, learned its characteristics during the enculturation process, and passed it on to their children. Living in America in the late twentieth century, I am apparently part of this culture as well.

Even though this formulation was an overt attempt to link the culturalist Georgian Order with capitalism, it went too far for many of the strict culturalists. For example, in a quick response, Anne Yentsch argued that capitalism was embedded within the Georgian worldview, not vice versa. As she said, "men and women in the medieval and post-medieval worlds do not live lives wholly or even primarily concerned with making monetary profits."[11] In other words, people must think Georgian before they can act capitalist.

When put in these simplistic terms, the culturalist viewpoint does seem to have merit. After all, where do people's thoughts originate? What makes people think they should do something one way and not another? One easy answer to such deep questions is the simplest one: culture makes people do what they do. This way of thinking is as comforting as it is mysterious. Culture appears as an ethereal cloud floating above us all, invisible yet there, unseen but acknowledged in everything we do. We express our culture in our actions and embody it in the things we make. Even our thoughts seem to be guided by our culture. And, where one culture's cloud ends, another begins, ready to exert its control over those men and women who live beneath it. Anthropologists have demonstrated time and again that the world exists as a mosaic of cultures, each of which is identifiable by its special characteristics, its unique way of doing things. As a result, we find hybrid cultures where the clouds come together, creolized creations hammered out of the overlap.

This account of culture is anthropologically satisfying. But though the culturalist vision seems comforting, it is far too simplistic to have lasting relevance to historical archaeology. As Deetz himself observed, in historical archaeology the simplest explanations may not always be the best,[12] and where the Georgian Order is concerned I would agree. As anthropologists we often find it convenient to have culture to fall back on, to make it the final explanation for all that happens. But historical archaeologists have another option, one that is more relevant to our eventual understanding of the modern world. This different way of interpreting the past involves the consideration of social relations, focusing on the actual ties that existed between real men and women.

Examples of the social relations perspective run throughout in this volume. For example, if we go back to the Maynard-Burgess House and to Gott's Court, we learn from Mark Warner that the African American community in Annapolis was not a cultural monolith. Instead, the residents of these sites made conscious choices that were socially charged and situationally meaningful. The use of tea is illustrative. As Warner points out, the Maynard household consciously selected tea drinking as a strategy designed to yield direct social benefits. Tea was not a cultural marker for African Americans in Annapolis. Rather, it forged and maintained certain social connections that had important meaning to the people within the household. In another example, Christopher Matthews tells us that the most influential advocate of the Georgian style of architecture was one man, Andrea Palladio. According to Matthews, to understand the Georgian style we must first understand Palladio. Thus, it appears that Palladio—this one man—held an important key to much of the Georgian mindset. Later, we learn from Matthews that one of the most important architects in colonial America—including Annapolis—was William Buckland. Buckland designed purely Georgian houses to be sure, but at least in the cases of the Chase-Lloyd and the Hammond-Harwood houses, he was also idiosyncratic. Only with difficulty could we ascribe the unusual architectural features to Buckland's culture. The same could be said of Nicholson's design of Annapolis as explained by Leone, Stabler, and Burlaga. The architecture was intended, not as a way to symbolize culture, but as a way to create, maintain, and symbolize social connections and to establish social boundaries between people.

Even given the apparent explanatory weakness of the Georgian Order, we would be foolish to suppose that the neat, symmetrical architectural style we now call Georgian did not appeal to America's colonial elites. Its neat designs were indeed intended to create artificial order from nature's apparent chaos. And maybe Deetz was right. Perhaps some kind of mental shift did indeed cause men and women of English heritage to change their thoughts from sloppy to neat, from asymmetrical to symmetrical. Something we can identify as culture exists even if we cannot touch it or exactly see it. But does culture, as a concept, have the most relevance to historical archaeology? The men and women who lived at the Maynard-

Burgess House and at Gott's Court, though they may have acted within culturally prescribed parameters, nonetheless constructed their daily lives around a series of shifting, changing interpersonal connections.

But an even greater weakness hides within the Georgian Order. This defect derives from its perhaps unwitting emphasis on elites. To explain, I will go far afield from Annapolis, to a distant but oddly related place. Since 1993, I have been conducting research in the green midlands of the Republic of Ireland on an estate once owned by the powerful, Anglo Irish Mahon family. Until the Great Famine struck Ireland in 1845, the estate consisted of three spatial elements: a huge mansion, a surrounding walled demesne, or park land, and hundreds of small farms outside the demesne on the estate's fifteen thousand acres. The peasant farmers, or cottiers, paid their hard-earned rents to head tenants who, in turn, paid Mahon. When the cottiers could not make rent, as happened during the Great Famine, the fortunes of the estate suffered. In 1847, Mahon decided to evict his starving nonrent-paying peasants in order to consolidate their small farms into broad grazing fields and larger, more productive farms operated by the head tenants. Mahon paid the cottiers' passage out of Ireland, and those who survived the horrors of the trip eventually landed at Quebec.[13]

Though far from Annapolis, Mahon's mansion is pertinent here because it represents a perfect example of Palladian architecture. As a result, the house is a distant cousin of the many Palladian buildings in Annapolis. The central residential core of Mahon's mansion is rigidly symmetrical. As one stands in front of the imposing structure, on the right side is the attached, vaulted stable, and on the left is the kitchen wing. The building is the very picture of symmetry and order, and in its whiteness it stands in stark contrast to the surrounding green of the demesne. The mansion makes a powerful statement, but it is much more than the sum of its physical appearance. In fact, its meaning runs even deeper because it conforms in every way to the ideals of the Protestant Ascendancy in Ireland. The term Protestant Ascendancy still has deep-seated political, social, and religious connotations in today's Ireland, but more important for us, "the most lasting creation of the Ascendancy" was the magnificence of its built environment.[14] The power of the Ascendancy is forever etched into Ireland, frozen in its mansions, geometrical gardens, walled demesnes, and urban townhouses. It is no accident that Georgian architecture constitutes an important element of this environment. Mahon's mansion is the very picture of Georgian neatness and control.

Without question, we could say if we wished that the Georgian Order maintains a strong presence on Mahon's estate, and really throughout Ireland. But when looking at the Mahon estate, we must ask ourselves this simple question: where is the relevance of the Georgian Order to the cottiers who formed the bulk of the Irish population? My guess is that while the residents of the Georgian mansions concerned themselves with painting, measuring time, and dining from matched tableware, life went on for the farmers in a decidedly non-Georgian, albeit nonmedieval, manner. Their lives were altered by the Georgian thoughts of the propertied landlords to be sure, especially when they were evicted in a fit of Georgian neatness. Some authors have even proposed that the building of Georgian structures helped the poor cottiers: "The building of an obelisk, the draining of a lake or bog, the enclosure of an estate by a perimeter wall, the planting of woodlands and extension of lawns all provided employment, and these works must not be dismissed as frivolous activity."[15] Clearly, Irish cottiers were affected by the thoughts of people who lived in Georgian-style mansions, but were they really any part of the elite's mindset?

It may indeed be compelling to examine the lives of the cottiers using the Georgian structures of the elites. But a more satisfying approach would result from focusing on the social relations maintained by the great mass of men and women who created history each and every day by the mundane connections they maintained. This perspective causes us to turn our attention away from those men and women who left behind lasting monuments to themselves—mansions, gardens, massive walls—and toward those who have been consistently overlooked by history. Though the study of the commonplace men and women has been a theme of much of Deetz's work,[16] his use of the Georgian Order clouds this interest.

I must make it clear, however, that the cottiers cannot be studied in isolation—removed from their landlords—and treated like remnants of some ancient Celtic culture. This approach would be as unsatisfying, and as culturalist, as the Georgian Order. The reason why we cannot study the cottiers in isolation rests with social relations.

The Triumph of Social Relations

The idea of focusing on social relations forms part of the quiet revolution in American historical archaeology. Recent publications—including this book—suggest that most Annapolitan archaeologists have left the Georgian Order behind. In a recent study, for example, Mark Leone, the Order's one-time champion, does not use the concept at all. Instead, he perceives the baroque and panoptic designs of Annapolis and Baltimore as expressions of social relations.[17] The social connections in both cities established, maintained, and symbolized the unequal relations between the real men and women who lived there. Their connections do not exactly describe culture, Georgian or otherwise.

The theoretical foundation for a perspective that foregrounds social relations derives from the work of several anthropologists. Over fifty years ago, A. R. Radcliffe-Brown wrote that a "particular social relation between two persons (unless they be Adam and Eve in the Garden of Eden) exists only as part of a wide network of social relations, involving many other persons." About twenty years later, Alexander Lesser argued that anthropologists could only understand human societies by recognizing that they consisted of a series of complex "weblike, netlike connections." Another twenty years later, Eric Wolf said that anthropologists should not see societies and cultures as taken-for-granted elements of human existence. Instead, he said that anthropologists should focus their attention on the "fields of relationships" that people create and dissolve.[18]

Several ethnographers became interested in social relations after Radcliffe-Brown's comments, and many went into the field to document the world's social networks. These anthropologists discovered that peoples around the world construct an infinite variety of networks, connecting themselves in ways that include, among other considerations, kinship, relations of power, economic strategies, class perceptions, and views on the environment.[19]

More recently, cultural anthropologist Michael Carrithers took these ideas about social relations one step further. Borrowing the term "mutualism" from social psychology, he argued that the relationships of interacting men and women have primary significance in group dynamics. Mutualism holds that people act and react in relation to one another rather than in direct response to some hazy, cultural abstraction. For culturalists, "people do things because of their culture," but for mutualists, people "do things with, to, and in respect of each other, using means that we can describe, if we wish, as cultural." In mutualism, social relations constitute "the basic stuff of human life."[20]

As soon as we put our analytical focus on the relationships people maintain rather than on the abstract culture they may carry in their heads, we understand humanity's unique potential. Other social animals—wolves and ants, for instance—tend to live in relation to one another, but humans produce relations *in order* to live. Because human life is metamorphic, men and women "produce culture and create history" in the relations they invent.[21] And, given the mutable nature of everyday experience, the relations are constantly changing.

Archaeologists find nothing new in the idea that men and women create their own histories. After all, V. Gordon Childe introduced the idea several decades ago in his stunning and widely read overviews of antiquity.[22] But what archaeologists have learned from Childe is that social relations gain expression in material things and on physical landscapes. Artifacts and landscapes, of course, are equally important to archaeologists, but in the remainder of this essay I focus specifically on physical landscapes to illustrate the significance of considering social relations in historical archaeology.[23]

Social Relations on the Landscape

Archaeologists' interest in landscapes is, of course, nothing new, and over the years archaeologists have adopted and invented diverse ways to study the subtle nuances of settlement patterning. Mutualism provides another way in which to view the meanings behind the locations of settlements. To understand the significance of thinking about landscapes as representative of social relations, we can start with the culturalist perspective. My critique of the culturalist perspective is pertinent because numerous historical archaeologists have adopted this approach in their settlement research, tending to incorporate its precepts as givens.

In a short but instructive paper, Deetz distinguished between a landscape—"the total terrestrial context in which archaeological study is pursued"—and a cultural landscape—"that part of the terrain which is modified according to a set of cultural plans." Cultural landscapes are the elements of the environment that interest anthropological archaeologists because it is here that we see the lasting, terrestrial effects of conscious human effort. Because men and women carry their cultural ideals around in their heads wherever they go, they tend to construct cultural landscapes that are familiar and comforting to them. When thinking this way, we are not surprised that "[a]t the southern tip of the African continent, one finds a little piece of England."[24] Our discovery of England in Africa seems to make perfect sense. After all, English colonists went to South Africa and settled in what was for them a new environment. In doing so, they created a cultural landscape that was familiarly reminiscent of the land they had left behind. By modifying South Africa to fit their cultural perceptions, the colonists in effect created tiny pieces of England in faraway Africa. They did this by holding the cultural ideals of their homeland securely in their heads during the long ocean voyage.

Based on this one example—and many more could be cited with ease— it appears that cultural landscapes indicate a people's understanding of how a terrain should be transformed to fit preconceived cultural ideals. This formulation is straightforward and easy to understand. Its only problem stems from its overwhelming reliance on culture. In this perspective, culture hovers over the landscapes colonists create, permitting them to construct houses that are unmistakably British. People do what they know, and what they know is cultural.

Though this viewpoint is again anthropologically comforting, a focus on social relations takes us out of this culturalist framework and allows us to envision a landscape that is more actively alive. It permits us to conceptualize landscapes that are spatial arenas upon which constantly changing social relations are created and recreated.

On any land surface, a people's relations can take both human-to-human and human-to-nature forms.[25] Human-to-human relations are both social and spatial. In hierarchical, capitalist societies—the sort studied by most historical archaeologists, including those at Annapolis—each kind of human-to-human relation necessarily incorporates relations of power. Power and power relations are complex issues that are far outside the scope of this brief essay. Its introduction here is necessary, however, because power forms an integral part of the built landscape. As philosopher Michel Foucault wrote, "space is fundamental in any exercise of power."[26] And, to complicate matters, existing side by side with power is another complex concept, ideology.

Ideology has been defined many ways, and this is not the place for a long, tiresome exegesis. Suffice it to say that most scholars agree that ideology works to hide and even to misrepresent social relations. Rather than to envision ideology as a force exerted on one class by another, the most sophisticated understandings see it as an element of social relations that is constantly being redefined. A society's power elite can use ideology to maintain its hold over nonelites, and leaders can use ideology to mystify their domination and to make their control seem natural and ahistorical. Nonelites can accept the ideology of the elites or they can transform it into an ideology of resistance.[27] Nonelites can also create their own ideologies. The clash of ideologies is necessarily an intriguing subject because it entails the creation of power relations.

Power relations and the struggles they engender always occur in a particular place and at a particular time. These places and the spaces that exist between them represent "spatiality," or the conscious creation of space. Spatiality is not a natural or an accidental phenomenon, but rather a "constituted objectivity, a 'lived' reality."[28] Space—the distance between things—is a social product, and spatiality "is really about the ordering of relations between people."[29] As a result, spatiality can be used as an ideological tool to hide the realities of social relations or make them appear to be something they are not. Spatiality can also be used to make landscapes seem natural and timeless, when in fact they are artificial and temporal.

These ideas about space and spatiality are compatible with a mutualist perspective and they are pertinent to archaeological research. Mutualism helps archaeologists to understand that past landscapes represent more than just where things were once located. The space between things—sites, villages, buildings, trash pits—represents the long-dead connections of past men and women. A mutualist perspective also can help archaeologists to comprehend the origin of spatially expressed ideology by keeping in mind that "we are not so much self-aware as self-and-other aware."[30] Spatiality is self-and-other awareness expressed on the landscape. What this means, then, is that the construction of modern landscapes is a function of the network of relations people maintained both with one another and with the natural environment around them. In creating landscapes, men and women are self-and-other aware. They are not merely the agents of their cultures.

To explain the relevance of the mutualist view of human settlement, we can return briefly to the Irish midlands. Here we can easily see spatiality in action. The Georgian mansion of the Mahons, with its huge demesne and formal, walled garden was one element of the built environment. But for all its grandeur, it could not exist if the estate's cottiers did not send their rents to Mahon from their tiny cottages. To be sure, the cottiers lived in a different landscape than did Mahon, but theirs was as connected to his as was the mansion's kitchen wing to its residential core. When Mahon left the safety of his neatly planned demesne, he entered a foreign landscape, one which he only tenuously controlled. When he traveled on the narrow roads of the countryside, he passed the one-roomed, thatched cabins of the cottiers, with their dung heaps piled near the door. When visiting the Irish countryside, early-nineteenth-century observers generally used the words "wretched" and "miserable" to describe the homes of the rural Irish farmers.[31] No one ever used such terms to describe Mahon's mansion. So, we can easily say that Mahon's estate was composed of at least two culturally designed landscapes. Or can we? These two landscapes—one ostensibly English and "modern," the other apparently Irish and "traditional"— were not mere reflections of English and Irish cultures. Rather, they were part and parcel of the same consciously created space, with each needing the other to survive as a settlement type. Without the farmers' rents, Mahon could not have built his Palladian mansion, and without Mahon, the cottiers would have been free to create an agricultural system built solely around subsistence. Each landscape was part of the other, and both were inexorably tied together by social relations. The social connections produced one Anglo-Irish place. What is intriguing to consider is how the material dimensions of these relations were created and recreated on a daily basis.

• • •

This brief visit to the Irish midlands brings us back to the Georgian Order. Little question exists that Mahon's mansion—like many of the homes in Annapolis—was built in a neat, symmetrical style. It did not look like the houses of traditional Ireland any more than the Georgian homes of Annapolis resembled the houses of Maryland's native peoples. I can fully accept that Mahon's construction of the mansion—along with its formal garden, its medieval folly, and its well-planned demesne—was intended to symbolize the smugness of his power within central Ireland. Mahon unquestionably ruled the estate, controlling the most lasting elements of its physical landscape. Control of the landscape was typical of landlords in pre-famine Ireland, and Mahon's power is not at all surprising.[32] But at the same time, we cannot easily envision Mahon's estate as existing within an ahistorical vacuum. When thinking about his neat, Georgian demesne, we must also think about the hundreds of men and women who lived outside its walls. These were the people who sent him their hard-won rents and who kept the fine transfer prints and shining crystal on his rich mahogany table. As soon as we think about the surrounding settlements, we must acknowledge the binding ties between Mahon and his tenants. To do otherwise is to ignore the way in which history was created in pre-famine Ireland. The Georgian Order, and its accompanying culturalist perspective, is not helpful in seeking to understand these connections. And, to bring the discussion back across the ocean to Annapolis, it does not appear useful there either.

Historical archaeology is an exciting field simply because the interpretations expressed by its practitioners matter so much. Oftentimes, given the closeness in time between the pasts we study and the realities of the contemporary world, our interpretations of sites sometimes seem to be interpretations of today. Though we historical archaeologists are not sociologists of the contemporary world, we cannot help but link past with present. In fact, mutualism shows that many of the ties that existed in the past still exist today. These connections stretch from the past and connect us to it. The Great Irish Famine of 1845–50 is not truly a thing of the past. It affects living men and women in Ireland, Great Britain, Australia, New Zealand, the United States, and Canada, and a hundred other places to which Irish immigrants traveled in their diaspora. The same connections can clearly be observed in today's Annapolis.

It would be naive to imagine that the interpretations that appear in this book are simply the stuff of academic scholarship. The quiet struggle that is currently being waged in American historical archaeology is reaching to the very soul of the field, for it will chart the course of our interpretations over the next several years. Historical archaeologists can take heart by the rise of social-relation, mutualist studies in their field because this approach promises—like this book—to advance our scholarship to new theoretical heights. It also promises to make our work directly relevant to thousands of our contemporary fellow citizens, who, like us, continue to create history through our social relations.

Notes

1. Brian M. Fagan, *Time Detectives: How Archaeologists Use Technology to Recapture the Past* (New York: Simon and Schuster, 1995), 245.
2. Brian M. Fagan, *Archaeology: A Brief Introduction*, 4th ed. (New York: Harper Collins, 1991), 38; Robert J. Sharer and Wendy Ashmore, *Archaeology: Discovering Our Past*, 2d ed. (Mountain View, Calif.: Mayfield, 1993), 31. See also Charles E. Orser Jr. and Fagan, *Historical Archaeology* (New York: Harper Collins, 1995), 48–49.

3. Kathleen M. Kenyon, *Beginning in Archaeology,* rev. ed. (New York: Praeger, 1970); Philip Rahtz, *Invitation to Archaeology,* 2d ed. (Oxford: Blackwell, 1991). A recent modification of European thought in regard to culture is perhaps best portrayed in Colin Renfrew and Paul Bahn, *Archaeology: Theories, Methods, and Practice* (London: Thames and Hudson, 1991).

4. Charles E. Orser Jr., *A Historical Archaeology of the Modern World* (New York: Plenum, 1996).

5. James Deetz, *In Small Things Forgotten: The Archaeology of Early American Life* (Garden City, N.Y.: Anchor Books, 1977); Deetz, "Scientific Humanism and Humanistic Science: A Plea for Paradigmatic Pluralism in Historical Archaeology," *Geoscience and Man* 23 (1983): 27–34; Deetz, "Material Culture and Worldview in Colonial Anglo-America," in *The Recovery of Meaning: Historical Archaeology in the Eastern United States,* ed. Mark P. Leone and Parker B. Potter Jr. (Washington, D.C.: Smithsonian Institution Press, 1988), 219–33.

6. Stephen Nissenbaum, "New England as Region and Nation," in *All Over the Map: Rethinking American Regions,* ed. Edward L. Ayers and Peter S. Onuf (Baltimore: Johns Hopkins Univ. Press, 1996), 38–39.

7. Mark P. Leone and Parker B. Potter Jr., "The Archaeology of the Georgian Worldview and the 18th-Century Beginnings of Modernity," in *The Recovery of Meaning,* ed. Leone and Potter, 211–12.

8. Mark P. Leone and Parker B. Potter Jr., "Introduction: Issues in Historical Archaeology," in *The Recovery of Meaning,* ed. Leone and Potter, 11; Parker B. Potter Jr., *Public Archaeology in Annapolis: A Critical Approach to History in Maryland's Ancient City* (Washington, D.C.: Smithsonian Institution Press, 1994), 141.

9. Mark P. Leone, "The Georgian Order as the Order of Merchant Capitalism in Annapolis, Maryland," in *The Recovery of Meaning,* ed. Leone and Potter, 235–61; Leone and Paul A. Shackel, "The Georgian Order in Annapolis," in New Perspectives on Maryland Historical Archaeology, issue ed. Barbara J. Little and Richard J. Dent, *Maryland Archaeology* 26 (1990): 69–84. A recent attempt to link Deetz's culturalism with capitalism appears in Matthew Johnson, *An Archaeology of Capitalism* (Oxford: Blackwell, 1996).

10. Leone, "Georgian Order and Merchant Capitalism," 237. Leone penned a somewhat less sympathetic position in "Symbolic, Structural, and Critical Archaeology," in *American Archaeology, Past and Future: A Celebration of the Society for American Archaeology, 1935–1985,* ed. David J. Meltzer, Don D. Fowler, and Jeremy A. Sabloff (Washington, D.C.: Smithsonian Institution Press, 1986), 424–26.

11. Anne Yentsch, "An Interpretive Study of the Use of Land and Space on Lot 83, Annapolis, Md.," in New Perspectives on Maryland Historical Archaeology, issue ed. Little and Dent, *Maryland Archeology* 26 (1&2) (1990), 25.

12. James Deetz, "Introduction: Archaeological Evidence of Sixteenth- and Seventeenth-Century Encounters," in *Historical Archaeology in Global Perspective,* ed. Lisa Falk (Washington, D.C.: Smithsonian Institution Press, 1991), 8.

13. Charles E. Orser Jr., "Can There Be an Archaeology of the Great Famine?" in *Fearful Realities: New Perspectives on the Famine,* ed. Chris Morash and Richard Hayes (Dublin: Irish Academic Press, 1996), 82–89; Orser, *A Historical Archaeology,* 94–

105. The story of Mahon's evictions is told in Cecil Woodham-Smith, *The Great Hunger: Ireland, 1845–1849* (London: Penguin, 1991), 228, 324–25, and in Stephen J. Campbell, *The Great Irish Famine: Words and Images from the Famine Museum, Strokestown Park, County Roscommon* (Strokestown: The Famine Museum, 1994), 40–44.

14. Roy F. Foster, *Modern Ireland, 1600–1972* (London: Penguin, 1989), 185–86.

15. Edward Malins and The Knight of Glin, *Lost Demesnes: Irish Landscape Gardening, 1660–1845* (London: Barrie and Jenkins, 1976), 1.

16. See, for example, Deetz, *In Small Things Forgotten*, 138–54. But, in contrast, see his comments throughout his most recent and unusual book, *Flowerdew Hundred: The Archaeology of a Virginia Plantation, 1619–1864* (Charlottesville: Univ. Press of Virginia, 1993).

17. Mark P. Leone, "A Historical Archaeology of Capitalism," *American Anthropologist* 97 (1995): 251–68.

18. A. R. Radcliffe-Brown, "On Social Relations," *Journal of the Royal Anthropological Society of Great Britain and Ireland* 70 (1940): 1–12; Alexander Lesser, "Social Fields and the Evolution of Society," *Southwestern Journal of Anthropology* 17 (1961): 40–48; Eric Wolf, "Culture: Panacea or Problem?" *American Antiquity* 49 (1984): 393–400.

19. J. A. Barnes, "Class and Committees in a Norwegian Island Parish," *Human Relations* 7 (1954): 39–58; D. Knoke and J. H. Kulkinski, *Network Analysis* (Newberry Park, Calif.: Sage, 1982).

20. Michael Carrithers, *Why Humans Have Cultures: Explaining Anthropology and Social Diversity* (Oxford: Oxford Univ. Press, 1992), 11, 34.

21. Maurice Godelier, *The Mental and the Material: Thought, Economy, and Society*, trans. Martin Thom (London: Verso, 1986), 1; Carrithers, *Why Humans Have Cultures*, 29.

22. The literature on Childe is vast and growing. For a good introduction, see V. Gordon Childe, *Man Makes Himself* (New York: New American Library, 1951).

23. My ideas about social relations and artifacts appear in Orser, *A Historical Archaeology*, 107–29.

24. James Deetz, "Landscapes as Cultural Statements," in *Earth Patterns: Essays in Landscape Archaeology*, ed. William M. Kelso and Rachel Most (Charlottesville: Univ. Press of Virginia, 1990), 1.

25. Godelier, *The Mental and the Material*; William H. Marquardt and Carole L. Crumley, "Theoretical Issues in the Analysis of Spatial Patterning," in *Regional Dynamics: Burgundian Landscapes in Historical Perspective*, ed. Carole L. Crumley and William H. Marquardt (San Diego: Academic Press, 1987).

26. Paul Rabinow, ed., *The Foucault Reader* (New York: Pantheon, 1984), 252; Allan Pred, *Making Histories and Constructing Human Geographies: The Local Transformation of Practice, Power Relations, and Consciousness* (Boulder: Westview, 1990), 9.

27. My use of the term ideology stems from the work of Randall H. McGuire, "Dialogues with the Dead: Ideology and the Cemetery," in *The Recovery of Meaning*, ed. Leone and Potter.

28. Edward W. Soja, *Postmodern Geographies: The Reassertion of Space in Critical Social Theory* (London: Verso, 1989), 79; A. Feenberg, "The Political Economy of Social Space," in *The Myths of Information: Technology and Postindustrial Culture,* ed. K. Woodward (Madison, Wisc.: Coda, 1980), 112.

29. Bill Hillier and Julienne Hanson, *The Social Logic of Space* (Cambridge: Cambridge Univ. Press, 1984), 2; Henri Lefebvre, "Space: Social Product and Use Value," in *Critical Sociology: European Perspectives,* ed. J. W. Freiberg (New York: Irvington, 1979).

30. Carrithers, *Why Humans Have Cultures,* 60.

31. Comments about rural housing in Ireland are abundant, but good portraits appear in Arthur Young, *A Tour of Ireland with General Observations on the Present State of that Kingdom made in the Years 1776, 1777, and 1778* (London: T. Cadell and J. Dodsley, 1780), 25–26, 184; Emmet Larkin, trans. and ed., *Alexis de Tocqueville's Journey in Ireland: July–August, 1835* (Washington, D.C.: Catholic Univ. of American Press, 1990), 39; Maria Edgeworth, *Castle Rackrent and Ennui,* ed. Marilyn Butler (London: Penguin, 1992), 186; Anthony Trollope, *Castle Richmond* (London: Penguin, 1993), 682–83.

32. T. Jones Hughes, "Society and Settlement in Nineteenth-Century Ireland," *Irish Geography* 5 (1965): 79.

Bibliography

Adorno, Theodor. *Negative Dialectics*. New York: Seabury, 1973.

Afro-American Ledger. Baltimore, Maryland.

Agnew, Jean-Christophe. "Coming Up for Air: Consumer Culture in Historical Perspective." *Intellectual History Newsletter* 12 (1990): 3–21.

Aiello, Elizabeth A., and John L. Seidel. *Three Hundred Years in Annapolis: Phase III Archaeological Investigations of the Anne Arundel County Courthouse Site (18AP63), Annapolis, Maryland*. Annapolis: Historic Annapolis Foundation, 1995.

Althusser, Louis. *For Marx*. New York: Pantheon, 1969.

Alverson, Hoyt. "Metaphor and Experience: Looking Over the Notion of Image Schema." In *Beyond Metaphor; The Theory of Tropes in Anthropology*, ed. James W. Fernandez, 94–117. Stanford: Stanford Univ. Press, 1991.

Ames, Kenneth. "Material Culture as Non-Verbal Communication." *Journal of American Culture* 3 (1980): 619–41.

Anderson, Benedict. *Imagined Communities: Reflections on the Origin and Spread of Nationalism*. London: Verso, 1991.

Anderson, Elizabeth B., and Christine Stevens. "Mount Clare: Introducing Baltimore to 18th-Century Splendor." *Maryland Archaeology* 26 (1–2) (1990): 86–94.

Anderson, Elizabeth B., and Michael P. Parker. *Annapolis: A Walk Through History.* Centreville, Md.: Tidewater Publishers, 1984.

Andrews, Lewis R., and J. Reaney Kelly. *The Hammond-Harwood House Cook Book.* Annapolis: The Hammond-Harwood House Association, 1963.

Anne Arundel County Court Land Records. Annapolis: Maryland State Archives.

Baker, Nancy. "Land Development in Annapolis, Maryland, 1670–1776." In "Annapolis and Anne Arundel County, Maryland: A Study of Urban Development in a Tobacco Economy, 1649–1776," ed. Lorena S. Walsh, N.E.H. Grant RS-20199-81-1955. Annapolis: Maryland State Archives, 1983.

———. "Annapolis, Maryland 1695–1730." *Maryland Historical Magazine* 81 (3) (1986): 191–209.

Barnes, J. A. "Class and Committees in a Norwegian Island Parish." *Human Relations* 7 (1954): 39–58.

Barth, Frederik. *Ethnic Groups and Boundaries.* Boston: Little Brown and Co., 1969.

Barthes, Roland. *Mythologies.* New York: Hill and Wang, 1972.

Bates, Wiley H. *Researches, Sayings and Life of Wiley H. Bates.* Annapolis: City Printing Co., 1928.

Beaudry, Mary C. "Archaeology and the Historical Household." *Man in the Northeast* 28 (1984): 27–38.

———. "The Archaeology of Historical Land Use in Massachusetts." *Historical Archaeology* 20 (2) (1986): 38–46.

———. "Words for Things: Linguistic Analysis of Probate Inventories." In *Documentary Archaeology in the New World,* ed. Mary C. Beaudry, 43–50. Cambridge: Cambridge Univ. Press, 1988.

———. "The Lowell Boott Mills Complex and its Housing: Material Expressions of Corporate Ideology." *Historical Archaeology* 23 (1) (1989): 19–32.

———, ed. *Documentary Archaeology in the New World.* Cambridge: Cambridge Univ. Press, 1988.

Beaudry, Mary C., and Stephen L. Mrozowski. "The Archaeology of Work and Homelife in Lowell, Massachusetts: An Interdisciplinary Study of the Boott Cotton Mills Corporation." *IA: The Journal of the Society for Industrial Archaeology* 14 (2) (1988): 1–22.

Beaudry, Mary C., Lauren J. Cook, and Stephen A. Mrozowski. "Artifacts and Active Voices: Material Culture as Social Discourse." In *The Archaeology of Inequality*, ed. Randall H. McGuire and Robert Paynter, 150–91. Cambridge: Basil Blackwell, 1991.

Beavan, Michele. *Analysis of Bottle Glass Recovered from Feature 12, Main Street (18AP44)*. Annapolis: Historic Annapolis Foundation, 1988.

The Bee. Washington, D.C.

Benjamin, Walter. *Illuminations*, ed. Hannah Arendt. New York: Harcourt, Brace and World, 1969.

———. *Reflections*. New York: Harcourt, Brace, Jovanovich, 1979.

Bierne, R. R. "The Chase House in Annapolis." *Maryland Historical Magazine* 44 (3) (1954): 177–95.

Bierne, R. R., and J. H. Scarff. *William Buckland, 1734–1774: Architect of Virginia and Maryland*. Annapolis: Board of Regents of Gunston Hall and Hammond-Harwood House Association, 1958.

Binford, Lewis R. "Dimensional Analysis of Behavior and Site Structure: Learning from an Eskimo Hunting Stand." *American Antiquity* 43 (3) (1978): 330–61.

———. *Nunamiut Ethnoarchaeology*. New York: Academic Press, 1978.

Board of Regents of Gunston Hall, ed. *Buckland: Master Builder of the Eighteenth Century*. Exhibition Pamphlet, 1977.

Borchert, James. *Alley Life in Washington: Family, Community, Religion and Folklife in the City, 1850–1970*. Urbana: Univ. of Illinois Press, 1982.

Botein, Stephen. "'Meer mechanics' and an Open Press: The Business and Political Strategies of Colonial American Printers." In *Perspectives in American History*, vol. 9, ed. D. Fleming and B. Bailyn, 127–225. Cambridge: Harvard Univ. Press, 1985.

Bourdieu, Pierre. *Outline of a Theory of Practice*. Cambridge: Cambridge Univ. Press, 1977.

Bowen, Joanne. "Faunal Remains and Urban Household Subsistence in New England." In *The Art and Mystery of Historical Archaeology, Essays in Honor of James Deetz*, ed. Anne E. Yentsch and Mary C. Beaudry, 267–81. Boca Raton, Fla.: CRC Press, 1992.

———. "A Comparative Analysis of the New England and Chesapeake Herding Systems." In *Historical Archaeology of the Chesapeake*, ed. Paul

A. Shackel and Barbara J. Little, 155–67. Washington, D.C.: Smithsonian Institution Press, 1994.

Brackett, Jeffrey R. "Progress of the Colored People of Maryland Since the War." In *Johns Hopkins University Studies in Historical and Political Science*, vol. 8, ed. Herbert B. Adams, 347–442. Baltimore: Johns Hopkins Univ. Press, 1890.

Bragdon, Kathleen, Edward Chappell, William Graham. "A Scant Urbanity: Jamestown in the 17th Century." In *The Archaeology of 17th-Century Virginia*, ed. Theodore R. Reinhart and Dennis Pogue, 223–49. Richmond: Archeological Society of Virginia, 1993.

Braudel, Fernand. *The Structures of Everyday Life: Civilization and Capitalism 15th–18th Century*, vol. 1. New York: Harper and Row, 1979.

Brenton, James J., ed. *Voices of the Press: A Collection of Sketches, Essays, and Poems*. New York: Practical Printers, 1850.

"Bric-A-Brac." *Spelman's Fancy Goods Graphic* 3 (3) (1883).

Bridenbaugh, Carl. *The Colonial Craftsman*. New York: New York Univ. Press, 1950.

Bronner, Stephen Eric, and Douglas MacKay Kellner, eds. *Critical Theory and Society: A Reader*. London: Routledge, 1989.

Brow, James. "Notes of Community, Hegemony, and the Uses of the Past." *Anthropology Quarterly* 63 (1990): 1–6.

Brown, Linda Keller, and Kay Mussell. "Introduction." In *Ethnic and Regional Foodways in the United States: The Performance of Group Identity*, ed. Linda Keller Brown and Kay Mussell, 3–15. Knoxville: Univ. of Tennessee Press, 1984.

Brown, Marley R. "Some Issues of Scale in Historical Archaeology." Paper presented at the Society for Historical Archaeology, 1987.

Brown, Marley R., and Patricia M. Samford. "Recent Evidence of Eighteenth-Century Gardening in Williamsburg, Virginia." In *Earth Patterns: Essays in Landscape Archaeology*, ed. William M. Kelso and Rachel Most, 103–22. Charlottesville: Univ. Press of Virginia, 1990.

Brown, Philip. *The Other Annapolis*. Annapolis: Annapolis Publishing Co., 1994.

Brown, Richard Harvey. *Society as Text*. Chicago: Univ. of Chicago, 1987.

Browne, Gary. *Baltimore in the Nation, 1789–1861*. Chapel Hill: Univ. of North Carolina Press, 1980.

Brugger, Robert J. *Maryland: A Middle Temperament, 1634–1980.* Baltimore: Johns Hopkins Univ. Press, 1988.

Bryant, V. M., Jr., and R. G. Holloway. "The Role of Palynology in Archaeology." In *Advances in Archaeological Method and Theory,* vol. 6, ed. Michael B. Schiffer, 191–224. New York: Academic Press, 1983.

Buchanan, William T., and Edward F. Heite. "The Hallowes Site: A Seventeenth-Century Yeoman's Cottage in Virginia." *Historical Archaeology* 5 (1971): 38–48.

Bullion, Brenda. "Early American Farming and Gardening Literature: 'Adapted to the Climates and Seasons of the United States.'" *Journal of Garden History* 12 (1) (1992): 29–51.

Burdick, William. *An Oration on the Nature and Effects of the Art of Printing.* Boston: Published by the author, 1802.

Bureau of the Census. *Population Schedules, Anne Arundel County, Maryland.* Annapolis: Maryland State Archives.

Campbell, Colin. *The Romantic Ethic and the Spirit of Modern Consumption.* Oxford: Basil Blackwell, 1987.

Campbell, Stephen J. *The Great Irish Famine: Words and Images from the Famine Museum, Strokestown Park, County Roscommon.* The Famine Museum, Strokestown, County Roscommon, Ireland, 1994.

Carrithers, Michael. *Why Humans Have Cultures: Explaining Anthropology and Social Diversity.* Oxford: Oxford Univ. Press, 1992.

Carroll Papers. Maryland Historical Society, Baltimore.

Carson, Cary, Norman F. Barka, William M. Kelso, Gary Wheeler Stone, and Dell Upton. "Impermanent Architecture in the Southern American Colonies." *Winterthur Portfolio* 16 (2–3) (1981): 135–96.

Cheek, Charles D., and Amy Friedlander. "Pottery and Pig's Feet: Space, Ethnicity, and Neighborhood in Washington, D.C., 1880–1940." *Historical Archaeology* 24 (2) (1990): 34–60.

Childe, V. Gordon. *Man Makes Himself.* New York: New American Library, 1951.

Clay, Grady. *Close-Up: How to Read the American City.* New York: Praeger, 1972.

Clemen, Rudolph. *The American Livestock and Meat Industry.* New York: Ronald Press, 1923.

Coffin, Robert S. *The Printer and Several Other Poems.* Boston, 1817.

Cook, Lauren J. "Tobacco-Related Material Culture and the Construction of

Working-Class Culture." In *Interdisciplinary Investigations of the Boott Mills, Lowell, Massachusetts, Volume III: The Boarding House System as a Way of Life,* ed. Mary C. Beaudry and Stephen A. Mrozowski, 209–30. Boston: National Park Service, 1989.

Cooper, David E. *Metaphor.* Aristotelian Society Series, vol. 5. Cambridge: Basil Blackwell, 1989.

Corner, James. "Representation and Landscape: Drawing and Making in the Landscape Medium." *Word and Image* 8 (3) (1992): 243–75.

Cornigan, J. J. "Binney and Ronaldson's First Type." *Printing and Graphic Arts* 1 (1953): 27–35.

Cowan, Ruth Schwartz. *More Work for Mother.* New York: Basic Books, 1983.

Cox, Warren J. "Four Men, the Four Books, and the Five-Part House." In *Building by the Book,* ed. M. di Valmarana. Charlottesville: Univ. Press of Virginia, 1986.

Crader, Diana C. "The Zooarchaeology of the Storehouse and the Dry Well at Monticello." *American Antiquity* 49 (3) (1984): 542–58.

Crary, Jonathan. *Techniques of the Observer: On Vision and Modernity in the Nineteenth Century.* Cambridge: MIT Press, 1990.

Creese, Walter L. *The Crowning of the American Landscape: Eight Great Spaces and Their Buildings.* Princeton: Princeton Univ. Press, 1985.

Cronan, William. *Changes in the Land.* New York: Hill and Wang, 1983.

Crosby, Constance A. *Excavations at the Victualling Warehouse, Jan. 14, 1982: Preliminary Report.* Annapolis: Historic Annapolis Foundation, 1982.

Cummings, Linda Scott. "Diet and Prehistoric Landscape During the 19th and Early 20th Centuries at Harpers Ferry, West Virginia: A View from the Old Master Armorer's Complex." *Historical Archaeology* 28 (4) (1994): 94–105.

de St. Mery, Moreau. *American Journey, 1793–1798,* ed. Kenneth Roberts and Anna Roberts. Garden City, N.Y.: Doubleday, 1947.

Deagan, Kathleen A. *Spanish St. Augustine: The Archaeology of a Colonial Creole Community.* New York: Academic Press, 1983.

Deering, Davis. *Annapolis Houses, 1700–1775.* New York: Architectural Book Publishing, 1941.

Deetz, James. *In Small Things Forgotten: The Archaeology of Early American Life.* Garden City, N.Y.: Anchor Books, 1977.

———. "Households: A Structural Key to Archaeological Explanation." *American Behavioral Scientist* 25 (6) (1982): 717–14.

————. "Scientific Humanism and Humanistic Science: A Plea for Paradigmatic Pluralism." *Geoscience and Man* 23 (1983): 27–34.

————. "Scale in Historical Archaeology." Paper presented at the Society for Historical Archaeology annual meeting, 1986.

————. "Material Culture and Worldview in Colonial Anglo-America." In *The Recovery of Meaning: Historical Archaeology in the Eastern United States,* ed. Mark P. Leone and Parker B. Potter Jr., 219–33. Washington, D.C.: Smithsonian Institution Press, 1988.

————. "Landscapes as Cultural Statements." In *Earth Patterns: Essays in Landscape Archaeology,* ed. William M. Kelso and Rachel Most, 1–4. Charlottesville: Univ. Press of Virginia, 1990.

————. "Introduction: Archaeological Evidence of Sixteenth- and Seventeenth-Century Encounters." In *Historical Archaeology in Global Perspective,* ed. Lisa Falk, 1–9. Washington, D.C.: Smithsonian Institution Press, 1991.

————. *Flowerdew Hundred: An Archaeology of a Virginia Plantation.* Charlottesville: Univ. Press of Virginia, 1993.

Desmond, Effingham C. "Matthias Hammond House, Part 1." In *Early Homes of New York and the Mid-Atlantic States.* New York: The Early American Society, 1977.

di Valmarana, M., ed. *Building by the Book.* Charlottesville: Univ. Press of Virginia. 1986.

Dixon, Wilfrid J., and Frank J. Massey. *Introduction to Statistical Analysis.* New York: McGraw-Hill, 1969.

Douglas, Mary. "Standard Social Uses of Food: Introduction." In *Food in the Social Order: Studies of Food and Festivities in Three American Communities,* ed. Mary Douglas, 1–39. New York: Russell Sage Foundation, 1984.

Douglas, Mary, and Baron Isherwood. *The World of Goods.* New York: Basic Books Inc., 1979.

Doyle-Read, Esther, Mark P. Leone, Barbara J. Little, Jean B. Russo, George C. Logan, and Brett Burk. *Archaeological Investigations Around State Circle in Annapolis, Maryland.* Annapolis: Historic Annapolis Foundation, 1990.

Du Bois, W. E. B. *The Negro American Family.* 1908. Reprint, New York: Negro Universities Press, 1969.

Duval, Ruby R. "Lot Number 71, Annapolis: A Brief Historical Sketch." *Maryland Historical Magazine* 54 (1) (1959): 104–11.

Eagleton, Terry. *The Ideology of the Aesthetic.* Cambridge, Mass.: Basil Blackwell, 1990.

Edgeworth, Maria. *Castle Rackrent and Ennui,* ed. Marilyn Butler. London: Penguin, 1992.

"Editorial." *The House Beautiful* 3 (2) (1898): 61–62.

Edwards, Andrew C., William E. Pittman, Gregory J. Brown, Mary Ellen Hodges, Marley Brown II, and Eric Voigt. *Hampton University Archaeological Project: A Report on the Findings.* Williamsburg, Va.: Colonial Williamsburg Foundation, 1989.

Edwards, Paul. *The Southern Urban Negro as a Consumer.* 1932. Reprint, New York: Negro Universities Press, 1969.

Eff, Elaine. *The Screen Painters.* VHS, Los Angeles: Direct Cinema, 1989.

Eisenstein, Elizabeth. *The Printing Press as an Agent of Change: Communications and Cultural Transformation in Early Modern Europe.* Cambridge: Cambridge Univ. Press, 1979.

———. *The Printing Revolution in Early Modern Europe.* Cambridge: Cambridge Univ. Press, 1983.

Epperson, Terrence W. "Race and the Disciplines of the Plantation." *Historical Archaeology* 24 (4) (1990): 29–36.

Ernstein, Julie H. *Historic Land Use and Cultural Development of 1601–1611 Thames Street: Block 1827 (Lots 61, 62, and 63) of the Fells Point National Historic District, Baltimore, Maryland.* Baltimore Center for Urban Archaeology Research Series Report No. 44. Baltimore: Baltimore Center for Urban Archaeology, 1992.

———. *Continuity and Change on an Urban Houselot: Archaeological Excavation at the 22 West Street Backlot (18AP51) of the Annapolis National Historic District, Anne Arundel County.* Annapolis: Historic Annapolis Foundation, 1994.

———. *Archaeological Reconnaissance at 18BC99, the 1609–1611 Thames Street Backlot, Block 1827 (Lots 63B and 63C) of the Fells Point National Historic District, Baltimore, Maryland.* Baltimore Center for Urban Archaeology Research Series Report No. 45. Baltimore: Baltimore Center for Urban Archaeology, 1995.

Evans, Robin. "Translations from Drawing to Building." *AA Files* 12 (1986): 13–18.

Ewen, Stuart. *Captains of Consciousness: Advertising and the Social Roots of Consumer Culture.* New York: McGraw-Hill, 1976.

Fagan, Brian. *Archaeology: A Brief Introduction*, 4th ed. New York: Harper Collins, 1991.

———. *Time Detectives: How Archeologists Use Technology to Recapture the Past*. New York: Simon and Schuster, 1995.

Faler, P. *Mechanics and Manufacture in the Early Industrial Revolution: Lynn, Massachusetts, 1780–1860*. Albany: State Univ. of New York Press, 1981.

Faulkner, Alaric. "Maintenance and Fabrication at Fort Pentagoet 1635–1654: Products of an Acadian Armorer's Workshop." *Historical Archaeology 20* (1) (1988): 63–94.

Febvre, L., and H. Martin. *The Coming of the Book: the Impact of Printing 1450–1800*. Trans. D. Gerard, ed. G. Nowell-Smith and D. Wootton. London: Atlantic Highlands Humanities Press, 1976.

Fee, Elizabeth, Linda Shopes, and Linda Zeidman, ed. *The Baltimore Book: New Views of Local History*. Philadelphia: Temple Univ. Press, 1991.

Feenberg, A. "The Political Economy of Social Space." In *The Myths of Information: Technology and Postindustrial Culture*, ed. Kathleen Woodward, 111–24. Madison, Wisc.: Coda, 1980.

Fields, Barbara J. *Slavery and Freedom on the Middle Ground: Maryland during the Nineteenth Century*. New Haven, Conn.: Yale Univ. Press, 1985.

Filkins, Sarah. "Notes on the Sands House, 130 Prince George Street." Annapolis: Historic Annapolis Foundation, 1988.

Fisher, William F., and Gerald K. Kelso. "The Use of Opal Phytolith Analysis in a Comprehensive Environmental Study: An Example from Lowell, Massachusetts." *Northeast Historical Archaeology* 16 (1987): 30–48.

Foster, Hal, ed. *Vision and Visuality*. Dia Art Foundation, Discussions in Contemporary Culture, no. 2. Seattle: Bay Press, 1988.

Foster, Roy F. *Modern Ireland, 1600–1972*. London, Penguin, 1989.

Foucault, Michel. *Discipline and Punish: The Birth of the Prison*. New York: Vintage Books, 1979.

Franklin, Wayne. *Discoverers, Explorers, Settlers; The Diligent Writers of Early America*. Chicago: Univ. of Chicago Press, 1979.

Fraser, Gertrude, and Reginald Butler. "Anatomy of a Disinterment: The Unmaking of Afro-American History." In *Presenting the Past: Essays on History and the Public*, ed. Susan Porter Benson, Stephen Brier, and Roy Rosenzweig, Philadelphia: Temple Univ. Press, 1986.

Freeman, Roland L. *The Arabbers of Baltimore.* Centreville, Md.: Tidewater Publishers, 1989.

Frissell H. B., and Isabel Bevier. *Dietary Studies of Negroes in Eastern Virginia in 1897 and 1898.* Washington, D.C.: U.S. Dept. of Agriculture, Office of Experiment Stations, Bulletin No. 71, 1899.

Fritz, John. "Chaco Canyon and Vijayanagara: Proposing Spatial Meaning in Two Societies." In *Mirror and Metaphor: Material and Social Constructions of Reality,* ed. Daniel W. Ingersoll and Gordon Bronitsky, 313–49. Lanham, Md.: Univ. Press of America, 1987.

Galke, Laura J. *Paca Garden Archaeological Testing, 18AP01, 186 Prince George Street, Annapolis, Maryland.* Annapolis: Historic Annapolis Foundation, 1990.

———. *A Quantitative Analysis of the Green Family Print Shop Site in Annapolis, Maryland.* Ann Arbor, Mich.: Univ. Microfilms International, 1995.

Gardner, Kelsey B. *Consumer Habits and Preferences in the Purchase and Consumption of Meat.* Washington, D.C.: U.S. Dept. of Agriculture, Dept. Bulletin 1443, Washington, D.C.: U.S. Government Printing Office, 1926.

Garrison, J. Ritchie. *Landscape and Material Life in Franklin County, Massachusetts, 1770–1860.* Knoxville: Univ. of Tennessee Press, 1991.

Gatewood, Willard B. *Aristocrats of Color: The Black Elite, 1880–1920.* Bloomington: Indiana Univ. Press, 1990.

Gibb, James G., and Julia A. King. "Gender, Activity Areas, and Homelots in the 17th-Century Chesapeake Region." *Historical Archaeology* 25 (4) (1991): 109–31.

Giddens, Anthony. *The Constitution of Society; Outline of the Theory of Structuration.* Berkeley: Univ. of California Press, 1984.

Glassie, Henry. *Folk Housing in Middle Virginia.* Knoxville: Univ. of Tennessee Press, 1975.

———. *Passing Time in Ballymore: Culture and History of an Ulster Community.* Philadelphia: Univ. of Pennsylvania Press, 1982.

———. "Vernacular Architecture and Society." In *Mirror and Metaphor: Material and Social Constructions of Reality,* ed. Daniel W. Ingersoll and Gordon Bronitsky, 229–45. Lanham, Md.: Univ. Press of America, 1987.

Godelier, Maurice. *The Mental and the Material: Thought, Economy, and Society.* Trans. Martin Thom. London: Verso, 1986.

Goldstein, Eric. *Surviving Together: African Americans and Jews in Annapolis, 1885–1968.* Annapolis: Historic Annapolis Foundation, 1991.

Goldstein, Leonard. *The Social and Cultural Roots of Linear Perspective.* Minneapolis: MEP Publications, 1988.

Goodwin, R. Christopher. *Phase II/III Archeological Investigations of the Gott's Court Parking Facility, Annapolis, Maryland.* Annapolis: Maryland Historic Trust, 1993.

Goody, Jack. "The Evolution of the Family." In *Household and Family in Past Time,* ed. P. Laslett and R. Wall, 103–24. London: Cambridge Univ. Press, 1972.

———. *Cooking, Cuisine, and Class: A Study in Comparative Sociology.* Cambridge: Cambridge Univ. Press, 1982.

Gramsci, Antonio. *Selections from the Prison Notebooks.* New York: International, 1971.

Grayson, Donald K. "Minimum Numbers and Sample Size in Vertebrate Faunal Analysis." *American Antiquity* 43 (1) (1978): 53–65.

Habermas, Jürgen. *Legitimation Crisis.* London: Heinemann, 1976.

———. *The Philosophical Discourse of Modernity.* Cambridge, Mass.: MIT Press, 1987.

Hall, Martin. "Small Things and the Mobile, Conflictual Fusion of Power, Fear, and Desire." In *The Art and Mystery of Historical Archaeology: Essays in Honor of James Deetz,* ed. Anne E. Yentsch and Mary C. Beaudry, 373–99. Boca Raton, Fla.: CRC Press, 1992.

Halsey, R. T. H. "Matthias Hammond House, Part 2." 1929. Reprint. *Early Homes of New York and the Mid-Atlantic States.* New York: The Early American Society, 1977.

Handlin, Oscar. *Boston's Immigrants: A Study in Acculturation.* Cambridge: Harvard Univ. Press, 1958.

Handsman, Russell G. "Historical Archaeology and Capitalism, Subscriptions and Separations: The Production of Individualism." *North American Archaeologist* 4 (1) (1983): 63–79.

———. "The Still-Hidden Histories of Color and Class: Public Archaeology and the Depot Village of West Kingston, Rhode Island." Paper presented at the Conference on New England Archaeology, 1995.

Harrington, Faith, ed. "The Archaeological Use of Landscape Treatments in Social, Economic, and Ideological Analyses." *Historical Archaeology* 23 (1) (1989).

Harris, Marvin. *The Sacred Cow and the Abominable Pig; Riddles of Food and Culture.* New York: Simon and Schuster, Inc., 1985.

Hayden, B., and A. Cannon, "Where the Garbage Goes: Refuse Disposal in the Mayan Highlands." *Journal of Anthropological Archaeology* 2 (1983): 117–63.

Heldman, Donald P. "Michigan's First Jewish Settlers: A View from the Solomon-Levy Trading House at Fort Michilimackinac, 1765–1781." *Journal of New World Archaeology* 6 (4) (1986): 21–33.

Herman, Bernard L. *Architecture and Rural Life in Central Delaware, 1700–1900.* Knoxville: Univ. of Tennessee Press, 1987.

———. "Fences." In *After Ratification: Material Life in Delaware, 1789–1820,* ed. J. Ritchie Garrison, Bernard L. Herman, and Barbara McLean Ward, 7–20. Newark: Museum Studies Program, Univ. of Delaware, 1988.

Hill, Sarah H. "An Examination of Manufacture-Deposition Lag for Glass Bottles form Late Historic Sites." In *Archaeology of Urban American: The Search for Pattern and Process,* ed. Roy S. Dickens Jr., 291–328. New York: Academic Press, 1982.

Hillier, Bill, and Julienne Hanson. *The Social Logic of Space.* Cambridge: Cambridge Univ. Press, 1984.

Hodder, Ian. *The Present Past.* New York: Pica Press, 1982.

———. *Reading the Past: Current Approaches to Interpretation in Archaeology.* Cambridge: Cambridge Univ. Press, 1986.

———, ed. *The Meaning of Things: Material Culture and Symbolic Expression.* London: Unwin Hyman, 1989.

Hoffman, Ronald. "'Marylando-Hibernus': Charles Carroll the Settler, 1660–1720." *William and Mary Quarterly* 45 (2) (1988): 207–36.

———. *"Anywhere so Long as there be Freedom": Charles Carroll of Carrollton, His Family and His Maryland.* Baltimore: Baltimore Museum of Art, 1993.

Holt, Cheryl A., and Louise A. Ackerson. "Mount Clare Orchard Planting Pattern." Baltimore: Baltimore Center for Urban Archaeology, 1986.

Hopley, Catherine Cooper. *Life in the South from the Commencement of the War.* 1863. Reprint, New York: Augustus M. Kelley, 1971.

Horkheimer, Max, and Theodor Adorno. *Dialectic of Enlightenment.* New York: Herder, 1972.

Horowitz, Daniel. *The Morality of Spending: Attitudes Toward the Consumer Society in America, 1875–1940.* Baltimore: Johns Hopkins Univ. Press, 1985.

Howson, Jean E. "Social Relations and Material Culture: A Critique of the Archaeology of Plantation Slavery." *Historical Archaeology* 24 (4) (1990): 70–78.

Hudgins, Carter L. "Robert 'King' Carter and the Landscape of Tidewater Virginia in the Eighteenth Century." In *Earth Patterns: Essays in Landscape Archaeology,* ed. William M. Kelso and Rachel Most, 59–70. Charlottesville: Univ. Press of Virginia, 1990.

Huey, Paul R. "The Dutch at Fort Orange." In *Historical Archaeology in Global Perspective,* ed. Lisa Falk, 21–67. Washington, D.C.: Smithsonian Institution Press, 1991.

Hunt, Frederick V. *Origins in Acoustics: The Science of Sound from Antiquity to the Age of Newton.* New Haven, Conn.: Yale Univ. Press, 1978.

Hunter, Albert. "Persistence of Local Sentiments in Mass Society." In *Perspectives on the American Community,* ed. Roland L. Warren, New York: Rand McNally, 1983.

Ingraham, J. H. *The Sunny South; or, The Southerner at Home.* Philadelphia: G. G. Evans, 1860.

Innes, Stephen, ed. *Work and Labor in Early America.* Chapel Hill: Univ. of North Carolina Press, 1988.

"Inside Southern Cabins." *Harper's Weekly* 24 (1246) (1880): 733–34.

"Internal Improvements." *Washington Quarterly Magazine* 1 (1823): 2–7.

Inventories. Maryland State Archives, Annapolis.

Isaac, Rhys. *The Transformation of Virginia, 1740–1790.* Chapel Hill: Univ. of North Carolina Press, 1982.

———. "Books and the Social Authority of Learning: The Case of Mid-eighteenth century Virginia." In *Printing and Society in Early America,* ed. W. L. Joyce, D. D. Hall, R. D. Brown, and J. B. Hench, 228–49. Worcester, Mass.: American Antiquarian Society, 1983.

Ives, Sallie. "Black Community Development in Annapolis, Maryland, 1870–1885." In *Geographical Perspectives on Maryland's Past,* ed. Robert D. Mitchell and Edward K. Muller, 129–49. College Park: Dept. of Geography, Univ. of Maryland, 1975.

Jackson, H. Edwin. "The Trouble with Transformations: Effects of Sample Size and Sample Composition on Meat Weight Estimates Based on Skeletal Mass Allometry." *Journal of Archaeological Science* 16 (1989): 601–10.

Jackson, John B. "A New Kind of Space." *Landscape* 18 (1969): 33–35.

James, Jamie. *The Music of the Spheres: Music, Science, and the Natural Order of the Universe.* New York: Grove Press, 1993.

Jensen, Ann. "Remembering Hell Point." *Annapolitan* (1989): 38–43, 62–66.

———. "Do You Know What I Have Been?" *Annapolitan* (1991): 36–42, 78, 92–94.

Johnson, Mark. *The Body in the Mind: The Bodily Basis of Meaning, Imagination, and Reason.* Chicago: Univ. of Chicago Press, 1987.

Johnson, Matthew. *An Archaeology of Capitalism.* Oxford: Blackwell, 1996.

Jones Hughes, T. "Society and Settlement in Nineteenth-Century Ireland." *Irish Geography* 5 (1965): 79–96.

Jopling, Hannah. Unpublished Oral History Interviews. Archaeology Laboratory, Dept. of Anthropology, Univ. of Maryland, College Park, 1991.

Kalčik, Susan. "Ethnic Foodways in America: Symbol and the Performance of Identity." In *Ethnic and Regional Foodways in the United States: The Performance of Group Identity,* ed. Linda Keller Brown and Kay Mussell, 37–65. Knoxville: Univ. of Tennessee Press, 1984.

Kasson, John F. *Civilizing the Machine; Technology and Republican Values in America, 1776–1900.* New York: Penguin Books, 1976.

Keeler, Robert. *The Homelot on the Seventeenth-Century Chesapeake Frontier.* Ann Arbor, Mich.: Univ. Microfilms International, 1977.

Kelso, Gerald. "Pollen-Record Formation Processes, Interdisciplinary Archaeology, and Land Use by Mill Workers and Managers: The Boott Mills Corporation, Lowell, Massachusetts, 1836–1942." *Historical Archaeology* 27 (1) (1993): 70–94.

Kelso, Gerald, and Mary Beaudry. "Pollen Analysis and Urban land Use: The Environs of Scottow's Dock in 17th, 18th, and Early 19th Century Boston." *Historical Archaeology* 24 (1) (1990): 61–81.

Kelso, William M. *Kingsmill Plantations, 1619–1800: Archaeology of Country Life in Colonial Virginia.* New York: Academic Press, 1984.

———. "Landscape Archaeology: A Key to Virginia's Cultivated Past." In *British and American Gardens in the Eighteenth Century: Eighteen Illustrated Essays on Garden History,* ed. R. P. Maccubbin and P. M. Partin, 159–69. Williamsburg, Va.: Colonial Williamsburg Foundation, 1984.

———. "Landscape Archaeology at Thomas Jefferson's Monticello." In *Earth Patterns: Essays in Landscape Archaeology,* ed. William M. Kelso and Rachel Most, 7–22. Charlottesville: Univ. Press of Virginia, 1990.

————. "Landscape Archaeology and Garden History Research: Success and Promise at Bacon's Castle, Monticello, and Poplar Forest, Virginia." In *Garden History: Issues, Approaches, Methods,* ed. John Dixon Hunt, 31–57. Washington, D.C.: Dumbarton Oaks, 1992.

Kelso, William M., and Rachel Most, ed. *Earth Patterns: Essays in Landscape Archaeology.* Charlottesville: Univ. Press of Virginia, 1990.

Kent, Susan. *Analyzing Activity Areas.* Albuquerque: Univ. of New Mexico Press, 1984.

————. "A Cross-Cultural Study of Segmentation, Architecture, and the Use of Space." In *Domestic Architecture and the Use of Space: An Interdisciplinary Cross-Cultural Study,* ed. Susan Kent, 127–52. New York: Cambridge Univ. Press, 1990.

Kenyon, Kathleen M. *Beginning in Archaeology,* rev. ed. New York: Praeger, 1970.

Kimball, Fiske. "A Landscape Garden on the James in 1723." *Landscape Architecture* 14 (2) (1924): 123.

King, Julia A. "A Comparative Midden Analysis of a Household and Inn in St. Mary's City, Maryland." *Historical Archaeology* 22 (2) (1988): 17–39.

————. *An Intrasite Spatial Analysis of the van Sweringen Site, St. Mary's City, Maryland.* Ann Arbor, Mich.: Univ. Microfilms International, 1990.

————. "Rural Landscape in the Mid-Nineteenth-Century Chesapeake." In *Historical Archaeology of the Chesapeake,* ed. Paul A. Shackel and Barbara J. Little, 283–99. Washington, D.C.: Smithsonian Institution Press, 1994.

King, Julia A., and Henry M. Miller. "The View from the Midden: An Analysis of Midden Distribution and Composition at the van Sweringen Site, St. Mary's City, Maryland." *Historical Archaeology* 21 (2) (1987): 37–59.

Kintigh, Keith. "Intrasite Spatial Analysis: A Commentary on Major Methods." In *Mathematics and Information Science in Archaeology: A Flexible Framework,* ed. A. Voorrips. *Studies in Modern Archaeology* 3: 165–200. Bonn: Holos, 1990.

Kintigh, Keith, and A. Ammerman. "Heuristic Approaches to Spatial Analysis in Archaeology." *American Antiquity* 47 (1) (1982): 31–63.

Klein, Richard G., and Kathryn Cruz-Uribe. *The Analysis of Animal Bones from Archaeological Sites.* Chicago: Univ. of Chicago Press, 1984.

Knoke, David, and James H. Kuklinski. *Network Analysis.* Newberry Park, Calif.: Sage, 1982.

Kryder-Reid, Elizabeth. *Landscape as Myth: The Contextual Archaeology of an Annapolis Landscape.* Ann Arbor, Mich.: Univ. Microfilms International, 1991.

————. "'As Is the Gardener, So Is the Garden': The Archaeology of Landscape as Myth." In *Historical Archaeology of the Chesapeake,* ed. Paul A. Shackel and Barbara J. Little, 131–48. Washington, D.C.: Smithsonian Institution Press, 1994.

————. "The Archaeology of Vision in Eighteenth-Century Chesapeake Gardens." *Journal of Garden History* 14 (1) (1994): 42–54.

Kubovy, Michael. *The Psychology of Perspective and Renaissance Art.* Cambridge: Cambridge Univ. Press, 1986.

Kuhn, Thomas S. *The Structure of Scientific Revolutions,* 2d ed. Chicago: Univ. of Chicago Press, 1970.

Lakoff, George. *Women, Fire, and Dangerous Things: What Categories Reveal About the Mind.* Chicago: Univ. of Chicago Press, 1987.

Lakoff, George, and Mark Johnson. *Metaphors We Live By.* Chicago: Univ. of Chicago Press, 1980.

Lamme, Ary J., III. *America's Historic Landscapes: Community Power and the Preservation of Four National Historic Sites.* Knoxville: Univ. of Tennessee Press, 1989.

Land, Aubrey, ed. *Letters from America by William Eddis.* Cambridge, Mass.: Harvard Univ. Press, 1969.

Langley, Batty. *New Principles of Gardening: Or the Laying out and Planning of Parterres, Groves, Wildernesses, Labyrinths, Avenues, Park, etc.* 1728. Reprint, England: Gregg International, 1971.

Larkin, Emmet, trans. and ed. *Alexis de Tocqueville's Journey in Ireland: July–August, 1835.* Washington, D.C.: Catholic Univ. of America Press, 1990.

Leeds, Anthony. "Locality of Power in Relation to Supralocal Power Institutions." In *Urban Anthropology: Cross-Cultural Studies of Urbanization,* ed. Aidan Southall, 15–41. New York: Oxford Univ. Press, 1973.

Lefebvre, Henri. "Space: Social Product and Use Value." In *Critical Sociology: European Perspectives,* ed. J. W. Freiberg, 285–95. New York: Irvington, 1979.

Leone, Mark P. "Archaeology as the Science of Technology: Mormon Town Plans and Fences." In *Research and Theory in Current Archaeology,* ed. Charles Redman, 125–50. New York: John Wiley and Sons, Inc., 1973.

————. "Archaeology's Relationship to the Present and the Past." In *Modern Material Culture: The Archaeology of Us,* ed. Richard A. Gould and Michael B. Schiffer, 5–13. New York: Academic Press, 1981.

————. "The Relationship Between Artifacts and the Public in Outdoor History Museums." In *The Research Potential of Anthropological Museum Collections,* ed. A. M. Cantwell, J. B. Griffin, and Nan Rothschild, 301–13. New York: Annals of the New York Academy of Sciences, 1981.

————. "Method as Message: Interpreting the Past with the Public." *Museum News* 62 (1) (1983): 34–41.

————. "The Role of Archaeology in Verifying American Identity: Giving a Tour Based on Archaeological Method." *Archaeological Review From Cambridge* 2 (1) (1983): 44–50.

————. "Interpreting Ideology in Historical Archaeology: Using the Rules of Perspective in the William Paca Garden in Annapolis, Maryland." In *Ideology, Power, and Prehistory,* ed. Daniel Miller and Christopher Tilley, 25–35. Cambridge: Cambridge Univ. Press, 1984.

————. "Symbolic, Structural, and Critical Archaeology." In *American Archaeology, Past and Present: A Celebration of the Society for American Archaeology, 1935–1985,* ed. David J. Meltzer, Don D. Fowler, and Jeremy A. Sabloff, 415–38. Washington, D.C.: Smithsonian Institution Press, 1986.

————. "Rule by Ostentation: The Relationship between Space and Sight in Eighteenth-Century Landscape Architecture in the Chesapeake Region of Maryland." In *Method and Theory for Activity Area Research—An Ethnoarchaeological Approach,* ed. Susan Kent, 604–33. New York: Columbia Univ. Press, 1987.

————. "The Georgian Order as the Order of Merchant Capitalism in Annapolis, Maryland." In *The Recovery of Meaning,* ed. Mark P. Leone and Parker B. Potter Jr., 235–61. Washington, D.C.: Smithsonian Institution Press, 1988.

————. "The Relationship Between Archaeological Data and the Documentary Record: 18th-Century Gardens in Annapolis, Maryland." *Historical Archaeology* 23 (1) (1989): 29–35.

————. "A Historical Archaeology of Capitalism." *American Anthropologist* 97 (2) (1995): 251–68.

Leone, Mark P., and Barbara J. Little. "Seeds of Sedition." *Archaeology* 43 (3) (1990): 36–40.

————. "Artifacts as Expressions of Society and Culture: Subversive Genealogy and the Value of History." In *History from Things: Essays on Material Culture,* ed. Steven Lubar and W. David Kingery, 160–81. Washington, D.C.: Smithsonian Institution Press, 1993.

Leone, Mark P., and George C. Logan. "Project Director Evaluation to the Maryland Humanities Council for Grant No. 032-L: Historical Archaeology and African American Heritage in Annapolis: A Program of Public Interpretation for the Community." Annapolis: Historic Annapolis Foundation, 1991.

Leone, Mark P., and Parker B. Potter Jr., eds. *The Recovery of Meaning: Historical Archaeology in the Eastern United States.* Washington, D.C.: Smithsonian Institution Press, 1988.

————. "Introduction: Issues in Historical Archaeology." In *The Recovery of Meaning: Historical Archaeology in the Eastern United States,* ed. Mark P. Leone and Parker B. Potter Jr., 1–22. Washington, D.C.: Smithsonian Institution Press, 1988.

————. "The Archaeology of the Georgian Worldview and the 18th-Century Beginnings of Modernity." In *The Recovery of Meaning: Historical Archaeology in the Eastern United States,* ed. Mark P. Leone and Parker B. Potter Jr., 211–17. Washington, D.C.: Smithsonian Institution Press, 1988.

Leone, Mark P., and Paul A. Shackel. "Archaeology of Town Planning in Annapolis, Maryland." Final Report to the National Geographic Society. Annapolis: Historic Annapolis Foundation, 1986.

————. "Forks, Clocks and Power." In *Mirror and Metaphor: Material and Social Constructions of Reality,* ed. Daniel Ingersoll and Gordon Bronitsky, 45–61. Lanham, Md.: Univ. Press of America, 1987.

————. "The Georgian Order in Annapolis, Maryland." *Maryland Archaeologist* 26, (1–2) (1990): 69–84.

————. "Plane and Solid Geometry in Colonial Gardens in Annapolis, Maryland." In *Earth Patterns: Essays in Landscape Archaeology,* ed. William M. Kelso and Rachel Most, 153–67. Charlottesville: Univ. Press of Virginia, 1990.

Leone, Mark P., Parker B. Potter Jr., and Paul A. Shackel. "Toward a Critical Archaeology." *Current Anthropology* 28 (3) (1987): 283–302.

Leone, Mark P., Julie H. Ernstein, Elizabeth Kryder-Reid, and Paul A. Shackel. "Power Gardens of Annapolis." *Archaeology* 42 (2) (1989): 34–37, 74–75.

Leone, Mark P., Paul R. Mullins, Marian C. Creveling, Laurence Hurst, Barbara Jackson-Nash, Lynn D. Jones, Hannah Jopling Kaiser, George C. Logan, and Mark S. Warner. "Can an African American Historical Archaeology Be an Alternative Voice?" In *Interpreting Archaeology: Finding Meaning in the Past,* ed. Ian Hodder, Micheal Shanks, Alexandra Alexandri, Victor Buchli, John Carman, Jonathan Last, and Gavin Lucas, 111–24. London: Routledge, 1995.

Leone, Mark P., Barbara J. Little, Mark S. Warner, Parker B. Potter Jr., Paul A. Shackel, George C. Logan, Paul R. Mullins, and Julie A. Ernstein. "The Constituencies for an Archaeology of African Americans in Annapolis, Maryland." In *"I Too Am America": Studies in African American Archaeology,* ed. Theresa Singleton. Charlottesville: Univ. Press of Virginia, in press.

Lesser, Alexander. "Social Fields and the Evolution of Society." *Southwestern Journal of Anthropology* 17 (1961): 40–48.

Lev-Tov, Justin S. E. "Intersite Faunal Analysis and Socioeconomic Status in Annapolis, Maryland." Paper presented at the Society for Historical and Underwater Archaeology Meetings, Richmond, Virginia, 1991.

Lewis, Kenneth E., and Helen W. Haskell. *The Middleton Place Privy: A Study of Discard Behavior and the Archaeological Record.* Columbia: South Carolina Institute for Archaeology and Anthropology, 1981.

Linenthal, Edward T. *Sacred Ground: Americans and Their Battlefields.* Chicago: Univ. of Illinois Press, 1993.

Lippson, Alice Jane, and Robert L. Lippson. *Life in the Chesapeake Bay.* Baltimore: Johns Hopkins Univ. Press, 1984.

Little, Barbara J. *AP29, Jonas Green Print Shop: Printers' Type from the 1983 Excavation.* Annapolis: Historic Annapolis Foundation, 1984.

———. *Ideology and Media: Historical Archaeology of Printing in Eighteenth-Century Annapolis, Maryland.* Ann Arbor, Mich.: Univ. Microfilms International, 1987.

———. "Craft and Culture Change in the 18th-Century Chesapeake." In *The Recovery of Meaning: Historical Archaeology in the Eastern United States,* ed. Mark P. Leone and Parker B. Potter Jr., 263–92. Washington, D.C.: Smithsonian Institution Press, 1988.

———. "Echoes and Forecasts: Group Tensions in Historical Archaeology." *International Journal of Group Tensions* 18 (1988): 243–57.

———, ed. *Text-Aided Archaeology.* Boca Raton, Fla.: CRC Press, 1992.

————. "Explicit and Implicit Meanings in Material Culture and Print Culture." *Historical Archaeology* 26 (3) (1992): 85–94.

————. "'She Was . . . an Example to Her Sex': Possibilities for a Feminist Historical Archaeology." In *Historical Archaeology of the Chesapeake*, ed. Paul A. Shackel and Barbara J. Little, 189–204. Washington, D.C.: Smithsonian Institution Press, 1994.

Little, Barbara J., and Paul A. Shackel. "Scales of Historical Anthropology: An Archaeology of Colonial Anglo-America." *Antiquity* 63 (240) (1989): 495–509.

Little, J. Glenn, II. "Archaeological Research on Paca Garden, 8 November 1967, 24 May 1968." Annapolis: Historic Annapolis Foundation.

Logan, George C., and Parker B. Potter Jr. *African American Archaeology in Annapolis, Maryland.* Brochure. Annapolis: Historic Annapolis Foundation, 1990.

Logan, George C., Thomas W. Bodor, Lynn D. Jones, and Marian C. Creveling. *1991 Archaeological Excavations at the Charles Carroll House in Annapolis, Maryland 18AP45.* Annapolis: Historic Annapolis Foundation, 1992.

Lott, Eric. *Love and Theft: Blackface Minstrelsy and the American Working Class.* New York: Oxford Univ. Press, 1995.

Louis Berger and Associates, Inc. *The Compton Site Circa 1651–1684: Calvert County, Maryland, 18CV279.* East Orange, N.J.: Louis Berger and Associates, 1989.

Lowenthal, David. *The Past Is a Foreign Country.* Cambridge: Cambridge Univ. Press, 1985.

Lowenthal, Leo. *Literature, Popular Culture and Society.* Englewood Cliffs, N.J.: Prentice-Hall, 1961.

Luccketti, Nicholas. "Archaeological Excavations at Bacon's Castle, Surry County, Virginia." In *Earth Patterns: Essays in Landscape Archaeology*, ed. William M. Kelso and Rachel Most, 23–42. Charlottesville: Univ. Press of Virginia, 1990.

Lukacs, George. *History and Class Consciousness.* Cambridge, Mass.: MIT Press, 1971.

Lyman, R. Lee. "Bone Density and Differential Survivorship of Fossil Classes." *Journal of Anthropological Archaeology* 3 (4) (1984): 259–99.

————. "On Zooarchaeological Measures of Socioeconomic Position and Cost-Efficient Meat Purchases." *Historical Archaeology* 21 (1) (1987): 58–66.

———. "Quantitative Units and Terminology in Zooarchaeology." *American Antiquity* 59 (1) (1994): 36–71.

Main, Jackson Turner. *The Social Structure of Revolutionary America.* Princeton: Princeton Univ. Press, 1965.

Malins, Edward, and The Knight of Glin. *Lost Demesnes: Irish Landscape Gardening, 1660–1845.* London: Barrie and Jenkins, 1976.

Mann, Robert, Douglas Owsley, and Paul A. Shackel. "A Reconstruction of 19th-Century Surgical Techniques: Bones in Dr. Thompson's Privy." *Historical Archaeology* 25 (1) (1991): 106–12.

Markland, J. *Typographia, An Ode on Printing.* Williamsburg, Va., 1736.

Marquardt, William H., and Carole L. Crumley. "Theoretical Issues in the Analysis of Spatial Patterning." In *Regional Dynamics: Burgundian Landscapes in Historical Perspectives,* ed. Carole L. Crumley and William H. Marquardt, 1–18. San Diego: Academic Press, 1987.

Martin, Ann Smart. "The Role of Pewter as Missing Artifact: Consumer Attitudes Toward Tablewares in Late 18th Century Virginia." *Historical Archaeology* 23 (2) (1989): 1–27.

———. *Buying into the World of Goods: Eighteenth-Century Consumerism and the Retail Trade from London to the Virginia Frontier.* Ann Arbor, Mich.: Univ. Microfilms International, 1993.

Martin, Peter. *Pleasure Gardens of Virginia.* Princeton: Princeton Univ. Press, 1991.

Marx, Karl. *Capital.* 1867. Reprint, New York: International Publishers, 1967.

Marx, Leo. *The Machine in the Garden: Technology and the Pastoral Ideal in America.* Oxford: Oxford Univ. Press, 1964.

Matthews, Christopher N. "A Reconstruction of Hell Point, Annapolis, Maryland: Material Culture and Memory." Unpublished manuscript.

Maryland Gazette. Annapolis, Md.

McCracken, Grant. *Culture and Consumption: New Approaches to the Symbolic Character of Consumer Goods and Activities.* Bloomington: Indiana Univ. Press, 1988.

McGuire, Randall H. "Dialogues with the Dead: Ideology and the Cemetery." In *The Recovery of Meaning: Historical Archaeology in the Eastern United States,* ed. Mark P. Leone and Parker B. Potter Jr., 375–406. Washington, D.C.: Smithsonian Institution Press, 1988.

———. *A Marxist Archaeology.* New York: Academic Press, 1992.

McGuire, Randall H., and Robert Paynter, eds. *The Archaeology of Inequality.* Cambridge: Basil Blackwell, 1991.

McKendrick, Neil, John Brewer, and J. H. Plumb. *The Birth of a Consumer Society: The Commercialization of Eighteenth-Century England.* Bloomington: Indiana Univ. Press, 1982.

McWilliams, Jane. "The Sands House—130 Prince George Street: Historical Summary." Annapolis: Historic Annapolis Foundation, 1970.

————. *163 Duke of Gloucester Street Research Report.* Unpublished document prepared for Port of Annapolis, Inc., Feb. 1991. Port of Annapolis, Inc., Annapolis, Md.

McWilliams, Jane, and Edward Papenfuse, eds. *Final Report: Appendix F, Lot Histories and Maps, 1971.* Annapolis: Maryland State Archives.

Meanley, Brooke. *Birds and Marshes of the Chesapeake Bay Country.* Centreville, Md.: Tidewater Publishers, 1975.

Miller, Daniel. *Material Culture and Mass Consumption.* Cambridge: Basil Blackwell, 1987.

————. "The Limits of Dominance." In *Domination and Resistance,* ed. Daniel Miller, Michael Rowlands, and Christopher Tilley, 63–79. London: Unwin Hyman, 1989.

Miller, Daniel, and Christopher Tilley. "Ideology, Power, and Prehistory: An Introduction." In *Ideology, Power, and Prehistory,* ed. Daniel Miller and Christopher Tilley, 1–15. Cambridge: Cambridge Univ. Press, 1984.

Miller, George L. "Classification and Economic Scaling of Nineteenth-Century Ceramics." *Historical Archaeology* 14 (1) (1980): 1–40.

————. "A Revised Set of CC Index Values for Classification and Economic Scaling of English Ceramics from 1787 to 1880." *Historical Archaeology* 25 (1) (1991): 1–25.

————. "Thoughts Towards A Users' Guide to Ceramic Assemblages." *Council for Northeast Historical Archaeology Newsletter* 18 (Apr. 1991): 2–5.

Miller, Henry M. "Pettus and Utopia: A Comparison of the Faunal Remains from Two Late Seventeenth Century Virginia Households." *Conference on Historic Site Archaeology Papers* 13 (1979): 158–79.

————. *Discovering Maryland's First City: A Summary Report on the 1981–1984 Archaeological Excavations in St. Mary's City, Maryland.* St. Mary's City, Md.: St. Mary's City Commission, 1986.

————. "An Archaeological Perspective on the Evolution of Diet in the Colonial Chesapeake 1620–1745." In *Colonial Chesapeake Society,* ed. Lois Green Carr, Phillip D. Morgan, and Jean B. Russo, 176–99. Chapel Hill: Univ. of North Carolina Press, 1988.

————. "Baroque Cities in the Wilderness: Archaeology and Urban Development in the Colonial Chesapeake." *Historical Archaeology* 22 (2) (1988): 57–73.

————. "The Country's House Site: An Archaeological Study of a Seventeenth-Century Domestic Landscape." In *Historical Archaeology of the Chesapeake,* ed. Paul A. Shackel and Barbara J. Little, 65–83. Washington, D.C.: Smithsonian Institution Press, 1994.

Mintz, Sidney W. *Sweetness and Power: The Place of Sugar in Modern History.* New York: Penguin Books, 1985.

Mrozowski, Stephen. "Exploring New England's Evolving Urban Landscape." In *Living in Cities: Current Research in Urban Archaeology,* ed. Edward Staski, 1–9. Historical Archaeology Special Publication No. 5, 1987.

Mudar, Karen. "The Effect of Socio-Cultural Variables on Food Preferences in Early 19th Century Detroit." *Conference on Historic Site Archaeology Papers* 12 (1978): 323–91.

Mullings, Leith. *Cities of the United States: Studies in Urban Anthropology.* New York: Columbia Univ. Press, 1987.

Mullins, Paul R. *Analysis of Feature 12 Ceramic Assemblage, Main Street Site (18AP44).* Annapolis: Historic Annapolis Foundation, 1988.

————. "'A Bold and Gorgeous Front': The Contradictions of African America and Consumer Culture, 1880–1930." Paper presented at the School of American Research Advanced Seminar "The Historical Archaeology of Capitalism," Santa Fe, New Mexico, Oct. 2–6, 1993.

————. "The Contradictions of Consumption: An Archaeology of African America and Consumer Culture, 1850–1930." Ph.D. diss., Univ. of Massachusetts, Amherst, 1996.

Mullins, Paul R., and Mark S. Warner. *Final Archaeological Investigations at the Maynard-Burgess House (18AP64), An 1850–1980 African-American Household in Annapolis, Maryland,* 2 vols. Annapolis: Historic Annapolis Foundation, 1993.

Munsell, Charles, ed. *A Collection of Songs of the American Press and Other Poems Relating to the Art of Printing.* Albany, N.Y., 1868.

Murphy, Peter, and Robert G. Scaife. "The Environmental Archaeology of Gardens." In *Garden Archaeology,* ed. A. E. Brown, 83–99. Council of British Archaeology Research Report, 78. London: Council of British Archaeology, 1991.

Nash, Gary B. *Red, White, and Black: The Peoples of Early America.* Englewood Cliffs, N.J.: Prentice-Hall, 1974.

————. *The Urban Crucible: The Northern Seaports and the Origins of the American Revolution.* Cambridge: Harvard Univ. Press, 1979.

The Negro Appeal. Annapolis, Md.

Neiman, Fraser D. "Domestic Architecture at the Clifts Plantation: The Social Context of Early Virginia Building," *Northern Neck of Virginia Historical Magazine* 28 (1978): 3096–3128.

————. *Field Archaeology of the Clifts Plantation Site, Westmoreland County, Virginia.* Stratford, Va.: The Robert E. Lee Memorial Association, 1980.

————. "Temporal Patterning in House Plans from the 17th-Century Chesapeake." In *The Archaeology of 17th-Century Virginia,* ed. Theodore R. Reinhart and Dennis Pogue, 251–83. Richmond: Archeological Society of Virginia, 1993.

Nichols, Frederick Doveton, and Ralph E. Griswold. *Thomas Jefferson, Landscape Architect.* Charlottesville: Univ. Press of Virginia, 1978.

Nickel, Cheryl. "The Semiotics of Andean Terracing." *Art Journal* 42 (3) (1982): 200–203.

Nietzsche, Friedrich. *The Portable Nietzsche,* ed. Walter Kaufmann. New York: Penguin Books, 1981.

Nissenbaum, Stephen. "New England as Region and Nation," in *All Over the Map: Rethinking American Regions,* ed. Edward L. Ayers and Peter S. Onuf, 38–61. Baltimore: Johns Hopkins Univ. Press, 1996.

Noël Hume, Ivor. "Matthews Manor." *Antiques Magazine* 40 (1966): 832–36.

Norris, Walter B. *Annapolis: Its Colonial and Naval Story.* New York: Thomas Y. Crowell, 1925.

O'Brien, Jay, and William Roseberry. *Golden Ages, Dark Ages: Imagining the Past in Anthropology and History* Berkeley: Univ. of California Press, 1991.

Ogburn, W., and M. F. Nimkoff. *Technology and the Changing Family.* Boston: Houghton Mifflin Company, 1955.

O'Malley, Therese. "Charles Willson Peale's Belfield: Its Place in American Garden History." In *New Perspectives on Charles Willson Peale,* ed. Lillian B. Miller and David C. Ward, Pittsburgh: Univ. of Pittsburgh Press, 1991.

————. "Appropriation and Adaptation: Early Gardening Literature in America." *The Huntington Library Quarterly* 55 (3) (1992): 401–31.

Onuf, Peter S., ed. *Maryland and the Empire, 1773: the Antilon-First Citizen Letters.* Baltimore: Johns Hopkins Univ. Press, 1974.

Orr, K. G., and R. G. Orr. *The Archaeological Situation at the William Paca Garden, Annapolis, Maryland: The Spring House and the Presumed Pavilion House Site.* Annapolis: Historic Annapolis Foundation, 1975.

Orser, Charles E., Jr. "The Archaeological Analysis of Plantation Society: Replacing Status and Caste with Economics and Power." *American Antiquity* 53 (4) (1988): 735–51.

———. *The Material Basis of the Postbellum Tenant Plantation: Historical Archaeology in the South Carolina Piedmont.* Athens: Univ. of Georgia Press, 1988.

———. "Toward a Theory of Power for Historical Archaeology: Plantations and Space." In *The Recovery of Meaning*, ed. Mark P. Leone and Parker B. Potter Jr., 314–44. Washington, D.C.: Smithsonian Institution Press, 1988.

———. "Beneath the Material Surface of Things: Commodities, Artifacts, and Slave Plantations." *Historical Archaeology* 26 (3) (1992): 95–104.

———. "Can There Be an Archaeology of the Great Famine?" In *Fearful Realities: New Perspectives on the Famine*, ed. Chris Morash and Richard Hayes, 77–89. Dublin: Irish Academic Press, 1996.

———. *A Historical Archaeology of the Modern World.* New York: Plenum, 1996.

Orser, Charles E., Jr., and Brian M. Fagan. *Historical Archaeology.* New York: Harper Collins, 1995.

Oswald, Dana Beth. "The Organization of Space in Residential Buildings: A Cross-Cultural Perspective." In *Method and Theory for Activity Area Research: An Ethnoarchaeological Approach*, ed. Susan Kent, 295–340. New York: Columbia Univ. Press, 1987.

Otto, John Solomon. *Status Differences and the Archaeological Record: A Comparison of Planter, Overseer, and Slave Sites from Cannon's Point Plantation (1794–1861), St. Simon's Island, Georgia.* Ann Arbor, Mich.: Univ. Microfilms International, 1975.

———. "Race and Class on Antebellum Plantations." In *Archaeological Perspectives on Ethnicity in America: Afro-American and Asian American Cultural History*, ed. Robert L. Schuyler, 3–13. Farmingdale, N.Y.: Baywood, 1980.

———. *Cannon's Point Plantation, 1794–1860: Living Conditions and Status Patterns in the Old South.* Orlando: Academic Press, 1984.

Outlaw, Alain Charles. *Governor's Land: Archaeology of Early Seventeenth-Century Virginia Settlements.* Charlottesville: Univ. Press of Virginia, 1990.

Paca-Steele, Barbara, with St. Clair Wright. "The Mathematics of an Eighteenth-Century Wilderness Garden." *Journal of Garden History* 6 (4) (1987): 299–320.

Palladio, Andreas. *The Four Books of Architecture.* New York: Dover Publications, Inc., 1965.

Panofsky, Erwin. *Meaning in the Visual Arts.* Garden City, N.Y.: Doubleday Anchor Books, 1955.

Papenfuse, Edward. *In Pursuit of Profit: The Annapolis Merchants in the Era of the American Revolution, 1763–1805.* Baltimore: Johns Hopkins Univ. Press, 1975.

Parker, Clara H. "The Use and Abuse of Ornamentation in the House." *The Boston Cooking School Magazine* 2 (1) (1897): 7–11.

Patterson, Thomas C. "Exploitation and Class Formation in the Inca State." *Culture* 5 (1985): 35–42.

Paynter, Robert. "Steps to an Archaeology of Capitalism: Material Change and Class Analysis." In *The Recovery of Meaning,* ed. Mark P. Leone and Parker B. Potter Jr., 407–33. Washington, D.C.: Smithsonian Institution Press, 1988.

———. "The Archaeology of Equality and Inequality." *Annual Review of Anthropology* 18 (1989): 369–99.

Peale, Charles Willson. *Diary.* American Philosophical Society, Philadelphia, Pa.

Pearson, Marlys J. *Archaeological Excavations at 18AP14: The Victualling Warehouse Site, 77 Main St., Annapolis, Maryland 1982–84.* Annapolis: Historic Annapolis Foundation, 1991.

Peterson, Roger Tory. *A Field Guide to the Birds of Eastern and Central North America.* Boston: Houghton Mifflin Company, 1980.

Pevsner, Nikolaus. *Northamptonshire.* Middlesex: Penguin Books, 1961.

Pierson, William H. *American Buildings and Their Architects, Volume 1.* Garden City, N.Y.: Doubleday and Company, Inc., 1970.

———. "The Hammond-Harwood House: A Colonial Masterpiece." *Antiques Magazine* 111 (1) (1977): 186–93.

Pinsky, Valerie, and Alison Wylie, eds. *Critical Traditions in Contemporary Archaeology.* Cambridge: Cambridge Univ. Press, 1989.

Pogue, Dennis J. "Anthrosols and the Analysis of Archaeological Sites in a Plowed Context: The King's Reach Site." *Northeast Historical Archaeology* 17 (1988): 1–15.

———. "Spatial Analysis of the King's Reach Plantation Homelot, ca. 1690–1715." *Historical Archaeology* 22 (2) (1988): 40–56.

Polk's Annapolis Directory. New York: R. L. Polk and Co., Inc., 1939.

Potter, Parker B., Jr. *Archaeology in Public in Annapolis: An Experiment in the Application of Critical Theory to Historical Archaeology.* Ann Arbor, Mich.: Univ. Microfilms International, 1989.

———. "Historical Archaeology and Identity in Modern America." Paper presented at School of American Research Advanced Seminar "The Historical Archaeology of Capitalism," Santa Fe, New Mexico, 1993.

———. *Public Archaeology in Annapolis: A Critical Approach to History in Maryland's "Ancient City."* Washington, D.C.: Smithsonian Institution Press, 1994.

Potter, Parker B., Jr., and Mark P. Leone. "Liberation Not Replication: 'Archaeology in Annapolis' Analyzed." *Journal of the Washington Academy of Sciences* 76 (2) (1986): 97–105.

Powell, B. B. *Archaeological Investigations of the Paca House Gardens, Annapolis, Maryland.* Annapolis: Historic Annapolis Foundation, 1966.

Praetzellis, Adrian, and Mary Praetzellis. "'Utility and Beauty Should Be One': The Landscape of Jack London's Ranch of Good Intentions." *Historical Archaeology* 23 (1) (1989): 33–45.

Pred, Allan. *Making Histories and Constructing Human Geographies: The Local Transformation of Practice, Power Relations, and Consciousness.* Boulder: Westview, 1990.

Pretzer, William. "Tramp Printers: Craft Culture, Trade Unions, and Technology." *Printing History* 6 (1984): 3–16.

Preucel, Robert W., ed. *Processual and Postprocessual Archaeologies: Multiple Ways of Knowing the Past.* Carbondale: Southern Illinois Univ., 1991.

———. "The Philosophy of Archaeology." In *Processual and Postprocessual Archaeologies: Multiple Ways of Knowing the Past,* ed. Robert W. Preucel, 17–29. Carbondale: Southern Illinois Univ., 1991.

Proceedings and Acts of the General Assembly of Maryland. Maryland State Archives, Annapolis.

Provinical Court Deeds. Maryland State Archives, Annapolis.

Prown, Jules David. "Mind in Matter: An Introduction to Material Culture Theory and Method." *Winterthur Portfolio* 17 (1982): 1–19.

Purser, Margaret. "Consumption as Communication in Nineteenth-Century Paradise Valley, Nevada." *Historical Archaeology* 26 (3) (1992): 105–16.

Quinn, Naomi. "The Cultural Basis of Metaphor." In *Beyond Metaphor: The Theory of Tropes in Anthropology*, ed. James W. Fernandez, 56–93. Stanford: Stanford Univ. Press, 1991.

Rabinow, Paul, ed. *The Foucault Reader.* New York: Pantheon, 1984.

Radcliffe-Brown, A. R. "On Social Structure." *Journal of the Royal Anthropological Society of Great Britain and Ireland* 70 (1940): 1–12.

Rahtz, Philip. *Invitation to Archaeology*, 2d ed. Oxford: Blackwell, 1991.

Rajchman, John. "Foucault's Art of Seeing." *October* 14 (1988): 89–119.

Ramirez, Constance Werner. *Urban History for Preservation Planning: The Annapolis Experience.* Ann Arbor, Mich.: Univ. Microfilms International, 1975.

Rapoport, Amos. *Human Aspects of Urban Form.* Oxford: Pergamon Press, 1977.

Reinhart, Theodore R., ed. *The Archaeology of Shirley Plantation,* Charlottesville: Univ. Press of Virginia, 1984.

Reitz, Elizabeth J. *Appendix I: Vertebrate Fauna from McCrady's Tavern and Longroom, Charleston, South Carolina.* Zooarchaeology Laboratory, Univ. of Georgia, 1982.

———. *Preliminary Analysis of Vertebrate Remains from Features 5 and 121, at the Calvert House, Annapolis, Maryland.* Interim Report No. 6. Annapolis: Historic Annapolis Foundation, 1987.

———. *Taphonomy and Socio-Economic Status from Faunal Assemblages.* Zooarchaeology Laboratory, Univ. of Georgia, 1987.

———. "Vertebrate Fauna and Socioeconomic Status." In *Consumer Choice in Historical Archaeology.* ed. Suzanne Spencer-Wood, 101–19. New York: Plenum, 1987.

———. "Zooarchaeological Analysis of a Free African Community: Gracia Real de Santa Teresa de Mose." *Historical Archaeology* 28 (1) (1994): 23–40.

Reitz, Elizabeth J., and C. Margaret Scarry. *Reconstructing Historic Subsistence with an Example from Sixteenth-Century Spanish Florida.* Special Publications Series, No. 3, Society for Historical Archaeology, 1985.

Reitz, Elizabeth J., and Martha A. Zierden. "Cattle Bones and Status from Charleston, South Carolina." In *Beamers, Bobwhites, and Blue-Points, Tributes to the Career of Paul W. Parmalee,* ed. James R. Purdue, Walter E. Klippel, and Bonnie W. Styles, 153–62. Springfield: Illinois State Museum, 1991.

Renfrew, Colin, and Paul Bahn. *Archaeology: Theories, Methods, and Practice.* London: Thames and Hudson, 1991.

Reps, John W. *The Making of Urban America: A History of City Planning in the United States.* Princeton: Princeton Univ. Press, 1965.

———. *Tidewater Towns: City Planning in Colonial Virginia and Maryland.* Williamsburg, Va.: The Colonial Williamsburg Foundation, 1972.

Riis, Jacob. *How the Other Half Lives.* New York: Dover Publications, 1971.

Riley, Elihu. *The Ancient City: A History of Annapolis, in Maryland 1649–1887.* Annapolis: Record Printing Office, 1887.

Robbins, C. Richard, and G. Carleton Ray. *A Field Guide to Atlantic Coast Fishes, North America.* Boston: Houghton Mifflin, 1986.

Roediger, David R. *The Wages of Whiteness: Race and the Making of the American Working Class.* New York: Verso, 1991.

Rorabaugh, W. J. *The Craft Apprentice: From Franklin to the Machine Age in America.* New York: Oxford Univ. Press, 1986.

Rorty, Richard. *Philosophy and the Mirror of Human Nature.* Princeton: Princeton Univ. Press, 1979.

———. *Contingency, Irony, and Solidarity.* Cambridge: Cambridge Univ. Press, 1989.

Roth, Rodris. *Tea Drinking in 18th-Century America: Its Etiquette and Equipage.* Washington, D.C.: Smithsonian Institution, 1961.

Rothschild, Nan A. *New York City Neighborhoods: The 18th Century.* New York: Academic Press, 1991.

Rothschild, Nan A., and Diana diZerega Rockman. "Method in Urban Archaeology." In *Archaeology of Urban America: The Search for Pattern and Process,* ed. Roy S. Dickens Jr., 3–18. New York: Academic Press, 1982.

Rovner, Irwin. "Macro- and Micro-ecological Reconstruction Using Plant Opal Phytolith Data from Archaeological Sediments." *Geoarchaeology* 3 (1988): 155–63.

———. "Fine-Tuning Floral History with plant Opal Phytolith Analysis."

In *Earth Patterns: Essays in Landscape Archaeology*, ed. William M. Kelso and Rachel Most, 23–42. Charlottesville: Univ. Press of Virginia, 1990.

———. "Floral History by the Back Door: A Test of Phytolith Analysis in Residential Yards at Harpers Ferry." *Historical Archaeology* 28 (4) (1994): 37–48.

Russo, Jean. "Economy of Anne Arundel County." In "Annapolis and Anne Arundel County, Maryland: A Study of Urban Development in a Tobacco Economy, 1649–1776," ed. Lorena S. Walsh, 1983, N.E.H. Grant RS-20199-81-1955, Maryland State Archives, Annapolis.

———. "The Public Thoroughfares of Annapolis." *Maryland Historical Magazine* 86 (1) (1991): 66–76.

Ryder, Robin. "Fluid Ethnicity: Archaeological Examinations of Diversity in Virginia from 1800–1900." Paper presented at Council of Virginia Archaeologists Symposium VII, 1993.

Salmon, William. *Palladio Londonensis*. 1738.

Sanborn Insurance Company. *Maps of Annapolis, Maryland*. Annapolis: Maryland State Archives.

Sanford, Douglas. "The Gardens at Germanna, Virginia." In *Earth Patterns: Essays in Landscape Archaeology*, ed. William M. Kelso and Rachel Most, 43–58. Charlottesville: Univ. Press of Virginia, 1990.

Sanjek, Roger. "Urban Anthropology in the 1980s: A World View." *Annual Review of Anthropology* 19 (1990): 151–85.

Sarudy, Barbara. "Eighteenth-Century Gardens of the Chesapeake." *Journal of Garden History* 9 (3) (1989): 104–59.

Savulis, Ellen-Rose. "Alternative Visions and Landscapes: Archaeology of the Shaker Social Order." In *Text-Aided Archaeology*, ed. Barbara J. Little, 195–203. Boca Raton, Fla.: CRC Press, 1992.

Schiffer, Michael B. *Behavioral Archeology*. New York: Academic Press, 1976.

———. *Formation Processes of the Archaeological Record*. Albuquerque: Univ. of New Mexico Press, 1987.

———. "Review of *Experiencing the Past:* On the Character of Archaeology." *American Antiquity* 59 (1) (1994): 158–59.

Schlereth, Thomas J. *Cultural History and Material Culture*. Ann Arbor, Mich.: UMI Research Press, 1990.

Schoenwetter, James. "A Method for the Application of Pollen Analysis in Landscape Archaeology." In *Earth Patterns: Essays in Landscape Archaeology*, ed. William M. Kelso and Rachel Most, 277–96. Charlottesville: Univ. Press of Virginia, 1990.

Schulz, Peter D., and Sherri M. Gust. "Faunal Remains and Social Status in 19th Century Sacramento." *Historical Archaeology* 17 (1) (1983): 44–53.

Scott, James. *Weapons of the Weak: Everyday Forms of Peasant Resistance.* New Haven, Conn.: Yale Univ. Press, 1985.

—————. *Domination and the Arts of Resistance: The Hidden Transcripts.* New Haven, Conn.: Yale Univ. Press, 1990.

Shackel, Paul A. *Archaeological Testing at the 193 Main Street Site, 18AP44, Annapolis, Maryland.* Annapolis: Historic Annapolis Foundation, 1986.

—————. *Personal Discipline and Material Culture: An Archaeology of Annapolis, Maryland, 1695–1870.* Knoxville: Univ. of Tennessee Press, 1993.

—————. "Town Plans and Everyday Material Culture: An Archaeology of Social Relations in Colonial Maryland's Capital Cities." In *Historical Archaeology of the Chesapeake,* ed. Paul A. Shackel and Barbara J. Little, 85–96. Washington, D.C.: Smithsonian Institution Press, 1994.

—————. "Archaeology of an Industrial Town: Harpers Ferry and the New Order of Manufacturing." *CRM* 17 (1) (1994): 16–19.

—————. "Interdisciplinary Approaches to the Meanings and Uses of Material Goods in Lower Town, Harpers Ferry." *Historical Archaeology* 28 (4) (1994): 3–15.

Shackel, Paul A., Joseph W. Hopkins, and Eileen Williams. *Excavations at The State House Inn, 18AP42, State Circle, Annapolis, Maryland. A Final Report.* Annapolis: Historic Annapolis Foundation, 1988.

Shanks, Michael. *Experiencing the Past: On the Character of Archaeology.* London: Routledge, 1992.

Shanks, Michael, and Christopher Tilley. *Re-Constructing Archaeology.* Cambridge: Cambridge Univ. Press, 1987.

Sharer, Robert J., and Wendy Ashmore. *Archaeology: Discovering Our Past,* 2d ed. Mountain View, Calif.: Mayfield, 1993.

Shorter, Edward. *Work and Community in the West.* New York: Harper and Row, 1973.

Silver, I. A. "The Ageing of Domestic Animals." In *Science in Archaeology,* ed. D. Brothwell and E. Higgs, 250–68. New York: Basic Books, Inc., 1969.

Singleton, Theresa A., ed. *The Archaeology of Slavery and Plantation Life.* Orlando: Academic Press, 1985.

Smith, Delos. "Annapolis, Maryland." 1929. Reprint, *Early Homes of New York and the Mid-Atlantic States.* New York: The Early American Society, 1977.

Smith, Gavin. "The Production of Culture in Local Rebellion." In *Golden Ages, Dark Ages: Imagining the Past in Anthropology and History,* ed. Jay O'Brien and William Roseberry, 180–208. Berkeley: Univ. of California Press, 1991.

Smith, William Loughton. *Journal of William Loughton Smith, 1790–1791.* ed. Albert Matthews. Cambridge: The Univ. Press, 1917.

Soja, Edward W. *Postmodern Geographies; The Reassertion of Space in Critical Social Theory.* New York: Verso, 1989.

South, Stanley. *The Paca House, Annapolis, Maryland.* Historic Annapolis Foundation, Annapolis, 1967.

———. *Method and Theory in Historical Archeology.* New York: Academic Press, 1977.

———. "Santa Elena: Threshold of Conquest." In *The Recovery of Meaning: Historical Archaeology in the Eastern United States,* ed. Mark P. Leone and Parker B. Potter Jr., 27–71. Washington, D.C.: Smithsonian Institution Press, 1988.

Spencer-Wood, Suzanne M., ed. *Consumer Choice in Historical Archaeology.* New York: Plenum Press, 1987.

St. George, Robert Blair. "'Set Thine House in Order': The Domestication of the Yeomanry in Seventeenth-Century New England." In *New England Begins,* 3 vols., ed. Jonathan L. Fairbanks and Robert F. Trent. Boston: Museum of Fine Arts, 1982.

———. "Maintenance Relationships and the Erotics of Property in Historical Thought." Paper presented at the American Historical Association meetings, Philadelphia, 1983.

———, ed. *Material Life in America, 1600–1860.* Boston: Northeastern Univ. Press, 1988.

Stevens, William Oliver. *Annapolis: Anne Arundel's Town.* New York: Dodd, Mead and Co., 1937.

Stewart, Susan. *On Longing: Narratives of the Miniature, the Gigantic, the Souvenir, the Collection.* Baltimore: Johns Hopkins Univ. Press, 1984.

Stilgoe, John R. *Common Landscape in America, 1580–1845.* New Haven, Conn.: Yale Univ. Press, 1982.

Stiverson, Gregory A., and Phebe R. Jacobsen. *William Paca, A Biography.* Baltimore: Maryland Historical Society, 1976.

Stone, Gary Wheeler, Henry Miller, Alexander H. Morrison II, and Emily Kutler. *The Clocker's Fancy Site, 18 ST1-65, on St. Andrew's Freehold: An Archaeological Survey.* St. Mary's City, Md.: St. Mary's City Commission, 1987.

Susman, Warren I. *Culture as History: The Transformation of American Society in the Twentieth Century.* New York: Pantheon, 1984.

Suttles, Gerald D. *The Social Order of the Slum.* Chicago: Chicago Univ. Press, 1968.

Switzer, Ronald R. *The Bertrand Bottles: A Study of 19th-Century Glass and Ceramic Containers.* Washington, D.C.: National Park Service, U.S. Dept. of the Interior, 1974.

Tabb, William K., and Larry Sawers. *Marxism and the Metropolis: New Perspectives in Urban Political Economy.* Oxford: Oxford Univ. Press, 1978.

Tatum, George B. "Great Houses from the Golden Age of Annapolis." *The Magazine Antiques* 111 (1) (1977): 174–85.

Thom, Alexander. *Megalithic Remains in Britain and Brittany.* London: Oxford Univ. Press 1978.

Thomas, David Hurst. "The Awful Truth About Statistics in Archaeology." *American Antiquity* 43 (2) (1978): 231–44.

———. *Refiguring Anthropology: First Principles of Probability and Statistics.* Prospect Heights, Ill.: Waveland Press, Inc., 1986.

Thompson, E. P. *The Making of the English Working Class.* New York: Pantheon, 1963.

———. "Time, Work-Discipline, and Industrial Capitalism." *Past and Present.* 38 (1967): 56–97.

Tilley, Christopher. "Interpreting Material Culture." In *The Meaning of Things,* ed. Ian Hodder, 185–94. London: Unwin Hyman, 1989.

Tooker, Elizabeth. "Foreword." In *Ethnography by Archaeologists.* 1978 Proceedings of the American Ethnological Society, ed. Elizabeth Tooker, vii–viii. Washington, D.C.: American Ethnological Society, 1982.

Trollope, Anthony. *Castle Richmond.* London: Penguin, 1993.

Twining, Thomas. *Travels in America 100 Years Ago.* New York: Harper and Brothers, 1893.

Tyler, Steven A. "Post-Modern Ethnography: From Document of the Occult to Occult Document." In *Writing Culture: The Poetics and Politics of Ethnography,* ed. James Clifford and George E. Marcus, 122–40. Berkeley: Univ. of California Press, 1986.

Upton, Dell. *Holy Things and Profane: Anglican Parish Churches in Colonial Virginia.* Cambridge, Mass.: MIT Press, 1986.

———. "White and Black Landscapes in Eighteenth-Century Virginia." In *Material Life in America, 1600–1860,* ed. Robert Blair St. George, 357–69. Boston: Northeastern Univ. Press, 1988.

———. "Imagining the early Virginia Landscape." In *Earth Patterns: Essays in Landscape Archaeology,* ed. William M. Kelso and Rachel Most, 71–86. Charlottesville: Univ. Press of Virginia (1990).

———. "Form and User: Style, Mode, Fashion, and the Artifact." In *Living in a Material World, Canadian and American Approaches to Material Culture,* ed. Gerald Pocius, 156–69. St. John's, Newfoundland: Institute of Social and Economic Research, 1991.

———. "The City as Material Culture." In *The Art and Mystery of Historical Archaeology: Essays in Honor of James Deetz,* ed. Anne E. Yentsch and Mary C. Beaudry, 51–74. Boca Raton, Fla.: CRC Press. 1992.

Ukers, W. H. *All About Tea.* New York: The Tea and Coffee Trade Journal Co., 1935.

Veblen, Thorstein. *The Theory of the Leisure Class.* 1899. Reprint, Boston: Houghton Mifflin, 1973.

Vincent, Joan. "The Structuring of Ethnicity." *Human Organization* 33 (1974): 375–79.

Wall, Diana diZerega. "The Separation of the House and Workplace in Early Nineteenth-Century New York City." *American Archeology* 5 (3) (1985): 185–89.

———. "Sacred Dinners and Secular Teas: Constructing Domesticity in Mid-19th-Century New York." *Historical Archaeology* 25 (4) (1991): 69–81.

Walsh, Lorena. "Annapolis and Anne Arundel County, Maryland: A Study of Urban Development in a Tobacco Economy, 1649–1776." In "Annapolis and Anne Arundel County, Maryland: A Study of Urban Development in a Tobacco Economy, 1649–1776," ed. Lorena S. Walsh, 1983, N.E.H. Grant RS-20199-81-1955, Maryland State Archives, Annapolis.

———. "Community Networks in Early Chesapeake." In *Colonial Chesapeake Society,* ed. Lois Green Carr, Philip D. Morgan, and Jean Russo, 200–241. Chapel Hill: Univ. of North Carolina Press, 1988.

Wallace, Anthony F. C. *Rockdale.* New York: W. W. Norton and Co., 1972.

Wapnish, Paula, and Brian Hesse. "Urbanization and the Organization of

Animal Production at Tell Jemmeh in the Middle Bronze Age Levant." *Journal of Near Eastern Studies* 47 (2) (1988): 81–94.

Warner, Mark S. *Test Excavations at Gott's Court Annapolis, Maryland, 18AP52.* Annapolis: Historic Annapolis Foundation, 1992.

Warner, Mark S., and Paul R. Mullins. "Community Activism and African-American Archaeology: Excavations at the Maynard-Burgess House, Annapolis." Paper presented at Third Annual Anne Arundel County Archaeology Conference, Annapolis, Maryland, Nov. 1992.

————. *Phase I–II Archaeological Investigations on the Courthouse Site (18AP63), An Historic African-American Neighborhood in Annapolis, Maryland.* Annapolis: Historic Annapolis Foundation, 1993.

Warner, Sam Bass. *The Private City.* Philadelphia: Univ. of Pennsylvania Press, 1968.

Warren, Mame. *Then Again . . . Annapolis, 1900–1965.* Annapolis: Time Exposures, Ltd., 1990.

Washington Bee. Washington, D.C., Public Library.

Webster, Noah. *A Compendious Dictionary of the English Language.* Hartford: Sidney's Press, 1806.

Westmacott, Richard. *African-American Gardens and Yards in the Rural South.* Knoxville: Univ. of Tennessee Press, 1992.

Whallon, Robert. "Unconstrained Clustering for the Analysis of Spatial Distributions in Archaeology." In *Intrasite Spatial Analysis in Archaeology,* ed. Harold Hietala, 242–77. Cambridge: Cambridge Univ. Press, 1984.

Wheeler, J. T. *A History of the Maryland Press, 1777–1790.* Baltimore: Maryland Historical Society, 1938.

White, Christopher P. *Chesapeake Bay, Nature of the Estuary: A Field Guide.* Centreville, Md.: Tidewater Publishers, 1989.

White, Clarence Marbury Sr., and Evangeline Kaiser White. *The Years Between.* New York: Exposition Press, 1957.

White, Theodore E. "A Method of Calculating the Dietary Percentage of Various Animals Utilized by Aboriginal Peoples." *American Antiquity* 18 (4) (1953): 396–399.

Whorf, Benjamin Lee. "Science and Linguistics." In *Language, Thought, and Reality,* ed. John B. Carroll, 207–19. Cambridge, Mass.: MIT Press, 1956. (Originally published in *Technology Review* 42 (6) (1940): 229–31, 247–48).

Wilke, Richard, and Michael B. Schiffer. "The Archaeology of Vacant Lots in Tucson, Arizona." *American Antiquity* 44 (3) (1979): 530–36.

Willey, Gordon R., and Jeremy Sabloff. *A History of American Archaeology*, 2d ed. London: Thames and Hudson, 1980.

Williams, Raymond. *Marxism and Literature*. Oxford: Oxford Univ. Press, 1977.

———. *Problems in Materialism and Culture*. London: Verso, 1980.

———. *The Country and the City*. London: The Hogarth Press, 1985.

Williams, Susan. *Savory Suppers and Fashionable Feasts: Dining in Victorian America*. New York: Pantheon Books, 1985. Reprint, Knoxville: Univ. of Tennessee Press, 1996.

Wittkower, Rudolf. *Architectural Principles in the Age of Humanism*. 1962. Reprint, New York: W. W. Norton, 1971.

Wolf, Eric. *Europe and the People without History*. Berkeley: Univ. of California Press, 1982.

———. "Culture: Panacea or Problem?" *American Antiquity* 49 (2) (1984): 393–400.

Wood, W. Raymond, and Donald L. Johnson. "A Survey of Disturbance Processes in Archaeological Site Formation." In *Advances in Archaeological Method and Theory*, vol. 1, ed. M. B. Schiffer, 315–81. New York: Academic Press, 1978.

Woodham-Smith, Cecil. *The Great Hunger: Ireland, 1845–1849*. London: Penguin, 1991.

Worthington, Thomas C. Collection. "1941 Valuation and Conclusions, Extension of the U.S. Naval Academy." Maryland State Archives, Annapolis.

Wright, James M. *The Free Negro in Maryland, 1634–1860*. 1921. Reprint, New York: Octagon Books, 1971.

Wroth, Lawrence C. *The Colonial Printer*. Portland, Maine: Southworth-Anthoesen Press, 1938.

Wylie, Alison. "The Interpretive Dilemma." In *Critical Traditions in Contemporary Archaeology*, ed. Valerie Pinsky and Alison Wylie, 18–27. Cambridge: Cambridge Univ. Press, 1989.

———. "The Interplay of Evidential Constraints and Political Interests: Recent Archaeological Research on Gender." *American Antiquity* 57 (1) (1992): 15–35.

Yamin, Rebecca, and Karen Bescherer Metheny, eds. *Landscape Archaeology: Reading and Interpreting the American Historical Landscape*. Knoxville: Univ. of Tennessee Press, 1996.

Yentsch, Anne E. "Spring House at Paca Garden, 16 March 1982." Letter. Annapolis: Historic Annapolis Foundation, 1982.

———. "An Interpretive Study of the Use of Land and Space on Lot 83, Annapolis, Md." *Maryland Archaeology* 26 (1–2) (1990): 21–53.

———. "The Calvert Orangery in Annapolis, Maryland: A Horticultural Symbol of Power and Prestige in an Early 18th-Century Community." In *Earth Patterns: Essays in Landscape Archaeology,* ed. William M. Kelso and Rachel Most, 169–87. Charlottesville: Univ. Press of Virginia, 1990.

———. "The Symbolic Divisions of Pottery: Sex-Related Attributes of English and Anglo-American Household Pots." In *The Archaeology of Inequality,* ed. Randall H. McGuire and Robert Paynter, 192–230. Cambridge: Basil Blackwell, 1991.

———. "Gudgeons, Mullet, and Proud Pigs: Historicity, Black Fishing, and Southern Myth." In *The Art and Mystery of Historical Archaeology, Essays in Honor of James Deetz,* ed. Anne E. Yentsch and Mary C. Beaudry, 283–314. Boca Raton, Fla.: CRC Press, 1992.

———. *A Chesapeake Family and Their Slaves.* Cambridge: Cambridge Univ. Press, 1994.

Yentsch, Anne E., and Mary C. Beaudry. "Introduction." In *The Art and Mystery of Historical Archaeology: Essays in Honor of James Deetz,* ed. Anne E. Yentsch and Mary C. Beaudry, 3–21. Boca Raton, Fla.: CRC Press, 1992.

Yentsch, Anne E., and Larry McKee. "Footprints of Buildings in 18th Century Annapolis." *American Archeology* 6 (1) (1987): 40–51.

Yentsch, Anne E., Naomi F. Miller, Barbara Paca, and Dolores Piperno. "Archaeologically Defining the Earlier Garden Landscapes at Morven: Preliminary Results." *Northeast Historical Archaeology* 16 (1987): 1–29.

Young, Arthur. *A Tour of Ireland with General Observations on the Present State of that Kingdom made in the Years 1776, 1777, and 1778.* London: T. Cadell and J. Dodsley, 1780.

Zeder, Melinda A. *Feeding Cities: Specialized Animal Economy in the Ancient Near East.* Washington, D.C.: Smithsonian Institution Press, 1993.

Zucker, Paul. *Town and Square, From the Agora to the Village Green.* New York: Columbia Univ. Press, 1959.

Contributors

Ann-Marie Burlaga received a B.A. from the department of anthropology, University of Maryland. She has since worked as a project archaeologist for Greenhorne & O'Mara in Greenbelt, Maryland. She is currently privately employed.

Julie H. Ernstein is completing her dissertation in archaeology at Boston University. She has taught at the University of Maryland and at George Mason University. She has also worked on projects for the Baltimore Center for Urban Archaeology.

Laura June Galke is an archaeologist at Jefferson Patterson Park and Museum in Southern Maryland. She was laboratory director for Historic Annapolis Foundation and the University of Maryland. Galke received her M.A. from the department of anthropology at Arizona State University.

Hannah Jopling is completing her Ph.D. at the department of anthropology, City University of New York. Her dissertation research is an oral history and historical ethnography of the African American community in Annapolis, Maryland, 1900–1950.

Elizabeth Kryder-Reid received her Ph.D. from the department of anthropology, Brown University, in 1991. Her research focused on the Carroll house and garden in Annapolis, Maryland. She has worked for the Center for Advancement Study in the Visual Arts, National Gallery of Arts. Kryder-Reid is currently working on a study of the California missions and their landscapes.

Mark P. Leone received his Ph.D. in anthropology from the University of Arizona in 1968. He is professor of anthropology in the department of anthropology, University of Maryland. Leone is director of the Archaeology in Annapolis project. He is author and coauthor of more than sixty articles and chapters in books, and five books, the most recent being *The Recovery of Meaning* and *Invisible America.*

Justin S. E. Lev-Tov is a Ph.D. candidate in anthropology, University of Tennessee. He has worked on zooarchaeological assemblages from the Chesapeake, Turkey, and Israel. Lev-Tov is currently conducting research in Israel.

Barbara J. Little is the archaeologist for the National Register of Historic Places, National Park Service. She received her Ph.D. in anthropology from the State University of New York at Buffalo in 1987. Little is author and coauthor of over twenty-five articles and chapters in books. She is editor of *Text-Aided Archaeology* and *Historical Archaeology of the Chesapeake.*

George C. Logan received his master's degree in education from the College of William and Mary, in 1992. He was a project director for the Archaeology in Annapolis project and was actively engaged in producing public interpretive programs. Logan is currently working for Woodward-Clyde Federal Services, in Gaithersburg, Maryland, performing cultural resource management projects.

Christopher N. Matthews is completing his dissertation in the department of anthropology, Columbia University. He has directed projects for the Archaeology in Annapolis project and is currently analyzing material from Annapolis, Maryland, for his dissertation. Matthews has taught at Northern Virginia Community College.

Paul R. Mullins is a visiting assistant professor in the anthropology program, George Mason University. Mullins received his Ph.D. in 1996 from the University of Massachusetts, Amherst. His research examines the relationship between racism and the emergent consumer culture between the Civil War and the New Deal. He is presently preparing a book entitled *Race and Affluence: An Archaeology of African America and Consumer Culture.*

Charles E. Orser Jr., professor of anthropology, Illinois State University, received the Ph.D. degree in 1980 from Southern Illinois State University at Carbondale. His most recent books are *Historical Archaeology* (with Brian Fagan) and *A Historical Archaeology of the Modern World.* He is founding editor of the *International Journal of Historical Archaeology.* He is currently directing a multiyear study of pre-Famine peasant life in the Republic of Ireland.

Parker B. Potter Jr. served as administrator of planning and registration and director of publications for the New Hampshire Division of Historical Resources. Potter received his Ph.D. in 1989 from the department of anthropology, Brown University. His work focused on the role of public interpretation in archaeology. He is author of many articles and is co-editor of *Recovery of Meaning* and is author of *Public Archaeology in Annapolis.*

Paul A. Shackel is assistant professor of anthropology at the University of Maryland. He received his Ph.D. from the department of anthropology, State University of New York at Buffalo, in 1987. He served as park archaeologist and directed a long-term interdisciplinary project at Harpers Ferry National Historical Park. His recent books include *Personal Discipline and Material Culture* and *Culture Change and the New Technology.*

Jennifer Stabler received her master's degree in applied anthropology from the department of anthropology, University of Maryland, in 1990. She is active in cultural resource management, working for companies in Texas and the Chesapeake Bay region. She has also excavated extensively at Caesarea Maritima.

Mark S. Warner is a visiting instructor in the department of sociology, gerontology, and anthropology at Miami University, Oxford, Ohio. He is completing his Ph.D. in anthropology from the University of Virginia. His dissertation research explores the historic symbolism of food and foodways among African Americans living in the Chesapeake region. He has worked for Gray & Pape, Inc., in Cincinnati and as a zooarchaeological contractor.

Index

Annapolis Pasts: Historical Archaeology in Annapolis, Maryland was designed and typeset on a Macintosh computer system using PageMaker software and set in Bodoni, Bauer Bodoni, and Gill Sans Bold. This book was designed and composed by Todd Duren and printed and bound by Thomson-Shore, Inc. The recycled paper used in this book is designed for an effective life of at least three hundred years.